75 YEARS WITH THE FIGHTING HAWKEYES

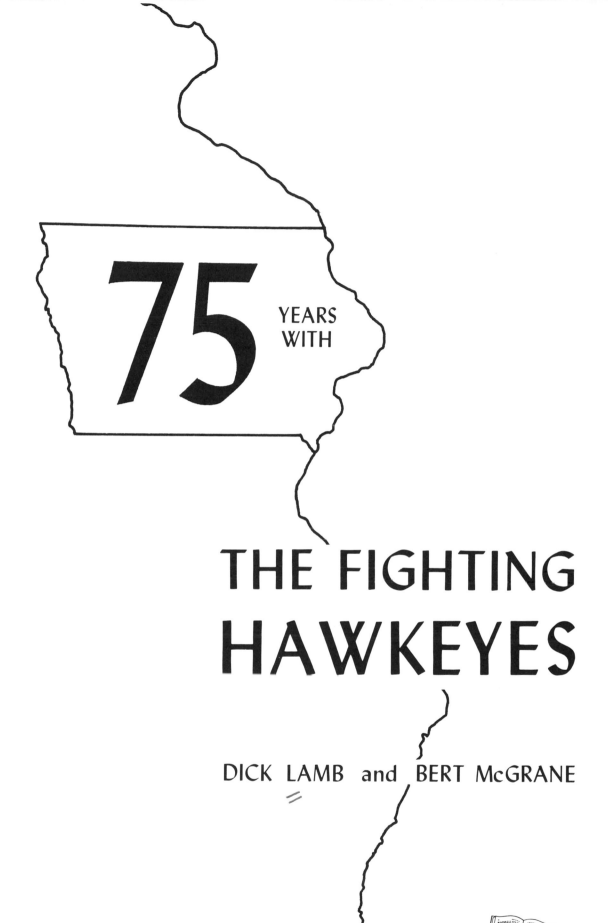

75 YEARS WITH

THE FIGHTING HAWKEYES

DICK LAMB and BERT McGRANE

WM. C. BROWN COMPANY PUBLISHERS
135 SOUTH LOCUST STREET • DUBUQUE, IOWA 52003

Manufactured by WM. C. BROWN CO. INC., Dubuque, Iowa
Printed in U. S. A.

Preface

"Rightly or wrongly, football is very definitely tied up with the status of a University.

"The majority of people who go to college . . . . they don't get that wider horizon or that better mental equilibrium. But they do get the opportunity. I think the same thing is true about football.

"While possibly the majority of boys don't get those subjective values that I mentioned, certainly the opportunity is there and I think the values they do get are perhaps more intensely brought out than they are in an educational system itself.

"As far as any activities I have been connected with are concerned, football has given me the opportunity to round out my philosophy and to change my thinking process more than any other activity with which I have been connected."

Nile Kinnick—All-American Halfback

Phi Beta Kappa Scholar
State University of Iowa

Football in American University life is misinterpreted if regarded solely as an athletic activity, detached or detachable from the purpose of the University. Today, the team and the game symbolize the University.

The critics of college football howl and charge that the game is over-emphasized. And yet none have successfully contended that anything but benefit results from witnessing and participating in a contest in which examples of courage, discipline, endurance, loyalty, mental alertness, teamwork and basic character are exhibited.

General Douglas MacArthur, one of the game's most outspoken supporters, has said:

"On the fields of friendly strife are sown the seeds that, upon other fields, on other days, will bear the fruits of victory."

The game has an unparalleled place in the consciousness of millions. In football is found a common denominator of unity and loyalty. As such, the football record of any institution deserves to be kept before the public.

The Diamond Anniversary of Iowa Hawkeye football seems an appropriate time to tell the story of the lives and times of the men who helped write her gridiron history. It has been with a firm resolve and a deep sense of obligation that the authors undertook the giant task of answering that need. It is fervently hoped that the spirit of unselfish sacrifice which motivated the wearers of the Old Gold down through the years has to some extent been captured on these pages.

The glory of victory, conference titles and national championship recognition has more than compensated for humiliating defeat, the shame of conference suspension or the personality conflicts and internal athletic department struggles which have been a prominent part of the 75 year Iowa gridiron saga.

It was at Iowa that football's first effigy hanging was executed. It was a Hawkeye who once scored eight touchdowns in a single game, and still another who caught a wind-blown punt in the opposition end zone for a touchdown. Twice Iowa games caused such bitter dispute that officials were forced to declare forfeit decisions. Another struggle is still carried as a victory by both sides.

Iowa coaches, too, added life to the story, both on and off the field. One, eminently successful, was also a physician and opera singer. After leaving coaching he became the nation's foremost writer of children's books. The intrigue and internal strife surrounding the tenure of two others has left an indelible mark, along with strained relationships. Still another Hawkeye coach was hired contingent upon his bringing a specifically named assistant. Even the legendary Knute Rockne figured prominently in Iowa coaching plans. He was receptive, signed an agreement, but never led the Hawkeyes.

This has been a pleasant task albeit not without difficulty nor free from sustained labor. Every attempt has been made to be as complete and accurate as possible. Every conceivable source of information has been consulted. It remains only to express heartfelt thanks to all of the many whose interest and cooperation have been so generously at our disposal.

For their support and suggestions in developing the original idea into a reality, grateful appreciation goes to the Iowa Board in Control of Athletics.

To Frank Paluka, head of the Archives Division of the University Library, and to Mrs. Lillian Bezanson, curator of the Special Collections section, we cannot find sufficient superlatives with which to express our gratitude for their splendid cooperation in allowing us free reign in their departments.

The same kindness and generosity was given during the past six years by Dr. William J. Peterson, superintendent of the Iowa State Historical Society. His patience, and that of his staff, was of inestimable help.

Long time Iowa photographer, Fred W. Kent, through his University photographic service, extended every courtesy at his command. The accompanying pictures are testimony to his efforts.

Special acknowledgment should also be given Mrs. Shirley Hamerlinck for her loyalty and efficiency in deciphering a multitude of notes, original drafts and hours of tape recordings. The final manuscript became a reality through her fingertips.

To these individuals and to more than two hundred others, the authors shall always carry with them the finest recollections of their helpfulness and understanding.

Dick Lamb
Bert McGrane

September, 1964

Introduction

The birth of football at the State University of Iowa, in the fall of 1872, was both in-auspicious and unpretentious. Indeed, the early years offered grave doubts that the game was at all welcome on the campus. And yet, though the beginning was not heralded and not spectacular, it was honest, it was earnest, and it was sincere.

However, it was seventeen years after those first seeds were sown that a formally recognized Iowa team played a game of intercollegiate football. Princeton and Rutgers fought in the first intercollege contest as early as 1869, although the game had been played informally since the early years of the nineteenth century.

But football at Iowa in the seventies and eighties was hardly reminiscent of the game today. There were 25 men on each side when the Iowa Academics and the College of Law fought in the first recorded game on the Iowa campus. The date was November 27, 1872.

Among the rules were those outlawing any passing or running with the ball. In addition, innings were used to denote periods of play. It was agreed that a game of seven innings would be played, but because the Academics easily won the first four, the Law students conceded the game, 4 — 0.

The first outside competition came in December of the same year when a group of Iowa City citizens played university students in the inaugural "Town vs. Gown" game. James G. Berryhill, most prominent of Iowa's earliest football heroes, wrote in glowing terms of the "honorable defeat" his teammates suffered, 5 goals to 4.

For the next ten years the game was primarily of the intramural variety. Many class games were played between the Laws and Medics, the Academics and Juniors, Freshmen and Sophomores, etc.

A popular campus ditty of the period evidenced the interest which football evoked among the students:

> Lawyer Charlie is my name,
> Playing football is my game.
> When I go out, some fun to see,
> Medics are the lads for me.

On October 20, 1882, the Senior Class team, university champions, represented Iowa in a game with Cornell College. The game was played at Mt. Vernon and might technically be called Iowa's first intercollegiate contest. The Seniors easily defeated their opponents and two weeks later duplicated the victory when Cornell journeyed to Iowa City.

Although no regular varsity teams were organized until 1889 the interclass champions were always given the honor of representing the university. A number of games were scheduled, primarily against Cornell, although it was also noted that the first "Alumni" game was played. The 1886 contest in Des Moines resulted in victory for the student players, three goals to one.

Various minor irritations developed during the period and were commonplace with Iowa City townspeople. Most amusing, perhaps, was this report of an incident in 1883:

"One evening last week the students collected on the football grounds just below the university to play football. During the process of their game the ball was kicked by accident into a yard nearby. Thereupon a representative of the property picked up the ball and thrust a knife into it, ending its usefulness and the game."

Football growth was handicapped at Iowa even during the early years that followed recognition by the university of a varsity eleven. Initially there was no athletic association to take charge of the game or to give it proper financial aid. There was no athletic park for the players, and games had to be played on vacant lots near the campus.

Finally in February, 1890, a permanent athletic association with constitution and bylaws was organized. The first intercollegiate game by an official University of Iowa team had been played and lost the previous fall. Lack of organization and no effective administration contributed to the overwhelming 24 — 0 defeat by Grinnell.

The first S.U.I. Athletic Association was entirely a student organization. A. H. Brown was elected interim president, with James Crossley, an influential member of the 1890 varsity, heading the organization in the fall.

It was soon recognized that this arrangement was not satisfactory and the following year a reorganization was made. An amended constitution vested authority in a dual body consisting of an advisory board and executive committee. Unlike the previous formation, university faculty members assumed control in conjunction with a student committee. All questions pertaining to athletics, including the composition of teams, were referred to this dual board. Professor Martin Sampson, chairman of the faculty group and unofficial coach of Iowa's first varsity eleven, stated that the new body would "bring the students and faculty into a closer relationship concerning athletics," and also that it would "insure a more equitable choice of university athletic teams because of the impartiality of the committee."

Although athletic administration was improved, actual decisions regarding teams and finances still remained in the hands of student captains and managers. As a result, criticism and a lack of over-all student interest continued to plague athletics in Iowa. The Athletic Association and the Athletic Advisory Committee proved to be little more than conservative consulting bodies.

Financial troubles soon became cause for concern. Professional coaches and lengthy interstate trips had drained the athletic treasury. Gate receipts did not match expenses and as a result several hundred dollars were lost during the 1893-94 year.

During this time uniforms were purchased by individual team members. In addition, interested townspeople contributed dollars and extended credit in order that Iowa's financial athletic storm might be weathered.

Another attempt to meet the crisis was made by not hiring a professional football coach in 1895. The plan backfired when Iowa was able to win only one of seven scheduled games and gate receipts fell short of defraying expenses.

The following year a professional coach again was secured and Iowa had its most successful season in terms of victories, winning the Western Intercollegiate Football Association championship as well as the state title. However, athletic expenses still exceeded income.

On February 6, 1897, a new Athletic Union was organized. Its main controlling body was an Advisory Board consisting of three members of the university faculty, the president of the Athletic Union, and the manager of the football, baseball and track teams.

It was required that all students taking part in athletics sign a declaration of eligibility slip signifying they had never violated any of the amateur rules and that they were bona fide students of the university. The faculty that same year passed a rule stating that any athlete found deficient in his academic work would be put on probation barring participation in all athletic activities if classroom work did not improve within a reasonable period of time.

Most important, however, was Article VII of the Constitution which required every varsity athlete to become a member of the Athletic Union at a cost of one dollar. Further, any student could join the organization for the same fee.

An athletic debt of close to $4,000 was outstanding, and although the University Board of Regents sold nearly 160 acres of S.U.I. land in Clay County with the hope of wiping out the deficit, slightly more than $1,000 remained unpaid. As a result, formal varsity competition was not permitted, and it remained unsanctioned until University President Schaeffer and three others gave their personal notes guaranteeing payment.

That same spring Athletic Park was formally purchased by Iowa for $6,000, even though it wasn't certain at the time whether the new grounds would be used for varsity or strictly intramural competition.

Although football showed a small profit in 1897, a complete athletic accounting at the close of the school year disclosed the debt remained unpaid. When the fall term of 1898 opened, the S.U.I. faculty committee passed the following resolution:

"Whereas, the student body of the State University of Iowa did, two years ago, promise to pay by June, 1898, a debt of $900 incurred in the interests of athletics, and whereas, the said debt of $900 has not yet been paid,

"Be it unanimously resolved by the faculty of the State University of Iowa, that no game of football or other athletic contest be permitted until at least $400 of the debt shall have been paid."

The money was raised by Thursday, September 29, two days prior to the first scheduled game. Season athletic tickets were sold to the public for the first time, at a cost of $5.00. The receipts from these sales had relieved the immediate financial pressure and allowed Iowa to complete its 1898 football schedule.

Although debts remained following the 1898 season, they had been reduced some $500. The turning point in athletics at Iowa had been reached, and within another year the entire financial obligation would be met.

In March, 1899, the Western Intercollegiate Football League met in Lincoln, Nebraska, to arrange a schedule for the fall season. Nebraska, Kansas and Missouri were represented. A resolution was drawn inviting Iowa to re-enter the League, and a schedule was made which included the Hawkeyes. However, the Athletic Advisory Board voted not to rejoin the organization, and it was perhaps this somewhat surprising decision which opened the door for entrance into the Western or Big Ten conference later in the year.

Acting President Currier, an outspoken advocate of athletics for each student, spoke in earnest terms at a May banquet when he said, "A director of athletics is most essential to an institution which sends out athletic teams. A physical director, indeed, should be as much a part of the faculty of a well equipped institution as a professor of language."

This undoubtedly was the first overt expression at Iowa in the direction of a physical culture department, and thirteen months after President Currier's suggestion it became a reality.

A new Constitution of the Athletic Union of the State University of Iowa was prepared and approved by the faculty in 1899. It went into effect on September 13. Dual responsibility remained under the new provisions, but the Iowa Board in Control of Athletics served as the primary legislative as well as executive body.

Thirteen members comprised the new Board, but included were two alumni members chosen by the alumni association and five faculty members appointed by the president of the university. The students were represented by the managers of the football, track, baseball and tennis teams. In addition, two officers of the Athletic Union were given places on the Board.

At this same time a committee was appointed by the University Board of Regents to report on the reorganization of athletics at Iowa. Among the recommendations were two which form the basis of Hawkeye athletic administration today.

It was suggested by the committee that athletic affairs be placed in the hands of the president, or the president and such committee or committees as he might constitute. Also, heeding the advice of President Currier, it was urged that a physical director be appointed.

On October 13, 1899, the faculty approved the proposal to place all athletic affairs in the hands of the University President and faculty members of the Board in Control. A few months later the Executive Committee of the Board of Regents recommended the establishment of a chair of physical culture. The board defined the powers of the director in a resolution passed on June 7, 1900:

1. The director shall be a member of the Board in Control of Athletics.

2. No student shall represent the university on any athletic team without the consent of the director.

3. The gymnasium and athletic park shall be under the direct control of the director.

Thus, by 1900, the program of centralized control of athletics had taken definite form. With the coming of Dr. Alden Knipe as football coach, and later as Director of Athletics, playing field fortunes improved and the Hawkeyes soon became a respected athletic power. In addition, the financial crisis was met, and athletics at Iowa became self-sufficient.

Administrative problems and financial turbulence had marked the first eleven years of intercollegiate football at the university. And yet, the Hawkeyes had won more than half of their games, including impressive victories over out-of-state rivals Missouri, Kansas, Nebraska, Illinois and Northwestern.

The control and regulation of athletics had already passed through three distinct stages of development: first, control by students; second, by students and faculty; and third, by faculty and alumni. Each succeeding phase had served to insure continued growth and a sound future for athletics at Iowa.

Table of Contents

75 YEARS WITH THE FIGHTING HAWKEYES

Football Pioneers in the Dawn of the Gay Nineties

From its humble beginning on the plain at Rutgers in 1869, intercollegiate football moved slowly across the country. Twenty years later the western two-thirds of the nation still had not witnessed a game between two collegiate elevens.

That fall, Martin Sampson, a graduate of Cincinnati, came to Iowa as an English instructor at the State University. He had never played football, but was familiar with the new game as contrasted to the soccer style which up to that time had prevailed in the "west."

On September 26 Sampson headed a meeting on the Iowa campus for the purpose of organizing an S.U.I. football team. His suggestion was heeded — and Martin Sampson himself, though he actually knew little about the game, was named "coach" and captain.

Other prime organizers for Iowa, each destined to contribute significantly to the growth and development of S.U.I. football, were Frank G. Pierce, William H. Bremner and A. G. Smith.

On October 6, 1889, the Vidette-Reporter, one of two campus student papers, printed the following announcement:

"The state university football team hereby challenges any college or other team in the State of Iowa to a game of football."

That obscure challenge soon found its way to Grinnell, then known as Iowa College. Rivalry between the two schools was not new. At infrequent intervals over a span of 20 years, baseball teams representing Grinnell and Iowa had met.

Grinnell had no football team, but the campus buzzed with the natural reaction to a challenge from Iowa. A student publication, The Pulse, added impetus to the activity by printing the rules of football, adding this advice:

"Let each football enthusiast carry a copy of these rules around in his pocket, to study at odd moments. You can't learn them too well. If there are chronic kickers unwilling to do this, then let us keep quiet and still retain the old worn-out back seat which we have hitherto held in respect to football."

The call was sounded and the men of Grinnell turned out for football.

Correspondence also grew between the managers of the rival teams and November 16 was agreed upon as the date for the first game. A site was not decided at the outset but finally Manager Swigert of Iowa, in a patronizing manner, wrote that Iowa would come to Grinnell "just to teach you boys how to play the game."

It was during this period of negotiations that the University of Iowa team actually played its first game of football. An eleven composed of Iowa City townsmen defeated the University gridders on October 15. According to the Vidette-Reporter, "although we did not win, the boys did admirably, developing an abundance of winning ability."

Unfortunately that first Hawkeye team, though determined and confident, was at best an enthusiastic though highly confused lot. The intricacies of play formations, the absence of teamwork and the lack of proper instruction and physical conditioning made preparations extremely difficult.

Such was hardly the situation at Grinnell. Although a team was not actually chosen until October 28, Grinnell was fortunate in having two men, Lou Van Giesen and Frank Everest, who had played the game previously at eastern prep schools. The experience and knowledge which Van Giesen and Everest brought to the campus enabled the Scarlet and Black to mold a reasonably cohesive unit by the time the Iowa game was scheduled.

From a financial standpoint, this first intercollegiate game was a surprising success. A committee had been organized to raise funds for the game. President Gates of Grinnell pledged 25 cents, while two affluent faculty members gave a dollar each. However, since no admission could be charged, the "hat" was passed both before and during the contest. After defraying all expenses attendant to the game, ten dollars remained as surplus. As will be noted later, collegiate football at Iowa was not always to be such a lucrative and profitable venture.

Among the rules governing Iowa's first intercollegiate game were the following:

1. Two halves of forty-five minutes each.
2. The playing field to be 330 feet in length.
3. The ball cannot be thrown forward.
4. A runner when stopped *must* cry "down."
5. Goals kicked from the field to count five points.
6. Touchdown to count four points.
7. Goal following touchdown to count two points.
8. Twenty-five yard penalty for roughness.
9. Quarterback must receive ball from "snapper-back" on every play. However

he must pass-off or hand-off to another back; i.e., quarterback could not carry the ball.

In addition, the rules of the game required that if "in three consecutive downs a team shall not have gained five yards or lost twenty yards, the ball shall go to the opponents." A team thereby could retain possession of the ball for a new series of downs either by gaining or losing yardage.

The Iowa team arrived in Grinnell attired in new uniforms made of heavy canvas. However, there was no padding. Neither did the players have the protection of helmets, shoulder or hip pads. The boys had to purchase their own suits, but the Iowa City clothing firm of Bloom & Mayer generously extended credit to them.

Only two of the Grinnell players had regulation-type football pants. Others, according to game accounts, wore "sweaters, gym jerseys, last summer outing shirts, bicycle pants, and one a pair of genuine blue-jean overalls."

At 2:30 on Saturday afternoon, with the sidelines thronged, intercollegiate football west of the Mississippi received its baptism. It was soon apparent that the nattily dressed Hawkeyes were no match for their football-wise hosts on the field of battle. One newspaper described the Grinnell "V" formation as being "similar to a medieval battering ram."

"By quick, hard rushes," the story continued, "the Iowa College team secured her first touchdown. It was then that the felicity of the occasion was marred by a misunderstanding between Allison of Grinnell and Pierce of Iowa. But peace was restored and the home team renewed her successful rushing tactics.

"At the close of the game excitement ran high. The Iowa College rush line with locked arms stood like a stone wall. After several abortive attempts by S.U.I., the game was over."

It should be noted that the Iowa gridders had devised a code or "signal" system for use in the Grinnell game. "Look Out" was yelled to denote a run around left end; "Ready" for a run around right end; and "All Right" meant a buck through center. Unfortunately, the huddle was not yet known to football and the Grinnell team easily heard the Iowa "signals." Since no variations of the system were used the Grinnellians quickly caught on and massed at the scrimmage line to thwart every Hawkeye effort.

The Pioneers smashed the rose-colored dreams of all S.U.I. followers and won by a score of 24 — 0.

A return game was immediately scheduled for Thanksgiving Day in Iowa City, but was cancelled at the last moment because of a storm. The season was over for both schools, and the first football championship of the state of Iowa, as well as the first football championship west of the Mississippi River, had been won by Grinnell.

1890

It wasn't until 1890 that Iowa was able to score its first touchdown, kick its first field

Arthur G. Smith

goal, and win its first game. Two contests were scheduled that fall and the Hawkeye gridders held formal practice sessions of two hours' dura-

tion each Tuesday, Thursday and Saturday afternoon. Arthur G. Smith, the "father of Iowa athletics," was elected captain by his teammates. Without the influence and vision of A. G. Smith, it is doubtful if S.U.I. athletic fortunes would have reached the heights which were attained under his leadership. However, such accomplishments were yet to come. Iowa hadn't yet won a football game.

Grinnell agreed to meet the Hawkeyes in the first Iowa City contest. Amid gusts of rain and a strong wind, the game was called for 3 p.m. on October 18.

Once again the Iowa College eleven proved too strong for the university team, winning the game 14 — 6. Martin Sampson, Iowa's football playing English instructor, recorded the first Hawkeye touchdown when he blocked a Grinnell kick, scooped up the ball and raced 70 yards to score.

Considerable improvement had been shown over the previous year by the home town Hawkeyes. However all was not serene on the Iowa campus. Discontent was voiced.

The S.U.I. Medics, "feeling keenly the disgrace brought upon our great institution by allowing a small academy to defeat our team, and desiring to convince the world that our team did not contain the best football material in the 'University'" requested a game with the S.U.I. team. Confident of their own ability the varsity agreed, only to be defeated by the Medics 22 — 10.

Changes of both personnel and playing tactics were instituted. A challenge was sent to Iowa Wesleyan proposing a Thanksgiving Day game. It was accepted, provided the game would be played in Mt. Pleasant. Iowa agreed. Fifteen hundred fans crowded Fairgrounds Park to watch the football inaugural at Wesleyan. Included in the stands were Senator John Harlan and Robert Lincoln, son of the President.

Playing under substantially the same rules as the previous year, including the awarding of four points for touchdowns, Iowa won 91 — 0. Wesleyan was unable to enter Hawkeye territory throughout the afternoon, while the win-

1. Michael R. Bailliet; 2. Lloyd L. Elliott; 3. Milton I. Powers; 4. David M. Knapp; 5. Matthew L. McEniry; 6. James J. Crossley; 7. F. H. Cutler; 8. Martin W. Sampson; 9. Albert P. Heald; 10. Capt. Arthur G. Smith; 11. Charles B. Smeltzer; 12. Arthur J. Cox; 13. Frank G. Pierce; 14. Allen T. Sanford; 15. William H. Bremner; 16. Fred W. Neal; 17. Unidentified.

ning Iowans ran for 19 touchdowns, five goals after touchdown, and a field goal. Dave Knapp and Albert Heald each contributed five touchdowns, while A. G. Smith kicked the first S.U.I. field goal.

The following two seasons were monumental ones for Iowa. Both were winning campaigns; the first professional coach was hired; the initial out-of-state game was played; Minnesota was met for the first time; and the strangest game in Iowa football was played — remaining unresolved to this day.

1891

The advantages of training, the mysteries of the whirling "V" formation and the rudiments of tackling were introduced to the Iowa varsity in the fall of 1891 by H. F. Kallenberg, the newly arrived Y.M.C.A. physical education director. Though not hired for his football knowledge, Kallenberg nevertheless was familiar with the game, having learned its rudiments from

Cartoon — 1890

Amos Alonzo Stagg at Chicago. In addition to counseling the Hawkeyes, he also filled the quarterback position on the 1891 team.

F. G. Pierce, playing his third season, was unanimously elected captain, and as such had charge of team strategy as well as the selection of all players.

Late in October Iowa opened its season by trouncing Cornell College, 64 – 6. Burt German, later to oppose the Hawkeyes as a member of the Iowa State varsity, paced the victory and notched an Iowa touchdown record which has never been equalled when he ran for eight scores.

Newspaper comment in the wake of the game included the following: "It was evident almost from the first that Cornell did not understand the game. We cannot, however, blame them, for this is their first season. Their foul tackles were numerous, but they had their own umpire."

Minnesota journeyed to Iowa the following week, administering the first of many one-sided defeats on the Hawkeyes, 42 – 4. It would be another 27 years before S.U.I. could record its first victory over the Gophers.

A week later Grinnell came from behind in the final minutes to gain its third straight win from Iowa. This time the score was 6 – 4. But many in Iowa City were dissatisfied. The student newspaper, Vidette-Reporter, commented tersely:

"The faculty at Grinnell should give Mr. Hoyt another day off so he can read the football rules before he attempts to umpire another game."

The final two games of the 1891 season found the Hawkeyes traveling beyond state boundaries for the first time. On Thanksgiving Day in Omaha, 2,000 watched the Iowans whitewash Nebraska 22 – 0. Football history of another sort was made, however, when it was revealed that the Nebraska coach, Theron Lyman, was the same Lyman who had played against Iowa less than three weeks before. He was an important cog in three straight Grinnell victories over S.U.I., and was lured by the

Cornhuskers who hoped such success would continue — as Nebraska's first recruited football coach.

Following the heartening victory, President Schaeffer of Iowa exclaimed proudly, if not prophetically:

"Nothing can do us more good in so short a time and at so little expense as a winning game of football. As a means of advertisement, athletic success cannot be equalled."

Seven hundred fans invaded Kansas City early in December to witness a game which to this day has not been resolved. Iowa carries the game as an 18 – 14 victory, but Kansas record books proclaim just as clearly that the Jayhawks won by a 14 – 12 score.

"The whirling V of Iowa, like Phoenix rising from the fire, went through the Kansas team like a Kansas cyclone." Such was the description "unbiased" Iowa papers presented.

However, midway through the second half Kansas held a narrow 14 – 12 lead. At that point, Bill Larrabee, son of an Iowa Governor, took the ball and raced to the Kansas 10 yard line before being tackled. Captain Kinzie of the Jayhawks protested violently that the ball had not been put into play fairly. When his objection was not sustained by the referee the Kansas captain withdrew his men from the field. Ten minutes remained. The referee motioned to Iowa to begin play, and with no interference (and no opponents on the field) Bailey walked for a touchdown. The game was called following the Hawkeye score, with both teams claiming victory.

The triumph by Iowa gave the Hawkeyes their first winning grid season. And, the win in Kansas records enabled the Jayhawks to record their first undefeated campaign.

On December 27, 1891, the Western Inter-State University Football Association was organized at Kansas City. Nebraska, Kansas, Missouri and Iowa were charter members. It was decreed at the first meeting that "no man shall play in this Association for more than five years." Also, that the 1892 championship series shall consist of "one game with each of the Universities of the Association."

1892

In October Iowa obtained the services of her first professional coach, E. A. Dalton of Princeton. Dalton, wearer of a striking handlebar mustache, was hired for ten days, completing his duties in Iowa City on the twenty-first of the month.

After experiencing little difficulty winning against Coe College, when Harl Myers romped for five touchdowns, and a week later over Knox, the Hawkeyes found themselves no match for Kansas or Missouri. The latter games were played within a period of two days early in November.

The Iowa City Citizen, attempting to analyze the defeats more blatantly, stated that

Head Football Coach — 1892
E. A. Dalton

Iowa lost the Missouri contest due to partiality shown fraternity men by the management of the team.

Three years of frustration came to an end a week later, however, and Iowa gained its first victory over Grinnell, 18 — 12. At that, the win-

ners had to drive from their own five yard line, 105 yards downfield, to score the winning touchdown and claim the state championship.

The annual Thanksgiving Day game with Nebraska resulted in a 10 — 10 stalemate, and Iowa closed its second consecutive winning season, this time under the leadership of Allen Sanford, with three wins, two losses and a tie.

Chancellor McClain toasted the S.U.I. team at a post-season banquet by stating "The college student is nothing if not manly. It is the coward who is not honest, and one of the best of antidotes for cowardice is the football team."

1893

There were not yet 1,000 students at Iowa when classes convened in the fall of 1893. At that, the number had increased nearly 50 per cent from the 657 enrolled in all departments just four years earlier.

Another professional coach, Ben "Sport" Donnelly, was brought to Iowa City late in September. He, like his predecessor at Iowa, had played for Princeton. But unlike E. A. Dalton, Donnelly managed to make himself generally disliked by the Hawkeye gridders. His contract was for two weeks only, and during that time Iowa opened the season with a decisive 56 — 0 victory over Coe College.

Three days after Donnelly left the team, Iowa succumbed to the Denver Athletic Club in Denver by an even more convincing 58 — 0 score.

Perhaps the most significant event of the year occurred on the Wednesday evening following S.U.I.'s shocking 36 — 14 loss at Grinnell. Football's first recorded "effigy" hanging greeted students and townspeople when captain and acting coach Lloyd Elliott was hanged on the telegraph wires near the city post office. Elliott was accused of "favoritism" in selecting players — primarily fraternity men — for the team, and this was said to be the principal factor in defeats at the hands of Denver, Kansas and Grinnell.

However, the following Saturday home town fans were delighted with a determined effort against Missouri, winning 34 — 12. Only a disappointing and controversial 20 — 18 loss to Nebraska on Thanksgiving kept the Hawkeyes from a third successive winning season.

Angered students were hardly pacified by the Vidette-Reporter account of the game:

"Iowa boys have the satisfaction of knowing that they played a clean, square game from

Head Football Coach — 1893
Ben Donnelly

start to finish. The defeat should have been on the other side. The idea of the referee entrusting the measurement of gains and losses to a reporter for a Lincoln paper is rather absurd to say the least. When after the cowardly tripping of Tyrrell and Myers, to enable Nebraska to score a touchdown, the referee runs down the field with a satisfied smile on his face and a wink to a reporter, things look somewhat peculiar."

Financially, football was quite successful. The team manager claimed that only $50.00 was lost during the entire season.

Lloyd Elliott, captain and acting coach of the Hawkeyes, deserves special mention as one

of Iowa's finest and most durable performers. He was the first gridder to play four complete varsity seasons. Elliott, along with Martin Sampson, A. G. Smith, Frank Pierce, William Bremner and Allen Sanford, was a significant tower of strength in pioneering Iowa football during its earliest years.

Intercollegiate football was still in its infancy, not only at Iowa, but throughout the country in general during the early 1890's. Although most of the larger eastern and midwestern schools had taken up the sport, problems were numerous. Financially the game was a burden to most. There was a universal lack of effective faculty control, poor officiating, as well as an absence of athletic conference affiliations to regulate and control such evils as professionalism, proselyting and brutality which had tainted the lessons and positive values of the game.

Iowa had a quasi-effective Athletic Association as well as an Athletic Advisory Board. The Association was a student organization and the Advisory Board was composed of faculty members. These two bodies worked together in overseeing athletics at the University of Iowa, but there was little communication between schools.

1894

That the values of football far outweighed its evils, at least at Iowa, was evident in 1894 when Roger Sherman of Michigan was named to coach the Hawkeyes during the entire season.

Prince Sawyer, climaxing three years of standout play for the Hawkeyes, was named both captain and quarterback. At the same time, sophomore Iver Iverson, playing the middle of Iowa's forward wall, began a career which would one day earn him recognition as the greatest center in early Iowa football history.

Three officials, an umpire, referee and linesman were used that fall. In addition, games were shortened to 70 minutes (35 minute halves) from the 90 minute contests of previous years.

Head Football Coach — 1894
Roger Sherman

Iowa State, then known as Ames, appeared on the Iowa schedule for the first time, and the Hawkeyes were surprised, losing 16 — 8. Burt German, Iowa's offensive might in 1891, and holder of the Hawkeye single game touchdown record, transferred to Ames and was both coach and captain of the Iowa State eleven. He scored half of his team's points against Iowa, and went on to become perhaps the single most important influence in the growth of early football and athletics generally at Iowa State.

Before another S.U.I. game was played, the first universally-accepted cheer was presented to the student body and formally adopted. Long since discarded, it went:

> Come right this way
> I   O   W   A
> Football we play
> Rush lines we break
> Touchdowns we make
> We take the cake
> Rah!   Rah!   Rah!

Cornell was swamped in the wake of Iowa's new yell, 60 — 0. Vic Littig, one of the most brilliant early day end performers, scored 32 points, making 4 touchdowns and 8 of 11 goals from touchdown. Scoring rules had still not been changed from the following:

> touchdowns — 4 points
> goals from touchdown — 2 points
> field goals — 5 points

Iowa looked eastward for the first time in 1894. The schedule as originally made up provided for games with Chicago and Northwestern as part of a Saturday-Monday road trip. It had been necessary to schedule the two games because of financial considerations, the guarantee from Mr. Stagg at Chicago being small. Two weeks before the trip Northwestern cancelled its game and Wisconsin was reluctantly but necessarily scheduled. The substitution of the powerful Badgers for smaller Northwestern presented a most difficult challenge to the upstart Iowans.

The result was an heroic effort against Stagg's Maroons, gaining a scoreboard tie, 18 — 18, but a decisive moral victory, when Chicago had to come from behind in the final minutes to deadlock the game. Two days later, however, the weary Hawkeyes were unable to stop Wisconsin, and the Badgers romped 44 — 0.

Two other '94 games deserve more than passing mention. Grinnell once again was the opponent in one, this time before an overflow Iowa City crowd of 900. About the middle of the second half, with the score tied 12 — 12, Darby of Grinnell stole the ball and raced 30 yards downfield to score the apparent leading touchdown.

However, the referee ordered the ball brought back, declaring that it had been whistled dead. Captain Arthur Crary of Grinnell stated that his team would quit unless the touchdown was allowed. Referee Stover waited the mandatory three minutes and then, according to the rules, gave the game and the state championship to Iowa, 6 — 0. Twenty-three minutes remained in the half.

Once again Iowa's student publication, Vidette-Reporter, fearlessly commented: "During the first half of the game, Stipp of Grinnell acted as referee, and twice our boys were robbed of the ball by his rank decisions, but they did not leave the field.

"It was during the second half. . . .that Grinnell threw up the game. Had the referee made several decisions which were very evidently unjust, there might be some excuse for their action. But since our team abided by the decisions of Stipp during the first half, it seems as though they should have abided by the decisions of Stover of S.U.I. during the second half."

President Schaeffer of Iowa and President Gates of Grinnell entered the controversy with an exchange of four letters. President Schaeffer wrote that "it is my duty to protest against the false attitude in which our players have been placed, and more especially against the false reports concerning the affair which have emanated from Grinnell.

". . . .a referee and an umpire were mutually agreed upon before the game began. . . . I can produce members of our Faculty who are thoroughly up on football matters, and who were very near to the point where the ball was picked up by an Iowa College man who distinctly heard our man call 'down.' I can further produce some of our players who made no attempt to tackle the Iowa College man with the ball, as they knew it was not in play."

It was not until years later that Grinnell changed its claimed 18 — 12 victory to an official 6 — 0 Iowa win, by forfeit.

The following week another controversy arose, this time in the Missouri game, played at Columbia. The Tigers overpowered Iowa 32 — 6, despite a noteworthy 70 yard touchdown run by Hawkeye R. C. Hayes, but the primary excitement was not generated by the players.

Once again the Iowa press reported from the scene of action:

"As soon as the crowd saw that a couple of the players were trying to exchange blows they rushed on the field from all sides. Canes were swung in a most vigorous manner, occasionally landing on the head of an Iowa man, and still others drew knives as they rushed upon the ground, either for the purpose of carving or of intimidation.

"In the meantime, three Iowa players had been arrested for causing the disturbance. Oh, etiquette, honor, justice, whither have you gone?"

Financially the 1894 season was a disastrous one for Iowa. Several hundred dollars were lost because gate receipts did not keep abreast of the large expenses brought about by lengthy interstate game trips, as well as the payments due Coach Sherman.

Had it not been for the loyalty and faithfulness of Iowa City clothier Max Mayer, it is doubtful if the financial storm during these years could have been weathered. Mayer, for

Max Mayer

many years referred to as the "grandfather of Iowa athletics," gave unselfishly of his time and his energies that athletics, particularly football, might continue. Max Mayer, beloved by all who knew him, will forever be remembered for his important role in the birth, the saving, and later the growth of athletics at Iowa.

Considerable agitation was heard in Iowa City about the merit and liability of hiring professional coaches. The student publication Quill commented:

"We believe that the coach could very well be done away with. Professional football coaches are not desired, at least not at the State University of Iowa."

1895

In June, 1895, a low ebb was reached when the Athletic Advisory Committee published a notice to the effect that the football team "will not be recognized until the finances of the team have been put upon a satisfactory basis."

When school convened in September the faculty approved a schedule provided the athletic debt be retired before any league games were played. Through the efforts of Max Mayer and other interested Iowa City businessmen, amounts covering the debt were pledged and Iowa played a full schedule.

However, no professional coach was secured that fall. Steve Coldren of the 1894 team was a pre-season advisor until Bill Larrabee, who had played with the 1891 and 1892 Hawkeyes, volunteered his services. But practices were highly disorganized, and Iowa was able to win only two of seven outings. The team was shut out in five games.

Kansas overpowered the Hawkeyes 52 – 0 at Lawrence, although Iowa reporters explained the loss by stating that "the gridiron was covered with about an inch of dust, which soon choked up our boys; and although the Kansans had a keg of water on the grounds they refused to give our boys a single drop, and thus with parched throats they were obliged to play until water was procured at almost a mile's distance."

Once again athletics at Iowa had proved to be a financial burden and student contributions as well as monetary support from the townspeople were necessary to continue inter-collegiate competition.

However, it was generally agreed that professional coaches must be hired if Iowa was to gain even a modest measure of athletic success, particularly against her more formidable rivals.

1896

School authorities again looked to the east for a football mentor, hiring A. E. Bull of Pennsylvania, one of the greatest centers the game had known, to lead the Iowans.

Bull was respected not only as a player but also as a likeable, conscientious football coach,

Head Football Coach — 1896
A. E. Bull

well grounded in the fundamentals of the game. The Hawkeyes responded to his teaching with seven victories, one loss and a tie, the finest season-long performance made up to that time by a team from the state of Iowa.

Three of the more prominent S.U.I. performers were captain and center Iver Iverson, halfbacks Joe Meyers and C. W. Holbrook. Meyers had helped defeat the Hawkeyes while playing for Iowa State in 1895. Kinney Holbrook, perhaps the state's first Negro gridder, must go down as one of the all-time greats at Iowa. He was a champion sprinter, the most dependable Hawk defensive man, as well as the team's leading scorer.

It was Holbrook who notched four touchdowns as Iowa trounced Drake 32 — 0 in the season opener. Powerful Chicago gained a hard-earned 6 — 0 victory from the Iowans a week later, but the Chicago Times-Herald paid particular recognition to the Hawkeye Negro: "Iowa's star work was done by Holbrook. It was brilliant. He made one run of forty yards through a forest of Chicago tackles, and a couple of sprints of thirty yards. Iowa always worked him when it was necessary to make a gain to keep the ball."

An unheard of crowd of 1,500 watched S.U.I. defeat Kansas 6 — 0 the following week. With only eight minutes remaining Holbrook raced 45 yards for the lone score. Iowa had caught the Jayhawks unprepared by lining up quickly and pitching the ball to Holbrook without signals. Hawkeye followers surged upon the field and mobbed the victors after the game. It was said to be "the most enthusiastic celebration ever seen in Iowa City."

Two weeks later another unfortunate incident took place on the field at Columbia, Missouri. Although the Hawkeyes won, 12 — 0, S.U.I. players carried only bitter memories of the contest. It was duly reported, however, that the agitation was triggered not by the Missouri team nor by the student body, but rather by alumni and townspeople.

Resentment was aimed primarily at Iowa's great Negro star, although when S.U.I. officials declared that there would be no game unless Holbrook were allowed to play, venom was directed at the entire team.

Shouts of derision were hurled throughout; unsportsmanlike penalties were the rule, not the exception; the referee was forced to leave the game after being hit in the face and behind the head by two Missouri players.

Through it all the Hawkeye goal line proved invincible, and with Holbrook and Meyers scoring Iowa touchdowns the 12 — 0 scoreboard victory was gained.

Grinnell and the Des Moines Y.M.C.A. teams fell victim to superior S.U.I. play in games that followed, with Nebraska scheduled as the traditional Thanksgiving Day opponent to close the season. The battle was played in rain, sleet and snow throughout, with neither team able to score.

Officials gathered immediately afterward, however, and decided to replay the game on Saturday. This time Iowa was able to register a touchdown, on a 30 yard dash by Holbrook, to win 6 — 0. It was the Negro star's twelfth score of the year, and the two game series was the first and only time the Hawkeyes ever played a team twice in one regular season.

Its most successful season, a state title, and championship honors in the Western Intercollegiate Football Association; those were the spoils of victory attained by Iowa's plucky 1896 gridders.

An important member of Hawkeye teams in 1895 and 1896 was left end "J. Brown." He earned major letters in football during both seasons. But, it wasn't until 30 years later that Iowa athletic authorities discovered that there actually never had been a "J. Brown."

It was true that diligent research had failed to disclose the class or address of any "J. Brown" in university records, but it was generally assumed that such records had simply been lost or otherwise misplaced.

The final twist to the strange case of "J. Brown" was revealed late in 1926 when the department of athletics received a letter from Dr. Charles W. Edmonds in Nebraska. Press dispatches, wrote Edmonds, had indicated that former athletes were to receive belated athletic letters at the fieldhouse dedication ceremonies January 14, 1927. Dr. Edmonds wanted just reward for his two years of football service.

The story began to unfold. Charles Edmonds and "J. Brown" were identical. The Nebraska physician explained that his parents had objected to the brutal game of football, forbidding him to play. But Edmonds, a natural athlete, had a persistent longing to make the team. It was suggested that he change his name, and "J. Brown" was the alias agreed upon.

In January, 1927, C. W. Edmonds returned to Iowa City to accept the two major football letters which he, in the name of "J. Brown," had earned more than thirty years before.

In spite of the playing field successes of 1896, football was still a financial burden at Iowa. Before the season had begun the school Board of Regents passed a motion whereby the regulation of athletic sports must thereafter be left with the college faculty. Positive action was deferred until after the 1896 season, but when football was unable to meet expenses with adequate receipts, the faculty passed a resolution stating that no University athletic team would be recognized until past debts of the Athletic Association were paid, and until an athletic organization was perfected to offer reasonable assurance that nothing resembling the then current state of affairs would recur.

Just a month earlier, in December, 1896, Iowa was "fired" from the Western Intercollegiate Football Association for 1. not having a representative at the Kansas City meeting, and 2. for failing to pay its annual association dues of $50.00.

The students, heretofore somewhat lethargic to rise in defense of athletics, were stirred to action. On February 6, 1897, a new Athletic Union was organized. It was a dual association of students and faculty, with the latter forming the Advisory Board. For the first time there was a membership fee, any student becoming a paid up member for one dollar. One hundred and seventy-five joined. In addition, a minstrel show was staged which brought in $200. The faculty contributed another $155. Most important, President Schaeffer, Max Mayer and two others agreed to give their personal notes guaranteeing payment of the athletic debt. Unfortunately, the three Iowa benefactors were unable to foresee continued financial troubles, and it was a considerable period of time before they were relieved of the obligation.

1897

Pennsylvania again was the early spawning ground of an Iowa football coach, Otto F. Wagonhurst accepting the position in 1897. Wagonhurst had played tackle for Quaker teams which won 38 of 41 collegiate games, and his arrival in Iowa City was received with enthusiasm and optimism.

Prior to the season scoring values were changed for the first time, a touchdown being increased from four to five points, and a successful goal or point after touchdown being reduced to a single point from its previous two point value. Field goals continued to count five points, while safeties remained two points.

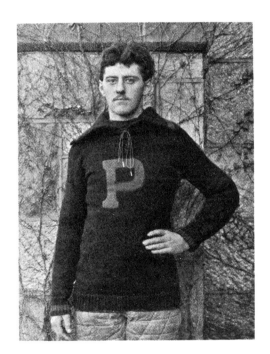

Head Football Coach — 1897
Otto Wagonhurst

The Hawkeyes opened the campaign with two victories, including a 12 — 6 win over Northwestern, the first ever over a Western Conference eleven.

Another week brought fireworks and the Physicians-Surgeons team from Chicago to

Iowa City. S.U.I. was shut out 14 — 0, but more than a few Iowans were unnerved by the rougher, more experienced visitors. Midway through the second half, P. and S. Negro star George Flippen, who had led Nebraska to victories over Iowa in 1893 and 1894, assaulted a Hawkeye spectator. He was placed under arrest following the game, and later fined $5.00 and costs, a total of $8.35, by Iowa City Judge Squire Leasure.

Kansas atoned for a 54 — 0 defeat by Iowa in 1895 with an overwhelming 56 — 0 verdict, and the battered Iowans regrouped their forces for Iowa State, Drake, Grinnell and Nebraska during the second half of the season.

The Cyclones were the first to be met, and the resultant battle left vivid memories and strained athletic relations. After a 4 — 0 S.U.I. lead at halftime, the two teams traded touchdowns early in the final period. Iowa led 10 — 6 when Parker of Ames raced 40 yards to score late in the game. The Hawkeyes claimed that Johnny Griffith had been deliberately fouled, enabling Parker to notch his touchdown. But when the umpire refused to allow Iowa's protest, explaining he had not seen the infraction, the Hawkeyes left the field, forfeiting to Iowa State, 6 — 0.

An Iowa City paper, presenting its own analysis of the game, commented:

". . . . the umpire, whose sole duty it is to observe such things, says he failed to see the play. Why? Either because he did not want to see it, or because he was grossly, not to say criminally, negligent. We believe the latter to be the true explanation.

"That he is endowed with at least normal vision, and could see when he made an effort to do so, is attested to in his other numerous decisions, every one of which was against Iowa."

The Hawkeyes rebounded strongly a week later by whipping Drake, 16 — 0, although the second half was shortened to only five minutes. The game began late in the afternoon, and with darkness enveloping the field as the second half started, it was decided to call the game after five minutes.

Traditional rival Grinnell traveled to Iowa City the next week and surrendered a hard fought 16 — 12 verdict to Wagonhurst's varsity. The Grinnellians held a 12 — 0 halftime lead, but Iowa rebounded for three second half scores and won with a touchdown in the final seconds.

An overflow crowd "went mad, stark-raving mad, yelling and dancing in very ecstasy," according to witnesses who viewed the post-game celebrations.

Thanksgiving Day, 1897, was both happy and sad in the annals of Iowa athletics. The football team was defeated by Nebraska 6 — 0 in a game played at Council Bluffs. But perhaps more important were the receipts totalling $536.65 which the Hawkeyes received.

For the first time in nine years of intercollegiate athletic competition at Iowa the indebtedness was not increased, and the football team had made an over-all profit of $12.06.

However, there were still outspoken critics of the game, many claiming that it was too rough a sport. The Cedar Rapids Gazette, in an editorial following the 1897 season, commented:

"The Iowa University football captain is against any changes in the rules, declaring the game is not brutal as played now. That fellow ought to be pulled out of college and used as a bumping post in some railway yard."

Dr. Knipe Builds Big Ten Champs

Although problems, financial and administrative, still were prevalent as the 1898-99 school year commenced, Iowa entertained high hopes of success when, for the third straight year, athletic officials secured a graduate of Pennsylvania to coach football.

Alden A. Knipe, quarterback-halfback-captain of Penn's national championship team of 1894, agreed to terms at Iowa, and arrived to begin his coaching duties on September 14.

Dr. Knipe, a respected physician as well as an operatic singer of note, was called by Pennsylvania's immortal George Woodruff "the greatest player I ever coached." He was to receive $50.00 a month as Hawkeye mentor in 1898.

Twelve hundred students were enrolled for classes, and 37 answered Dr. Knipe's opening call for practice. A training room was used for the first time when Kenyon and Hamm, proprietors of an Iowa City laundry, generously donated a portion of their basement facilities.

The following Monday, September 19, Dr. Knipe conducted the first secret football practice at Iowa.

A stern disciplinarian and fervent advocate of training rules, Coach Knipe began immediately to lay the groundwork of football success at Iowa which has never been exceeded.

But, in the immediate future, problems confronted the new leader.

After an opening scoreless tie with Knox College, followed by a 38 — 0 defeat at the hands

Head Football Coach — 1898-1902
Athletic Director — 1901-1903
Alden Knipe

of Chicago and its great all-American, Clarence Herschberger, the initial Varsity-Alumni game was scheduled.

Hawkeye heroes of other years returned to the campus — at their own expense — and, although disorganized, held the Varsity to an 11 − 0 score. Coach Knipe played with the Alumni, and he was aided by old time stars Vic Littig, Kalita Leighton, Lloyd Elliott, Kinney Holbrook and others.

Evidence of internal difficulties within the ranks of Iowa's varsity squad was observed later in the week, and friction was particularly noticeable between the coach and a number of the older players. Knipe wanted faster men and he also felt that his linemen should take a crouching position rather than a straight up stance. Drake University took advantage of the situation by upsetting the Knipe men 18 − 5. Ray Morton contributed 75 and 90 yard touchdown dashes enabling the disorganized Hawkeyes to split their next two games, winning from Upper Iowa but losing to Rush College.

A week later, State Normal (now State College of Iowa) shocked mid-western football followers by handing S.U.I. a convincing 11 − 5 setback. After the game five members of the Iowa varsity revolted and left the squad. Not one ever wore an Iowa uniform again.

Those taking part in the internal uprising declared that the team had been "grievously neglected, in that suitable clothing and equipment had not been given them."

However, a campus publication, The Quill, reported that the "Blackmore Revolt" was maliciously inspired because the deserters "could not advise Coach Knipe of where certain players should be placed on the team."

The mass withdrawal may have been a blessing in disguise for Iowa, however. An inexperienced, but determined group of underclassmen were immediately promoted to first team status. Such famous names as Clyde Williams, Joe Warner, and Ray "Buck" Morton became the backbone of Knipe teams which were not to lose another game in three years. More impressive, from the date of the 1898 revolt until midway through the 1901 season, only a

single touchdown was scored against the Hawkeyes.

Grinnell, an old grid nemesis, managed a game tying field goal in the waning minutes to hold the Iowans 5 − 5, but the following week S.U.I. defeated Simpson College 12 − 0. Captain Sam Hobbs, and still another early Iowa football hero, Moray Eby, gained major plaudits from Knipe.

Council Bluffs was again the scene of Iowa's traditional Thanksgiving Day game against powerful Nebraska. The Cornhuskers, coached by the immortal Fielding Yost, had defeated such teams as Missouri, Kansas and Iowa State handily. They were heavy favorites against Iowa.

Two thousand fans witnessed a startling 6 − 5 Hawkeye victory, referred to by Captain Hobbs many years later as "the real birth of Iowa football glory which was to follow."

The Hawkeyes had come from behind to tie the score, kick goal, and then hold the Nebraskans inside the Iowa five yard line as the game ended.

Iowa City papers hailed the S.U.I. triumph with prophetic praise:

"Our football team has won glory unexcelled, a gem of unparalleled brilliance, in defeating Nebraska by a 6 − 5 score. No other explanation can be given but that Dr. Knipe has succeeded in bringing together a team united in action, united in spirit, and united in determination to do or die."

The victorious 1898 team was honored at a university banquet the following Monday. Professor Currier led the speechmaking and commented strongly on the importance of athletics in the educational curriculum at Iowa.

It was announced early in December that Dr. Knipe would remain in Iowa City during the winter and spring to help with the University track team. Further, he agreed to coach Iowa football for a second year, in the fall of 1899.

Not to be overlooked is the fact that football gate receipts exceeded expenses by $241.75 during the 1898 season. In addition, yearbook subscriptions and individual contributions decreased the total athletic debt by January, 1899, to only $676.

The first memorable era of Iowa football had begun and would reach its zenith in accomplishment during the following two seasons.

1899

Little did anyone realize as the 1899 season approached that the accomplishments of this team and its twin counterpart, the 1900 eleven, would rank favorably with any ever produced at the University of Iowa. Fewer still even considered the thought that no Hawkeye teams would ever, albeit could ever, exceed the 1899 and 1900 defensive record against touchdowns.

Dr. Alden Knipe had been retained at the close of the 1898 season and elected an assistant instructor in athletics for the following school year. His monthly salary, from August 15 to June 15, was $50.00. Dr. Knipe thus became the first football coach to serve two consecutive seasons.

Further evidence of athletic recognition within the University was shown when Sam Hobbs, captain of the 1898 eleven, was appointed assistant coach by the Iowa board.

More than forty candidates reported for practice in September, although 17 men, including Captain Moray Eby, had been training since late in August at Linder's boathouse on the northern outskirts of Iowa City.

Once again season athletic tickets were sold, this time providing chairs for the women, standing room for the men. Students as well as townspeople were eligible to purchase the athletic yearbooks.

Two other innovations were adopted for the first time. A four foot wire fence was erected around the playing field to keep out all "illegitimate spectators." Also, ticket booths were constructed and used at all home games.

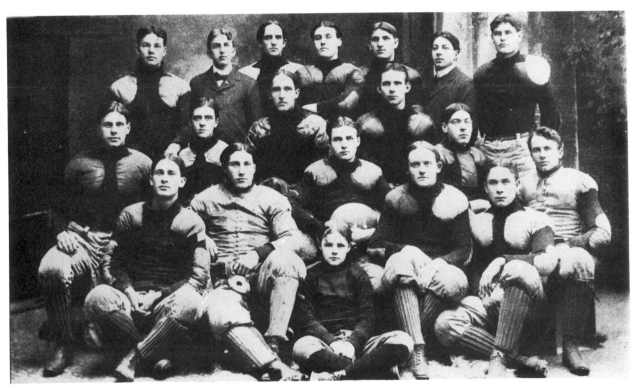

1899 Team

| Little | McCutchen (Mgr.) | Warner | Baker | Weiland | Knipe (Coach) | Howell |

Stratford   Watters   Brockway   Eby (Capt.)   Burrier   F. A. Williams   Edson

S. C. Williams   Morton   'Spike'   Griffith   Hoover

On Thursday and Friday preceding the season opener, an operetta, "The Mikado," was presented for the benefit of the football team finances. The opera house was filled both evenings, and one of the outstanding performances was that given by Head Coach Knipe, appearing as Ko-Ko, Lord High Executioner of Titipus. Almost $400 was realized for the athletic fund, with $381.60 being turned over to the Athletic Union.

Iowa opened the season by trouncing State Normal 22 — 0. Billy Edson, a transfer from Ames, scored two touchdowns, one on a run of 60 yards, to pace the winning Hawkeyes.

After whitewashing the Alumni 30 — 0 the following week, Iowa prepared in earnest for the Chicago Maroons of Alonzo Stagg. Western Conference champions the preceding year, and 26 — 6 victors over Notre Dame a week prior to the Iowa game, the midway eleven were heavy favorites over the yet untested Hawks.

But Chicago was unable to cross the Iowa goal that afternoon. Only a 25 yard field goal gave the Staggmen five points and a tie with the determined Iowans who gained their points on a first half touchdown.

According to the University of Chicago Weekly: "The tackling of the Iowa team as a whole was the best ever witnessed on Marshall Field."

After news of the final score was flashed in Iowa City, students celebrated by building bonfires and marching to the home of University President MacLean. The president appeared, acknowledged the moral victory, and later joined in the celebration of cheers for Coach Knipe and the team.

Penn College was next to fall before the Hawkeyes. Of interest, however, was the name Simon Hester in the Penn lineup. A month earlier he had come out for varsity football at Iowa, remained for ten days, and then returned without cause to Penn where he had starred the previous year. Considerable controversy was raised, although even Hester's inside knowledge could not slow the S.U.I. attack and Iowa triumphed, 35 — 0.

Rush College of Chicago, although outweighing the Hawkeyes more than thirty pounds per man, proved no match for the speedy Iowans, and became victim Number 4, 17 — 0.

Two thousand fans, the largest crowd to witness a football game in Iowa City, saw Coach Knipe's heroes gain a fiercely fought 5 — 0 decision from Iowa State the following week. Ironically, former Iowa halfback Joe Meyers was coach of the Ames team, while Billy Edson of the Hawkeyes had played for Iowa State in 1898.

Jim Brockway, stalwart Hawk right guard, was pushed over for the only score of the game and Iowa remained undefeated.

Clyde Williams, Joe Warner and Johnny Griffith stood out in a surprisingly easy 30 — 0 victory over Nebraska in a game Knipe attributed directly to the over-all teamwork of his charges. A. E. Branch, coach of the Cornhuskers, said "the Iowa team is a wonder and has a right to the prominent position it occupies in the football world this season."

Mark Baker, Iowa's center, scored the final touchdown when he fell on a loose ball in the Nebraska end zone. Baker was the only Hawk pivotman to score until Dayton Perry of the championship 1960 eleven grabbed an errant Purdue fumble and raced 80 yards to paydirt.

Grinnell, fresh from a startling 5 — 5 tie with perennial power Minnesota, invaded Iowa City in mid-November and succumbed before the Hawkeyes, 16 — 0, and this victory was followed by a 33 — 0 romp over Knox College.

Simpson was to have been played the next week, five days before the season finale against Illinois, but the Iowa athletic board cancelled the game out of respect to Winfred Stephenson of Des Moines who was fatally injured making a tackle in a junior-senior class game on the campus.

Rock Island, Illinois, was the site of Iowa's battle with Illinois. The game, played on Thanksgiving, was attended by nearly 6,000 fans, including 500 who made the trip by special train from Iowa City.

If the stamp of greatness had not been placed upon the Hawkeyes before the Illinois game, it was indelibly accorded them after it. Ten touchdowns were notched by Iowa enroute to a 58 point victory margin. The Illini were held scoreless. Further, because of the rout, it was mutually agreed to shorten the second half by ten minutes.

Individually, Billy Edson raced for five touchdowns, including runs of 55 and 65 yards. Johnny Griffith, pint-sized 150 pound fullback, returned a punt 85 yards for the most spectacular score, and durable Joe Warner, one of the greatest of all Iowa linemen, kicked 8 of 10 goals after touchdown, in addition to averaging fifty yards punting.

Charles Hollister, head coach at Northwestern and umpire in the game, commented: "Iowa has the best team for its weight that I ever saw." Referee R. T. Hoagland of Princeton said: "Iowa has a quickness of playing that excels any team I have seen. The generalship and judgment of quarterback Williams were excellent. The dodging run of Griffith down the field for a touchdown was the best piece of individual playing that I ever saw. The men are all stars; they make the best team I ever saw."

No team across the nation could match Iowa's defensive record of an uncrossed goal line in 1899. Financially, football receipts exceeded expenses by more than a thousand dollars, and the Athletic Union was to stand without a dollar indebtedness.

Immediately after the Illinois game Professor A. G. Smith, long a tower of strength in the formation and growth of Hawkeye athletics, represented the university at an important meeting of the Western Intercollegiate Conference at the Chicago Beach Hotel. Member schools, including Chicago, Illinois, Wisconsin, Minnesota, Michigan, Purdue and Northwestern, voted to admit both Iowa and Indiana to full conference affiliation. The date was December 1, 1899.

Thus, within a period of twenty-four hours Iowa had completed its first undefeated season; erased a financial debt which had plagued all athletics for more than ten years; and gained admittance to what would soon become the ranking athletic conference in the nation.

Caspar Whitney, most prominent sportswriter of the day, recognized the heroics of Coach Knipe and his players by stating in Harpers Weekly: "There is no other team in the West to approach Iowa and Chicago.

"Clyde Williams was the only good all-around quarterback and field general in the middlewest.

"Johnny Griffith was better for all around fullback service than Pat O'Dea of Wisconsin."

But what of Dr. A. A. Knipe? Who was he, and what methods did he use to mold a group of native, corn-fed Iowans into a cohesive, well disciplined and successful football team?

It is probably true to say that Iowa's early football fortunes were spawned and nurtured on the playing fields of the University of Pennsylvania.

Knipe, a disciple of Penn's Hall of Fame coach George Woodruff, introduced the Pennsylvania system of football to the midwest, even though he had been preceded at Iowa by two former Woodruff pupils, A. E. Bull in 1896 and Otto Wagonhurst in 1897.

But it was Alden Arthur Knipe who brought renown and gridiron prestige to the Hawkeyes. Quarterback and halfback sparkplug of Pennsylvania's national championship 1894 eleven, Knipe was without peer among his contemporary football field generals. Through his senior season the Quakers were undefeated in twelve games, scoring more than 300 points to 20 for the opposition.

After spending two years as assistant coach under Woodruff at Penn during which time he earned his degree in medicine, Knipe accepted the coaching challenge at Iowa.

The style of play which he brought to the Middle West was not long taking hold. Although essentially a swift, open running attack, the most significant feature was employment of the Pennsylvania system known as "guards back." Knipe pulled his guards, or his tackles, out of the line of scrimmage before the ball was snapped, thus giving the offense more versatility and placing greater stress on the defense.

In the guards back formation, the two guards were stationed in tandem to the immediate right or left of the quarterback. From this position they could be used on devastating power plays straight ahead or, by employing variations, the backs could be given the ball on wide sweeping runs.

Iowa's basic formation showed this lineup:

```
LE  LT  C  RT  RE
        Q  RG
        F  LG
     LH     RH
```

Knipe interchanged his tackles and guards. At times he placed only a single guard or tackle in the backfield. Still another maneuver, called by Chicago Coach Stagg "Iowa's Flying Interference Play," was highly reminiscent of the end run keeper-pitchout of modern football. Only the set formation differed to any degree:

```
LG  C  RG  RT  RE  F  LT  LE
    Q
LH     RH
```

The backfield alignment of early football in many respects closely paralleled the "T" formation style of attack which gained nationwide popularity in the forties, and with modern variations since that time. With the exception of punt plays, there was no direct pass from center. Until 1910 it was a rule of the game that the ball must be handed off or passed off on every play; therefore the quarterback, though he received the ball, was rarely, if ever, the ball carrier.

Iowa's impregnable defense against touchdowns in 1899 and 1900 was the result of a fierce and determined pride coupled with disciplined teamwork. Dr. Knipe installed a basic seven man line with four fast, mobile backers-up. The primary formation, designed to stop only running plays since there was yet no forward passing, concentrated no defenders more than five yards from the line of scrimmage. The 1900 Iowa-Northwestern game program outlined the defensive formation as follows:

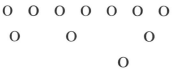

The rules specified that a team must relinquish the ball if five yards were not gained in three downs. However, a quirk in the laws allowed a team to retain possession for a second series of downs if it lost twenty yards or more. This section was rescinded following the 1903 season.

BEST OF THE DECADE — 1889 — 1899

Ends	Moray L. Eby	1897-1898-1899-1900
	Victor L. Littig	1893-1894
Tackles	Allen T. Sanford	1890-1891-1892
	Joseph S. Warner	1897-1898-1899-1900
Guards	James M. Brockway	1898-1899-1900
	Kalita Leighton	1894-1895-1896
	James C. Walker	1895 1896-1897
Center	Iver Iverson	1894-1895-1896
Quarterback	Prince Sawyer	1892-1893-1894
Halfbacks	Willis Edson	1899-1900
	Lloyd L. Elliott	1890-1891-1892-1893
	C. W. (Kinney) Holbrook	1895-1896
	Ray Morton	1898-1899-1900
Fullbacks	Samuel W. Hobbs	1895-1896-1897-1898
	Frank G. Pierce	1889-1890-1891

1900

With nine regulars returning for duty, Iowa followers looked forward with anticipation to the 1900 season. On June 7, Coach Knipe had been appointed the first athletic director at a salary of $1,800, and the University Board of Regents had signalled further confidence in Hawkeye athletics by appropriating $1,500 for the improvement of Athletic Park.

The field, subscribed for and eventually purchased in sections, was first discussed at Iowa by Professor Isaac Loos during 1891.

Options were taken in 1892 on what was then called the Metzger lot, and a year later on Englert Park. The south half of old Iowa Field, Sullivan Pasture, was contracted for in 1895.

The University did not actually gain title to these properties until 1897, and by late summer of 1898 the Athletic Park debt had been reduced from its original $6,000 to $3,695.

Shortly after practice began the last week in August, 1900, Midwestern grid experts, writing in the Chicago Tribune, proclaimed that "the team to be selected this year will be the strongest that ever represented Iowa on the gridiron."

The Hawkeyes opened the season by whitewashing Upper Iowa 57 — 0, with tackles Warner, Little and Coulthard smashing for five touchdowns.

Athletic Park was formally dedicated the following week against State College of Iowa, and Knipe's gridders responded with an overpowering 68 — 0 win. Ray Morton scored four touchdowns, while Johnny "Red" Griffith notched two, along with seven extra points.

Next, Simpson was run over 47 — 0 in a game featuring four touchdowns by Billy Edson and a brilliant 65 yard punt return by quarterback and playmaker Clyde Williams.

With a scheduled game against Iowa State cancelled due to an outbreak of typhoid fever on the Ames campus, Iowa had an additional week to prepare for Drake. After being held to a 5 — 0 score at halftime, the Hawks broke the game open early in the second period and won easily, 26 — 0.

But Chicago and Michigan loomed large in the path of Coach Knipe and his stalwart band of Iowans. The Maroons had already played Minnesota's behemoths a 6 — 6 tie, and this was the same Gopher team which would finish the

The Hawkeye playing field in 1900, showing Old Capitol in the upper left center of the picture.

1900 season undefeated. Michigan, a giant in football circles for some twenty years, hardly expected serious trouble from the upstart Hawkeyes. But Iowa was committed to play. . .perhaps the two biggest games of its twelve-year football history. . .within a period of eight days.

An official party of twenty, along with some 150 supporters, entrained for Chicago on Thursday before the game. More than once they were reminded that a Stagg coached team had never tasted defeat by Iowa.

The two teams battled on even terms throughout the first half, although the Maroons had a favorable wind advantage which would go to the Hawkeyes in the second 35 minutes. Four minutes after the second half kickoff, Moray Eby plunged for the first touchdown. Moments later Edson dashed five yards for another, and Joe Warner climaxed the Iowa scoring by kicking a 33 yard field goal. The jubilant Hawks had shut out the Maroons 17 — 0, Chicago never penetrating the Iowa 25 yard line.

Immediately following the game the Hawkeye athletic party headed for Lakeside Inn, a summer resort hotel located about twenty miles north of Detroit, on Lake St. Clair. The entire week was spent there, preparing in earnest for Michigan.

Writing about the preparations years later, Iowa guard James Brockway said: "In that week Coach Knipe worked a miracle. Michigan had scheduled an open date the day we played Chicago and the whole Michigan team was there to size up our team and each player's opponent.

"Knipe changed our entire system. Not once did we use the Pennsylvania system of guards or tackles back which we had worked so well against Chicago. Instead of resorting principally to power plays from his guards and tackles back formation, Coach Knipe concentrated on surprising the Wolverines with an outside attack, utilizing the speed and mobility of his pony-sized backs."

Michigan was caught unprepared, having based its defense on stopping the mass formation plays used so successfully against Chicago. Iowa recovered a fumble in the opening minute of play, scored on a burst through center by Eby, and led 6 — 0 when Joe Warner kicked the extra point.

Clyde Williams returned a punt 55 yards to set up the second Iowa score, and by half-time Edson had notched another to give the Hawkeyes a commanding 17 — 0 lead.

The relentless Iowa surge continued in the second half and only a last minute Wolverine field goal enabled Michigan to escape being shut out. The final score read: Iowa 28, Michigan 5.

Area papers heaped deserved praise on the valiant Iowans. The Detroit News-Tribune commented on Sunday: "Beaten clearly and undisputably, outclassed in every department of the great college game, Michigan yesterday went down to defeat at Bennett Park before the meteoric team from the prairies — the players from Iowa. Detroit has never seen such football as Iowa played. The Iowans are in a class by themselves, and beat Michigan beyond all conjecture. The team is without equal in the West."

Even more descriptive was this tribute in the Detroit Free Press: "Michigan met them in friendly controversy Saturday. The visitors were a most gentlemanly set of young giants, though anything but gentle when in action. They showed magnificent education and training from the tips of their long scalp locks to the soles of their perniciously active feet. Their brains worked like greased lightning set to clock-work. They were shrewder than a strategy board and could mobilize in less time than is employed in an owl's wink. When they charged it was like a bunch of wing-footed elephants, and when they tackled one of the enemy it was like the embrace of a grizzly. They could kick harder than a gray mule with years of experience, and with the accuracy of a globe-sight rifle. Michigan recognizes that Iowa is setting the pace in the West. So, it's hats off to Iowa."

Back in Iowa City wild crowds invaded the campus and downtown area. Bands played ragtime music and a massive bonfire was built. The heat was so intense, plate-glass windows were cracked and the flames for a time threatened an entire block of the business district. A snake-walking torch parade was held through the streets in a celebration that lasted well into the night.

Iowa's university band, two city bands and more than 2,000 people crowded the railroad platform to welcome the champions home on Monday morning. Two new cheers permeated the campus throughout the day and enlivened a formal city-wide parade headed by President MacLean, Dr. Knipe and their wives. The spontaneous though quickly adopted yells included:

"Who's the Best, we're the best,
We're the Champions of the West."

"Merrily we roll them up, roll them up,
Merrily we roll them up, twenty-eight
to five."

Enthusiasm was maintained at a fever high pitch throughout the week, with Grinnell next in sight for the high flying Hawkeyes. The objective was not only a victory, but in particular a more decisive triumph than the 26 − 0 defeat Minnesota had handed the Pioneers earlier in the season.

The Iowa offensive machine responded with an impressive 63 points, while the defense allowed no enemy touchdowns for the sixteenth straight game.

Seven different Hawks scored before the end of the first half, and the intermission margin was 40 points. Grinnell was awarded a gift safety late in the game, but otherwise the Pioneers were no match for the smoothly working Knipe machine. In the wake of Iowa's 63 − 2 win, the Grinnell student paper, Scarlet and Black, called the Hawkeye team "the greatest eleven that ever played in the Hawkeye state, if not the greatest the West has ever seen."

Only one official hurdle remained between Iowa and a second consecutive undefeated season. Northwestern would provide the challenge.

But there were already off-the-record discussions regarding the possibility of a post-season game matching the Hawkeyes and either Wisconsin or Minnesota. Dr. Knipe quieted the rumors by stating that "post-season games put athletics on a professional basis." The Athletic Board also announced that it was against any games played after the regular schedule. Besides, Iowa had not finished its current season.

Rock Island was again selected for the Thanksgiving Day finale. A victory or a tie against the Wildcats would give Iowa at least a share of the coveted Western Conference title. The team, including the Iowa band, arrived in Davenport on Wednesday. The St. James Hotel, still a landmark overlooking the Mississippi River, housed Iowa's official party.

Northwestern, accompanied by 300 fans, also arrived on Wednesday, staying at Rock Island's downtown Harper House.

An overflow crowd of more than 5,000, expecting to see Iowa win comfortably, set the Watch Hill Road ball park ablaze with golden streamers and yellow chrysanthemums.

Iowa scored midway in the first half following a mixup of signals in the Northwestern backfield. Moray Eby picked up a Wildcat fumble and raced 47 yards to give the Hawks a 5 − 0 lead which was maintained at intermission.

Northwestern employed a baffling tandem formation which was sprung on the Iowans by surprise. Instead of deploying his halfbacks parallel to the line of scrimmage, or flanking the quarterback, Coach Hollister stationed all four backs in tandem, directly behind the center.

The plucky, determined Hawkeyes preserved their shutout record against touchdowns, but a 30 yard field goal late in the game gave the visitors five points and a 5 − 5 deadlock.

There was much speculation following the game about the inability of Iowa to win. Many claimed that overconfidence and lethargy were the cause. However, those close to the situation offered a different, more plausible explanation. Billy Edson, the last living member of the team, wrote that "there was not a question of taking the game lightly. We were not that kind of fellows.

"All we ever learned was that the chef at the hotel had taken some bets that Iowa would not win 40 − 0. We had creamed potatoes the night before the game. My roommate, Johnny

Griffith, was the only man who didn't eat any. The men's room was at the corner of the hall. When I got there at four o'clock in the morning, it was full up and more coming. All of us except Griffith had stomach cramps that were very severe. We were not any of us in shape to go on the field, and I don't see yet how we stayed in to the end of the game."

Iowa never played another football game in Rock Island, but that mysterious Thanksgiving Day game of 1900, closing a second straight undefeated season for the Hawkeyes, had fanned rather than extinguished the talk of post-season football.

In mid-December D. W. Hitchcock of California proposed that Knipe's team play two games with the University of California, one at San Francisco on Christmas, and the other in Los Angeles on New Year's Day.

The Iowa team voted unanimously in favor of the trip and immediately began full scale practice sessions. President MacLean was also enthusiastic about the proposal, explaining that "it would be a fine opportunity for the university to advertise itself on the Pacific Coast." MacLean stressed, however, in a wire to the Des Moines Leader, that "these games would not be post-season games, but holiday games."

The Iowa Board in Control of Athletics, at a lengthy evening meeting on December 18, voted 9 to 1 in favor of accepting the proposition.

Coach Knipe and the Iowa team prepared to leave Iowa City by train the following day. However, early in the afternoon a message was received to await further authorization from the University of California.

1900 Team

Coulthard   Briggs   Hart   Ely   Warner   Little   Melton
McCutchen, Gen. Mgr.   Eby   Burrier   Siberts   Brockway   Herbert   McClain, Manager
Morton   Dye   Hobbs, Asst. Coach   Dr. A. A. Knipe, Coach   Watters   Cogswell
Edson   Griffith, Capt.   Williams

Three hours later President MacLean received the following telegram:

Berkeley, Cal. Dec. 19, 1900

Pres. Geo. E. MacLean
Iowa City, Iowa

Impossible to arrange games. Manager says team cannot get ready.

Victor Henderson
Sec'y to President Wheeler
University of California

When the final message came it was taken to Athletic Park where the Iowa team was completing its final practice before entraining that evening. Universal disappointment prevailed, plans were cancelled, and what might have been the first East-West Tournament of Roses Bowl game was postponed until the following year when Fielding Yost led his 1901 "point-a-minute" Michigan team to victory over Stanford.

Officially the 1900 playing season was closed, and the first of three great football eras at Iowa showed two successive undefeated seasons; two consecutive years, seventeen straight games, in which the Hawkaye goal was uncrossed; and a Western Conference football championship in its first year of affiliation. These impressive credentials serve as lasting monuments to Dr. Alden A. Knipe and his fighting band of gridiron gladiators.

Dr. Henry L. Williams of Minnesota, along with Chicago's Stagg the most prominent football teacher in the West, eulogized the Iowa accomplishments under Knipe when he wrote:

"From the standpoint of attack, brilliancy and rapidity of execution, and general efficiency, Iowa's game is unsurpassed by that of any college in the country. No football has been played East or West of a higher type than that which has been shown for the past two years by Iowa."

Four members of the Iowa eleven were recognized by the Chicago Post with positions on the All-Western team. Three of the four backfield positions were given to Hawkeyes.

Quarterback Clyde Williams was captain of the honor group, while Ray Morton and Billy Edson were named halfbacks. Joe Warner earned a first team tackle berth.

Morton, playing three seasons for the Hawkeyes, notched eighteen career touchdowns, and using six point touchdowns as a measurement he became one of an elite group to garner more than one hundred markers.

Billy Edson, Iowa's speedy right halfback, will long be remembered for his brilliant open-field running. Seven times during his two year varsity career as a Hawkeye Edson raced for touchdowns from beyond fifty yards, and on sixteen other occasions he crossed the enemy goal from shorter range.

Tackle Joe Warner bulwarked Iowa's invincible forward wall. But more than that, Joe

Clyde Williams

Warner, while playing tackle, was also a scoring leader in both 1899 and 1900. Each season he tallied three touchdowns, and during the two years he also kicked 50 successful extra points.

Clyde Williams was accorded national prominence by football's foremost authority, Walter Camp. The "father of American football" placed Williams on his third team All-American — the first player west of the Mississippi to attain such distinguished recognition.

Over-all financial profits from the 1900 grid season amounted to $1,431.28. The previous track, baseball and tennis teams had lost a total of $637.77.

Late in February the operetta "Mikado" was again presented on behalf of the Athletic Union. Dr. Knipe, who had been named Director of Music at the university, managed the production and once more sang the role of Ko-Ko.

He was also made Professor and Director of Physical Training and Athletics by the Board of Regents in April. This was done in recognition of his valuable services to the university. Dr. Knipe thus was given a seat on the collegiate faculty and the university council.

An important revision of the Athletic Union constitution was adopted the following month. The new make-up of the Board in Control included the captains, in addition to the managers, of the football, baseball and track teams. This was done, according to the Board, to "give strength to the administration of athletic affairs."

Of the seventeen total members, nine would now be students, while faculty and alumni memberships numbered eight. As future events would indicate, the shift of control back to the hands of the students signalled the beginning of a new period of athletic stress and difficulty at Iowa.

1901

Only three holdover members of Coach Knipe's championship 1900 team were available when practice opened prior to the 1901 season. Fortunately, playing field coach Clyde Williams was one, along with linemen Bert Watters and Emmett Burrier.

Athletic Park was refurbished with a new grandstand seating more than 4,000. Season football tickets to all home games were sold for three dollars. Also, an obscure item in the September 24 Daily Iowan announced that, "Hereafter, except on Fridays, football practice will be strictly secret, no one being admitted to the grounds but the players in uniform, the coaches and the managers."

Dedication of the new athletic field grandstand and Billy Edson's return to Iowa City as assistant coach of the State College of Iowa (then State Normal) team highlighted activities in the season opener. The Hawkeyes shut out the visitors 16 — 0, and the following week, with Coach Knipe officiating at Minnesota, they were fortunate to edge Drake 6 — 5 in Des Moines.

The Gopher game was still two weeks away, and before it Iowa entertained an undefeated Iowa State eleven, winning 12 — 0. Dr. Henry L. Williams of Minnesota returned the visit of Dr. Knipe to Minneapolis by serving as an official in the game.

A round-trip railway fare of five dollars was offered by railroad officials to what was billed the "game of the year" at Minnesota. A torchlight parade and rally were held on the Iowa campus prior to the entourage northward.

Friday night before the game Minnesota authorities complained to Hawkeye officials that Captain Clyde Williams had played summer baseball in North Dakota under an assumed name. Iowa admitted the charge, but denied that he received any monetary remuneration. Minnesota did not lodge a formal protest against Williams, but twenty-five minutes before the game informed Iowa that such a protest would be made if Williams were put on the field.

Since the matter could not be settled amicably, the Iowa athletic committee decided to withdraw Williams and lay the matter directly before conference officials.

The Hawkeyes without Williams were a physically and psychologically outmanned football team. An overflow crowd of nearly 13,000 watched the Gophers notch forty-two first downs to four for Iowa, enroute to a 16 — 0 triumph. Only two minutes remained in a scoreless first half when Minnesota tallied a touchdown. It was the first time the Iowa goal line had been crossed since 1898.

Eleven days later conference officials declared that Clyde Williams was ineligible to compete further in intercollegiate athletics. The board was of the unanimous belief that Williams acted honestly in claiming that the offense arose because of a misinterpretation of conference rules over playing under an assumed name. However, though the ruling had been adopted to reduce or eliminate the illegal acceptance of pay, which Clyde Williams was not accused of receiving, the conference board believed it best to establish a precedent for the strictest application of the rules.

The football playing career of Iowa's most prominent early-day athlete was over. However, his later influence as an athletic administrator at Iowa State, and as an important member of the national rules committee for ten years, were further evidence of his stature. Clyde Williams' Field at Ames is named in his honor.

Four-year veteran lineman Emmett Burrier was named to captain the Hawkeyes the remainder of the season. Although both Knox and Grinnell were defeated following the loss of Williams, Illinois and Michigan whitewashed the Hawkeyes handily. The Michigan game was played in Chicago on Thanksgiving morning.

Coach Stagg of Chicago expressed his particular unhappiness toward the Wolverines and Hawkeyes for daring to play a game of football in Chicago on Thanksgiving Day. His Maroons were to entertain Wisconsin that afternoon, also in the Windy City.

According to one newspaper account, "Mr. Stagg was most displeased at the infringement of his divine right to the territory embraced in the environs of Chicago and the District of Lake Michigan."

The 50 — 0 triumph by Coach Yost was the final Wolverine victory before a 49 — 0 romp over Stanford in the first Tournament of Roses game on New Year's Day. During the season Michigan won eleven straight games, scoring 550 points to none for the opposition.

Iowa, winning five games and losing three, gained a measure of consolation for the conference defeats when national writer Caspar Whitney ranked the Hawkeyes nineteenth in the country at the end of the year.

1902

The 1902 season contained few highlights of the cherished variety. Although the team won five of nine games, disaster at the hands of Michigan and Illinois soured the taste of a winning season.

Dr. Knipe, beginning his final year with the Hawkeyes, had both Sam Hobbs and Clyde Williams as assistant coaches. Hobbs was completing his medical studies, while Williams was a dental student.

A Daily Iowan reporter, assigned to cover pre-season workouts, viewed Knipe's rigorous conditioning program with some doubt when he wrote:

"During the early practice sessions, one of the interesting antics was for the players to lie down on their backs and raise their feet a ridiculously large number of times."

A torrential downpour forced cancellation of the season opener against State College of Iowa, although Iowa agreed to reimburse any expenses of the Cedar Falls team if they would play on the following Tuesday. State College agreed, but gave up eleven touchdowns and eight extra points as Iowa gained an easy 63 — 5 victory.

Drake and Simpson were also Hawkeye victims before powerful Minnesota invaded Iowa City and outclassed the undermanned Iowans, 34 — 0.

A Cedar Rapids Gazette editorial the next day took exception to the Iowa performance:

"The football team of the state university is very poor this year, and the deterioration makes The Gazette tremble for the future of the bench, the pulpit and the school of physicians. Whenever the young men of Iowa are so weak that they cannot grow hair nineteen inches long, they supply abundant proof that the human race has hit the toboggan."

Coach A. W. Ristine of Iowa State, referring to his own team's 16 – 0 loss at Minnesota, predicted a smashing Ames victory weeks before the Iowa battle. On the eve of the game he said, "We are going to win. We are giving it to you straight. We are sure of it. We will not lose to Iowa."

However, after a 6 – 0 Iowa State lead at halftime, the Hawkeyes tied the score and then, with less than a minute remaining, Dwight Griffith returned an Ames punt 65 yards for the winning score.

A new Iowa cheer, unveiled during the game, may have inspired Knipe's gridders to the 12 – 6 victory:

Allah – Ka – Zoo   Ka – Zee   Ka – Zay
I – O – W – A
Hoo – Rah!   Hoo – Ray!
Iowa!   Iowa!
Ioway!

On November 8 in Ann Arbor, Big Ten scoring records were smashed in the most overpowering blitzkrieg ever displayed in an interconference game. The Wolverines, scoring at will behind the drives of Hall of Famers Willie Heston and Neil Snow, increased a 65 – 0 halftime lead to an astronomical 107 – 0 final score.

According to the Iowa State Register account of the game, "Owing to Coach Yost's absence from the battle scene the Michigan players were more anxious than ever to pile up a big victory. Today's score is the largest one any big college ever made on another."

Rumors of dissension filtered through the Iowa campus during the following week, although Knipe rallied his players for a 61 – 0 victory over Washington University of St. Louis.

After Missouri eked out a narrow 6 – 0 triumph, Illinois gave Iowa its second worst grid setback 80 – 0. The most disastrous winning season in all football was over, and one of the finest over-all won-lost coaching records at Iowa also was ended. Knipe teams lost only eleven games during his five years.

Immediately after the Thanksgiving Day game with Illinois, Dr. Knipe left the team for Philadelphia. There he married long-time family friend Nellie B. Kennedy. It was Knipe's second marriage and culminated a series of problems he had had with certain members of the Iowa Athletic Board and University Board of Regents.

Parker Holbrook of the Regents was outwardly disturbed over Knipe's marital difficulty, and suggested strongly to the Hawkeye coach that he not marry for a second time because the "whispered talk such a marriage would provoke would be bad for Iowa."

The internal conflict also included difficulties with Dr. James Gilchrist of the Medical Homeopathic Department. Gilchrist had long wanted to reduce the authority of the Director of Athletics and had been openly critical of Knipe.

However, an understanding friend and supporter of Dr. Knipe was University President George MacLean. The Iowa coach tendered his resignation in a letter to MacLean from New York City early in February, 1903. In it he expressed his concern over the future of athletics at Iowa and stated that he wished that he could be on the campus for the fight:

"I have no doubt that there will be difficulties springing from many sources to prevent anyone from looking after athletics, and there will be opposition from the Homeops; but let us hope that it will be as attenuated as is the rest of their theory."

President MacLean answered the letter on February 12 remarking that he was sorry Knipe felt "constrained to present the resignation, and yet, as you well know, I have foreseen that it was altogether likely that you would take the step.

"I trust that the future will fully justify my faith in your rising career."

Dr. Knipe never returned to the University, although his deeds of accomplishment were just begun. Named the finest halfback in the nation in 1894, he is considered today one of the great players in Pennsylvania football history.

Pre-eminent as a scholar, he was the holder of a degree in medicine, although never engaged as a practicing physician in Iowa City. But, as the builder of two nationally recognized grid teams at Iowa, the school's first athletic director, as well as the first director of music at the university, Knipe most certainly left an indelible mark of achievment.

Yet, upon leaving Iowa, Dr. Alden A. Knipe forsook the football coaching ranks and further association with athletics. He never pursued a promising career in music, and he decided against entering the active practice of medicine.

Instead, for the next 47 years he and his wife collaborated in the writing and illustration of children's books, both attaining foremost recognition in Who's Who in America during the period.

An examination of athletic department finances at Iowa early in 1903 revealed that once again considerable debt had been incurred. The 1902 football season had failed to meet expenses by more than $2,000.

A hastily arranged meeting was held in February and it was announced that no more athletic teams would be fielded until the athletic debt was erased. Following President MacLean's subscription of $100, an athletic ball was held, alumni were contacted, and Iowa City businessmen were asked to contribute. By April 3 the amount pledged was $4,011.56, and a month later this figure had swelled to $5,099.78. Athletics once again were saved at Iowa.

The Lean Years -- 1903-1909

The problem of a successor to Alden A. Knipe resolved itself first into the important decision of whether Iowa was interested in hiring a man from the east as in the past, or an alumnus of the university. Among alumni mentioned were Dr. Sam Hobbs, captain of the 1898 Hawkeyes and Dr. Knipe's assistant since that time; John Griffith, captain of the 1900 team and then athletic director at the University of Idaho; S. Clyde Williams; Willis Edson and Paul Coldron.

Early in June announcement was made of the appointment of John G. Chalmers, athletic director at Franklin & Marshall College, to the directorship of physical training and athletics at Iowa.

Chalmers, one of the finest all-around athletes in Lafayette history, agreed to terms giving him $1,500 a year, his duties to include serving as head football coach.

A particularly cold and wet fall hampered Hawkeye game preparations during September and October. Following victories over Cornell and Coe on muddy fields, the State College game had to be played on the old circus grounds south of the city. Although Iowa won the battle 29 — 0, largely on the strength of four touchdowns and five extra points by Nyle Jones, contrasting weather conditions which ranged from bright sunshine to cloudy weather, and during the last half a steady downpour of rain, troubled both teams.

Evidence of continued difficulties within the athletic board was heightened early in October when Professors E. A. Wilcox and C. C. Nut-

Head Football Coach and
Athletic Director — 1903-1906
John Chalmers

ting resigned. Wilcox, president of the board for three years, had prepared and presented the brief on behalf of Clyde Williams at the Western conference meeting in 1902, while

Nutting was chairman of the eligibility committee. Both felt strongly that the 1901 revision of the athletic constitution, giving controlling policy back to the students, had removed any effective legislative efforts from the faculty group. It would be another year, however, before the warnings of Wilcox and Nutting would be heeded.

At the same time, harmony was the byword on the football field. Coach Chalmers had recorded shutout victories in his first three games, and the winning streak was extended to four before Minnesota drove the Hawks into submission 75 — 0. The Gophers were held for downs only once during the game.

Again the Hawkeyes bounced back, however, and won three of the next four games. With a respectable seven victories in nine outings, elaborate preparations were made for the biggest game ever staged in Iowa City. Illinois was the opposition, and all Iowa remembered well the humiliating 80 — 0 defeat administered by the Illini a year before.

The determined Hawks throttled their visitors early in the game, drove the length of the field to score, and maintained a surprising 6 — 0 lead at halftime. Another touchdown following the second half kickoff, coupled with fierce defensive play throughout, gave Iowa a convincing 12 — 0 verdict. It was the first triumph ever registered over a Big Ten opponent in Iowa City, and the Daily Iowan student paper acknowledged the occasion by appearing on downtown streets twenty minutes after the game with its pages in Old Gold.

Earle McGowan, captain of the 1905 Hawkeyes, and holder of Iowa scoring records for a single season, gave major credit to the spontaneous enthusiasm of Iowa fans for the upset victory. Writing in the Iowa Alumnus nine years later, McGowan said, "The eleven men had done their best, but the twelfth man on the team, in the person of the loyal and spirited Iowa rooter, had won the game for S.U.I."

A week later John Chalmers' heroes won their ninth victory in eleven games. No future Iowa team would exceed that number of triumphs in a single season.

Thirteen "I"s were awarded by the Board in Control of Athletics, and the Board also voted to award "I"s each year to those who earned them in track and baseball. It thus became possible for the first time for an athlete to win as many as twelve total letters. This was an important departure from the former procedure of awarding "I"s but once in each sport.

A financial accounting at the close of the 1903-04 year disclosed that the over-all debt from athletics had risen to more than $4,000. The University Board of Regents was asked to take over supervision of athletic monetary affairs, but the Board declined, saying that it would be unwise to take part in any management of athletics. Most important, the Regents refused to take any official action in connection with the Athletic Board.

A month later, Stephen H. Bush, secretary of the Board in Control of Athletics, wrote to University President MacLean regarding the distressing situation:

"I see no way out except in some way to take away financial control entirely from the students. We face the music, the students vote the expenses. I want to do my part but I cannot be any longer responsible for the improper and even practically dishonest methods which will keep the Athletic Union under its present cloud as long as athletics are managed under its present system. I fear we will get into trouble as soon as the preliminary season begins. The students demand a two weeks' outing up the river. I do not believe such extravagances honest and cannot lend my good name to that kind of business methods."

Then Professor Bush, along with A. G. Smith, President of the Board, and Mr. Walter Davis resigned from the Board in Control. Shortly thereafter it was agreed that the accounting of funds should not be left alone to the manager of athletics, but that the secretary of the Board of Regents should be the accountant and all reports of athletic management filed with him. Professors Smith and Bush, along with Mr. Davis, were asked to return to the Board and accepted. Thus the last important piece of student control was once again removed and transferred to faculty jurisdiction.

1904

The 1904 season, although not as successful in terms of victories as the previous year, found the Hawks winning seven of eleven games, including a noteworthy performance against Minnesota.

The Gopher game, originally contracted to be played in Davenport, was changed to Cedar Rapids two weeks prior to the Thanksgiving

Advertisement of
Iowa — Minnesota Game

playing date. It would have been necessary for the university to erect bleachers seating at least 3,000 fans if Davenport were to host the game. When both Minnesota and Iowa authorities suggested Cedar Rapids as a possible playing site, a group of businessmen from that city agreed to erect bleachers at no cost to Iowa.

Although the Hawkeyes were defeated 11 – 0, newspapers lavished praise on the fighting Iowans. One paper commented: "No Iowa team ever covered itself with so much glory as did the Iowa players when they met the big Gophers. Minnesota was held to eleven points, and was not able to score at all in the first half, so perfect was the Iowa defense."

The Gophers continued unbeaten in twelve contests, but the Iowa game point total was their lowest of the year.

Earlier in the season Iowa had trampled Cornell College 88 to 0, scoring a record ten touchdowns in the first half. Andy "Sagwaw" Chalmers finished the game with four touchdowns and twelve of fourteen extra points.

However, Hawkeye jubilation turned to humiliation and subsequent anger when it was announced three days later that Cornell had sent its second team to Iowa City for the game. The Mt. Vernon story declared that "This is Cornell's first experience in playing her subs against the conference teams, and it has made a week of merriment."

The following week Iowa journeyed to Des Moines to meet Drake in the dedicatory game of the new Bulldog stadium. Dignitaries including Governor Cummins and the presidents of both schools were on hand, but the home inaugural was spoiled when Iowa triumphed 17 – 0.

Still later in the season, Walter Eckersall of Chicago, not used by Coach Stagg in the first half against Iowa, came off the bench to return the second half kickoff 90 yards for a touchdown and the Maroons went on to shut out the Hawkeyes by 39 points.

The Iowa State battle captured more statewide interest than any, both before and after the game was played. An overflow mass meeting was held in Iowa City on Thursday preceding the clash. President MacLean gave a stirring charge to the varsity, and this was followed by a snake dance through downtown streets.

Ames scored within fifteen seconds of the opening kickoff when Iowa fumbled. The ball was picked up by Cyclone Preston Daniels who carried it into the Hawkeye end zone. "Germany" Schwin and Dwight Griffith countered with Iowa scores moments later, after which the two teams battled on even terms the remainder of the game. Iowa had won 10 — 6, and students staged a wild demonstration through the night. But repercussions were also being heard.

Sportswriter C. E. Harris, writing in the Iowa State Register, commented: "Quite the worst thing of the entire season was the use Iowa made of an ear-splitting steam-whistle during the game. This contrivance, situated at the south end of the grand stand, seriously interfered with the visitors' signals. So far as I can recall the home team was never greatly handicapped in this manner. Even more disgusting was the continual exhibition of this noise making device whenever the loyal rooters of Ames sought to encourage their team by good, wholesome cheering."

Coach John Chalmers was offered a third term as Iowa football mentor, but the Board was unable to raise his salary from the $2,000 it had been paying him. Since Chalmers was completing law studies at the university, in addition to his coaching duties, he accepted for another year.

The abilities and far-reaching influence of Prof. A. G. Smith were concretely recognized when he was elected president of the Western Conference at a meeting held in Chicago following the 1904 season. At the same time the conference adopted the "one semester rule," barring freshmen from athletic participation until they "shall have been a student in the school for at least one semester."

1905

An important change in scoring had been adopted for use at the beginning of the 1904 season. The value of a field goal was reduced from five to four points. In 1905 the rules were further revised, stating that a player who was substituted for could not re-enter the game at any time.

Earle McGowan, playing his third year with the Hawkeyes was named captain, and it was largely because of his record breaking scoring efforts that Iowa was able to win eight games against only two defeats. McGowan notched an impressive 19 touchdowns and 19 extra points to set a state scoring mark which has never been equalled in Iowa. His biggest single afternoon came in mid-November against Drake, then coached by Michigan's famed Willie Heston, when the powerful fullback crashed for five touchdowns and kicked five extra points.

Iowa shut out six opponents in 1905, but in the only two conference games, against Minnesota and Walter Eckersall-led Chicago, the Hawkeyes were whitewashed while giving up seventy-one points.

The longest field goal in the midwest, and one of the longest in the nation during the season, was kicked by Iowa's versatile sophomore quarterback, Maury Kent. Kent's tape-measure effort, one of two kicked against St. Louis University, was forty-five yards.

Early the following January Mark Catlin, captain of the championship Chicago grid team of 1905, was named Iowa's track coach and assistant in football. Three months later John Chalmers resigned his position as physical director and football coach. Chalmers had attained his legal degree, formed a law partnership and planned to practice in Dubuque beginning in July.

However, at the suggestion of the Iowa Athletic Board he agreed to return to Iowa City early in September to handle the 1906 Hawkeyes through the season. His salary was to be $800. Catlin, heir apparent to Chalmers, was immediately appointed physical director.

At the spring meetings of the Western Conference, perhaps the most important sessions held up to that time, drastic changes were proposed and adopted by the faculty representatives. Six of the more significant and far-reaching provisions were destined to alter the course of football and athletics within the conference for a period of years. Those six regulations:

1. The number of intercollegiate football games limited to five.
2. No graduate student eligible to compete.
3. No one may play intercollegiate athletics for more than three years.
4. No training table or training quarters permitted.
5. The six month residence rule of 1904 extended to a full year before eligibility.
6. That steps be taken to reduce receipts and expenses of athletic contests.

Never again would a conference school be permitted unlimited latitude in the number of games it scheduled. As such, the twenty-two

Head Football Coach — 1907-1908
Athletic Director — 1906-1909
Mark Catlin

games played by Chicago in 1894 would stand forever as a Big Ten high, and one of the most ambitious single season schedules ever undertaken by a collegiate team.

Iowa was opposed to the first three provisions, and as a result of the adoption of the second and third, such fine performers as Andy Chalmers, Fred Schwin and Maury Kent would have their Hawkeye athletic careers shortened.

In addition to the newly created Western Conference regulations, the most revolutionary changes ever introduced to football became a part of the game in 1906 — a year which stands as perhaps the most important in the history of the sport.

A storm of criticism had followed the 1905 season. The rough, exhausting type of game which had prevailed contributed to an increasing number of serious injuries. The brutality and danger of football, along with the overemphasis placed upon it by the larger universities was the subject of lengthy editorial comment. Several schools abolished the game, including Northwestern within the conference. President Theodore Roosevelt, who felt that the game had too many beneficial features to be banished, used his influence to save the sport.

Following a hastily arranged meeting of the President and football's most influential leaders, significant alterations were made. Among them was the formation of the National Collegiate Athletic Association as controlling and chief legislative body for colleges and universities throughout the country.

In addition, the football rules committee modified the game radically. Most important of the new rules were the following:

1. Length of games reduced to sixty minutes, divided into two halves of thirty minutes each.
2. Distance to be gained from scrimmage in three downs increased to ten yards.
3. Forward pass introduced and formally legalized.
   a. One forward pass allowed on each series of downs.
   b. If a forward pass hits the ground before being touched by a player of either side, the ball shall go to the opponents on the spot where the pass was made.
   c. A pass touched but not caught could be recovered by either side (having the same effect as a completion, or an interception).

1906

It was necessary to hold three separate elections for the purpose of selecting an Iowa captain prior to the 1906 season. Fred "Germany" Schwin was named to the position following the 1905 campaign, but subsequent conference legislation made him ineligible for the position. In the spring Andy "Sagwaw" Chalmers was elected team captain, but he too was denied further competition, having played the three previous seasons. Late in September halfback George Allen received the honor of captaining the 1906 Hawkeyes.

In view of conference restrictions limiting the season to five games, Iowa did not face varsity competition until the final Saturday in October. The abnormally long pre-season practice was gratefully accepted by Coaches Chalmers and Catlin, however. Of the twenty-five Hawkeyes eligible for action, only five had represented the university in a game before 1906.

Iowa divided its first two contests, winning from Missouri but losing to Wisconsin. The following week one of the most spectacular games ever seen on Iowa Field took place. Coe College, heretofore never having made a touchdown against the Hawkeyes, provided the opposition. Iowa scored within the first three minutes, but lost the lead when Morrow of Coe returned a punt sixty yards to tie the game. The Cedar Rapids eleven scored a second time and led 12 — 5 with less than ten minutes remaining in the game. The Hawkeyes drove the length of the field to score, and shortly thereafter were stopped on the Coe six-inch line. The jubilant Kohawks held a slim 12 — 11 lead with less than a minute to play as they punted from out of their end zone. However, Iowa called for a fair catch and Maury Kent quickly kicked the game winning field goal to snatch the victory from Coe, 15 — 12.

Visiting officials insisted that the game had been allowed to continue long after time had run out. Some even suggested that six minutes additional time had been permitted. It was heatedly pointed out that the official time-keeper was an Iowa official. Further, a regular watch was used with time-outs simply being subtracted on a piece of paper. Even Iowa players casually admitted that the final half was unusually long; but by that time the 15 — 12 Hawkeye score had been permanently affixed in the football record book.

A ferocious defensive performance highlighted the Iowa — Iowa State battle two weeks later. Clyde Williams, Iowa's most decorated early grid hero, had moved to Ames as assistant to head coach "Shady" Ristine.

Only three first downs were notched by the two teams that afternoon. Further, the ball was punted a total of 45 times, 23 of the kicks from the foot of Hawkeye Maury Kent. The two teams attempted six field goals, all failures.

The single break in the game came midway in the first half when a blocked Iowa punt was downed in the Hawk end zone. Ames was awarded a safety and won the game, 2 — 0.

A week later the largest crowd to watch an Iowa athletic team in action, 15,000, cheered the most highly developed use of the forward pass ever seen up to that time. St. Louis University, coached by the renowned Eddie Cochems, bewildered the Iowans with a devastating array of double passes, forward passes and revolving plays beyond anything the Hawkeyes had ever seen. The home town Billikens, undefeated throughout the season, gained a convincing 39 — 0 victory.

Iowa returned from St. Louis' playing field losers but with sufficient gate receipts to retire every debt of the athletic department as well as long standing notes which had been contracted nine years earlier when Athletic Park was purchased.

The Hawkeyes' share of the St. Louis game receipts was $4,637,50. At the December meeting of the Athletic Association, Board President A. G. Smith stated that total athletic income now exceeded $15,000, with football receipts amounting to more than $10,000. Notes and drafts of more than $4,500 were paid off, and interest bearing certificates worth $3,000 were purchased as assets of the association.

Early in January, 1907, representatives of Kansas, Missouri, Nebraska, Washington of St. Louis and Iowa met in Kansas City to discuss the formation of a new athletic conference. A month later, February 16, 1907, the five schools formally organized the Missouri Valley Conference.

Iowa, although a charter member, was a part of the new league for only four years, finding affiliation with two athletic conferences difficult and unwieldy.

John Chalmers had left Iowa City to spend the next fifty-six years as a prominent attorney and judge in Dubuque. During his four years with the Hawkeyes, Iowa was defeated only eleven times, winning 26 of 37 games. Mark Catlin, previously named athletic director, was elevated to the head coaching position.

Although Chalmers and Catlin had worked together harmoniously during the 1906 season, their football backgrounds and teaching philosophies differed in many ways. Chalmers, an easterner, had played the game at Lafayette and was well indoctrinated in the eastern style of play. As such he spent considerable time coaching his players as individuals, striving for thoroughness and technical competence. Kindly and highly respected by his players as well as university officials, John Chalmers fostered and strengthened those friendships throughout his life.

Mark Catlin, also congenial both on and off the field, learned his football at Chicago under Amos Alonzo Stagg. Because he advocated the aggressive, more open western style of football, Catlin spent less time coaching his players as individuals. His own great natural ability and football instinct probably hindered Mark Catlin during his early coaching years. Few athletes were endowed with the physical and instinctive qualities of Catlin. Carrying his own playing field experience to the coaching ranks, the new Iowa coach therefore devoted less time to individual detail and basic football knowledge. Unfortunately, Western Conference legislation of 1906 and 1907 made such teaching philosophy difficult and hazardous.

1907

The conference ruling that no more than three years of varsity football could be played, and that no freshmen were eligible, in effect barred seniors and first year men in 1907. The smallest squads and most inexperienced teams in the history of the conference, composed of sophomores and juniors, greeted Catlin and his coaching brothers when practice convened late in September.

John "Reddy" Griffith, a backfield star of Iowa's undefeated 1899 and 1900 teams, was appointed assistant coach. Two modifications of the rules provided that 1) the length of each game was again increased to seventy minutes; and 2) forward passes which fell to the ground without being touched drew a 15-yard penalty rather than loss of the ball.

Although Maury Kent had been the first to use the forward pass at Iowa, it was Chick Kirk, generally recognized the finest Hawkeye backfield performer between Clyde Williams and Aubrey Devine, who first exploited the pass effectively. Kirk, a full game performer, was Iowa's first triple-threat gridder. And in addition to his running, passing and punting feats, Chick Kirk drop-kicked field goals and extra points and did the kicking off.

After a successful 9 — 0 outing against an alumni team, the Hawkeyes opened their regular season with an impressive 21 — 6 triumph over Missouri. Iowa notched 37 first downs in the game, with Kirk scoring one touchdown, kicking a field goal and three extra points.

Drake was a 25 — 4 victim the following week, and early in November Wisconsin was met in Iowa City. The Badgers came from a 5 — 0 halftime deficit to win 6 — 5 in the highly publicized "rabbit game."

Coach Catlin and the Hawkeyes felt that Iowa had been jinxed by a rabbit just prior to the start of the second half. As the two teams lined up for the kickoff the bad-omen cottontail raced from Wisconsin's goal the length of the field, passing between the Iowa goal posts. This was claimed to be the forerunner of the Badger player who followed late in the game with a long touchdown run. Harlan "Biddy" Rogers fielded a high, wind-blown punt and carried it into the Hawkeye end zone for the tying score. Goal was kicked and Wisconsin captured the victory. Each team fumbled twelve times during the game, but Iowans felt it was the 110-yard rabbit run which had sealed their fate.

Feature of activities in preparation for the Illinois game was an announcement by Catlin that an extensive rabbit hunt would precede practice on Wednesday. The Iowa coach shot the villain at the north end of Iowa field after his players had dislodged it from beneath the grandstand. The left hind foot of the rabbit was touched by each player, and the carcass hung on the fence of Iowa field — emblematic of Illinois' fate on Saturday.

A second consecutive victory was credited to the mystic powers of Iowa's now famous rabbit when the Hawkeyes ambushed the favored Illini 25 — 12. Catlin exploited the open game to its fullest, and with Chick Kirk completing 12 passes for 195 yards, Iowa dominated the game.

The following Saturday history of another sort was written in the annals of Iowa football. No game caused more statewide controversy and eventual repercussions than the bitter 1907 struggle between Iowa and Iowa State. A crowd of close to 5,000, including bands from both schools, jammed the field at Ames. Tension had been electric all week but feelings became even more strained on the morning of the game when it was rumored, and later confirmed, that Coach Mark Catlin had received an anonymous call the night before warning that star halfback Chick Kirk would be "put out of the game early."

Shortly after the opening kickoff Kirk was sent back to receive an Ames punt. He signalled for a fair catch. Reppert, playing end for Iowa State, thundered down field, saw Kirk ready to make the catch, left his feet and dove into the Iowa star. A Des Moines newspaper story described the incident in this paragraph:

An historical football photo of the 1907 Iowa team lined up in the T formation with split right end.

"After Kirk had signalled for a fair catch, Reppert jumped into him with terrific force, much as he jumped into Nebraska's captain earlier in the season (for which he was removed from the game). For two minutes Kirk was stretched lifeless on the turf. Reppert was taken from the game. The halfback who had been the sensation of the gridiron this year continued to play, but with Chick Kirk injured Iowa's offense was shattered. The injury was irreparable."

And from Ames came staunch defense of Reppert. Loyal Cyclone students praised him as a hard, clean player unjustly criticized. This article carried an Ames dateline:

"A great deal of indignation is felt here over the scathing Reppert is receiving in the newspapers over the Kirk incident. Reppert is one of the best defensive players Ames ever had. He tackles low, sure and hard, but he is never dirty. No one doubts here that he did not see Kirk signal for a free catch and so tackled him."

In speaking of the incident, Reppert said:

"We were told before the game to look out for Kirk. If we could break up his plays and down him in his tracks for the first 15 minutes, we would discourage him and he would be no worse to us than any other man on the team. I saw Kirk was about to receive the punt but I did not see him signal for the free catch when I lowered my head to dive for him. I started to dive before he had the ball in his arms because I was afraid he'd get away from me if I waited. I had no thought of laying him out."

Chick Kirk, though ineffective the remainder of the game as a runner or passer, kicked two field goals to give Iowa early leads. However, Ames retaliated each time and held off a last minute Hawkeye surge on their own five to win 20 — 14.

Immediately after the game charges and counter charges were hurled from all sides. After more than half a century of deliberation, the jury of public opinion has yet to issue a clear cut decision on whether Reppert was a powerful defensive football player who became a victim of circumstances, or a man who went out to "get" the star of the opposing

team. However, the thud of his resounding tackle will echo forever.

Shortly before the Iowa Athletic Board was to meet regarding the "Ames-Iowa, Reppert-Kirk" incident, a startling story came to light that Tod Willetts, Iowa State fullback, had played at Grinnell in 1902 and 1903, transferred to Ames, and competed there in 1904, 1905, 1906 and 1907.

On Friday evening January 10, 1908, the Board in Control of Athletics met and severed

Chick Kirk

all athletic relations with Iowa State. Chairman of the Board A. G. Smith made the announcement:

"The breaking of athletic relations with the Iowa Agricultural College by Iowa is caused by the fact that the Ames management must have had knowledge of the ineligibility of a member of the football eleven which met Iowa. The fullback on the Ames team, Thomas K. Willett, was a member of the Grinnell College and Ames athletic teams for a greater length of time than the rules allow.

"As the present trainer of the Ames football team, Mr. Watson, had charge of Willett when they both were at Grinnell, the Ames authorities must have known of the questionable stand of the athlete. The action taken is not based on the Kirk-Reppert incident, but upon the playing of Willett in the Ames-Iowa game."

A formal apology regarding the Willett incident was sent from Professor S. M. Beyer of Ames, Chairman of the Faculty Committee in Charge of Athletics. It was received and accepted by the Iowa Board on January 16.

Deserved recognition was given Chick Kirk at the close of the 1907 season. In addition to all-America mention, he was a unanimous all-western choice. The Chicago Record-Herald in announcing its selection, commented:

"Kirk is a scoring machine in himself, being, besides a great man with the forward pass, one of the most accurate drop kickers in the west. In all other departments of the game he qualifies as a star."

His teammates, recognizing the versatile abilities of Kirk, elected him captain of the 1908 football squad, and he was also named to captain the 1908 baseball team.

There was considerable adverse criticism within the conference over the "reform" legislation of 1906 and 1907. Particularly controversial was the rule limiting the period of competition to three years, and later making the restriction retroactive. This meant that senior year men who had played as freshmen were ineligible. Certain conference schools felt that their member institutions were put at a disadvantage in competition with schools which did not observe such strict regulation. Michigan, geographically and traditionally interested in continuing successful competition with eastern teams, led the opposition. When the majority refused to change their previously enacted legislation, Michigan withdrew entirely from the Western Conference.

1908

Sixty-five candidates reported to head coach Mark Catlin when practice opened late in September. It was the largest pre-season turnout in twenty years of Iowa football.

Perhaps the most interesting development surrounding practice sessions in 1908, however, was the presence of "Burch," Iowa's first mascot. The four month old bear cub was obtained from the Idaho hills and lived under the newly

"Burch" the Mascot

constructed cement bleachers at Iowa Field. Referred to as "one of the boys" by members of the Hawkeye team, Burch occupied a prominent position near the Iowa bench at all home games during the 1908 and 1909 seasons.

After a 16 to 0 victory in the first varsity-alumni game for many years, Iowa completely annihilated Coe College 92 — 0. The Old Gold, determined to "pour it on" in answer to the unfavorable publicity which arose following the controversial 1906 game, scored 15 touchdowns,

13 extra points and one field goal. Outstanding performances were given by Chick Kirk and Peck Hazard. Kirk notched three touchdowns, seven extra points and a 45 yard field goal, while Hazard scored four times, once on a 105 yard kickoff return.

Unfortunately, disaster was born out of that overwhelming grudge game triumph. Five prominent Hawkeyes, including backfield mainstays Kirk and Walter "Stub" Stewart, were badly injured, their effectiveness never fully regained during the balance of the season.

Iowa was able to win only one of six remaining contests, and included in the defeats was a surprising 12 – 6 loss to Drake. Most spectacular feature of the game was a record-setting 65 yard scoring pass from Chick Kirk to H. R. Gross in the final minutes.

Kirk, although physically handicapped during the season, was again a unanimous All-Western selection, receiving the honor from Collier's Magazine, Fielding Yost, Walter Eckersall and others. This recognition was gained in spite of his team's winning only two of seven games.

Aaron "Fat" Seidel, powerful three year guard, was honored for the second year in a row on Collier's All-Western second team.

One week prior to the close of the 1908 season a significant meeting of the Athletic Union was held in the Old Capitol building. At this time dissolution of the original governing body was voted and a transfer was made of all rights and property to the Board in Control of Athletics.

A month later, December 21, 1908, the Board in Control of Athletics was incorporated. The powers of the Board were outlined in Article II of the Articles of Incorporation:

"The powers of this corporation shall be to direct, manage and have general charge of athletic contests given under the auspices of said University, whether such contests be between members of said University or between such members and other persons; to make contracts with reference to such contests; to provide for instruction in athletics; to transact any business of any nature in any way connected with athletics referred to said Board; and to transact all business of any nature or to do any act which, in the opinion of said Board, will further the athletic interests of said University, including the acquisition and disposition of property."

The new Board was to consist of twelve persons, chosen as follows:

"Five members of the staff of instruction of the University, to be appointed by the acting President of the University; the Director of Athletics; two alumni of the University; cap-

Head Football Coach — 1909
Athletic Director — 1909-1910
John G. Griffith

tains of the university football, baseball, track and basketball teams."

Thus ended the last effective control of athletics by students at Iowa, although undergraduate dissatisfaction and unrest during the next two years openly challenged the "conservative policies and bureaucratic control" of the new Board.

Shortly after the first of the year athletic relations with Iowa State were resumed, and late in February, 1909, Mark Catlin tendered his resignation, effective at the close of the school year. His brief two year coaching tenure at

Iowa showed five victories against seven defeats.

The Iowa Athletic Board, considering the complexities of both coaching and managing athletics, acted to separate the duties by elevating Assistant Football Coach John G. Griffith to the head coaching position. Griffith, the first of only two Iowa graduates to coach football at the university, accepted the grid and basketball posts for $1,300. Until the athletic directorship was filled, all management decisions would be resolved by the Board in Control.

1909

Disappointment again was the byword used to sum up Iowa football fortunes in 1909. The team won only two of seven games, as well as a 6 — 6 tie with Nebraska on the strength of twelve and thirty-seven yard field goals by Mike Hyland. This was the first year in which field goals counted three points.

Minnesota, with its famous Lisle Johnson scoring five touchdowns, smashed any early season Iowa dreams by winning 41 — 0 in the opener. Johnson included 55 and 65 yard punt returns in his quintet of markers. Never has his record been exceeded in a Western Conference game, and never has it been matched by a conference player against Iowa. Lisle Johnson, one of the finest of many great Gopher athletes, died tragically in 1913, at the age of twenty-five. A monument to his memory stands prominently on the Minnesota campus.

Missouri escaped with a narrow one-point victory, 13 — 12, despite two touchdowns by dependable Ray Murphy. The Daily Iowan story of the game included this revealing account by an eagle-eyed reporter:

"Missouri's kick for goal after the first touchdown landed on the 'Merry Widow' of a startled feminine spectator at the north end of the field."

The first intentional safety in Iowa, and one of the first in American football, helped Drake defeat the Hawkeyes 17 — 14. For the second straight game Ray Murphy and Mike Hyland scored all S.U.I. points, but a fumble on the Bulldog four late in the game led to the winning strategy. Drake coach John L. Griffith, later commissioner of the Big Ten conference, and Tom Burcham, who had kicked two long field goals earlier in the game, conceived the idea of giving Iowa two points by intentionally grounding the ball behind the goal-line. Under rules at the time the Bulldogs would retain

Walter L. (Stub) Stewart

possession of the ball. Drake led by five points, 17 — 12, and conceded a game-saving safety, but with less than four minutes remaining Iowa could get no closer than 17 — 14 .

The Hawkeyes gained ample revenge the following week by surprising a heavily favored Iowa State team 16 — 0 before 5,500, the largest crowd to see a game in Iowa City up to that time.

In describing the victory, one newspaper commented that "the Hawkeyes won by being superior in every department of the game, playing rings and concentric circles around their opponents."

Iowa made thirty-five first downs, Ames but four. Captain Gross, Archie Alexander and Ray Murphy were offensive standouts, with Murphy notching a brace of touchdowns for the third straight game. Mike Hyland's accurate punting kept the Cyclones at bay, while the spirited generalship of quarterback Stub Stewart ignited the play of every Hawkeye.

The active athletic career of Stewart, most versatile "small man" ever to compete at Iowa, came to a close following the 1909-10 school year. A nine letter winner, he never weighed more than 130 pounds and in addition to captaining the varsity baseball and basketball teams, was a second team All-Western selection in football.

Stub Stewart remained at Iowa after earning his undergraduate degree. While studying for his Ll.B. he served on the varsity coaching staff in all three sports, and was head coach of the baseball and basketball teams in 1911-12. Stewart maintained his abiding interest in Iowa athletics by faithfully serving as a member of the Board in Control of Athletics for nearly thirty years.

At the mid-November Athletic Board meeting requirements for winning an "I" in football were changed. Henceforth it was necessary for a player to participate in at least three halves of Western Conference games or five halves of games with Missouri Valley conference opponents. Participation was defined as playing the entire half unless removed from the game because of injury.

The second decade of Hawkeye football, from 1900 thru 1909, found Iowa winning fifty games, losing 29 and tying two. However, in Western Conference competition the record showed only four victories, sixteen losses and a tie.

Over-all, since the first game in 1889, S.U.I. grid teams were victorious eighty-eight times against fifty-seven losses and eight ties — winning 60 per cent of their games.

Intimately involved with Hawkeye athletic successes and failures since the day a ball was first discovered on the Iowa campus was a be-

"Jimmie" Barry

loved old man, Jimmie Barry. No University of Iowa student, supporter or school administrator before or since has been held in higher affection than Jimmie, nor has any served the university over a longer period of years. Not blessed with the opportunity of gaining any formal education, Jimmie Barry nevertheless was saluted by his university president, honored at dinners, and recognized as guest of honor at football games. The venerable guardian of Iowa Field celebrated his seventy-eighth birthday on St. Pat-

BEST OF THE DECADE — 1900 — 1909

Ends	Mark W. Hyland	1908-1909-1910
	Jack N. Streff	1904-1905-1906
	L. Bert Watters	1899-1900-1901-1903
	Roy A. (Cresco) White	1904-1905-1907
Tackles	Archie A. Alexander	1909-1910-1911
	Fred W. Schwin	1903-1904-1905
Guards	Emmett F. Burrier	1898-1899-1900-1901
	Aaron E. Seidel	1907-1908
Centers	Irving H. Hastings	1906-1907-1908
	Fred Moore	1904-1905
Quarter-backs	Walter L. Stewart	1907-1908-1909
	S. Clyde Williams	1898-1899-1900-1901
Half-backs	Maurice A. Kent	1904-1905-1906
	Carrol N. (Chick) Kirk	1906-1907-1908
Fullback	Earle A. McGowan	1903-1904-1905

rick's Day, 1910. That date also marked fifty-two years of service in Iowa City.

The Athletic Board voted a ten dollar honorary payment to Jimmie following the 1909 season "for the faithful feeding and caring of 'Burch' over an eighteen month period."

The black bear mascot, imported from Idaho in 1908, was found drowned in the Iowa River in March, 1910. His head was mounted and placed among the archives of the university museum.

Financially, the 1909-10 athletic year showed an over-all loss of $46.86. Football receipts of more than $12,000 exceeded expenses by $3,700. However, track, baseball and basketball were conducted at a loss. The Athletic Board financial statement revealed a cash equity of $310.14 at the close of the year.

John Griffith had been offered an extension of his football contract through the 1910 season, but he resigned the position in July to return to the University of Idaho as football coach and head of the school Entomology Department.

Jess Hawley Takes Over — 1910-1912

1910

Severe and pointed attacks were directed at the Iowa Board in Control of Athletics by undergraduate students who demanded a more liberal policy in regard to athletics. They wanted a one-man directorate, and they wanted a prominent voice in the athletic management through a student athletic association. Charges and counter charges were hurled by both sides, although the Board survived the discontent without altering its course or its control.

At the same time the State Board of Education launched an attack, not at the Board in Control but at all forms of intercollegiate athletics. James H. Trewin, President of the State Board, stated that he did not believe it appropriate or within the provisions of the constitution of the State Board to use public funds for the purpose of maintaining intercollegiate athletics. Trewin then advocated the abolishment of football and all intercollegiate athletics, and although his suggestion was not sustained, the Iowa Board passed a drastic revision of its own by establishing the controversial "two-sport rule."

This rule prohibited any athlete from competing in more than two major sports. Foot-

**Head Football Coach — 1910-1915
Jess B. Hawley**

ball, basketball, baseball and track were designated major sports. It was aimed at preventing a student from devoting too much time to athletics at the expense of his classroom studies. However, while the purpose was exemplary, intercollegiate athletics suffered, without any appreciable change in the scholastic ranking of Iowa athletes. As a result, the rule was rescinded in 1913.

Early in September, 1910, two men were named to the Iowa athletic staff. Each was destined to make an everlasting contribution to the growth and development of athletics on the campus, within the state, and within the Western Conference.

Nelson Kellogg, one of the foremost distance runners in the nation shortly after the turn of the century, accepted the position of head track coach and manager of athletics at a salary of $1,600. The Iowa Board agreed that this figure would be increased to $1,800 the second year. Only two other men were considered by the Board. The first was S. Clyde Williams, one of the greatest athletes ever to perform for the Hawkeyes. The other was John L. Griffith, then athletic director at Drake University and later the first commissioner of the Western or Big Ten conference. Neither was able to consider an offer from the Iowa athletic board.

The position of head football coach was filled when Jess Hawley, a graduate of Dartmouth College, accepted terms providing $1,050 for the 1910 season and $1,300 for both 1911 and 1912 if his first year work were found satisfactory. Before the 1910 season had ended, the athletic board re-signed Hawley for the 1911 campaign, this time for $1,800.

Jess Hawley came to Iowa highly recommended as a player, coach and leader. Although actively engaged in business, a continuing interest in football and young men prompted his decision in favor of Iowa.

Significant football rule changes were proposed and subsequently adopted prior to the 1910 season. Playing time was reduced to sixty minutes, consisting of four fifteen minute periods. At least seven players were required to be on the offensive line of scrimmage. A quirk in the laws stated that a forward pass traveling more than twenty yards beyond the scrimmage line was not allowed. Interlocking interference was finally abolished, along with pushing or pulling the ball carrier forward. In addition, it became legal for the player who first received the ball from center to run with it from any point. This provision, although not highly publicized at the time, opened the door of opportunity for football innovators such as Hawley, Pop Warner, Knute Rockne and others to devise offensive formations which soon revolutionized the game.

Two weeks before Iowa's first game, Jess Hawley greeted an alarmingly small group of

Athletic Director — 1910-1917
Nelson Kellogg

football candidates. The new coach was a disciple of sound fundamentals, attention to details and well grounded organization.

Three sections of concrete bleachers, each holding 720 fans, were dedicated before the opening game. In addition, Iowa's first press box, constructed during the summer, was opened to reporters. The Hawkeyes responded with a 12 — 0 win over Morningside College, but a week later were defeated by Northwestern, 10 — 5.

On Wednesday following the Wildcat game, Iowa City high school played the varsity a 30-minute practice game. The light, inexperienced high schoolers dominated the session and held Hawley's unit scoreless.

Well placed concern was evident. A serious and all-important mass meeting was held the next day, at which Coach Hawley attributed the poor showing of the Hawkeyes to an almost "complete lack of fighting spirit in the men."

"We have only 22 men out for football," said Hawley, "and we should have 60 to 70."

Three more varsity players left the team prior to its departure for Columbia, Mo., and further disappointment arose when it was announced by Missouri that Archie Alexander, giant Negro tackle, would not be permitted to play against the Tigers. Iowa lost 5 — 0, but in view of the pre-game announcement, as well as the unsportsmanlike treatment given the Hawkeye team, Coach Hawley declared that never again would he field a team against Missouri.

The Iowans rebounded with a vengeance the following week, scoring a decisive 16 — 0 victory over Purdue in the first conference game played in Iowa City in three years. Iron Mike Hyland and Ray Murphy led the Hawkeye attack which outrushed the Boilermakers 434 yards to 50 and outdowned them, 19 — 4.

Cold and bleak was that November afternoon when Jess Hawley led his gridders to Ames for the annual struggle with Iowa State. Clyde Williams, Iowa's greatest early day performer, was head coach of the Cyclones.

An Iowa City paper began its report of the bitter struggle: "The long suffering farmers got it in the same old place today, Iowa defeating Ames by a score of 2 — 0."

Ames never penetrated the Hawkeye 25 yard line, although they did attempt four field goals. In the first period Iowa got the only two points of the game when State's Smith fumbled a bad pass from center while attempting to punt from his own goal line. He was smothered by charging Iowa linemen, and downed in the end zone for a safety.

A week later Iowa won its first undisputed state championship since 1905 by decisively defeating Drake, 21 — 0.

Willis "Fat" O'Brien made his debut as a drop-kicker and his initial effort, from the Bulldog 45 yard line, matched a placement field goal by Maury Kent against Washington of St. Louis in 1905.

Ray Murphy, playing his junior season for Iowa, electrified the Iowa City crowd early in the first period with a brilliant 65 yard touchdown dash, the longest of his career and the longest of the season for the Hawkeyes.

The seventh and concluding game, against Washington of St. Louis, resulted in a 38 — 0 Iowa victory. Mike Hyland climaxed his meteoric career by notching three touchdowns and a trio of conversions. The popular Hyland was selected the outstanding player in the state. He was Iowa's leading scorer for the year with five touchdowns and nine extra points.

At the December meeting of Western Conference representatives a resolution was adopted prohibiting any conference athletic team from scheduling games with schools which previously had been members of the conference. The resolution obviously was aimed at the University of Michigan which severed connections with the conference in 1908.

More important, perhaps, was legislation requiring each conference school to schedule four football games with other affiliated institutions. Prof. A. G. Smith, the Iowa representative, characterized this as the "most significant of recent years, since it now unites the conference as it has never been united before."

Early in 1911 considerable public print was given to a "break" in athletic relations between Iowa and Drake. The Hawkeyes had originally desired to play Drake in mid-October of 1911. Drake preferred a November date which from a financial standpoint would be much more profitable.

Iowa, feeling committed to the Western Conference, requested that a firm November date not be settled until after the February conference meetings in Chicago. Following these meetings Manager Kellogg wrote Drake coach John Griffith that Iowa would prefer the October date.

Drake was incensed, feeling that Iowa had broken an agreement to play a mid-November game after Drake had kept such a date open for the Hawkeyes. Coach Griffith then said that Drake would agree to the October date for 1911 only if Iowa would consent to a November date in 1912, both games to be played in Des Moines. Kellogg refused and no further games were played between the two schools for more than thirty years.

On May 24, 1911, the Iowa Board in Control of Athletics met in an historic session which culminated with the resignation of Iowa from the Missouri Valley Conference two days later. In a carefully prepared statement, the Iowa Board stated that the multiplicity of events in both conferences "makes it impossible for any institution to participate fully as a member in both of these organizations unless athletics are to be given an undue prominence in the University.

"The result is Iowa is placed in the position of being unable to carry out the entire duties of a member in both these conferences simultaneously.

"The University of Iowa therefore, with a warm appreciation of the many kind favors received from the several members of the Missouri Valley Conference, tenders its resignation from this Conference."

Thus, charter member Iowa, after a brief and somewhat stormy four year existence, closed its affiliation with the Missouri Valley Conference in favor of a stronger, more enduring, and hopefully, a more successful venture in the Western Intercollegiate Conference.

1911

With victories in its last four games in 1910, coupled with a veteran nucleus for 1911, indications pointed toward a successful campaign — the second under Jess Hawley.

Moray Eby, star of an earlier Hawkeye era, was named assistant coach, while hard-charging Ray Murphy was captain. Only the uncon-querable fighting spirit of Mike Hyland was absent when practice convened.

Hawley worked in earnest, fighting an unaccountable lethargy which was to plague the Iowa squad through its first four games. Morningside College battled the Hawkeyes on even terms before losing a lack-lustre 11 — 5 verdict in the opener.

A week later Cornell shocked the state and surprised even her most optimistic followers by defeating the uninspired Hawley men 3 — 0. A field goal by Cornell's West in the final three minutes sealed the victory.

Willis "Fat" O'Brien gained national acclaim in a losing cause the following Saturday. His two Paul Bunyon-like field goals, one of 45 yards, and the other from 52 yards afield, were the only Iowa scores in an otherwise decisive Minnesota victory, 24 — 6. They were the first points S.U.I. had registered against the Gophers since 1892, and the 52 yard O'Brien field goal was the longest in the nation in 1911.

After a 12 — 0 shutout loss to Wisconsin, desperation began to assert itself in the Hawkeye camp. Their spirit, broken by early disasters, was welded into a new fury. But Purdue, object of the grim preparations, and led by one of football's all-time greats, Elmer Oliphant, presented a formidable foe.

Following a scoreless first half, an Iowa touchdown, coupled between 35 and 43 yard field goals by Fat O'Brien, gave victory to the Hawkeyes, 11 — 0. An impregnable Iowa defense throughout the game permitted the Boilermakers only one first down.

Eight thousand fans, the largest crowd ever to see a game in Iowa City, braved unseasonable weather to watch the annual battle with Ames. Statistically the Hawkeyes dominated play, but costly fumbles and errors of judgment negated any effective offensive effort as State triumphed, 9 — 0.

Iowa closed the season against Northwestern, climaxing the game with a furious rally in the final minutes to score and shut out the Wildcats, 6 — 0. Once again a series of misfortunes had thwarted the Hawkeyes — three touch-

Willis O'Brien

downs being lost because of penalties. The victory, however, marked the first time since 1900 that Iowa had defeated two Western Conference opponents in a single season.

The playing career of Willis "Fat" O'Brien was highlighted following the campaign by his selection to various honor elevens. Walter Eckersall, foremost midwestern authority, wrote that "in O'Brien, Iowa had a kicker and all-around player who was the peer of any pivot man in the West."

Outing Magazine named the burly Hawkeye "one of the three outstanding centers in America, on account of his great work in breaking up the defense of opposing teams, his accurate passing, his brilliant defensive work, and above all his marvelous dexterity in dropkicking."

Away from the gridiron, Iowa was involved in two conference proposals of considerable import. Northwestern, having abolished football temporarily following the 1905 season, suggested three plans designed to remove the

"overemphasis" and "Big Business" labels which had already been hurled at the game's most successful proponents. The specific Wildcat proposals were to:

1. cut down the number of games each season to three;
2. abandon the use of all coaches, and
3. reduce all admissions to a maximum of twenty-five cents.

Each suggestion was defeated by a vote of member conference schools, with Iowa disapproving of all three.

Ohio State, which had applied for membership in January, was formally accepted as an affiliate of the Western Conference in April. Iowa had opposed its admittance, feeling that additional members might make the organization less effective and more unwieldy.

The last drastic revisions by the football rules committee were formally adopted prior to the playing season of 1912. Considerable agitation had been raised regarding the rules since the significant changes of 1906 and 1910 which had legalized the forward pass, increased the distance to be gained from scrimmage in only three downs to ten yards, and made it mandatory that at least seven players on offense be on the line of scrimmage. The contention was voiced that the running game, long a basic necessity for success, was no longer a requirement which would insure victory.

After the changes of 1912, however, the game finally appeared to be stabilized. Most important of the revisions were those which 1) increased the number of downs required to advance the ball ten yards from three to four; 2) reduced the playing field to 100 yards, plus two ten yard end zones; 3) changed the value of a touchdown from five to six points; 4) abolished the 20 yard limit on forward passes — any distance now being legal, including catching touchdown passes in the end zone. Of particular interest was the insertion of the only rule calling for a 25 yard penalty which the game has known. It was inflicted on any team not ready to play at the start of the second half.

1912

Financial problems, seldom a cause for concern since before 1900, once again beset the athletic department. An accounting as the 1912-13 school year began showed an athletic debt of close to $4,000. Receipts had become constant, while the expense of fielding representative teams increased each year. Improvement was not immediately ahead, however.

With only three home football games scheduled, the Hawkeye athletic board authorized season athletic books to be issued for $5.00. The purchaser was entitled to attend all contests during the school year.

Iowa opened the campaign with victories in its first two games, but success disintegrated before the furious fourth quarter passing barrage of Chicago a week later, 34 — 14. The Hawks had held a narrow 14 — 13 lead as the last period began, due primarily to the offensive determination of Leo Dick, Charley Parsons and Ralph McGinnis. But the physically outmanned Iowans were no match for Stagg's Maroons late in the game.

Minnesota overwhelmed Hawley's men the following week, but conference history was made early in November as Iowa met Indiana in the first game between the two teams. Dick and McGinnis scored Hawkeye touchdowns enroute to a 13 — 6 victory, although it was Hoosier Mickey Erehart who electrified the partisan Indianapolis crowd by racing 108 yards to put his name in the record books.

Writing of his marathon feat nearly fifty years later, Erehart recalled "we had held Iowa for downs on our two yard line and I was in position to punt, deep in our end zone. I had received the ball and had taken my step forward to punt when I saw the Iowa right end ready to jump in front of me. So, I hesitated a second, went around the open position, sidestepped three men, and was in the clear." It was the nation's longest scrimmage run during the year, longest ever in the Western Conference, and one of the longest dashes from scrimmage in the history of football.

Ames was a logical favorite over Iowa when the two State schools clashed. Minnesota, the only team to halt the Cyclones, had squeezed out a 5 — 0 victory as a result of a field goal and a safety. The same Gopher team had bewildered Iowa, 56 — 7.

However, the fundamentally sound Hawkeyes played their finest game of the year and earned a decisive 20 — 7 victory. Left halfback Leo Dick dashed 55 yards around his right end from Jess Hawley's famous spread formation for the game's most brilliant single play.

Hawley, one of football's greatest innovators, exploited the speed and quickness of his 1912 and 1913 teams by devising a number of successful maneuvers from the following basic spread formation:

E   T   G   C   G   T   E

QB

HB   FB   HB

In the foregoing formation was a spread of seven yards between the center and Iowa's guards. In addition, the halfbacks and fullback were stationed ten yards behind the Hawkeye linemen.

All week following the Ames battle preparations were made for Iowa's first annual Homecoming game and celebration. Unfortunately, one of the great teams in Western Conference history would provide the opposition. Wisconsin, averaging more than 43 points a game, scored twice within the first ten minutes and notched its sixth straight victory of the season, 28 — 10.

Midwestern football critic, Walter Eckersall, paid everlasting tribute to Coach Bill Juneau's devastating team when he announced his all-Big Ten selections at the close of the season. Nine Badgers were given first team recognition, a mythical all-star team monopoly which has never been approached by another conference school.

But, deserved honors were also given two prominent Iowa players. Capt. Henry Hanson was named on two all-Western and three all-Conference first teams. His running mate at tackle, Jim Trickey, was picked by the immortal

Jim Trickey

Walter Camp to his second team all-American. This was the highest recognition given a Hawkeye up to that time by Camp, and would rank

him with Aubrey Devine, Gordon Locke and Duke Slater as the only four Iowans selected by the "father of American football" to his first or second all-America teams.

Tragically, less than a year after learning of his all-American honor, Jim Trickey was dead. He succumbed early in December, 1913, as a result of an operation followed by peritonitis.

A graduate of Iowa Falls High School, Trickey entered the university in 1909. As a means of defraying a portion of the cost of his education, he preached on Sundays in churches near Iowa City. He played guard on the Hawkeye varsity as a sophomore and junior. Then, surprisingly, he asked to be excused from further participation in football. He wanted to devote his entire senior year to classroom studies.

Students at Iowa voiced a pleading protest. The football team needed Trickey. A petition was prepared, signed by 1,600 students, and presented to him. The next afternoon Trickey was in uniform on the football field. As if in reward for the sacrifice, his sterling play attracted the attention and gained the plaudits of critics from coast to coast.

Off the gridiron his kindness and personality were so well recognized that his fellow students elected Jim Trickey president of the senior class by unanimous vote, a majority never before accorded a student in the university.

Many who knew him speak of the admirable qualities which distinguished Jim Trickey from the ordinary man. The contributions he made to his university, both on and off the football field, remain his epitaph.

1913: One of the Greatest

Jess Hawley was offered a salary increase, calling for payment of $2,000, if he would agree to return as head football coach in the fall of 1913. The taciturn but likeable business executive agreed and welcomed 50 candidates, including ten veterans, when practice opened late in September.

On the tenth of that month, the Iowa Alumni Athletic Association was formally incorporated. Two of its prime purposes were the advancement of clean and successful athletics, along with the hope that more good Iowa athletes would remain within the state and attend the university.

School enrollment exceeded 2,500 for the first time, and the sale of season athletic books reached an all-time high when it was announced that 1,224 had been purchased.

And, a last relic of the ancient football laws was finally eliminated from the rulebooks. Legislation which formerly read that the ball be passed from center "by one quick continuous motion of the hands or of the foot" was changed by cutting out the words "or of the foot."

Their mark of accomplishment, which is the heritage left by Jess Hawley's 1913 stalwarts, indicates that this team must rank with the finest ever produced at Iowa. A season record showing two losses in seven games fails to remove the lustre which Barron, Kirk, Gunderson,

Carberry, Brueckner, Houghton, Gross, Dick, McGinnis, Parsons, Penningroth and others gave to Iowa's football history.

An overwhelming 45 — 3 victory over Upper Iowa in the opener was hardly cause for undue optimism. Nor was the smashing 76 — 0 win from Cornell a week later, even though the Hawkeyes displayed a versatility of attack and a toughened defense. Youth and lack of numbers hampered Upper Iowa, while injuries, illness and anti-fraternity legislation played havoc with Cornell hopes.

A week later, co-national champion (with Harvard) Chicago, taking advantage of an inexperienced Iowa quarterback playing his first important game, swept to 16 points before Hawley could reorganize his rudderless offense. A 23 — 6 defeat resulted, but sophomore Sammy Gross, destined to become one of the great play-makers in Hawkeye grid annals, had fired a second half Iowa surge which outplayed the vaunted Maroons.

Prior to the Northwestern game the following week, an official mass meeting was held on the campus. It was called "Jimmie's Mass Meeting" in honor of the venerable guardian of Iowa Field, Jimmie Barry.

The ancient Jimmie gave a memorable charge to his beloved gridders, promising that he would lock the gates of Iowa Field and plant potatoes

1913 Team

1. Penningroth, Walter; 2. Carberry, Joseph L.; 3. Gilliland; 4. Hamilton; 5. Bowen, Carl T.; 6. Garretson, Herman John; 7. Von Lackum, Herman LeRoy; 8. Oxley; 9. Gross, Samuel E.; 10. Wills, Ernest C.; 11. Scholte; 12. Hanson, Henry D.; 13. Kellogg, Ath. Mgr.; 14. Mann, Asst. Train.; 15. Donnelly, William L.; 16. Kirk, Archie; 17. Houghton, Max; 18. Correll; 19. Mortimore; 20. Barron, Irving J. (Stub); 21. Baird, Burton A.; 22. Adams, Asst. Coach; 23. Gunderson, Arthur; 24. Wilson, J. Max; 25. Brueckner, Carl; 26. Eason; 27. Paradise; 28. Dick, Leo G.; 29. Parsons, Charles L.; 30. Eby, Asst. Coach; 31. Hawley, Coach; 32. "Jimmie" Barry; 33. McGinnis, Ralph A., Capt.; 34. Watson, Trainer; 35. Carmichael; 36. Gaimes; 37. Swisher; 38. Osborne, Dr.

and onions on the grounds if his team should lose in Evanston.

The Hawkeyes paid heed. On October 25 the most overwhelming conference victory in Iowa football resulted when "Jimmie's charges" scored eleven touchdowns enroute to an unbelievable 78 — 6 win. A slashing Iowa offense, coupled with a superb defense, led referee Walter Eckersall to write glowingly of the exhibition. Eckersall dwelt at length with the performances of McGinnis, Gross and Dick in the backfield, and of Kirk in the line.

Offensively, McGinnis powered his way to five touchdowns, tying a Western Conference scoring record which has not been exceeded. Quarterback Gross added three scores, and the exciting Dick had 74 and 42 yard runs, along with a brace of touchdowns. Carl Brueckner, called upon for place-kicking duties when Charley Parsons was injured, converted nine

extra points, in addition to a 30 yard field goal.

Northwestern has never suffered a more decisive defeat in seventy-seven years of intercollegiate football.

Two weeks later, Alonzo Stagg's national champion Chicago eleven, endeavoring to equal the Iowa margin, trimmed the Wildcats, but only 14 — 0.

After an open date, Iowa's hurricane offense struck again. Indiana, fresh from a victory over Ohio State, invaded Iowa City. Hardened football critics were astounded by the 60 — 0 Hawkeye victory.

Seven different players scored, led by Gross with three touchdowns and Penningroth with two. Late in the second period, one of the strangest incidents in the long history of football occurred. Indiana had held Iowa for downs within the shadows of its goal posts.

The Hoosiers went back to kick, their punter deep in the end zone. A terrific wind was blowing; accounts of the game called it a 50-mile gale. The Indiana punter got his kick high into the air — inches away from the finger tips of Iowa's onrushing Brueckner.

Leo Dick, playing safety for Iowa, was back about 25 yards. He recalled that the "ball advanced about twenty yards and then was caught by the adverse north wind." Dick, advancing goalward, followed the ball during its descent, "catching it behind the Indiana goal for a touchdown."

Football records no other time a successful punt was actually caught by the punt receiver . . .in the opposition's end zone.

The two Iowa victories broke state, conference and national marks for total points scored in two consecutive major games. The records have never been equalled.

The 60 — 0 Indiana defeat has only been exceeded by a 63 — 0 Hoosier loss to Michigan in 1925 — a team Fielding Yost called "the greatest I ever coached."

Football enthusiasm reached a fever pitch in Iowa City as preparations were made for the intrastate game with Ames. An enthusiastic torchlight parade through the streets highlighted Iowa's second annual Homecoming festivities.

The official game program, dedicated to Jimmie Barry, and featuring his life story, described the personable Irishman as "the man better known than any man ever connected with the University."

The largest crowd ever to see a game in Iowa City, 8,300, jammed old Iowa Field. They witnessed a 45 — 7 Hawkeye victory, the most one-sided battle in the long Iowa — Ames rivalry.

Led by the brilliant open-field running of Dick, and bolstered by Ralph McGinnis' furious line smashing, the winners were invincible. Captain McGinnis tallied four touchdowns, bringing his season total to 14, and Iowa had scored a total of 178 points in three straight games against major opposition.

Early the following week an announcement was made by Thomas Brown, manager of Iowa

City's American Theatre, that moving pictures of the Iowa — Ames game were being processed for public showing. One-thousand feet of film were taken of the Homecoming victory, the first time such pictures had ever been made of an Iowa athletic event.

A disappointing 12 — 0 loss at the hands of powerful Nebraska closed the 1913 season. Misfortune continually throttled the Hawkeyes as they had one touchdown called back, and on three other occasions were stopped after fighting to within five yards of the Cornhusker goal. However, for Jumbo Stiehm's Nebraskans, the Iowa victory was but one of 34 consecutive games without defeat.

A capsule review of Iowa's 1913 achievements is worthwhile.

1. The Hawkeyes scored 310 points during the season. Undefeated, and co-national champions Chicago and Harvard counted 124 and 225 total points respectively. Nebraska, also unbeaten, scored 138, while undefeated Notre Dame, led by the passing tandem, Dorais to Rockne, notched 268. Iowa was unchallenged as the highest scoring team in the nation.

2. The 44 point per game average of the 1913 Hawkeyes has been exceeded by only one Western Conference team since that time.

3. Iowa scored 138 points in two consecutive major games, defeating Northwestern 78 — 6, and Indiana 60 — 0. This was, and remains, a national record. In December, 1954, an NCAA Service Bureau release erroneously stated: "UCLA set an all-time record by rolling up 133 points in two consecutive major games, beating Stanford 72 — 0 and Oregon State 61 — 0."

4. Against their only two common opponents, Northwestern and Indiana, Iowa scored 103 more points than Alonzo Stagg's national champion Chicagoans. The Maroons defeated Northwestern 14 — 0 and downed Indiana 21 — 7.

5. All Hawkeye game and partial game scoring records for conference games were made in 1913. The 28 first quarter points, 41 points at halftime, and 78 final score points registered

against Northwestern are tops. The third quarter mark of 54 points was set against Indiana.

6. The five touchdowns made by Captain Ralph McGinnis against Northwestern tied a Western Conference record which has not been exceeded.

Midwestern critics recognized the deeds of four individual Hawkeyes by giving them places on all-Western and all-conference teams. Archie "Bunt" Kirk was a consensus selection to the first conference eleven, and International News Service authority Frank Menke tabbed him for the first all-Western team. End Art Gunderson gained first team conference honors, while McGinnis and Dick were accorded second team berths.

In 1914 a new uprising occurred. This time the revolt originated in alumni circles and was aimed at Nelson A. Kellogg, business manager and director of athletics. Kellogg was charged with incompetency by alumni in cities outside the state.

Specifically, the accusations aimed at Kellogg were to the effect that he was not interested in the scholastic record or physical welfare of students; that athletics at Iowa were conducted according to a slipshod system; that there had been consistent financial loss under his management; that trips were poorly managed; that there was lack of harmony with coaches and students; that he induced students to attend the University of Michigan; that he did not look after alumni returning to games; and that he spent no time with prospective students or students interested in non-intercollegiate sports. Finally, the alumni petition stated, "no one but an alumnus can be a satisfactory manager."

The student body at Iowa, as well as the faculty, stood behind Kellogg, and the Board in Control of Athletics also gave him a strong vote of confidence.

In June a proposed amendment to the articles of incorporation of the Athletic Board was adopted. The provision provided that the Board in Control consist of a faculty representative appointed by the president from each of the six colleges of the university. In addition, captains of the football, baseball, basketball and track teams, the director of athletics, an alumnus appointed by the alumni association, and a student representative selected by the Iowa Union or such other organization as the board might designate were to have a voice in Hawkeye athletics.

By the change, which actually reduced alumni representation, the board hoped to give campus faculty and students a more significant part in the over-all legislation and execution of athletics.

1914

Jess Hawley, returning for his fifth straight season, was greeted with the unfortunate news that captain elect Leo Dick would play no more football — giving up a third season to devote all possible time to his dental school studies. Arthur "King" Gunderson was selected to replace Dick as captain.

Shortly before the opening game it was announced that all Hawkeye players would wear numbers for the first time. Iowa, along with other Western Conference schools, became one of the first to number players, the idea not becoming mandatory by action of the national football rules committee until 1937.

An all time scoring record was established in the opener against Normal (now State College of Iowa). For the third time in history the Hawks topped ninety points, but the ninety-five against Normal exceeded both the 92 — 0 victory over Coe in 1908 and the 91 — 0 win from Iowa Wesleyan in 1890. In addition, the 81 points registered during the first three periods set another all-time mark.

Coach Hawley used thirty-six Hawkeye players in the Normal game, the most ever used in a single contest up to that time. Charley "Poss" Parsons, a fine all-around performer and one of the few nine-letter winners, scored 29 points, making four touchdowns and five extra points in the one-sided skirmish.

An easy 49 — 0 victory over Cornell the following week extracted its toll when Irving "Stub" Barron, an important bulwark in the

Iowa line, suffered a broken arm. The injury to Barron was of particular significance in the next two games, both fiercely contested defensive battles, against Chicago and Minnesota. Both were lost by 7 — 0 scores. Pete Russell returned an Iowa punt 55 yards for the Chicago touchdown while the Gophers scored early, then held the Hawkeyes for downs on their own seven yard line late in the fourth period to preserve the Minnesota victory.

Iowa rebounded impressively with a decisive 27 — 0 triumph over Northwestern, but it was the ingenuity and resourcefulness of quarterback Sammy Gross which has caused the game to be remembered affectionately through the years.

The able Gross was the instigator of the trick "penalty" play in football. Writing of the play a number of years later, Gross stated: "During the first half of the game, played at Evanston, I had occasionally crabbed to the official concerning some alleged violation by Northwestern. As a result, I received some kidding from my opponents to the effect that I was a 'cry baby,' etc.

"The huddle was not in vogue at this time, and the signals were called vocally in the open. Immediately after the preceding scrimmage I called a signal, resulting in a balanced line, and after I observed the line in position I approached the referee and asked that a penalty be imposed upon the Northwestern left end for illegal holding, pointing to him.

"This particular end, being entirely innocent, vociferously denied any guilt. The referee, pointing his finger at me, said, 'Play ball.'

"I walked up to our center, who was on one knee listening to the conversation, and said, 'Give me the ball — I'll take the penalty myself.' He picked up the ball and handed it backwards to me.

"Then I walked up to the line of scrimmage and started pacing off the penalty toward the opponents' goal.

"As it happened the opposing defensive fullback was directly in front of me, about three yards back. When I reached him, I paused momentarily and then pushed him to the side.

"Immediately I broke for the open toward the left side line. The only man then between me and the goal was the defensive quarterback. I was able to dodge him and carried the ball 55 yards down field before being pushed out of bounds inside the Northwestern ten yard line."

Few plays in football have succeeded under such bizzare circumstances as those surrounding the lengthy run which Sammy Gross devised and carried out against Northwestern in 1914.

A week later, close to 10,000 fans braved threatening clouds and jammed the newly built concrete stands of State Field in Ames for the annual battle between Iowa's two largest schools. After a bitterly contested first quarter in which both teams scored, the Hawkeyes, with Gunderson, Gross and Parsons leading the play, dominated the remainder of the game, winning 26 — 6.

Nebraska closed Iowa's season, and once again the all-winning Cornhuskers whipped the Hawkeyes 16 — 7. Vic Halligan, recognized one of the finest gridders ever to attend the Lincoln school, kicked 25, 30 and 33 yard field goals, in addition to setting up the lone Nebraska touchdown.

A second successive winning season was recorded by Hawley's men and, in addition, three linemen, Captain Gunderson, Bunt Kirk and Stub Barron were given recognition on various all conference teams.

Early in December the Western Conference formally adopted a proposal that a conference medal be given to the senior from each school who "has attained greatest proficiency in athletics and scholastic work." The medal, an annual award, is the only conference recognition of scholastic ability. The first Iowa recipient was H. L. Von Lackum, a prominent member of the football and baseball teams, and later a successful physician-surgeon.

That same month Jess Hawley was offered a new contract calling for $2,500 to coach the Iowa football team in 1915. Hawley demanded $3,000 but agreed to coach for one more season — at a compromise salary of $2,750. During the off-season he was highly successful as manager of the bond department in a large Chicago investment firm.

1915

Football prospects at Iowa, rosy at the start of the 1915 campaign, became less encouraging as the season progressed. With what appeared to be a good nucleus from the 1914 team available, Jess Hawley hoped to develop a strong lineup. But the season fell short of expectations. Perhaps the loss of both ends, Gunderson and Carberry, halfback Parsons, Kirk, Houghton and Brueckner should have been viewed with more concern, although Gross, Donnelly and Garretson in the backfield, along with Captain Stub Barron in the line, were returning for another year of competition. In addition, Hawley greeted two first year players, Chuck Laun and John E. "Waddy" Davis, each destined to gain future all-conference and all-Western recognition.

Lights were installed on Iowa Field for the first time, enabling the Hawkeyes to schedule night workouts. The season opened with victories over both Cornell and Morningside, and these triumphs were followed by a hard fought, but well deserved 9 – 6 win from Northwestern.

Sophomore Davis supplied the scoring punch for Iowa by virtue of his already educated right foot. The plucky halfback notched three field goals in eight attempts, accounting for all Hawkeye points. Before his career would be completed, Waddy Davis would lead the nation in goal kicking and establish himself an all-time great in Iowa football.

One of the dark days of Hawkeye athletics, in which high hopes were disastrously crashed to the ground, took place a week later on Northrup Field in Minneapolis. Once optimistic Iowans watched in dismay as the Gophers, led by halfback Bernie Bierman and left end Bert Baston, rolled to an easy 51 – 13 victory.

Next, Purdue broke a scoring drought against Iowa with a fourth quarter touchdown to snatch its first victory from the Hawkeyes, 19 – 13.

Another standing room crowd, the largest ever to see a game in the state, was on hand when Ames and Iowa took the field in Iowa City. More than 11,000 fans watched as seven sophomore Cyclone starters paced the visitors to a stunning 16 – 0 win.

But, the game was a financial success. Gate receipts of more than $12,000 accounted for one-half of Iowa's football income and 35 percent of the University's total athletic income for the year.

Nevertheless, rumblings of discontent were being heard, and when Nebraska followed with a 52 – 7 victory, largely on the strength of a one-man, five-touchdown performance by Hall of Famer Guy Chamberlin, the outcries became louder.

Students and alumni demanded an explanation for the late season downfall. Fuel was added to an already heated situation when it was pointed out that eleven of the best players in the conference, all of them Iowans, were playing for other member schools.

Minnesota, boasting an undefeated season, included four Iowans in its starting lineup. Chicago won five of seven games, with three Iowa natives on its team. In addition, Northwestern had three and the star of Wisconsin's 1915 team was an Iowan.

Further, it was pointedly noted that of the five Iowans named to the all-conference teams following the season, only one, Stub Barron, actually played for the Hawkeyes.

The Iowa Board in Control of Athletics, in a letter to university President MacBride, stated: "There has not been a season during the past ten years when there was not a full eleven of Iowa men playing on the teams of Iowa's competitors."

The letter continued: "This is the most important problem to be solved, and until it is solved by the alumni in the home towns making it their business to see that these boys attend their own state university, the University of Iowa cannot hope to have anything but mediocre teams."

Those opposing Jess Hawley voiced little objection to his coaching ability. However, they were outspoken in their stand against his spending only ten weeks on the campus each year. A "full-time" coach was a necessity if Iowa were to succeed in keeping Iowa boys in Iowa, and if the football team were to succeed as a representative member of the Western Conference.

Jess Hawley, having signified his intention to devote all of his time to his investment business, closed his career at Iowa with an over-all record of 24 victories against only 18 defeats. But, within the conference his teams could win only 8 of 19 games.

Although quiet and reserved to the point of antagonizing many, his abilities stamp Hawley as one of football's finest offensive coaches. His credentials in this area became even more definitive in the mid-twenties when he re-entered the football coaching ranks to lead Dartmouth to the national championship. In six years at the Hanover school, Hawley teams lost only ten games. Throughout his twelve year collegiate coaching career at Iowa and Dartmouth, Jess Hawley elevens averaged nearly 25 points — more than four touchdowns a game.

His offensive maneuvers at Iowa emphasized both a balanced and unbalanced line, as well as a highly successful spread formation. Perhaps his most effective plays were those which featured a split buck through the weak side of the line with cross blocking. Knute Rockne based his entire Notre Dame system on this ingenius Hawley idea of attacking through the short side of the line with cross blocking.

After moving to Dartmouth, Hawley soon became widely acclaimed for introducing a revolutionary passing offense based on split-second timing with precision passing and receiving patterns.

Grantland Rice, writing of this attack in 1925, stated: "We can recall no attack in modern football history that has piled up as many points in feature contests, or that has shown as much versatility and as much power and speed. Above that, no team in the history of the new game has ever put the forward pass to as brilliant use as Jess Hawley's lineup."

After six years at Dartmouth, Hawley retired from coaching to prosper in private business. He died in 1948, but is referred to today by three former Iowa captains who played or coached with him as "never one to socialize or fraternize with his players, but one of the great offensive coaches of football."

CHAPTER

6

Birth of a Dynasty

By mid-December, 1915, the Board in Control of Athletics had taken positive action to improve the distressing situation which confronted Iowa and its athletic future.

First, an alumni committee of former Hawkeye captains was formed to work closely with Iowa letter winners and other prominent graduates throughout the state in an effort to interest high school athletes in going to Iowa. A YMCA employment bureau was established,

Head Football Coach — 1916-1923
Athletic Director — 1917-1924
Howard Jones

with the cooperation of the athletic department, to aid those who indicated a need for financial assistance. Also, a full-time football coach was secured under a long-term contract.

His name was Jones. Even though he was a graduate of Yale, the cradle of American football, Iowans received the news of his appointment with guarded optimism. After all, Howard Jones had coached during only four of the eight years since his graduation, at three different schools, and only in an unofficial "advisory" capacity the two seasons prior to signing an Iowa contract.

However, the impact which Howard Harding Jones would leave upon football during the next twenty-five years clearly stamps him one of the dozen greatest coaches the game has known. Indeed, only three coaches in the long history of intercollegiate football would exceed Jones' record of three victories in each four decisions over twenty-nine seasons of head coaching.

And yet, were it not for a boyhood association with a prominent member of the Iowa Athletic Board, Howard Jones never would have coached on the Hawkeye campus, and in all probability he never would later have gained football immortality at the University of Southern California.

J. Reed Lane of Davenport, alumni representative on the Athletic Board, spent a year with Jones at Phillips Exeter, an exclusive Yale preparatory school near New Haven. The two continued their friendship even though each went his separate way after leaving Exeter — Lane to Iowa, and Jones to Yale where he was to letter three years on Bulldog teams which were undefeated in thirty games.

Reed Lane, well acquainted with Howard Jones as a man and as an athlete, had also followed his somewhat sporadic but successful career as a coach. He strongly advised that Jones be considered for the Iowa football vacancy.

When the Athletic Board agreed, he was invited to Iowa City to discuss the football position as well as the Iowa athletic situation in general.

Howard Jones arrived in Iowa, met with athletic authorities and, after a unanimous vote by the Iowa Board in Control of Athletics, agreed to terms of a 5 year contract as head football coach, beginning in September, 1916.

Provisions of the agreement guaranteed that Jones would receive $4,500 during each of his first two years, $5,000 during his third season, and $5,500 for the fourth and fifth years.

Between February 1 and June 1, 1916, Jones would work with the athletic department in Iowa City, in addition to spending time throughout the state looking for prospective university athletes. He was to be paid $2,250 during this period.

Never before had Iowa entered into such a long term commitment, and never before had so much money been pledged to gain the services of an athletic coach.

However, a football dynasty had been born at Iowa with the signing of Howard Jones. Two consecutive Big Ten titles, a pair of unbeaten teams, and a national championship — these would be only three of the hallmarks of Jones' teams during the next eight years.

But, playing field successes were not an immediate reality. The necessary groundwork would take time, and to Howard Jones it was an agonizingly long time.

The years of 1916 and 1917 would be ones of development, of change and counter-change

at Iowa. Over-all the record was not distasteful: seven victories against eight defeats. But a 67 − 0 loss to Minnesota in 1916, and a 47 − 0 rout at the hands of Nebraska the following year were bitter lessons to acknowledge. They were the worst setbacks in Howard Jones' career, but he would avenge both. Nebraska never scored again against a Jones' coached team, and Minnesota suffered five straight defeats at the hands of his Iowa elevens.

1916

After opening with two nonconference victories over Cornell and Grinnell in 1916, the Hawkeyes continued their winning ways with a convincing 24 − 6 triumph from Purdue. Feature of the game was an 85 yard punt return for the first score by Bert Jenkins. It was the nation's longest during the year.

Disaster in the form of Minnesota's 67 − 0 avalanche buried Iowa dreams a week later. Led by a quartet of touchdowns by halfback Joe Sprafka, the Gophers dominated every phase of play. An impregnable defense held the Iowans without a first down until the final period.

Tragedy of a different form pierced the hearts of every Hawkeye when it was learned that the "father of Iowa athletics," A. G. Smith, had died in the early morning hours of November 5.

Leukemia, or cancer of the blood, dreaded because of its slow, yet inevitable conclusion, had forced Professor Smith to resign his duties as Chairman of the Iowa Athletic Board in 1914. However, he courageously refused confinement until only three weeks prior to his death, sacrificing time and energy which he could ill afford for the betterment of athletics.

In his student years, A. G. Smith was one of the finest athletes at the university, captaining the 1890 football team. He was a tower of strength in carrying Iowa through the difficult years of the nineties. He represented his school when Iowa was admitted to the Western Conference in 1899, and continued to be its official spokesman until 1914. Before his retirement he was vice-chairman of the NCAA, chairman of the Western Conference, and the single most important personality in the building of constructive athletics at his university and within the Conference.

Following his death, the Western Conference formally incorporated a resolution of tribute to be included in its minutes. The resolution referred to the "conspicuous ability and sound judgment" of A. G. Smith, and further stated: "It is safe to say that no one has rendered a more valuable constructive service to the Intercollegiate Conference than Professor Smith."

Perhaps this philosophy concerning intercollegiate athletics, written by A. G. Smith in 1911, best exemplifies the man, and the athletic course he charted for Iowa.

"All college sports must work to the development of character. As such, no man may become a member of an athletic team unless he can control himself and work with his teammates. He must learn to give all that is in him and to give it unselfishly; and with this end in view the profit is great when he has striven to the limit. To be a member of an intercollegiate team is a privilege given by the university. Therefore, the college has the right to impose scholarship requirements upon those so privileged.

"However, the university also recognizes that it is as much a part of modern education to teach sports as to teach other subjects in the curriculum."

A disheartened Iowa football team journeyed to Evanston the week following A. G. Smith's death. Northwestern, playing before the largest crowd in its history, defeated the Hawkeyes, 20 – 13, on a fourth quarter touchdown which broke a 13 – 13 tie. Waddy Davis, starring offensively for Iowa, kicked a pair of field goals, his fourth and fifth against the Wildcats in two years.

Dedication keynoted practices prior to the traditional Ames clash, still the most important single battle on the Hawkeye schedule. Not a touchdown had been scored on the Cyclones prior to its mid-November meeting with Iowa.

Another record crowd, this time approaching 15,000, added to the excitement in Ames.

In one of the great high-tension struggles ever waged by the two schools, the Hawks were able to gain a memorable 19 – 16 victory.

Waddy Davis, Chuck Laun and Fred Becker were most prominent stalwarts for Iowa. Davis

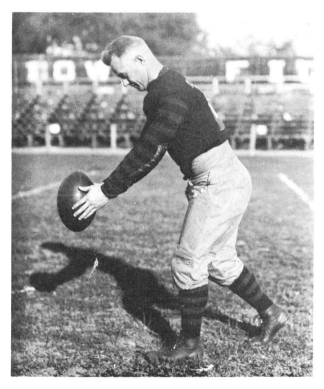

John E. (Waddy) Davis

again kicked a field goal, a pair of extra points, and helped set up one touchdown by carrying a Laun pass to the Cyclone one. The dependable Laun, long remembered as one of the half dozen great Hawkeye punters, also stood out on defense, and as the key blocker in Jones' offensive system.

Fred Becker, who would gain all-American recognition before his death in World War I, was just embarking on his sensational career. The play of Becker, brilliant throughout, bulwarked Iowa's forward wall. With his team holding a narrow 17 – 10 lead in the fourth period against Ames, Fred Becker crashed through to block two Cyclone punts, one giving the Hawkeyes an insurance safety, and the other to keep the surging hosts deep in their own territory. Only one other Iowan shares Becker's distinction of blocking two enemy punts in a single game. Ironman Mike Enich, an all-American himself twenty-four years later, led an Iowa defensive charge against Purdue in 1939 when he blocked two Boilermaker efforts each resulting in safeties and a 4 — 0 win.

Nebraska closed the 1916 season by trouncing Iowa 34 — 17. Hugo Otopalik, later wrestling coach at Iowa State, scored four times for the Cornhuskers who roared from a 10 — 0 deficit to defeat the Old Gold. Waddy Davis tallied eleven of Iowa's points on a 40 yard field goal, one touchdown and two extra points.

Davis was given deserved recognition for his sterling play in 1916, Walter Eckersall selecting the Iowa junior to his second all-Western team.

Fred Becker, although only a sophomore, gained everlasting honor when Eckersall named him to his all-America first team. In writing about Becker, Eckersall commented: "No matter where he was placed his work was a feature. He was strong and powerful and quick to size up the attack of his opponents. He seldom failed to open holes for the backs and was on top of the play all year."

Few Iowans have received such exalted recognition in their sophomore seasons, and none attained the honor from as prominent and recognized critic as Walter Eckersall. This is the playing field distinction of Fred Becker through seventy-five years of Iowa football.

But, fate decreed that Becker's football achievements would end after only one season. Within a month after the United States entered World War I, Fred Becker enlisted. He sailed for France in September, and ten months later, July 18, 1918, was killed in action. The Waterloo, Iowa, native, referred to by Eckersall as "unparalleled in Iowa football annals," was awarded the Belgian War Cross, the Croix de Guerre, highest French decoration given solely for battlefield heroism, and the American Distinguished Service Cross, exceeded in importance by only the Congressional Medal of Honor.

The War Years — 1917-1919

The trials of 1916 were light compared with the problems which were uncovered by the outbreak of World War I early in 1917. In May athletic director Nelson Kellogg left Iowa for military service at Fort Snelling. The likeable Kellogg, subject of attack and controversy at various times during his six and one-half years in Iowa City, nevertheless made his own significant contributions while serving the university.

It was Kellogg who 1. inaugurated the season athletic ticket; 2. worked continuously to obtain better schedules for all intercollegiate sports; 3. improved both the interscholastic track meet and the annual basketball tournament; and 4. instigated and supervised the various improvements which were made of the athletic field.

After completing his military service in 1919, Nelson Kellogg was successful in gaining the athletic directorship at Purdue, and he remained in that position for twelve years, building Boilermaker athletics to conference leadership in the late twenties and early thirties.

A month after Kellogg had left Iowa for army duty, the Iowa Board in Control of Athletics suggested the appointment of Howard Jones to the position of athletic director. The recommendation was approved on September 14, effective from September 1.

The football season was long and disappointing for Iowa. After an opening win over Cornell, 22 — 13, the Hawkeyes were shut out against Nebraska, Grinnell and Wisconsin.

Even in the Cornell game Iowa was forced to rebound from a 13 — 0 deficit, largely on the strength of a twenty point effort by Waddy Davis, to gain the victory.

Nebraska romped easily, 47 — 0. Most notable, perhaps, was the introduction by the Cornhuskers of three girl cheer leaders, an entirely new innovation to football, although one which soon gained universal acceptance throughout the nation.

Grinnell capitalized on Iowa mistakes to notch a 10 — 0 triumph in the final game played between the two schools which in 1889 had started intercollegiate football west of the Mississippi. Twenty-eight years and seventeen games later, the record showed the Hawkeyes with 11 victories, five losses and a tie.

After Wisconsin had beaten Iowa by three touchdowns the following week, a Daily Iowan editor remained unconvinced. His banner headline, which greeted Sunday morning readers, has become a classic journalistic example of over extended loyalty: "HAWKEYES SURPRISE BADGERS WITH STRONG DEFENSE — SCORE 20 to 0."

Jimmy Counzelman of Great Lakes thwarted a fourth period Hawkeye scoring march and broke open a 16 — 14 game by intercepting an Iowa pass and racing 85 yards to lead the sailors to a thrilling 23 — 14 win.

During the week prior to the South Dakota game, word was passed that venerable Jimmie Barry had missed two days of duty at Iowa Field. Jimmie, who had been honored in April on the occasion of his eighty-fifth birthday, had never before been absent. Concern turned to relief late in the week however, and "the ouldist mimber of the facultee," as Jimmie referred to himself, was back, fully recovered and "feelin' foine, jist foine."

Chuck Laun had his biggest scoring day against South Dakota and Iowa won its second game in five starts, 35 — 0. Laun scored three touchdowns and a pair of extra points.

After Northwestern had unleashed a 19 point second period flurry to outscore the Hawkeyes, 25 — 14, preparations were made for the season finale against Ames. The Cyclone record showed only a single defeat when the two teams lined up to face one another.

A furious defensive struggle was waged, and neither team was able to score a touchdown. Waddy Davis, playing his final game for Iowa, kicked two wide angle field goals, the last splitting the uprights in the final minutes of the fourth period, and the Hawkeyes had earned a narrow 6 — 3 triumph.

Howard Jones used no substitutes during the game, the first time an Old Gold eleven had ever played sixty minutes without substitution.

Chuck Laun and Waddy Davis closed their football careers at Iowa. Laun was named to all-Western and all-conference teams for his play during the 1917 season.

Davis, the most prolific field goal kicker in Iowa annals, also was one of few Hawkeyes to notch more than one-hundred points during his career. He made 106 total markers, scoring seven touchdowns, thirteen field goals and twenty five extra points. His seven field goals in 1916 led the nation and is a single season high at Iowa. Also, Davis' thirteen career three-pointers is five more than any other Hawkeye has registered.

Late in November the Big Ten became a reality for the first time. Michigan, which had voluntarily withdrawn from the conference in 1908, accepted an invitation to resume membership.

Examination of the athletic financial statement at the close of the 1917-18 school year disclosed that football and over-all athletic receipts were the lowest in five years. In addition, disbursements once again exceeded income, and an indebtedness of $10,000 was shown.

Football held a position of secondary importance in the fall of 1918 when the western front thundered with some of the mightiest battles of World War I. Gone from the college campuses of Iowa and other states were most of the rugged athletes of previous years. In their place was a new group of youths who comprised the Student Army Training Corps. They wore the same khaki as those in active service overseas, were subject to military discipline and training, but were permitted to combine their military preparations with regular classroom studies.

By action of September 26, 1918, the Big Ten conference suspended control "for the duration" to the War Department. The following rules for athletic regulation were submitted to the Conference:

1. All members of S. A. T. C. shall be eligible for competition.

2. One and one-half hours each day shall be set apart for athletic training, but all practice for football or other sports by soldiers must be in recreation periods and not decrease time allotted for drill and study.

3. No games involving absence for a night may be played before November 1 — scheduling only local Saturday games calling for trips that can be made on Saturday afternoons.

4. Two trips in November shall be allowed, a squad not to exceed twenty-five men to be excused from military duties from Friday afternoon to Sunday afternoon.

Eligibility rules of other years were discarded. A man who reported for football was allowed to compete with no questions asked. No residence requirements were enforced, freshmen were eligible and the competition was not to be charged against any player. As a result, the squad was augmented by two former Jess Hawley players — Homer Scott and Bill Donnelly.

Also enrolled at Iowa were many men who were destined to reach stardom in Hawkeye athletics. Among them were Fred (Duke) Slater, Lester Belding, Johnny Heldt, Bill Kelly, Fred Lohman, J. B. Synhorst and others.

Even though the effects of World War I disrupted football throughout the country, it might have been just another season at Iowa except for three memorable incidents.

It was in 1918 that Iowa scored its first football victory over Minnesota. It was in 1918 that the Hawkeyes played a game in which no spectators were allowed. It was also 1918 that Iowa played what then was described "the greatest gridiron battle of the season in Iowa." Strangely enough, that game has been "lost" from official University of Iowa records, as well as the record books of football.

Over-all, the season was highly successful for Iowa. Six of the nine opponents were held scoreless, and it was the first time in thirteen years that a Hawkeye team won as many as six games.

The Hawkeyes opened their season early, meeting Great Lakes only three days after practices had commenced. The lack of preparations hurt Iowa and the older, more experienced sailors won, 10 — 0.

Early in November a long period of frustration ended with a hard fought 6 — 0 victory over Minnesota, the first ever over the Gophers in a series extending back 27 years, to 1891. Along the way the powerful Norsemen had smashed earlier Hawkeye elevens by 75 — 0 and 67 — 0 scores. But in this one the Gophers could not penetrate Iowa's 30 yard line. Fred Lohman, Howard Jones' dependable crashing fullback, gave Iowa victory with a third quarter touchdown.

Captain Ronald Reed, writing of the game years later, said that "the entire Iowa season was shaped by Coach Jones toward the Minnesota game." The Gopher shift was stopped so successfully that Dr. Williams' eleven could notch only two first downs all afternoon. Peace and tranquility were not restored in Iowa City for a week after the upset victory.

A month before, Iowa and Coe College clashed behind locked gates in front of which there were armed guards stationed to keep spectators away. An epidemic of Spanish influenza had spread over the state early in October, and in order to reduce the possibility of further illness Iowa authorities were advised by the War Department that if the game were to be sanctioned it would have to be played with all doors padlocked. A number with powerful field glasses attempted to watch the play from the Iowa River bridges and from the high hills on the west side of the river, but all nonplaying personnel were barred from the field itself.

Accounts of the battle were sketchy, but the bigger, more experienced Hawkeyes apparently triumphed, 27 — 0.

Iowa closed the 1918 season with a highly publicized skirmish against Camp Dodge. The since "forgotten" game was played in Drake stadium, Des Moines. Critic Walter Eckersall was referee. Howard Jones' eleven kept the ball in soldier territory most of the afternoon, twice striking within the Camp Dodge 5 yard line. But, the Hawkeyes lacked the necessary scoring punch and the game ended in a scoreless stalemate. Duke Slater, Les Belding and Ronald Reed starred for Iowa, and the play of Reed prompted Eckersall to label him "the finest end in the West" following the season.

In other games Iowa romped over Cornell, 34 — 0, defeated Northwestern, 23 — 7, and Ames, 21 — 0, but fell before conference champion Illinois, 19 — 0. The team also shut out Nebraska, 12 — 0, Iowa's first victory over the Cornhuskers in 19 years.

Ronald Reed and Harry Hunzelman were selected to the Big Ten conference first team by Walter Eckersall, with quarterback Bill Kelly and fullback Fred Lohman gaining second team honors. When the all-Iowa mythical team was announced, eight Hawkeyes were awarded first team berths.

After the signing of the Armistice, the Big Ten conference declared its former authority in effect as of December 7, 1918. This opened the era of greatest expansion and success of intercollegiate athletics within the conference.

The university campus was deeply saddened on January 2, 1919. Eighty-six year old Jimmie Barry died peacefully after an illness which had confined him for six weeks.

Perhaps no person connected with the University, either before or since, had a wider circle of acquaintances or made more friends among both students and faculty than Jimmie.

Born in Ireland in 1832, Jimmie Barry came to Iowa City and began service with the University in 1866. On his beloved Iowa Field he ruled supreme, and no one dared challenge his authority.

"Sacred practice tiday! Go on wid ye! I know ye, I know every wan of ye — I know wan of ye anyhow," was the vocal outburst which any would-be trespasser faced if caught inside the gates of his sanctuary. And it was Jimmie who warned each Hawkeye squad that he would surely plant a potato patch on his beloved turf should the Ames warriors defeat his gridders.

Although his daily life was a pattern of frugality and steady work, Jimmie Barry met his measure of duty with an honesty and cheerfulness which endeared him to all.

Two boys and two girls, children of Jimmie, all received the formal education which never was available to their father from the university of Iowa.

A. G. Smith spoke for many when he said of Jimmie Barry in 1913, "He is now famous, and deservedly so, as one of the best known and best loved traditions of Iowa."

Before the 1919 fall semester began, evidence of uneasy internal troubles within the athletic board were seen. Specifically, it was charged that Athletic Director Howard Jones did not present matters pertaining to minor sports in a business-like manner to the Board.

Later in the year there were other areas of controversy, this time over the advisability of retaining trainer Jack Watson. Jones felt that Watson was the best conditioner of athletes he had ever worked with; that he was a very important and valuable man during the football season. Others on the Board did not agree, and an obvious split within the administration was opened, with Director of Athletics — Football Coach Howard Jones on one side and Athletic Board Chairman B. J. Lambert on the other.

Within five years Jones would resign at Iowa to continue his football coaching success at the University of Southern California. Before that time, however, Hawkeye athletic and gridiron fortunes under his leadership would prosper in national recognition as never before.

1919

The 1919 season opened with a second straight shutout victory over Nebraska, 18 — 0. Duke Slater and Ben Synhorst spearheaded an impregnable defense, while Iowa's most famous football brother combination, Aubrey and Glenn Devine, sparked the offense.

Next came a memorable game with Illinois, when Synhorst, the great left tackle, was declared ineligible just sixteen hours before the teams took the field. He had been protested on the grounds that he already held a B.A. degree from Central College, received in 1918. When the question of his eligibility had come up previously, the conference committee ruled that Central College was not a fully accredited school. However, further review of the case by the Conference committee on eligibility brought about the changed decision.

On the playing field fate also turned against the Hawkeyes. In the second period, with Iowa leading, 7—0, the Illini scored on a freak though prearranged play. The ball was on Iowa's 33 yard line, fourth down, when an on-side kick signal was called. The rules of football at the time allowed the kicking team to recover a punted ball provided the man recovering was behind his punter at the time the kick was made. As the ball was passed from center, Walquist, the Illinois halfback, stepped back toward his own goal in order to be back of the kicker when the ball was punted. The kick was very high and Iowa's safety man, realizing the disastrous result of a fumble, elected to allow the ball to hit the ground, never dreaming of the on-side kick maneuver. The ball bounded straight up. Walquist grabbed it and lunged into the end zone unmolested. The old, seldom used play had been resurrected, and when the Illini countered later with a field goal, victory was theirs, 9 — 7.

A week later Iowa rebounded with a game winning 33 yard field goal by Aubrey Devine to gain its first win in history at Minneapolis, 9 — 6.

An obscure Daily Iowan story intrigued readers on the eve of the Hawkeyes' 26 — 13 triumph over South Dakota. Beneath a headline which read, "To Try New Iowa Song," was a brief announcement that Waterloo Attorney Robert Law had composed both the words and music to "On Iowa," which would be presented to the student body at a mass meeting that evening.

Law, a 1904 Iowa graduate, offered the fight song to the university in 1917, when a prize was given for the best entry. It did not win at that time, but by mid-November 1919 the rendition was formally adopted by the university.

Aubrey Devine and Captain Fred Lohman paced Iowa to a narrow 14 — 7 victory over Northwestern at Evanston. Devine scored both touchdowns and kicked the extra points.

Another heartbreaking loss, this time at the hands of Chicago, 9 — 6, cost Iowa its finest season record since 1900. After a 20 yard fourth period field goal had put the Maroons ahead, Iowa, behind the line smashing of Lohman and the passing of Devine, drove to a first down on the Chicago two yard line. Less than thirty seconds remained and time ran out with the Hawkeyes holding the ball on third down, inches from the Chicago goal line.

A furious intrastate battle between once beaten Ames and the twice clipped Hawks closed the season in Iowa City. Following an early first quarter touchdown pass, Aubrey Devine to Guerdon Parker, the game was a bruising defensive struggle with neither team scoring until the final minute when Devine dropkicked his third field goal of the year to seal a 10 — 0 victory.

Deserved accolades were given to five different Hawkeyes at the close of the season. Aubrey Devine and Harry Hunzelman were both recognized on various all-conference teams, while Duke Slater, Les Belding and Fred Lohman were accorded higher honors.

Belding, a consensus all-western selectee, was named to the first team all-America of Frank Menke for Newspaper Features Syndicate. Walter Eckersall placed the Iowa wingman on his third team all-America.

Duke Slater, giant Negro tackle, was a unanimous all-Western performer, and was further honored by both Walter Camp and Eckersall. The mid-western critic gave Slater a second team all-America berth, while Camp nominated him to his third team.

Fred Lohman, described by Eckersall as "the main cog in the Iowa offense," was a strong all-conference first team member, joining both Belding and Slater on Eckersall's all Big Ten and all-Western elevens.

BEST OF THE DECADE — 1910 - 1919

Ends	Arthur H. Gunderson	1912-1913-1914
	Charles E. Laun	1915-1916-1917
Tackles	Irving (Stub) Barron	1913-1914-1915
	Archie Kirk	1912-1913-1914
Guards	Henry D. Hanson	1909-1911-1912
	James J. Trickey	1910-1911-1912
Center	Willis J. O'Brien	1909-1910-1911
Quarterback	Samuel E. Gross	1913-1914-1915
Halfbacks	John E. (Waddy) Davis	1915-1916-1917
	Leo G. Dick	1912-1913
	Ralph A. McGinnis	1911-1912-1913
Fullback	J. Ray Murphy	1909-1910-1911

A third decade of Iowa football had ended. An over-all record showing 42 victories, thirty losses and one tie reflected years of both achievement and frustration. Within the Western Conference the ledger was still weighted against the Hawkeyes — fourteen wins against seventeen defeats. However, the record was markedly improved from the four victories in twenty-one Big Ten games played between 1900 and 1910.

Conference leadership followed by athletic humiliation would await Iowa in the twenties.

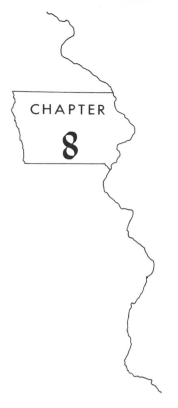

Two Conference Titles and Twenty Straight Victories — 1920-1923

The taste of moderate success that came during the early years of the Howard Jones' regime was hardly enough to compensate for the many less productive years that had preceded him. From the glories of the 1900 team through fifteen seasons that followed, prosperity was rare at Iowa and never sustained. During seven of the fifteen years the Hawkeyes were unable to win a Conference game. The turn toward better days might be dated from the third season of Jones' tenure when the wartime team of 1918 lost only two of nine games in finishing with a 6 — 2 — 1 record. But the real climb lay ahead.

It was midway through the 1920 season that Iowa thundered into a stretch of sustained greatness that never has lost its luster. Through two full seasons and parts of two others the Howard Jones Hawkeyes stacked up triumph after triumph until they had won 20 consecutive games, two Big Ten championships in a row, and a rare look from the Rose Bowl authorities, who had an eye on the Hawks. Conference rules prevented what otherwise might have been the first Iowa appearance at Pasadena. As they stormed through the most spectacular winning streak in their history the Hawkeyes conquered Minnesota, Notre Dame, Yale, Northwestern, Illinois, Purdue, Indiana and Ohio State, among others. All of them fell

in that ruthless march, some of them three times.

Commanding the Hawks was the wiry, unemotional Coach Jones, a man of fierce concentration who, in the course of a football season, featured the well known "one-track" mind, and it was geared to football. He was quiet, even reticent, until the demands of football called for fiery action.

William S. Kelly, a Minneapolis insurance executive who captained one Jones team (1920) had this to say of him long after the famous coach had departed from Iowa:

"He liked clean, hard football. He never would stand for anything out of line. He never was known to swear. He was a terrific disciplinarian. For him to 'go after' one of his players was something never to be forgotten. He was a hard man to get close to. He never had more than 40 men on his Iowa squads and during most of his years he was athletic director as well as coach. Many times, he actually was selling tickets up to within an hour or so of game time."

Jones coached at Iowa for eight seasons and his record of 42 games won, 17 lost and one tied assures him a place among the most successful of Iowa coaches.

In addition to a good nucleus of lettermen returning from the 1919 team, including the Devines, Lawrence Block, Bob Kauffman, Duke

Aubrey Devine

Slater, Joe Sykes and Captain Bill Kelly, Howard Jones welcomed a promising group of sophomores that included Max Kadesky, Gordon Locke, Craven Shuttleworth, Paul Minick, Chet Mead and George Thompson.

Expectations of a long-awaited conference championship were high, particularly so when it was recalled that only five points separated Iowa from claiming the Big Ten title the year before. Three days before the season opener Coach Jones was offered and accepted a new five-year contract calling for $7,500 a year.

Highlighted by the line plunging of Gordon Locke and the accurate passing of Aubrey Devine the Hawkeyes opened with a hard fought 14 — 7 victory over Indiana at Bloomington. Devine scored once and passed 25 yards to Max Kadesky for the game winner.

Seven first half touchdowns, including a 34-point flurry in the second quarter, carried

Iowa to an easy 63 — 0 conquest of Cornell College the following week in Iowa City.

Next, Illinois broke open a tight defensive struggle with 17 points in the third quarter to push Bob Zuppke's eleven to a 20 — 3 triumph, and a week later Chicago, taking advantage of fumbles and an inconsistent Iowa attack, shut out the Hawkeyes, 10 — 0. Disappointing as the loss was, it would be the last suffered by an Iowa team for three years.

The Northwestern Wildcats were the first of 20 consecutive victims, falling before the Iowans in a rain drenched and mud-spattered battle, 20 — 0. Minnesota closed the conference season, determined not to drop a third straight decision to Iowa. Never in her long football history had a Minnesota team been defeated three years in a row by an opponent. The Gophers scored early and held a 7 — 0 lead as the second quarter began. However, Iowa dominated play in the final three periods and the brilliant all-around play of Devine, coupled with the line plunging of Locke, carried the Hawks to four touchdowns and a satisfying 28 — 7 victory. In the season finale an unexpectedly stubborn Ames team battled the more highly rated Hawkeyes throughout, succumbing in the face of three pass interceptions made, a touchdown scored and another thrown — all by the brilliant Aubrey Devine. Les Belding was on the receiving end of the 23 yard scoring pass. Polly Wallace, recognized as the greatest of all Iowa State linemen, stood out for his defensive play and was named the finest center in the nation by many prominent selectors, including the respected authority Walter Eckersall.

The Devine brothers, Aubrey and Glenn, along with Les Belding and Duke Slater, earned high post-season recognition. Belding, who gained his first varsity letter as a 17-year old freshman, received all-American, all-Western and all Big Ten honors. He was the only Iowan to be named to a nationally recognized all-America, being picked by Walter Eckersall and The Chicago Tribune as a second team end. Slater, like Belding playing his third season, was all-Western and consensus all-Conference at tackle. Glenn Devine, a defensive and blocking standout, was a second team all-Western pick of Colliers' Magazine, and brother Aubrey was a unanimous selection on both the all-Western and all Big Ten first units. The versatile quarterback, although only a junior, rushed for more than 600 yards during the season and added an additional 500 as a result of his passing. For the second year in a row he led the Hawkeyes in rushing, passing and scoring.

1921

The year 1921 brought Iowa its first undisputed Big Ten football championship. But more than that, it also brought the Hawkeyes national championship recognition and an invitation to the Rose Bowl.

It is indeed difficult to present an all-inclusive summary of the achievements carved by Howard Jones' 1921 warriors. The team itself

was unbeaten and said by many to be the nation's finest eleven; Coach Jones has since been justly recognized as one of football's greatest mentors; and four of the starting eleven gained all-America stature at the close of the season.

Other significant points provide additional lustre to the all-winning record: all members of the first two varsity elevens came from the state of Iowa. The first, second and fourth leading scorers in the Big Ten were all Hawkeyes. Notre Dame coach Knute Rockne's longest winning streak, 20 games, was stopped by the 1921 Iowans. Also, Purdue tested its worst football defeat, and Minnesota surrendered in the face of the most points which had ever been scored on a Gopher team. When the all-state of Iowa mythical teams were announced following the season, six Hawkeyes were listed on the first unit and all eleven starters were selected on one of the first three teams.

Individually, the greatest two-game performance in more than fifty years of Big Ten play

Gordon Locke gains yardage as Duke Slater blocks out four Notre Dame linemen. Irish captain Eddie Anderson, later head coach of the Hawkeyes, is shown to the right of the play.

was turned in by Aubrey Devine. The versatile Iowa captain and quarterback scored 57 total points against Minnesota and Indiana in a period of eight days. Not even the legendary feats of Red Grange, Herb Joesting, Pug Lund, Tom Harmon, or any of a host of great backs of recent years could approach Devine's mark. Called by critic Walter Eckersall "the best exponent of the triple threat the Middle West has seen since the coming of the forward pass in 1906," the incomparable Devine gains near unanimous support from those who saw him play as the greatest player ever to wear a Hawkeye uniform.

Iowa opened the season as expected, with an easy 52 — 14 ambush of outclassed Knox college, but their sights were already set upon the much heralded battle with Notre Dame scheduled the next week.

In one of the classic games of Hawkeye football history the powerful Rockne coached Irish were beaten, 10 — 7. Not since 1918 had Notre Dame tasted defeat, and not until the waning seconds when a pass interception thwarted the final Irish threat was the game settled.

Iowa scored all of its points in the first period, Gordon Locke hitting for a touchdown on a fourth down smash from inside the Notre Dame one. On the next Hawk series Locke and Devine drove to the Irish 30 from where Aubrey kicked a field goal. The ball was drop-kicked from the 38 yard line. Notre Dame retaliated with a score of its own in the second quarter when Johnny Mohardt completed a pass to Roger Kiley on the Iowa 30 and the All-American end carried the ball the remaining distance.

Two more Fighting Irish threats were stopped in the final half and Iowa had earned one of its most cherished victories, 10 — 7 The Notre Dame right end and team captain was a Mason City, Iowa, native — Eddie Anderson. Eighteen years later that same Eddie Anderson would be involved in another memorable Hawkeye-Irish battle, then as coach of the immortal 1939 "Ironmen."

Five consecutive Big Ten opponents were yet to be faced by Howard Jones' heroes as

they turned their thoughts toward a meeting with Illinois. The resulting 14 — 2 victory was comforting, but most instrumental was the pile-driving fury of Gordon Locke. The Iowa fullback was called upon 37 times during the game and he responded with a record 202 yards rushing and both Hawk touchdowns. All eleven Iowa starters played the full sixty minutes.

Purdue was victim Number 4. Playing on a gridiron covered with water Aubrey Devine again took charge. He passed to Les Belding for one score and then raced 33 yards through the entire Boilermaker team with a punt return for the winning touchdown in a close 13 — 6 game. Veteran coach and authority Clark Shaughnessy, writing in 1943, called Devine's brilliant punt return "one of the 12 greatest individual plays in the history of football."

A Minneapolis date with perennial rival Minnesota loomed as another tough challenge. It wasn't, because Iowa had Devine. In the greatest single performance by a Hawkeye gridder the Iowa captain passed for two touchdowns, scored four touchdowns himself, and kicked five extra points. He raced for 162 yards from scrimmage, returned punts and kickoffs an additional 180 yards and passed for 122 more. The 464 total yards gained caused Hall of Fame Gopher coach Dr. Henry L. Williams to refer to Devine as "the greatest football player who ever stepped on Northrup Field." The Hawkeyes won, 41 — 7.

Iowa and the incomparable Devine continued their 1921 title drive in the home windup against Indiana. The Hoosiers were smashed, 41 — 0. Aubrey Devine rushed for 183 yards from scrimmage, completed seven passes for 102 more, scored four touchdowns and kicked four extra points during the first three periods. He saw no action in the final quarter.

Duke Slater, Les Belding and the Devine brothers closed their careers a week later against Northwestern at Evanston. The resulting 14 — 0 victory, coupled with Illinois' defeat of Ohio State, gave Iowa its first undisputed Conference championship and its last such title for another 35 years. Just 36 points were scored against the Hawkeyes who averaged more than

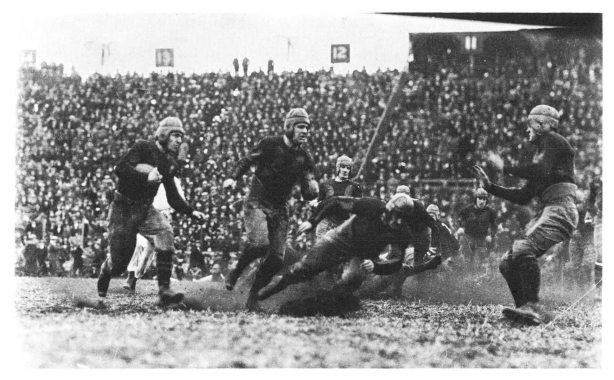

Aubrey Devine carrying the ball behind blockers Gordon Locke and Craven Shuttleworth. Devine scored 29 points and threw two touchdown passes as Iowa defeated Minnesota, 41 — 7.

four touchdowns themselves in each of seven games.

Only two men, Locke and Devine, carried the ball on offense. The other backfield pair, Glenn Devine and Craven Shuttleworth, were used as blockers. Forty years later another highly successful exponent of this style of attack molded his offense in the same way. Ohio State, under the tutelage of Woody Hayes, utilized the quarterback or fullback on 522 of 584 total plays in 1960. The Buckeye halfbacks were used almost exclusively as blockers, carrying the ball less than seven times a game. Ironically, a defeat by Iowa near the close of the 1960 season cost Ohio State the undisputed Big Ten title — giving the championship instead to the Hawkeyes and Minnesota.

After the season opener against Knox there were only three touchdowns scored on the 1921 champions. Following the final game came rumors of a post season contest. Howard Jones was called into conference with a committee repre-

senting the California Tournament of Roses Association to discuss the possibility of the Iowa team going west to meet the leading team of the Pacific Coast on New Year's Day.

On November 21 Athletic Board chairman B. J. Lambert acknowledged that Iowa was in receipt of an invitation to play the football champions of the Far West on the following January 1.

Nine days later the Iowa Board in Control of Athletics met in "special session" with Dr. William Duffield of Los Angeles, representing the Tournament of Roses Committee. Would Iowa be interested in a Rose Bowl appearance against the University of California? Unfortunately for the record the Hawkeyes were not interested because: 1. the Board opposed post-season competition and, 2. a Big Ten ruling adopted six months earlier prevented such a possibility, although a review of the Iowa invitation by the Conference was made. The indications were present that had the Conference agreed to permit Iowa to make the trip, the Iowa Board would have approved the January 1 game.

Four Hawkeyes, Devine, Locke, Slater and Belding were named to various all-America teams. Walter Camp, football's foremost authority, gave Aubrey Devine the game's highest honor: selection as quarterback on his first honor team. No other Iowan had ever been given first team recognition by the "father of American football." With his career completed Devine could look back on a score of achievements. His single game deeds against Minnesota may never be approached, nor the two-game records established against the Gophers and Indiana within an eight day period. He led the Iowa team in rushing, passing and scoring during each of his three years of varsity competition. His 895 yards rushing in 1921 stands as an Iowa single season mark, and his 1316 yards total offense has been exceeded only once. The 161 career points scored rank third in the Iowa record book. His total passing yardage, although made with a more difficult ball to control and at a time when passing rules were much more confining, was enough to place him in the Hawkeye top ten when compilations were made more than forty years later. No one has topped the 1961 yards Devine gained rushing during his Iowa career. He also kicked six

field goals during his three years of play. No Iowan has matched that number since. And he is the only Hawkeye to exceed 3,000 yards in total offense during a career. Randy Duncan, who played 35 years later, ranks second, nearly 500 yards away. No other Iowa player accumulated yardage within one-thousand of Devine.

Years after he left Iowa City Howard Jones evaluated Aubrey Devine in this fashion: "The greatest all-around backfield man I have ever coached or seen in the modern game. Others may have been as great in open field running, there may have been better punters or drop kickers, but I have never known any backfield man whose accomplishments in running, punting, drop-kicking and forward passing combined equal those of Aubrey Devine. In addition, he was a leader and field general of the highest type."

Gordon Locke, only a junior in 1921, was named to the all-America first team of Norman Brown, the second team of Walter Eckersall and the Chicago Tribune, as well as a consensus all-Western and all Big Ten selection. Second in scoring in the Conference, Locke rushed for more than seven hundred yards, his most successful afternoon being more than 200 against Illinois.

Lester Belding, fourth leading Big Ten scorer, was also a consensus all-Western and all Big

1921 Team

Lineman — Belding   Slater   Kriz   Heldt   Minick   Thompson   Kadesky   Mead
Backs — G. Devine   Locke   A. Devine   G. Miller   Shuttleworth

Ten team member, in addition to gaining numerous all-America second and third team awards.

Giant Fred (Duke) Slater, the greatest offensive tackle ever to play for Iowa and one of the finest football has known, earned a first team all-America berth on most elevens, including those of Eckersall, Walter Trumbull of the New York Herald, I.N.S. and the N.E.A. Walter Camp, having placed Aubrey Devine on his number one unit, gave Slater a second team spot. Most critics disagreed with Camp. Walter Eckersall said: "Slater is so powerful that one man cannot handle him and opposing elevens

Fred (Duke) Slater

have found it necessary to send two men against him every time a play was sent off his side of the line."

H. O. (Fritz) Crisler, a tower of strength to football and athletics for more than forty years,

played against Duke Slater. His comments about him were equally impressive: "Duke Slater was the best tackle I ever played against. I tried to block him throughout my college career but never once did I impede his progress to the ball carrier."

Duke Slater, always a gentleman on and off the gridiron, was chosen on the all-time all-America football team by Glenn (Pop) Warner. In 1946, 600 sports writers throughout the nation named him a member of their all-time all-America eleven. Five years later he was further honored by being selected to the National Football Hall of Fame.

There were other Iowans whose football stature reached maturity in 1921. Craven Shuttleworth and Glenn Devine, halfbacks, paved the way as offensive blockers and linebacking stalwarts. The Iowa forwards, impregnable and unmovable according to modern terminology, included Belding and Max Kadesky at the ends, Slater and George Thompson at tackle, Paul Minick and Chet Mead the guards, and fireplug Johnny Heldt at center.

Seven of the starters would return in 1922, but Howard Jones was faced with the task of filling the shoes of both Devines, Duke Slater and Les Belding.

Early in 1922 the Iowa Board in Control of Athletics met twice to consider the possibility of hiring Notre Dame's outstanding end and captain, Eddie Anderson, as an assistant football coach. The suggestion was rejected on the advice of Howard Jones.

In June the first informal discussions were held on the advisability and feasability of establishing an athletic field on the west side of the Iowa River. It was unanimously agreed that available seating at Iowa Field was inadequate to handle the demand of fans to see the Hawkeye gridders. In an effort to temporarily alleviate the problem the seating capacity was increased by 9,600 with the construction of new steel bleachers. Capacity was raised to 22,000.

Within the Big Ten legislation was adopted whereby the office of a Commissioner would be established "to assist in the enforcement of amateur rules, to aid and assist in the promo-

The Howard Jones' offense was built almost exclusively around Devine and Locke. Two of the more successful plays, each utilizing the abilities of his all-America stars, consistently humbled all opposition.

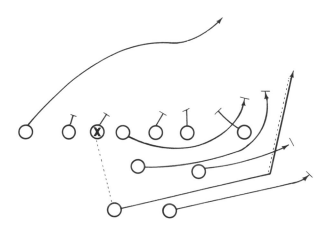

This play, designed especially for Aubrey Devine, began following a shift which placed the Iowa quarterback in the tailback position. After a direct pass from center Devine started to his right behind four interferers. He maintained the option of carrying out an end run or, as the defense committed, to call for a pass play.

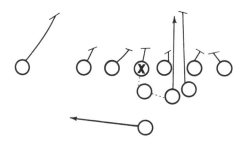

Fullback Gordon Locke was invariably called upon when difficult short yardage was needed. Most successful, perhaps, was this play in which Locke took a handoff from the quarterback and smashed over the interior right or left side of the Iowa offensive line, bolstered in 1921 by all-time Hawkeyes Slater, Heldt, Minick and Thompson, and in 1922 by the returning latter trio.

tion of the amateur spirit and principles, and to carry on research in intercollegiate athletic problems." This was an outgrowth of a suggestion first made by Michigan coach and Director of Athletics, Fielding Yost. A short time later a committee of directors recommended that long time Drake University athletic director Major John L. Griffith be named to the position. Griffith accepted and held the post until his death in 1944.

1922

Fifty-one candidates reported to Coach Howard Jones when practice convened in mid-September, 1922. Names most prominently mentioned to fill the places left vacant by graduation losses were sophomore Leland Parkin, Glenn Miller and Ed Rich in the backfield, along with Lowell Otte, John Hancock and Karl Engeldinger in the line. These men, in addition to the seven returning starters from 1921, formed the backbone of Iowa's hopes as they embarked upon the task of defending the Big Ten championship.

Knox College was scheduled as the opening opponent and offered little more than an opportunity for Coach Jones to view the quality of his over-all team depth along with the specific abilities of some inexperienced second and third team members. Iowa trampled the Illinois college under a 61 — 0 score, Gordon Locke scoring four times and the Hawkeye ground attack smashing for 471 yards.

One of the nation's top football classics of 1922 was played the following week when Iowa met Yale University in the famed Yale Bowl. The traditionally powerful Bulldogs had never lost to a western team in New Haven. The eyes of the entire football world were focused on the Yale-Iowa meeting which was not only a battle of western versus eastern prestige, but also pitted the coaching abilities of two Yale graduates, Howard Jones and his brother Tad Jones, against one another. It was only the second time in collegiate football history that two brothers had faced one another as opposing coaches.

The bruising, high tension defensive struggle which took place resulted in one of the most prized Iowa football victories. So significant and important was the game that The Chicago Sunday Tribune bannered the front page of its general news sections: IOWA ELEVEN SMASHES YALE.

The 6 — 0 final score offered little indication of the superiority which the Hawkeyes displayed throughout. Yale was held without a first down during the first half. The only touchdown was made early in the second period when Gordon Locke and sophomore quarterback Lee Parkin carried the ball to the Yale four. A penalty moved it to the nine, but Parkin met the challenge with a touchdown dash around left end for the six points and victory. Parkin was the rushing and passing leader for Iowa with more than 125 yards gained. Only 26 men played in the game, Yale using three substitutes and Iowa substituting just once.

Walter Camp referred to the game two years later with a comment of historical significance when he wrote: "One of the features of the season which has provoked probably more discussion than almost any other, is that of the use of the 'huddle system' in giving signals. Those Easterners who saw Iowa defeat Yale a couple of years ago were first given an illustration of this system which is becoming quite popular in the Middle West."

A long train ride back to Iowa City left the Hawkeyes with only three days to practice for what proved to be the most difficult game of the year — with Illinois. Coach Zuppke had skipped the Illinois-Butler game to scout the Iowa battle in New Haven. The result was an upset loss by his Illini at the hands of the smaller Indiana team, but an important notebook of information by Zuppke on how to stop Iowa. Lacking power and experience the Illini held the Hawks without a touchdown in the first half. However, an 18 yard scoring dash by Locke in the third quarter, coupled with an

1922 Team

Hill   Jenkins   Fieseler   Roberts   Otte   McIntyre   Jones   Bresnahan   Kelly
Wade   White   Lindsey   Moldenhauer   Jaqua   Barrett   Thom   James   Frank   Fisher
Hancock   Kriz   Engeldinger   Mead   Heldt   Minick   Thompson   Kadesky   Johnstone
Nugent   Seiling   Parkin   Miller   Locke   Shuttleworth   Rich   Yerkes

Chicago Sunday Tribune

THE WORLD'S GREATEST NEWSPAPER

VOLUME LXXXI—NO. 42   [COPYRIGHT 1922 BY THE CHICAGO TRIBUNE]   OCTOBER 15, 1922.   ★ SEVEN CENTS IN CHICAGO AND 20 MILE RADIUS | TEN CENTS ELSEWHERE.

IOWA ELEVEN SMASHES YALE

RAIL WAY MEN GET PAY BOOST OF $22,125,562

Rate Raised 2 Cents an Hour by Board.

Pay of railroad maintenance of way employes was yesterday increased 2 cents an hour by the United States railway labor board. The increase will affect 461,911 men and will amount to $22,125,562 in a year.

Ben W. Hooper, chairman of the board, declared that the action was taken because of the definite upward trend of wages in other lines of industry, particularly common labor. There was no pronounced increase in the cost of living, he said.

"The board does not feel that it is receding from its decision of last spring, as at that time the wage increase ordered was just and reasonable," he said. "The reasons and issues leading to the present increase will be fully set out when the official decision is rendered.

Ruling Breaks Deadlock.

The decision of the board, which breaks a deadlock extending over a period of several weeks, in which the members were unable to agree upon the amount of an increase, will make the minimum rates of pay for main tenance of way workers from 23 to 27 cents an hour, effective Oct. 14. This is

NEWS SUMMARY

LOCAL.

United States railway labor board increases wages of maintenance of way men 2 cents an hour, totaling $22,125,-562 yearly for 461,911 employes.

Police redouble efforts to run down persons responsible for robbery of vital gland from Joseph Wozniak, whose varying versions of affair add to mystery.

Health Commissioner Bundesen captures moron who, posing as dentist sent by health department, examined children of Dore school.

Senator Arthur Capper of Kansas in Chicago, after tour of central west, predicts Republican success in November.

Brig. Gen. Mosely urges establishment of a training base for the Reserve Officers' Training corps at Fort Sheridan, which he asserts is ideal location of middle west.

Reports to the department of labor show that employment is on the increase and traveling salesmen report that the pickup in business is quite general.

FOREIGN.

Prime Minister Lloyd George challenges foes to enter election test; defends his near east policies, which he says kept France from engaging in a new war.

Kemal Pasha makes triumphal entry into Brusa, ancient Turkish capital.

DOMESTIC.

All records for speed beaten in air races at Mount Clemens, Mich., army aviators carrying off honors.

New prohibition ruling immediately dries up all American ships, government and private, but gives all foreign vessels one more damp week.

Gov. Edwards expected to direct inquiry into slaying of New Jersey

THE FOUR ENEMIES OF GOOD GOVERNMENT

[Copyright: 1922: By The Chicago Tribune]

HAWKEYE LINE ATTACK BRINGS 6 TO 0 VICTORY

Parkin Star; Scores Only Touchdown.

IOWA-YALE LINEUP

IOWA (6).		YALE (0).
R. E.	Hancock, Eddy	L. E.
R. T.	Engdahger, Green, Gazzla	L. T.
R. G.	Kriz Cruikshank	L. G.
C.	Heldt Levelor, Lovejoy	C.
L. G.	Minnick Cross	R. G.
L. T.	Thompson Diller	R. T.
L. E.	Raspany Holtman	R. E.
Q. B.	Parkin, Kilb Neidinger	Q. B.
R. H. B.	Shuttleworth Wiglet	L. H. B.
L. H. B.	Miller Hans, Cochrane	R. H. B.
F. B.	Locke [Capt.]	F. B.
	Mallory	

Touchdown — Parkin. Referee—H. J. O'Brien [Tufts]. Umpire—Dave Fultz [Brown]. Head linesman—Frank E. Birch [Earlham]. Field judge—Magidsohn [Michigan].

BY HUGH FULLERTON

New Haven, Conn., Oct. 14.—How ard is champion of the Jones family.

In one of the most desperately contested battles ever fought in Yale's historic bowl the west today triumphed over the east and smashed all the history of football.

Iowa, ripping and tearing through, scored a touchdown when Leland Parkin, a new hero in the football

Races in Coma to Set World Air Record

Selfridge Field, Mount Clemens, Mich., Oct. 14.—[Special.]—Lieut. R. L. Maughan, flying a Curtiss high speed pursuit plane, a United States army entry, won the Pulitzer trophy here in a race in which all world's records, officially and unofficially, were broken for 50, 100, and 200 kilometer courses.

The fastest lap in the race, which was flown in three flights, was made by Lieut. L. J. Maitland, who flew a sister ship to Maughan's and also an army entry. He made the first lap at a speed of 216.1 miles an hour. Maitland finished second in the race.

Maughan's average speed for the five laps was 206 miles an hour.

Army Flyers Triumph.

The triumph of the army flyers was witnessed by a crowd of 50,000, who literally went wild as the aviators made the hazardous turns at the Pylon in front of the grandstand with their planes almost upside down.

In the spectacular race today, replete with thrills, two planes were forced down. The navy's "mystery ship" was forced to the ground by motor trouble. Capt. St. Claire Streett, an army entry, also was forced down.

Lieut. Maughan was exhausted by his race and leaned against his plane for a few minutes until he had revived. Then he told how all through the race he had been thinking of a telegram he was expecting to receive at any moment announcing the birth of a child to his wife.

Feet Went to Sleep.

"I got just four time in the race," said Maughan. "I was stunned more or less at each of the fifteen turns

LLOYD GEORGE PUTS FATE IN PEOPLE'S HANDS

Contends He Kept Peace in Europe.

BY JOHN STEELE

[Chicago Tribune Foreign News Service.]

[Copyright: 1922: By The Chicago Tribune.]

MANCHESTER, Oct. 14.—"I cast myself on the people whose cause I have never betrayed in thirty-two years of strenuous public life. They are a just and generous people. They will see fair play."

These were the words of Prime Minister Lloyd George here today as he hurled defiance at his enemies and foreshadowed an early appeal to the people at the polls, which he is confident will result in a triumphant vindication.

There has been a quick change over night in the British domestic situation as a result of the reception this morning of Austen Chamberlain's speech. All Tory newspapers are dissatisfied and the younger Tories are clamoring for a dissolution of the coalition, which both Mr. Lloyd George and the Tory leaders are anxious to maintain. Under the circumstances the leaders are not looking forward joyfully to a conference of the national and conservative clubs on Nov. 14, at which it is feared their leadership may be

The Hawkeyes reap national headlines.

Jubilation following victory.

all-important safety, proved to be enough for Iowa to escape, 8 — 7.

Purdue paid dearly for the disappointing performance displayed against Illinois. Nine touchdowns were scored by the perfectly executed Iowa attack. The Boilermakers never penetrated the Hawk 30 yard line in the face of their worst football defeat, 56 — 0.

A record breaking crowd jammed Iowa Field the following week to watch the undefeated Hawkeyes subdue Minnesota for the fifth consecutive time. The Jonesmen, powered by a three touchdown salvo from Gordon Locke, ran up 28 points before the half, then substituted freely and won, 28 — 14.

Locke firmly established his all-America calibre against Ohio State in Columbus as Iowa

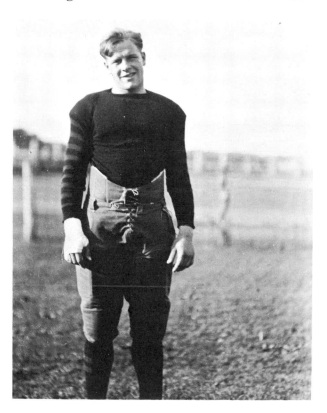

Paul Minick

earned a viciously fought 12 — 9 verdict over the Buckeyes. The durable Hawk captain scored both touchdowns, smashed for 126 yards from scrimmage and returned three kickoffs for an additional 91 yards. Iowa was forced to

come from behind for the first time in two years when a field goal and touchdown pass by Buck great Nick Workman gave the host eleven brief leads in each of the first two quarters.

A six touchdown flurry, again paced by Gordon Locke who notched four, provided Iowa a seventh straight victory, a second consecutive Big Ten title and recognition by many as the nation's finest college eleven. Northwestern succumbed, 37 — 3, in the season finale and Howard Jones' Hawks had stretched their winning streak to an impressive seventeen straight games.

Accolades were thrown in the direction of the Iowa team as well as her individual players following the season. No other eleven in the country was able to offer a more persuasive claim to the national title than the Hawkeyes. Only Princeton in the East and California in the West went through the year unscathed. However, midwestern critics pointed out that Princeton was outplayed by Chicago of the Big Ten and was unable to score a touchdown against Yale, although defeating the Bulldogs, 3 — 0. California was untested by a team from the Midwest or East, meeting no competition from outside of the Pacific Coast area.

Four Hawkeyes, Gordon Locke, Paul Minick, Max Kadesky and John Heldt, were selected on one or more all-America teams. Seven gained recognition on the all Big Ten teams chosen by Walter Eckersall and, for the second year in a row, eleven Iowa starters were given berths on the Iowa All-State honor elevens.

Center Johnny Heldt, completing his third season, was selected by eastern authority Charley Brickley and by the Chicago Daily News to the all-America first team. Senior guard Paul Minick gained first team honors from respected writer Norman Brown, and was a second team choice of both Brickley and The Chicago Daily News. End Max Kadesky, a first team honoree of veteran writer Heywood Broun, gained further renown when Walter Camp named the plucky wingman to his third all-American unit. George Thompson, Craven Shuttleworth, Ed Rich, Glenn Miller, Leo Kriz,

Lee Parkin and Chet Mead were others who gained distinction following the season.

Most decorated Hawkeye, however, was Gordon Locke, captain and driving force behind the 1922 champions. During three years of varsity competition Locke was called upon to carry the ball 430 times. He was thrown for

John C. Heldt

losses totalling only eleven yards, grinding out nearly two-thousand by virtue of his punishing pile-driving thrusts. Six times in his career Locke blasted opposing defenses for 125 yards or more rushing and twice he piled up more than 200 yards, the only Hawkeye ever to top the 200 yard mark. In addition, Locke scored four touchdowns in four different games during his career. No Iowan since 1928 has tallied a quartet of scores even once.

Gordon Locke set a Big Ten scoring record in 1922 that neither Red Grange nor Tom Harmon, two of the most unforgettable backs in conference history, could equal. That mark, (12 touchdowns for 72 points in five conference games) stood for more than 20 years, until the late Tony Butkovich of Purdue erased the

Big Ten record by scoring 78 points against the weak wartime teams of 1943.

At Iowa, his 32 touchdowns in three seasons are seven more than any other Hawkeye has scored. Further, no Iowan has approached the 192 total points registered by Locke and he is one of only five Hawks to garner more than 2,000 yards total offense in a career.

What did the widely known football commentators of the time think of Gordon Locke? John Heisman, for whom the Heisman Trophy is awarded each year, said: "Powerful is an inadequate adjective to use in describing his strength and ramming talents. He had the legs that gave the drive the momentum of a battle tank. . ."

In the Athletic World: ". . .Locke of Iowa. . .was the most consistent ground gainer in the country. He not only can run the ends to advantage but he can buck a line with tremendous power. . .he has an individual style, carrying the knees high, toes hardly touching the

Gordon C. Locke

ground, and can turn, dodge and reverse with remarkable speed."

Walter Camp recognized the Iowa stalwart by placing him on his first all-America team. Walter Eckersall did the same, selecting him as captain of the first unit.

Away from the gridiron Locke was also a leader. He was credited with a better than "B" average through his liberal arts course. Advancing to the law college, he finished within the top three in his graduating class.

He also won the Big Ten medal for scholastic achievement and athletic prowess. Forty years after beginning his varsity playing at Iowa, Gordon Locke was given football's highest honor: election to the National Football Foundation and Hall of Fame.

With a second straight perfect season, embellished by the intersectional win over Yale and a second consecutive conference crown, Howard Jones reached the peak at Iowa. There was little reason to suspect he was nearing the end of his Iowa career, but such was the case.

1923

The winning streak remained unbroken going into 1923, but two rugged battles, each of which was lost, soon disfigured it. Before that time, however, Oklahoma A & M, Knox and Purdue fell before the surprisingly strong Hawkeyes. Gone was the offensive and defensive might of Jones' championship teams, and in their place were inexperienced sophomores along with a sprinkling of juniors. Brightest of the newcomers was a powerfully built linesmashing runner from Manning, Wes Fry by name. At season's end Fry would stamp himself the greatest sophomore ground gainer and total offense leader in Iowa history.

Other sophomores destined to play big roles for the Hawkeyes were end Dick Romey, Don Graham, John Schirmer, Ray Dauber and Tubby Griffen.

After twenty consecutive victories, extending from the middle of the 1920 season through the first three games of the 1923 campaign, Iowa was pitted against powerful Illinois, featuring another highly touted sophomore, Harold (Red) Grange. After trailing the Illini through the first three quarters, the result of a king-size 47 yard field goal by Earl Britton, the Hawkeyes scored early in the fourth period to lead, 6 − 3. A 25 yard scoring pass, Fry to Romey, put Iowa ahead but only briefly. Less than five minutes remained. Illinois took possession of the ball on its own 19, 81 yards from a touchdown. Britton faded back and passed 29 yards to Grange. He threw to him for two, another for 21, and still a fourth for 26 yards. The ball rested on Iowa's three. Grange was called upon to run and he responded with a dash around end for the winning touchdown.

Writing about the 1923 Iowa game long after his playing career had ended, Grange said: "I can honestly say that my greatest thrill in football came against Iowa in 1923 when I held the ball for Earl Britton on his sensational field goal from the 47 yard line. There was such power to that kick it shot out almost on a line as it cleared the uprights."

A battered and crippled Iowa team journeyed to Columbus the following week and blasted Ohio State, 21 − 0. Two first quarter field goals by Darrell Fisher, a touchdown by Wilbur Scantlebury and another score following a 40 yard dash with a recovered fumble by tackle John Hancock gave the Hawks an easy victory.

Michigan's Wolverines, coached by Fielding Yost and led by all-American Harry Kipke, dealt Iowa a heartbreaking loss in a late season Iowa City game. Matching field goals, one by Fisher for Iowa and the other by Kipke, were only an indication of the evenness which the two teams showed. Earlier, however, one of the most frustrating plays in Iowa football had given Michigan a somewhat tainted touchdown. John Schommer, one of the officials in the game, presented his account in a 1929 issue of the Big Ten Weekly under the heading: The Toughest Decision I Ever Made.

. . ."I'll never forget the Michigan-Iowa game at Iowa City in 1923," Schommer wrote. ". . .The winning play came as Michigan punted, as I recall, and it was Kipke who got off the kick. As he did so, an Iowa end or tackle broke through and, as I recall, it was Hancock. He made a wild leap for the ball and barely got his finger tips on it. He didn't block the punt and it continued on its course as though it had not been touched. . .I was the umpire and was stationed a few yards behind the defensive line. I saw and heard the contact of the ball on Hancock's finger tips and immediately called as loud as I could, 'Free ball! Onside!' That was customary in those days. Blott, the Michigan center, was near me and raced down the field to recover the ball. It rolled slowly over the goal line and I think it was Miller of Iowa who watched it roll, preferring to take a touchback rather than be downed inside the ten-yard line. He had not heard me call 'free ball,' evidently. . .Blott got there and the instant the ball crossed the goal he pounced on it for the touchdown that let Michigan win, 9 — 3. I won't forget leaving that field.

"Before I could get to the dressing room I was surrounded by a thousand men, most of them, I think, being townsfolk rather than students. Each one of them was ready to swing the second punch, but none the first blow and with the protection of the Iowa squad, I got to safety. I began wondering if there would not be some way to slip out of town without going to the depot for the usual train, but when I got back to town after the game I found that Coach Howard Jones had sent members of his team to the hotel lobby, cigar stores, drug stores and places of meeting in every part of the city — to inform the crowds that I had made the proper decision and that he stood back of me. That's the kind of a square shooter and solid sportsman Howard Jones is."

(John W. Hancock, director of athletics at Colorado State College, verified Schommer's version in 1956, specifying that the kicked ball was a punt by Kipke and that he, Hancock, was the man who touched the ball. This play led to a change in the rules.)

Junior Leland Parkin, one of the most prominent lights on the 1922 championship team, had seen no action in four of Iowa's first six games. Prone to injury throughout much of his career, his loss in what was termed a "rebuilding year" in 1923 was particularly damaging.

Minnesota scored its first victory over Iowa since 1916 when the Gophers dominated the play to win, 20 — 7. The final game of the season, and the last of Howard Jones' eight year stretch at Iowa, was a winning one, 17 — 14 over Northwestern. The over-all season record showed five victories against three defeats and it was Jones' seventh winning season.

Lowell Otte, tackle Leo Kriz and guard Bill Fleckenstein were recognized by various midwestern selections with berths on the all Big Ten first team. Wes Fry, with 791 yards rushing and 1232 yards total offense, placed himself among the all-time Iowa offensive leaders. Four times during the 1923 season, twice against Big Ten opposition, Fry rushed for more than 125 yards, including a top of 188 yards against Knox.

Jones-Lambert Clash

During the year action designed to strengthen the staff of the physical education department academically was introduced. A study of the department at that time showed that the staff of the department was limited to four persons, only two of whom had bachelor of arts or bachelor of science degrees, with none holding higher degrees. The department actually was in its infancy. Members of the staff were Coach Jones, E. G. (Dad) Schroeder, James Ashmore and David A. Armbruster. The department was a unit of the College of Liberal Arts.

Plans tending to transform the physical education staff into a unit with higher academic standing began to take definite shape in 1923. The consolidation of the departments of intercollegiate athletics and of physical education for men and women was proposed, with a single head in charge. There were other proposals, consideration of which brought out differences of opinion. A particular disagreement arose between Howard Jones and B. J. Lambert, chairman of the Board in Control of Athletics. Jones apparently had no great interest in increasing the emphasis on academic work in physical education, and the impression that Lambert had only passing interest in the intercollegiate athletic effort was assumed in some circles.

After what he termed "a little unpleasantness" during a Board meeting, Chairman

Lambert wrote President Jessup, submitting his resignation from the Board. He said: . . ."Among other things I was charged by Director Jones with not working in harmony with his office or with him. . .From certain things Mr. Jones said I feel that he holds me personally responsible for the Board's desire to combine the Departments of Athletics and Physical Education under a man other than himself. . ."

Lambert was persuaded to remain on the Board, but it was no secret that his long standing difficulties with Jones were being compounded. The first signs of tension between the two men had occurred years before when Lambert expressed his outspoken opposition to Jones' use of and confidence in long-time trainer Jack Watson. Two years later the coach asked that his assistant coaches be given salary increases. After objections were raised by Lambert the raises were not forthcoming. Also during 1923, Jones raised strong objection to the right of the Board chairman to accompany the team to football games.

It was also true that Howard Jones was deeply concerned over the unhappiness of his wife and her dislike of Iowa City. In mid-December, following the 1923 season, he proceeded to his old home in Excello, Ohio, where he reviewed his role at Iowa. The worsening troubles with B. J. Lambert, as well as his desire to salvage his marriage, undoubtedly were paramount in Jones' mind when he dispatched the following letter to Prof. R. A. Kuever, secretary of the Board in Control of Athletics, on December 22:

"Since I have arrived home I have had opportunity to give thought to the situation which has arisen relative to my position at the University," he wrote.

"After taking everything into consideration I earnestly request that the Board accept my resignation of the position of Football Coach and Athletic Director. . .to take effect September 1st, 1924. . . If, after acting upon the above request, the Board wishes to consider engaging me as football coach for the period of the football season and spring practice, will you let me know by wire here, before the twenty-seventh, or at the Georgian Terrace Hotel, Atlanta, before the twenty-ninth."

When Walter A. Jessup, president of the University, was informed of Jones' action, he immediately wired the coach:

"Just learned of your difficulty. Don't let anything cloud the fact of our unswerving devotion to you and our full expectation of a permanent future for you here. I want to see you when you return. . ."

To Jones also went a telegram from Athletic Board Secretary Kuever, saying:

"The Board and President are firmly of the opinion that conditions can be adjusted so as to be thoroughly satisfactory to you. We ask therefore that you hold the matter in abeyance until your return. . ."

The coach responded by declaring his appreciation of the attitude of the Board and saying he would hold the matter in abeyance. Coach Jones returned to Iowa City and on January 8, 1924, met with the Board in another executive session, in the Law building. Deliberations lasting more than six hours brought no definite decisions and the meeting was adjourned, to reconvene the following day. This formal acknowledgment of the discussions was issued:

"Informal discussion on Mr. Jones' resignation. A conference of one hour was held with President Jessup. Mr. Jones was called in and it developed that he desired to terminate his present contract and make a new one for a period of five years at $10,000 per year, with essentially five and one-half months' service for each fiscal year, as follows: the last half of September, all of October, November, December up to the holiday recess, as much of April as is necessary for spring practice (Mr. Jones suggested approximately two weeks) all of June and the first half of July. After prolonged informal discussion and another conference with President Jessup it was decided to adjourn until the following day.

R. A. Kuever
Secretary"

That Coach Jones was adamant in his demand for a new contract was indicated with the resumption of the adjourned meeting in the Law building on January 9, 1924. Jones again was present. This report of the meeting appeared over the signature of Board Secretary Kuever:

". . .Another long conference was held with Mr. Jones during which he insisted upon having his present contract terminated and a new one drawn, on a part time basis, provided he is to be retained at Iowa. After another prolonged discussion and a third conference with President Jessup it was found that Mr. Jones' financial request could be met but not his request for part-time services and the Board, feeling that Mr. Jones has just reasons for asking that his contract be terminated, voted unanimously to do so and to have it take effect the first of September, or on an earlier date if Mr. Jones so desired. . ."

Alumni reaction to the Board's move to release Coach Jones from his contract was prompt and persuasive. On January 12, 1924, the Board again went into executive session, this time at the suggestion of alumni who felt that there still was a possibility of retaining Coach Jones. This action resulted:

". .After an informal discussion it was moved, seconded and carried, as follows:

"1) That Mr. Jones' contract be continued in force until its expiration and that he be given such leaves of absence as the Board may direct;

"2) That he be given an option which shall terminate on January 15, 1926, of a contract of five years, dating from the expiration of his present contract, such contract to carry a salary of $10,000 per year, to be on a full time basis and his status under this new contract shall be determined not later than January 15, 1926;

"3) That the above clauses be submitted to the President for his approval.

"The board then adjourned to confer with President Jessup at his house, where it was decided to hold the above matter in abeyance for perhaps twenty-four hours until more thorough consideration could be given to it and a full meeting of the Board could be had. . ."

The busy Board members met again the following day, in the office of Secretary Kuever, and were informed that Coach Jones already had wired Trinity College of Durham, N. C., (later to be known as Duke University) accepting an offer to coach at Trinity. This report of the day's meeting came from Secretary Kuever:

". . .Kuever and Beye reported that on the evening previous, January 12th., Mr. Jones had wired the North Carolina institution definitely accepting their proposition, and that Trinity College had wired him a reply, which he received Sunday morning, January 13, acknowledging his acceptance of the position.

"After an informal discussion it was found that no further action could be taken or would be advisable and the meeting then was adjourned."

Two days later another bombshell exploded, this time in the form of a letter from Board Chairman B. J. Lambert to Howard Jones. The letter follows:

January 15, 1924

Mr. H. H. Jones
City.

My dear Mr. Jones:

I have asked the President to release me at once from my work on the Board in Control of Athletics and he has assented. I am sure that you, as well as the President and the other members of the Board will all feel as gratified over this as I am.

I am giving you this information at once as it will no doubt influence you in your decision to remain at Iowa. From the statement given to the press over your signature, one was led to believe that change of climate and part time work were the main factors that caused you to wish a change. But today your friends are telling me that my presence on the Board has been given as the real reason that you cannot keep your contract with the University.

Under all the circumstances that have arisen in the past year, since I first tendered my resignation and was then only influenced to remain by the seemingly earnest expressions of yourself and the other members of the Board, I can only say that now it is really a pleasure to give way to your wishes.

I trust that your reputation for fairness, honesty and good sportsmanship will not be questioned and that nothing now stands in the way of your fulfillment of your contract.

Very respectfully,
(Signed) B. J. Lambert

Howard Jones still was in the Iowa picture and he remained so as late as February 10, 1924, when another Board meeting revealed these procedures:

"After an informal discussion of the Jones situation the following motion was unanimously passed:

"In the event that Howard H. Jones obtains a release from the contractural relations into which he has entered with another institution, the Board in Control of Athletics will reinstate the contract between Mr. Jones and the Board which has recently been terminated. Under this contract, however, Mr. Jones will be relieved from his duties as Director of Athletics and will be given such leaves of absence as the Board may direct.

"Future relations between Mr. Jones and the Board will be determined only at the expiration of the present contract and no promises, expressed or implied, are made with reference to the terms and conditions of such future contract, but the Board places itself on record as being opposed to the principle of part-time services.

"In view of the fact that the time for spring practice is almost at hand, the Board requests from Mr. Jones a decision, in writing, on or before February 20. . ."

The climax of the discussions of the Jones' contract was quick to arrive. On February 13, 1924, a copy of a message from Howard Jones went into the records of the Board. It read:

"In accordance with my conversation with Mr. Pelzer this afternoon, regarding the date my resignation should become effective, will say that I should be very glad to have the Board in Control of Athletics state the date, any time prior to March 1, 1924, which they deem it desirable to set."

The Board immediately notified Secretary Kuever to advise Mr. Jones that his resignation would become effective on February 29, 1924. And on that date the Howard Jones' regime formally ended at Iowa. During eight seasons, his Hawkeye teams won 42 games, lost 17 and tied one.

A final postscript was added shortly thereafter when resigned Board Chairman B. J. Lambert wrote university President Jessup:

"It is unnecessary to go into the matter leading to the late unpleasantness and the conditions now existing.

"It is now my firm conviction, and I think time will prove this, that what is now happening will be, not a hindrance, but a great help to our general athletic situation here.

"I have often, in my office, tried to make a paper outline of an organization capable of doing work as great or even greater than say, Illinois or Michigan are either now doing or have in contemplation. No such plan has ever been sent to you for the simple reason that I never could see where Mr. Jones would fit into the scheme except as a Football Coach, and that only for Intercollegiate work.

"You know how I feel about this *indispensible* stuff. It simply never works out that way. It is all right for newspaper material and general conversation, but deep down in my heart I can only feel that the University now has a chance for a certain development that otherwise might have been delayed a number of years.

"I am sorry all this has happened, and yet I am glad."

Trinity, now known as Duke University, secured the coaching services of Howard Jones in 1924, after which he moved on to the University of Southern California. His tenure there, which included five Rose Bowl victories, was incomparably successful. His remarkable overall coaching career spanned twenty-nine seasons and included 194 victories, only 64 defeats and 21 ties.

Howard Harding Jones died of a heart attack July 27, 1941, at his home in Los Angeles, generally recognized as one of the half-dozen greatest coaches of intercollegiate football.

The Knute Rockne — Iowa Affair

With the departure of Coach Jones, the finding of another coach of similar stature who could keep the Hawkeyes among the nation's leaders was of first concern and Iowa was "thinking big." In a matter of days a little-known incident in Iowa history came to light.

At Notre Dame, the famous Four Horsemen were on the fringe of the national scene and charging hard toward the front. The Fighting Irish were moving into the fabulous era that established them with the greats of all time in football. The man who built the Notre Dame teams and their growing prestige attracted the attention of Iowa authorities. Quietly, although perhaps not quietly enough, Hawkeye negotiators approached Knute Rockne. The discussions, which brought Rockne to Iowa City for a meeting with the Board in Control of Athletics, had progressed for a period of nearly two weeks when the Chicago Tribune startled the football world with this headline:

"Events Point to Rockne as Iowa Coach Deal is in Effect Closed."

It was the morning of March 23, 1924, that the famed newspaper spread the word of a possible switch of the great coach. It was a speculative report, based on the facts available at the time, but subsequent happenings suggested that there was more to the story than mere rumor. The Tribune headline was true — for a

time — but later developments changed the picture and the publicity occasioned by the headline itself seems now to stand as the basic reason why Knute Rockne did not become the head football coach at Iowa. But, let's move ahead a few months and try to piece out the picture.

Shortly after the close of the 1925 football season, Coach Rockne was in New York City and during his visit he conferred with representatives of Columbia University over the possibility of his assuming the head coaching role at Columbia. There were published reports that Rockne was likely to make the switch. Now let's reproduce a part of a story that appeared 16, 1925:

". . .When the story came out in the east in the Iowa City Press-Citizen on December that Rockne would leave Notre Dame and hereafter see his name on a Columbia door, the story was painted all over the country in newspaper headlines and it brought a bad taste into the mouth of at least one Iowa alumnus. King Thompson of Cedar Rapids read of Knute's latest newspaper activity and he recalled an incident in March, 1924, when officials of the University of Iowa were hunting a man to fill the shoes which Howard Jones suddenly left out in the cold. Alumni of Iowa demanded a man with a reputation, since Jones had turned out two or three teams which will always be dear to Iowa hearts.

"Thompson evidently knew more about Iowa's negotiations with Rockne than anyone suspected and, until he got mad the other day and gave out a newspaper story which hinted at pretty near the whole truth, very few football followers actually knew how close the Iowa men came to getting Rockne here.

"Following the resignation of Jones, it was universally known that Iowa was desperately in need of a football coach and one weekend in March, 1924, the semi-bald pate of the famous Rockne made its appearance here.

"Later in the week Dr. Paul E. Belting, director of athletics, met Rockne in Chicago and in their conference in the Windy City Knute loosened up and admitted that, providing the ante was high enough, he'd come to the Hawkeye institution. Dr. Belting sweetened the pot with the promise of a few thousand shekels per annum and Knute called. Dr. Belting then returned to Iowa City with the verbal understanding that Rockne would come here as head football coach, providing the matter did not receive too much publicity since the famous Swede (Rockne was a Norwegian) seemed to fear the persuasive powers of Notre Dame representatives if the matter became too prominently mentioned in the news columns.

"Several days later Rockne again communicated with Dr. Belting, only to inform the chief of Iowa athletics that as far as he was concerned the negotiations were off. With the affairs in that situation President Jessup evidenced an interest in the matter and a week after Dr. Belting's conference. . .returned home with the understanding that Rockne would come here providing relations with Notre Dame could be concluded . . . . .

"With the matter apparently settled, although not ripe for publicity, President Jessup and Dr. Belting were confident Rockne would be the next Iowa coach, although at no time in the dealings had a written contract been signed. . ."

This lightly treated and perhaps slightly slanted account of events seems to have been in error in one major respect. There WAS it seems, a written agreement by Rockne to become head coach at Iowa, contingent apparently on certain conditions. That agreement is in the hands of Dr. Walter R. Fieseler, then Medical Supervisor for the Iowa athletic department and a prominent part of the Rockne negotiations. Fieseler, for many years a leading Fort Dodge physician, currently lives in retirement at Okoboji, Iowa.

Additional research has developed the fact that Rockne was in Iowa City on March 10 and 11, 1924, to discuss the coaching vacancy with the Iowa Board. The Chicago Tribune headline suggesting Rockne as the new Iowa coach made its appearence on March 23 but during the interim the South Bend Tribune, on March 20, had telegraphed a source close to the Iowa administration inquiring:

"When will Rockne actually begin work in Iowa City?" The subject was becoming "hot" from a newspaper standpoint. Resulting publicity apparently was contrary to the wishes and the agreement of the interested parties and embarrassing to Coach Rockne.

The Iowa Board was called into session in the athletic department March 25, 1924, and the following telegram, undisclosed for more than 40 years, was read into the record:

"SOUTH BEND   IND   MAR 25, 1924
PRES JESSUP
UNIVERSITY OF IOWA   IOWA CITY
IOWA

BELTING AND FIESELER BOTH PROMISED ABSOLUTELY NO PUBLICITY   MY DUTY NOW LIES HERE   FURTHER DISCUSSION IS USELESS   I VOLUNTARILY SIGNED NEW TEN YEAR AGREEMENT ON SAME TERMS AS IN PAST AND WHOLE MATTER IS NOW CLOSED   GOOD LUCK
                    K K ROCKNE"

Belting was Iowa's newly appointed athletic director, and Medical Supervisor Fieseler had been an acquaintance of Rockne for many years. What had triggered the breakoff in negotiations, and what was the chain of events surrounding this interesting but little known chapter in University of Iowa athletics? According to Rockne's final telegram, ill-timed publicity was a primary reason. But there were other interesting developments which highlighted the suspense-filled two weeks.

The original contact with Rockne was made by R. A. Kuever, then dean of the Iowa College of Pharmacy and secretary of the Board in Control of Athletics. Regarding the affair, Kuever wrote: "It was I who called him by telephone at Notre Dame University to ask him to come to Iowa City for a conference with respect to the football vacancy that then existed at Iowa. I made the call at the suggestion of Dr. Walter A. Jessup who was then president of the University."

President Jessup himself shed further light upon the situation when he wrote, in a letter dated April 3, 1924: "We had a signed contract which Rockne drew up. . . .very much as outlined in Eckersall's article in The Tribune. We were greatly surprised to find that he had changed his plans. When he was here to talk over the matter with us we came to a definite understanding as to the details of his service, but before he got back home, the alumni of his own institution visited his wife and built up such a backfire as to ultimately break up the whole proposition. I made a trip to New York City to attempt to break down the opposition, but finally he cut the knot himself by withdrawing from his contract with us."

Another Iowa official who had a part in the Rockne discussions was George T. Bresnahan, then Hawkeye track coach and a member of the faculty in the department of physical education. Bresnahan has written: "In addition to coaching football, he volunteered to join me in the coaching of track at Iowa. There was one impediment (at that time) to his coming. He had promised orally to one of the Regents that he would not leave Notre Dame without first discussing the change with him. A leading administrator at Iowa, after a trip to New York City to meet this Regent, obtained the go-ahead sign."

The Bresnahan letter undoubtedly refers to the trip of President Jessup to New York in an effort to solidify Iowa's efforts to obtain Rockne. Other messages bearing upon the possible alliance between the Notre Dame coach and Iowa included these telegrams:

JACKSON   MICH   MAR 17 1924

PRESIDENT JESSUP

UNIVERSITY OF IOWA   IOWA CITY IOWA

WIFE NOT FEELING WELL ENOUGH TO COME MAKING SPEECH HERE TONIGHT CALLED ALUMNI ON PHONE AND HE INSISTS ON HOLDING ME ABSOLUTELY TO MY PROMISE OF LAST SATURDAY SO WE HAD BETTER DROP WHOLE MATTER WITH EVERY GOOD WISH

ROCKNE
826P

Additional activity was noted within a day or two. On March 20 President Jessup, while in New York, received this telegram from W. R. Fieseler, Iowa's Medical Supervisor, who had taken a prominent part in the negotiations.

A CHICAGO ILL   153P   MAR 20, 1924

W A JESSUP

WOODSTOCK HOTEL   NEW YORK   NY WILL STAY HERE UNTIL I HEAR FROM YOU

W R FIESELER
301P

The following day Fieseler, waiting in Chicago to see Rockne, sent another message to Jessup:

CHICAGO ILL   1226P   MAR 21 1924

W A JESSUP

WOODSTOCK HOTEL   NEW YORK   NY I WILL SEE ROCKNE TONIGHT DID MCDONALD REFUSE TO RELEASE ROCKNE

W R FIESELER
139P

President Jessup's reply (copied in his own handwriting)

Dr. W. R. Fieseler

Auditorium Hotel, Mich. Blvd., Chicago

Rockne had talked to McDonald Thursday over phone. McDonald says that they are working at Notre Dame to fix everything there to Rockne's entire satisfaction. He doesn't think that Rockne thinks our future is better. He is entirely free to make a choice. Now that the road is clear I feel sure of the outcome.

W. A. Jessup

Another message from Dr. Fieseler:

CHICAGO   ILL   220P   MAR 21 1924

W A JESSUP

WOODSTOCK HOTEL   NEW YORK   NY
ROCKNE IS CALLING MCDONALD THIS
AFTERNOON

W R FIESELER
331P

And finally this closing telegram:

CHICAGO   ILL   943P   MAR 21 1924

W A JESSUP

WOODSTOCK HOTEL   NEW YORK   NY
ROCKNE WIRED   HAVE DECIDED FOR
OWN PEACE OF MIND EVERYTHING ALL
OFF   WILL STAY HERE   THIS IS FINAL
CANNOT   EXPLAIN   FURTHER   WITH
EVERY GOOD WISH   AM LEAVING AT
TWELVE FIFTY

W R FIESELER

Pertinent to the negotiations with both Howard Jones and Knute Rockne were these excerpts from a letter written April 8, 1924, by President Jessup to W. Earl Hall of the Mason City Globe-Gazette. The excerpts are taken from an original draft of a letter which had been revised and hand corrected on its margins by President Jessup:

My Dear Earl:

". . .As you know, every attempt was made to retain the services of Mr. Jones, even to the point of offering him more money than was ever paid to a coach in the Big Ten Conference.

"The Board next turned to Mr. Rockne, and after putting forth every known effort, *a contract with him to come in 1925 was secured.* Such pressure was brought to bear upon him, however, after a tentative announcement in the Chicago Tribune, that he broke this contract.

"The Athletic Board had over seventy written applications for the position. In arriving at a decision, football experts were widely interviewed, and it was finally decided that Ingwersen was better fitted to do this particular task than any other available man in the country.

"As you know, this coach must work with Mr. Bresnahan, Dr. Fieseler and Coach Barry, as well as other members of the coaching staff. These three men have been unusually successful in their athletic endeavors for the University; and in view of their keen interest in the whole athletic situation and knowledge of the importance of it all, the Athletic Board decided at the beginning that these men should have a voice in the selection of a coach.

"I am very glad to be able to say that the entire coaching staff and the Athletic Board are all set for next year's heavy schedule, and I believe that nothing is more likely to lose our chances for a successful season than lack of support at this time, which will break down the morale of either the new coach or the team. . .

"The Iowa team is not to blame for Jones' leaving or for Rockne's breaking his contract, thus necessitating the securing of a coach without a national reputation, but if every last one of us will pocket our disappointment and 'pitch in' I believe the boys will give a fine account of themselves next year. As a member of the team said to me this morning, 'We sure can beat Illinois this year.' This is the spirit of Iowa. . ."

CHAPTER 11

The Arrival of Burt Ingwersen and Paul Belting

In the period of transition that followed the departure of Howard Jones, basic changes of athletic administration in 1924 preceded a crushing climax five years later. As successors to Jones, the University had selected two University of Illinois graduates and the first to arrive was Dr. Paul E. Belting, who assumed his duties on March 13, 1924. Within three weeks after his arrival Belting concluded the search for a football coach by signing Burton A. Ingwersen to head the staff.

That Dr. Belting's early days on the Iowa campus were pleasant is suggested by excerpts taken from a University bulletin entitled "Physical Education and Athletic Coaching" and dated May 21, 1926. This was two years after Dr. Belting's Iowa association began.

A sketch headed "P. E. Belting — Organizer, Director, Builder" states:

"Architects' plans and complicated specifications have become the hobby of a man who, some months ago, was considered primarily as a specialist in athletics and physical education.

"In the office of Doctor Paul E. Belting, Director of the Division of Physical Education, may be found complete sets of plans. There are those of the Iowa fieldhouse which when completed in the fall of 1926 will be the largest structure of its kind in the country. The director is always ready to discuss these plans . . .for they represent the culmination of a cherished dream of expansion — a dream, the fulfillment of which will raise the Hawkeye physical education plant to an even higher level.

"It was the first task of Doctor Paul E. Belting to reorganize the physical education situ-

Athletic Director — 1924-1929
Paul Belting

Head Football Coach — 1924-1931
Burt Ingwersen

ation at the University. . . . During the summer he worked quietly and well, and in the fall there was a smoothly-working combination of the department of athletics, department of physical education for men and the similar department for women. Formerly without coherence and under three heads, these important departments were united under the title of the Division of Physical Education.

"The new organization functioning like a machine, its workers including men and women of the finest caliber, Doctor Belting was not content to sit back and cast a mildly supervisory eye over the situation. He drew up courses of study, plotted out the intricate details and soon presented to the University faculty his plans for the formulation of a semi-professional curriculum which would lead to the degree of Bachelor of Science in Physical Education. So sound were his theories, so practical and progressive were his plans that the committee on courses of study showed no hesitancy in placing their approval on the new curriculum. . .

"A brief review of Doctor Belting's career before he came to the University shows that he was principal of the Oskaloosa, Iowa, high school; principal of the Globe, Arizona, high school, and that he filled a similar position in Martinsville, Illinois. Then in the years between 1917 and 1920, he was director of games for boys at the Horace Mann school in New York City. The University of Illinois next secured his services and there he was a member of the staff of the college of education, in charge of secondary education.

"No office-bound director is Doctor Belting. He admits that games of all sorts have a fascination for him and football in particular is his delight. Possibly this is for the reason that, while at Illinois, he was one of the stars in the Illini line during 1910 and 1911. (Belting previously had played in the backfield of the Eastern Illinois State Teachers College teams of 1907 and 1908.) A thorough knowledge and keen interest in the game enabled him to coach the Oskaloosa high school eleven to an Iowa state championship in 1916, and this same knowledge and sustained interest gives him all the feelings of the star player and trained coach as he watches Iowa's battles from a seat on the sideline bench. . ."

So much for the University Bulletin's appraisal of Dr. Belting as of May 21, 1926. Almost three years to the day farther along, when Iowa's suspension from Big Ten competition struck the sports world like a bomb, varying opinions of the Director were volunteered. Meanwhile, however, the same issue of the University Bulletin (New Series No. 359) offered this comment on Burt Ingwersen, the man who took charge of football when the departed Jones went elsewhere.

". . .For two years now (The Bulletin said) a forceful young man, Burton A. Ingwersen, fearing no other Conference coach no matter how impressive may be his past history, has been responsible for the making of Iowa elevens. It is not possible to point to the background of ten or more years of coaching because it has been only seven seasons since this same Ingwersen was an all-Western tackle for Bob Zuppke of the Illini. Much can be told, however, of the Hawkeye teams of 1924 and 1925 which are testimonials of the skill of Coach Ingwersen and his right-hand man, the illustrious Locke, who was Walter Camp's all-American quarterback in 1922. These two teams have trotted out upon gridirons no less than seventeen times and on twelve of these occasions have trudged happily from the field of battle exulting in victory. . .''

With this bit of background on the men chosen to lead the Hawkeyes through their athletic highs and lows of the middle and late twenties, the records of the University provide other timely historical bits. Since 1914, the supervision of the assorted affairs of the physical education department had been in the hands of a Senate Board in Control of Athletics, composed of a representative of each of the University's colleges, appointed by the President. The separate departments of physical education for men and women included a division of academic instruction under the Dean of the Liberal Arts college. Administration of athletics had progressed from the earliest days of student control to control by faculty and alumni, with the desired goal of strict faculty control making only modest strides.

Under Belting, a move toward the main objective was made with the consolidation of all three divisions covering physical education and athletics into one department. As its head, Dr. Belting was charged with the responsibility of conducting intercollegiate athletics. The day was gone when the captains of the football, baseball, basketball and track teams were invited to sit in on athletic board meetings.

It was the breakdown of negotiations with Knute Rockne that first brought Burt Ingwersen into the considerations of the University. The selecting of a coach was the first order of business for Belting, the new director of athletics. Several possibilities were considered. A telephone call brought Ingwersen to the Iowa campus for an interview and the Board was

sufficiently interested to invite him back a second time. Then, on April 5, 1924, Ingwersen was offered a three-year contract as head football coach at Iowa, at an annual salary of $5,000. The appointment carried with it faculty rank of assistant professor of physical education. Ingwersen signed the contract.

Criticism of his appointment was not long in coming from friends of the University who had sought a "name" coach. Ingwersen had been born in Bryant, Iowa, a community a few miles from the city of Clinton, Iowa, where he played his high school football. The complaint went up that Ingwersen was an Iowa born athlete who had turned his back on his native state to engage in athletics at the University of Illinois. There was this justifying situation, however: The Ingwersen family had moved across the Mississippi to Fulton, Illinois, while the new Iowa coach was in grade school. He returned to Clinton to attend high school because he wanted to compete in football and Fulton did not provide an interscholastic athletic program at that time.

1924

In the face of misgivings in some quarters, Ingwersen swung into his Iowa career. He screened the squad and found a number of men who had played the 1923 campaign under Coach Jones. On hand were Leland Parkin, Don Graham, Forrest Olson, Tubby Griffin, Wilbur Scantlebury, Ray Dauber, Wes Fry, Dick Romey, John Hancock and others. Around men of this caliber Ingwersen built his first Hawkeye team, and he built well. His Hawks were undefeated through three games, sandwiching a scoreless tie with Ohio State between victories over Southeastern Oklahoma and Lawrence. Minnesota provided the opposition at Homecoming a week later, and with quarterback Parkin sparking a potent Iowa offense the Old Gold triumphed, 13 — 0. Parkin rushed for 163 yards in 38 attempts from scrimmage, scoring the lone Hawkeye touchdown on a 37 yard run. John Hancock added 13 and

The Corn Monument — A Long Time
Homecoming Tradition

21 yard field goals to seal the victory. Captain Parkin was even more brilliant against Wisconsin. He personally gained 170 yards rushing, scored twice on 17 and 25 yard runs, and set up a third score by dashing 63 yards to the Badger one foot line. Iowa won, 21 — 7. Ingwersen's team also beat Michigan, 9 — 2, along with a 7 — 0 win over nonconference Butler. The victory over Michigan and Fielding Yost was a particular highlight of Burt Ingwersen's first season. Most instrumental was the clutch punting of Iowa's Don Graham, including a game preserving 76 yard effort in the closing minutes which rolled to a stop at the Wolverine eight. When the 1924 season was over Iowa had a 6 — 1 — 1 record, tops in the league, and the cheers drowned out the jeers of all save those who pointed to the one defeat. Illinois, with Red Grange and his mates in action, smashed Iowa 36 — 0.

Years later in his career Ingwersen recalled the "master-pupil" struggle in which his former boss, Bob Zuppke, dished out a convincing lesson. In describing it, Ingwersen set the date of the Illinois defeat as "the day of the big wind." Big and frustrating it must have been.

"I remember," Ingwersen recalled, "Illinois won the toss and took the wind. We received,

Old Iowa Field as it appeared in 1924. The Hawkeye campus is pictured in the background.

and got the ball behind our goal line. We took it out to the 20-yard line and Parkin went about 15 yards on the first play but we were called for being in motion. We had to punt and Don Graham was a great punter. He got back there and kicked — but it went right out of bounds. I believe it may have even been behind our line of scrimmage, and Illinois got a quick touchdown. They scored three times in the first quarter with the wind in their favor. And I remember how they scored another touchdown. Wes Fry was catching the second half kickoff and he fumbled behind the goal line. Illinois fell on it for its fourth touchdown."

Big John Hancock, his playing career abbreviated because of injury, had contributed mightily to the Iowa cause, both as a lineman and field goal kicker. His five successful efforts in 1924 stand as the most in one season since Waddy Davis notched seven in 1916.

Lowell Otte, Phi Beta Kappa scholar and end on the '24 team, closed his career with recognition to the first team all-Conference and all-Western elevens of Walter Eckersall. The Chicago Tribune authority named Leland Parkin "captain" of his all-Big Ten team, calling him "a natural leader and an excellent field general. He knows the game thoroughly, catches punts well and is dependable as a safety man."

Parkin, workhorse of the Iowa team, averaged 25 carries a game during the season, picking up 864 yards rushing. The mark has not been equalled since. By gaining more than 1900 yards rushing and passing during his three injury-hampered years Parkin entered his name among the top half-dozen all-time total offense leaders at Iowa.

Burt Ingwersen coached football at Iowa through eight seasons and he had only two losing years and one of the two was his last, 1931, after the bottom had been knocked out of Iowa football by suspension from athletic participation within the Big Ten Conference. Other than that disastrous season, Ingwersen knew only one year, 1926, when he failed to win at least half of his games.

1925

The new Iowa coach earned a share of second place in the conference his first season. His second campaign began even more auspiciously, with the Hawks unbeaten going into their sixth game and holding victories over Ohio State and Illinois. The smooth sailing ended in the last three battles when Wisconsin, Minnesota and Southern California dumped Iowa in successive games. But the season of 1925 must not be dismissed as merely another campaign.

Bob Zuppke still coached at Illinois and Red Grange still was thundering goalward in his backfield. Burt Ingwersen continued to smart from the pounding his team had taken at Champaign the year before. The Hawks had warmed up for the Illinois arrival with victories over Arkansas and St. Louis University. The previous year Illinois had scored 36 of a total of 50 points given up by Iowa's rugged defense. As Iowa prepared to take the field in 1925 a telegram was delivered to the team from Ledrue Galloway, Negro tackle of the 1924 eleven who was fighting from a sickbed, a victim of tuberculosis. The message said simply: "There will be twelve Iowa men on the field to beat Illinois. I am with you."

Galloway never recovered from his illness, succumbing less than a year later. Iowa players vowed privately to meet the test for their stricken teammate, rated by coach Ingwersen as "one of the finest linemen I had at Iowa."

Grange opened the much-heralded 1925 Iowa-Illinois game by receiving the opening kickoff and racing 89 yards for a touchdown. Not a hand touched him. Despairing Iowa fans foresaw a possible repeat of the 1924 rout, but such was not to be. The Hawkeyes had a mission, and they also had a little-known new halfback named Nick (Cowboy) Kutsch, who had transferred from Trinity College in Sioux City. Kutsch had the antidote for Grange. He battered the Illini, kicked two 25-yard field goals and rammed over for the winning touchdown in the final minute to gain a 12 — 10 win for Iowa. Kutsch had gained 144 yards rushing and scored all of the Hawkeye points. A record Iowa City crowd of 27,721 looked on

Nicholas (Cowboy) Kutsch

as Ingwersen and his heroes had their revenge.

Nick Kutsch had played his first three games for Iowa. During that time he scored 50 points, raced for 427 yards, sparkled as a passer and averaged nearly eight yards each time he carried the ball. Ohio State was next, and after one quarter of play a battered Nick Kutsch was led from the rain drenched field, crippled beyond repair. Wes Fry took over the role of executioner and his two touchdowns, plus a field goal by Buzz Hogan accounted for all the points in the 15 — 0 Iowa victory. The record was now 5— 0, but a Wisconsin challenge without Kutsch was the next conference start. Many years have passed since that early November game but it, and the blizzard that enveloped it, still come readily to mind when older heads gather. There were no such things as sidelines or yardlines. The storm obliterated every trace. Players were indistinguishable and spectators, few in number and stung by the driving snow, were limited to visibility that covered less than half the field. Fred Kent, long a photographer in Iowa City, had three cameras at his disposal when the game started but ice on the lenses made two useless. Thirty-four fumbles were recorded in the game, eighteen in the opening quarter. Yet Wisconsin managed to score a lone touchdown and its 6 — 0 victory

Iowa 0 — Wisconsin 6, in the long remembered snow blizzard of 1925.

was the first blot of 1925 on the Iowa record. Burt Ingwersen's 11 — 1 — 1 mark going into that game absorbed defeat Number 2 and touched off a string of reversals that included a 33 — 0 pasting by Minnesota and an 18 — 0 reverse in the windup game against Southern California. The Trojans were coached by Howard Jones and assisted by former Hawkeye stars Aubrey Devine, Paul Minick and Doc Van-Metre. Iowa had been shut out in its last three games, closing with a 5 — 3 record.

Wes Fry, Dick Romey and Nick Kutsch earned special mention following the season, each gaining recognition on various all conference first teams. Romey, along with Lowell Otte, the finest end to play for Ingwersen, was given special honor by Collier's and Grantland Rice, with a berth on the magazine's second all-America team. Wes Fry, closing a three year career which had been hampered by injuries, totalled more than 1300 yards rushing at Iowa. Kutsch, never fully recovered from the injury which disabled him at Ohio State, still led the team in both rushing and scoring. But Iowa was able to win only one game, a non-conference date with Wabash, after his injury.

Prior to the 1926 season the football rules committee again altered the forward pass rule to the extent that a penalty of five yards (in addition to the loss of a down) was to be made in each instance where a team had more than one incomplete forward pass during the same series of four downs. Another change, brought about primarily as a result of two Drake University games in 1925, made it mandatory that a team which had scored a safety would put the ball in play by a kick to its opponents. Previously the team which gave up the safety retained possession of the ball.

Three nonconference victories, over Colorado Teachers, North Dakota and Carroll College, hardly atoned for a dismal conference record which found Iowa the victim of five straight conference defeats. Nick Kutsch was back to pace the Hawk offense, while tackle Emerson (Spike) Nelson led the forward wall, but Ingwersen's charges were unable to muster the offensive or defensive strength needed to meet

Big Ten calibre competition successfully. Illinois, although unable to stop Kutsch, fought off all but one Hawk scoring surge and won, 13 — 6. Cowboy Nick rushed for 147 yards and scored the Iowa touchdown on a sixty yard burst. Ohio State leveled the next blast, 23 — 6, and Minnesota followed with a crushing 41 — 0 victory in Iowa City. The Gophers completely dominated the game, racing to a 22 — 0 first quarter lead, gaining 25 first downs while holding Iowa to only two. It was the first Minnesota triumph on Iowa field in twelve years. Wisconsin and Northwestern buried the Hawks in the Big Ten cellar with 20 — 10 and 13 — 6 victories, respectively. Home attendance dropped alarmingly in 1926. An average of only 8,627 fans saw each of the five Iowa City games.

Emerson (Spike) Nelson was named by George Trevor and the New York Sun to the first all-America team, while both he and Kutsch were picked by Big Ten coaches to the

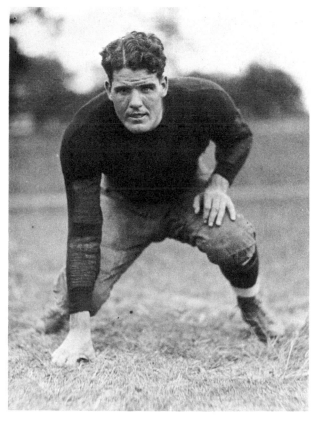

Emerson Nelson

first all-Conference unit. Nick Kutsch closed his meteoric two-year career at Iowa with 781 yards rushing in 1926. He averaged slightly less than six yards each time he carried the ball for the Hawkeyes in 1925 and 1926, and in five different games he smashed for more than 140 yards. No two year performer has approached either record.

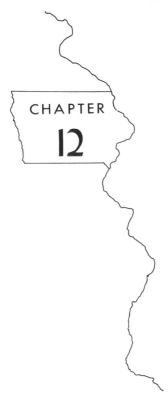

Prelude to Catastrophe

(*Author's note. The suspension, perhaps the most important single legislative bombshell to rock the Big Ten Conference in its more than 70 years of existence, is told here in all of its ramifications. Included is a supplementary account of the internal maneuverings as related by a member of the Iowa Athletic Board who was particularly close to certain aspects of the situation. The authors have included all details of the suspension in the light of heretofore unpublished and uncirculated findings which are presented here for the first time.*)

Away from the gridiron, unrest was apparent in Iowa. Unrest, in fact, never had quite disappeared following the departure of Howard Jones and the appointment of Ingwersen. There were alumni at that time who felt that the Board in Control of Athletics had withheld facts bearing on the Jones' resignation. Ingwersen's appointment and the installation of Paul Belting as head of the department had not stilled all of the critics.

Burt Ingwersen's career at Iowa had barely begun when a group of alumni in Sioux City voiced dissatisfaction and petitioned the University, on April 9, 1924, protesting the selection of Ingwersen. In answer to that objection Professor R. A. Kuever, secretary of the Board in Control of Athletics, answered the petitioners by letter, under date of April 14, 1924:

"This is in reply to your petition of April 9 which states that you cannot support the selection of Burton E. (sic) Ingwersen as football coach at the University. We thank you very kindly for your interest in this important situation. We believe, therefore, that you perhaps are not in possession of all the facts that have led to his selection, hence we are pleased to have this opportunity to make the following explanation:

"Since Mr. Jones' resignation on December 19th a dozen men from the Board, the administration and coaching staff have studied this perplexing problem and each step that has been taken has first been given the most thorough study because of the important position and the peculiar responsibility that was involved.

"Our first effort was to keep Mr. Jones at Iowa. In this we failed for reasons over which we had no control. Then we made every endeavor to obtain the services of Coach Rockne. We know now that we never had a chance to get him. The opinion in the newspapers to the contrary notwithstanding this position was only offered to Rockne and then to Ingwersen.

"Mr. Ingwersen was selected after a very deliberate and careful consideration had been given to the available men. We had some seventy applications. Men from all parts of the country were interviewed. The Board, the administration and the coaching staff are unanimous, after studying the situation for more than two months, that he is, by far, the most desirable man available.

"Mr. Ingwersen has been Mr. Zuppke's brightest pupil and his assistant for four years. He has scouted every team in the conference. He knows the style and system of play of every conference team. He knows the strength and weakness of every conference player. He has made a reputation at Illinois as a coach, as a teacher of subjects in physical education, and as a square, clean fellow. He is known for his leadership. The players like him, and while he is only twenty-six years of age, they take his coaching and advice as seriously as that of Zuppke himself; he is unafraid with youth, ambition, ability, brains, and the proper spirit on his side. . . ."

Coach Ingwersen's early success did much to quiet his critics but the smouldering discord flamed again when the 1926 team went winless in Big Ten play. In November the Mason City, Iowa Globe-Gazette published an editorial which said:

"Not a few alumni and friends of the University of Iowa have reached the conclusion that perhaps a new football coach is needed. The Hawkeyes haven't won a conference game this season and it takes a sanguine person to predict a victory in either of the two remaining Big Ten games. Iowa is represented this year by its weakest team in the past ten years. That much must be admitted. But there are some things to be said in Mr. Ingwersen's behalf.

"Last week Iowa was trimmed by Minnesota to the tune of 41 to 0. Ten years ago Iowa was beaten by the score of sixty-something to nothing with Howard Jones as coach. And in the previous year under Jesse Hawley, the Gophers won 51 to 13. Then they cry went up: 'Can Hawley!' and 'Can Jones!' Hawley left and gained fame at Dartmouth where last year his team won the eastern championship.

"Jones stayed, but it wasn't a bed of roses for him. The writer remembers sitting in on a meeting of lettermen in 1920 or 1921 when just

such a wave of dissatisfaction against the coach as is evident today had submerged Howard Jones. His team had just lost a game to Chicago which alumni felt should not have been lost. The I-Club members were unanimously for the coach, however, and ways and means were discussed to overcome the criticism which had been directed at him.

"It was Coach Jones himself, though, who allayed the rising tide of discontent. That afternoon his team won from Illinois and not for almost three years was an Iowa team beaten. Those who once were willing to sacrifice Howard Jones on the altar stayed to lead the chorus in singing the praises for him. Such is the fickleness of an athletic constituency.

"Ingwersen came to Iowa three years ago. He was young and his selection was opposed by many — by none more strenuously than this writer. But the first year his team finished high in the conference standing. Last year after a brilliant start against Illinois and Ohio, there was a letdown and the Hawkeyes were trounced by three opponents. This year, with a nucleus of only four or five lettermen, the team has been weak. One Chicago sportswriter stated that not more than two of the Iowa eleven could win positions on the Minnesota team and he wasn't far from right. None but a confirmed optimist would have predicted a brilliant record for the Iowa team this fall.

". . .at least six teams out of the Big Ten have larger student bodies than the University of Iowa. This means a larger body of men from which to draw for football teams. For Iowans to hope every year to head the conference, or, putting it another way, for Iowans to expect never to be near the foot of the standings is obviously foolish. It's contrary to the established principles of mathematics. Coaches may modify Iowa's arithmetical handicap to some extent, but they can't eliminate it. Dismissal of Coach Ingwersen at this time would be unfair to him and to the University's athletic future. He is working this year under a handicap of material that couldn't, we are certain, be overcome by any coach. Next year he will have a strong freshman team coming on. Much better it would be to judge him on the basis of his team's showing then. . ."

Alumni attitudes reflected one view of the athletic scene at Iowa. The Board in Control meanwhile was striving to strengthen other bulwarks. It deemed a change advisable in the management of athletics and so informed President Jessup under date of June 21, 1924.

". . .the Board in Control of Athletics makes the following recommendations:

"(1) That the Board. . .deems that a reorganization of the management of athletics at the State University of Iowa is advisable, with a view, (a) to give the Director more permanent and a more academic status, and (b) to give him wider authority and a standing compatible with such a status:

"(2) That the Board further expresses its willingness to cooperate or take any steps necessary to bring about such reorganization.

"Be it resolved: That the Board in Control of Athletics hereby cease to function as a controlling body and that the control and management of all athletics at the State University of Iowa be vested in the Director.

"The Board in Control further recommends that a Board consisting of faculty members and a representative of the Alumni Association be appointed to serve in an advisory capacity.

"The above action was taken at an executive session of the Board held. . .June 21st, at the Athletic Department. Pelzer presiding — present Beye, Horack, Fenton and Kuever.

"A copy of this communication is being sent to Director Belting.

(signed) R. A. Kuever, secretary."

CHAPTER

13

The Suspension

Events leading toward the upheaval of 1929, which temporarily cost Iowa its place in Conference activities, were beginning to shape up. Ten days before the Board in Control notified President Jessup of its resolution, at his request, to cease functioning as a controlling body, and vest control of the department in the hands of the Director of Athletics, a letter arrived from Major John L. Griffith, commissioner of the Conference, directed to Dr. P. E. Belting, the new Iowa director. Dated June 11, 1924, it found its way eventually into University files. A part of the letter is reproduced here:

"Dear Dr. Belting:

I was sorry that you could not sit in with the Directors at their meeting here last Friday. I am sending you under separate cover a copy of my report and Mr. Stagg will no doubt mail you the minutes of the meeting. There was a great deal of discussion, however, that was of interest and I wish you might have shared in the deliberations.

"As you know, the Directors two years ago took upon themselves the responsibility of enforcing the Conference amateur rule and last year they also set about the task of trying to eliminate illegitimate recruiting. I feel that the Directors are the proper persons to initiate and carry through athletic reforms and I also

am convinced that they are doing very good work in handling these and other problems.

"The thing that I wanted to take up with you especially is this: Last summer I made quite a survey of athletic conditions in the middle west and I found. . . .that alumni in some of the schools had been unduly active in aiding athletes. I am not disposed to criticize the alumni very severely because until last year the Conference rules practically endorsed alumni recruiting because the rule stated that it was not possible nor desirable to prevent alumni from recruiting athletes and the rule does not specify between legitimate and illegitimate recruiting. The alumni consequently from the different universities believing that it was a common practice sometimes became overly enthusiastic. This was true, I found, regarding some of the Iowa alumni.

"I am convinced that quite a number of the Iowa alumni were asked to subscribe to a fund which was used in helping athletes to make their way through a state university. The fund, I am advised, was administered by the alumni and that the athletic authorities had nothing whatsoever to do with it. I think that both Col. Mumma and Howard Jones had suspicions but am sure that neither had anything to do with it, and further, I think that both felt that some things were being done that possibly were not just right. I am convinced further that the money was not as a rule paid direct to the athletes but that it was paid through local businessmen who would give employment to the boys who received it. The boys further, I am told, were not required to work full time for the money that was paid them. That is, their pay went on when they were practicing or were away with the teams.

"I had wanted to go over these things with you in person because it is hard to write the details and further it is more or less of a confidential matter. . .However, I plan to leave here June 19th for the Olympic games and will not be back until late in the summer and I wanted you to know the situation before I left.

"So far, when I have received information of this sort regarding any violations, I have taken it up only with the Director concerned and everything has been handled confidentially. However, at the meeting last Friday the Directors agreed that they would like to have me at the next meeting lay all of my facts regarding the ten members on the table so that if one or two members of the Conference were not making headway in educating the alumni in accordance with the Directors' ideals that further steps be taken to bring about common enforcement of the rules. Most of the Directors have sent letters to their alumni requesting that they play the game according to the rules. If there is anything that you care to take up with me regarding this matter, I will be glad to hear from you further.

Yours very sincerely,
John L. Griffith."

This advice, strongly but carefully worded, already evidenced the concern which Griffith and the conference shared. It may also have influenced Director Belting to transfer considerable funds from the athletic department to a trustee fund, commonly referred to as the "Belting Fund."

Late in 1926 two memorandums on the subject of "Recruiting" were sent to the athletic directors and presidents of the Western Conference. These were prepared by Commissioner Griffith. He was disturbed about the practice within the Big Ten and fuel was added when one of the Conference university presidents wrote:

"If I am to judge by the rumors that keep floating, recruiting by fraternities and alumni is growing more persistent and more active, and the methods used are becoming more questionable. If there be any truth in these rumors it seems to me that it is time we engaged in a widespread, co-operative move to eliminate the improper and unfortunate phases of the movement, for already it is cultivating suspicion."

Early the following year Commissioner Griffith issued an eleven page "Report on the Recruiting Situation in the Intercollegiate Conference." He again expressed concern by stating:

"From reports and from my own personal studies it is clear that there is very little recruiting being done by individuals from certain universities while in other universities in the Conference conditions are not so good."

Iowa may or may not have been under Griffith's scrutiny at the time, but there was evidence of dissatisfaction in other areas. By 1927 the matter of Iowa's inability to obtain its share of home games against Conference teams was brought to the attention of President Jessup by H. J. Prentiss, who wrote:

"As an ex-chairman of the Athletic Board of the University of Iowa, on looking over the schedule for games in the Conference for members for '28, '29 and '30. . .it seems to me that it is most unfair to the undergraduates of this University that only two Conference games are to be played in Iowa City while the remainder are to be played away. In '28 we play two Conference games in Iowa City and three away. In '29 we play two Conference games in Iowa City and four away. In '30 we play two Conference games in Iowa City and four away.

"It may be good business to have such a schedule but it seems to me that if athletics are to be a part of the undergraduate interest, as a sportsmanlike proposition it is most unfair and I would like to register an objection. When I was a member of the Faculty representation of the Big Ten, I, as the Iowa representative, objected to the football coaches making the schedule. My conferees stated that when Iowa proved herself she would have no trouble in making a proper schedule. Iowa has certainly proved herself as of athletic ability and it seems to me that the same old condition which we have fought is again creeping in.

                                    H. J. Prentiss."

A notation at the bottom of the Prentiss letter, signed by Wilbur J. Teeters and Percy Bordwell, said:

"I wish to O.K. the above. Feel very strongly against the abandonment of the Home and Home game policy that the Board pursued for years."

There was more unrest. Letters which occasionally arrived from alumni expressing discontent with Dr. Belting as Director inclined toward hostility after a time. By 1927 alumni in several cities had submitted petitions requesting the removal of both Dr. Belting and Coach Ingwersen. Early in 1928 alumni residing in Fort Dodge, Waterloo, Cedar Rapids, Fort Madison and Des Moines prepared an invitation to alumni throughout the state to attend a meeting at Hotel Fort Des Moines on January 14, 1928, for the purpose of discussing the athletic situation at the University of Iowa. The invitation was headed: "Proposed Organization of an Athletic Association for Alumni and Friends of the University of Iowa." County organizations were urged to send representatives.

Before the Des Moines meeting was held the clamor of the alumni was given new impetus when word went out that the "Athletic Council" informed President Jessup that it had "listened to the judgment expressed in person, by letter, and in petitions from the members of the faculty, the alumni, former prominent athletes who are conversant with the athletic situation, members of the student body and the present varsity and freshman football squads" and were "unanimously of the opinion that for the best interest of Intercollegiate Athletics at Iowa, present and future, the head football coach be given an additional year."

New and widespread interest now surrounded the scheduled meeting in Des Moines. In an atmosphere "of urgency" as one writer described it, the meeting was held and the Federation of University of Iowa Alumni Associations was formed. Robert Bannister of Des Moines was elected president, Martin W. Smith of Davenport, vice-president, and Dr. Sumner B. Chase of Fort Dodge secretary. A resolution adopted during the meeting said in part:

"In the field of competitive athletics, we take this occasion to commend George Bresnahan, Coach of Field and Track; Justin (Sam) Barry, Coach of Basketball, and Otto Vogel, Coach of Baseball. . .

"We deplore the tendency which has been manifested during the past few years by the refusal of the Athletic Council and the Department of Athletics to co-operate with, or to consider the wishes of the great body of graduates, former students and many enthusiastic supporters in reference to football. . .

"BE IT THEREFORE RESOLVED, that we do hereby request the resignation of Coach Burton Ingwersen, and recommend the employment of a Coach of recognized and proven ability.

"Be it further resolved that it be recommended that this association be given at least three representatives on the Board in Control of Athletics and such representatives be selected by the executive committee of this association."

In answer to the action of the Des Moines meeting President Jessup remained silent. A campus poll to determine student sentiment produced heavy voting but was declared void by the Student Council when "an unidentified dark man" ran away with one of the ballot boxes. This was an outdoor campus poll of the students, held on January 18, 1928. No subsequent student poll of campus opinion is on record.

The matter of alumni representation on the Board in Control of Athletics remained a live issue, however, and on February 14 a petition was presented orally to the Iowa State Board of Education. It was indicated that alumni representation appointed by the State Board of Education would satisfy the alumni but appointees selected by the Board in Control of Athletics would not be satisfactory. A petition in writing, filed with the Board of Education on March 2, 1928, was tabled at that time.

Alumni representation on athletic boards was not unprecedented in the Western Conference, Michigan and Purdue having had such representatives for some time. Precedent thus gave support to the action of President Jessup in October, when he appointed three alumni members to the Iowa Board in Control of Athletics. The new appointees were W. Earl Hall of Mason City, Rush G. Butler of Chicago and F. G. Higbee, then acting secretary of the Alumni Association.

That Major John L. Griffith, the Western Conference Commissioner, was keeping a close eye on athletic department affairs was indicated on several occasions, one of them December 6, 1927, when he wrote President Jessup that "some newspapers and Iowa alumni were of the opinion that Burt Ingwersen was not competent to coach the University of Iowa football team and were starting a movement to have him ousted."

The letter also included the following from Griffith:

"They (some alumni) said that others were of the opinion that Ingwersen was a good football coach but that Dr. Belting (athletic director) and Dr. Fieseler (medical supervisor) had interfered with him to such an extent that he had been unable to produce the desired re-

1. Wickhorst; 2. Barry; 3. Ingwersen; 4. Williams; 5. Mead; 6. Lloyd Jensvold; 7. Pignatelli; 8. Reedquist; 9. Fuhrman; 10. Magnussen; 11. Tousey; 12. Mitchell; 13. Haberkamp; 14. Hauge; 15. Wallace; 16. Hilton; 17. Wendel; 18. Thomas; 19. Elting; 20. Carson; 21. Cox; 22. J. Carlsen; 23. Myers; 24. Gilchrist; 25. Westra; 26. McIntyre; 27. T. Smith; 28. Hay; 29. N. Smith; 30. Hagerty; 31. Smedes; 32. Higdon; 33. Madden; 34. Cummins; 35. Armil; 36. Farroh; 37. McLain; 38. Schmidt; 39. Wilcox; 40. Bunn; 41. Leo Jensvold; 42. Leeka; 43. Grimm; 44. Kelsh; 45. Kosek; 46. McMahon; 47. Ely; 48. Brown, Capt.; 49. Roberts; 50. Glassgow; 51. O. Carlsen; 52. Rogge; 53. Pape.

sults. Consequently they were trying to force Dr. Belting to resign.

"I told these men. . .that perhaps some people were actuated by a desire to wreak vengeance on the athletic men and to in a sense secure revenge because these individuals had been disappointed this last fall.

"I suggested that my chief consideration was for the University of Iowa and that I was concerned lest a few sports writers and certain emotional and hysterical alumni and a few disgruntled gamblers should make enough disturbance to affect the smooth running of Iowa's athletics.

". . .Further, I told these men that in my judgment the University of Iowa alumni were more to blame for the situation at the University today than the men at the head of athletics. . .

"If I was guilty of mixing into matters which concern only the University of Iowa I trust that you will believe that I was actuated only by one motive and that was to try to help the authorities at the University."

This, or the June 11, 1924, letter from Commissioner Griffith to Director Belting must have been the "letter of warning" which Commissioner Griffith and other Conference officials spoke of as being influential in the action which subsequently was taken in May, 1929.

The Commissioner, in another letter on January 26, 1928, told Dr. Belting that Judge Michael L. McKinley of Chicago had called him several times concerning his efforts, and the efforts of Robert Bannister, Frank Comfort and Walter L. Stewart of Des Moines, to advance alumni interests in the administration of athletics at Iowa.

Meanwhile, as recorded in "Athletics, A Story in Twelve Chapters" by Louis Pelzer, "there had developed on the campus. . .a very strong but not publicly voiced criticism of Dr. Belting. This feeling finally became so pronounced that it reached the President through the members of the physical education staff, students, athletic board and faculty. . ." When Justin (Sam) Barry resigned as head basketball coach at Iowa to follow Howard Jones to

Southern California in April of 1929, the resignation was interpreted in some quarters as an evidence of the unpopularity of Dr. Belting. Jessup met with Belting and offered the suggestion that, because he was the subject of so much controversy as Director, perhaps he could best serve the University in the capacity of professor in the field of Physical Education but apart from athletic administration.

Dr. Belting, in a letter to President Jessup dated April 26, 1929, pointed to some of the accomplishments of his administration, then, in a startling conclusion to the letter, submitted his irrevocable resignation to take effect at the end of his five years of service. The letter:

*   *   *

My dear President Jessup:

*   *   *

This year I am completing a five year program of educational service as the Director of the Division of Physical Education in the State University of Iowa. Under this new organization the indebtedness on the old stadium was paid; the Field House was built; the golf course was developed, and the new Stadium was begun and is now under rapid construction.

The required courses in physical education have been revised; the semi-professional curricula in physical education were initiated, and numbers of men and women who are graduates of these courses have received good positions in public schools and colleges throughout the country.

The graduate work in physical education that has been developed under my direction is unsurpassed in any college or university in the United States. The program of intramural games has reached a high point of development, and the intercollegiate teams have achieved distinction. Much of this accomplishment has been paid for out of the careful management of the net proceeds from intercollegiate football.

To this program of achievement I point with pride. Naturally, continued opposition, dissension, and jealousy have developed over a program that not only has moved so rapidly but also has had only educational aims in view. I would gladly see the Stadium through to final completion but these dissensions have been embarrassing to the University and disheartening to me.

I therefore tender my resignation to take effect at the completion of this five year program.

Very truly yours,
Paul E. Belting

＊　＊　＊

On May 7, 1929, President Jessup went before the Board in Control of Athletics and read Dr. Belting's resignation. The Board voted to accept it but urged the President to find a place for Dr. Belting in the Division of Physical Education, where his work had been termed "excellent." In a matter of days the resignation of Dr. Belting was accepted by the State Board of Education and announcement was made that Dr. Edward H. Lauer would succeed Dr. Belting as director of physical education. Belting refused to accept any other position at Iowa. A post of director of intercollegiate athletics, not previously included within the department, was filled with the appointment of George T. Bresnahan, the track coach. This new division of administrative authority and responsibility aroused curiosity and concern among those who read into the change a possible yielding to critical alumni, who had been termed in Conference circles "interferers."

In Professor Louis Pelzer's "Athletics, A Story in Twelve Chapters," it is recorded that Dr. Lauer paid a call on Dr. Belting within a day or two after Lauer's appointment. He had in mind a conference about matters incident to the switch. Belting suggested that Dr. Lauer take over the duties June 1, 1929, rather than July 1, as he had expected to do. Belting told Lauer he would call him and arrange a conference to discuss affairs of the department. No call was forthcoming. Dr. Lauer then learned of a meeting of Directors of the Western Conference to be held in Chicago May 25, 1929, and again called Dr. Belting. The scheduling of football games from two to four years ahead,

rather than on a yearly basis, presumably was to be the chief item of business and Dr. Lauer sought assurance that Dr. Belting would be on hand to provide his experience in schedule making. Belting said he would attend. He agreed once more to meet with Dr. Lauer to discuss departmental affairs but when Lauer took over the office he had held no such conference with Belting and reports were heard that the athletic files had been rifled and were empty.

On the morning of May 25 and the meeting which was to precede a tremendous blow to Iowa, Dr. Lauer and Dr. Belting were in the lobby of the Morrison Hotel, Chicago, where the Directors were to meet. However, when the hour of the meeting arrived, Belting had not reappeared and Dr. Lauer went to the meeting room alone. Not possessing the necessary credentials, Lauer obtained the proper admission card from Commissioner Griffith and entered the meeting. When Dr. Belting did not appear, Dr. Lauer welcomed a suggestion in the form of a motion that the making of a four year football schedule be deferred pending a general discussion of recruiting problems. Later, in his writings, Professor Pelzer noted the irony in the action of the Iowa representative at the meeting who "supported a perfectly harmless looking action which in fact led to Iowa's suspension." By the time scheduling was again an order of business Iowa was no longer a significant part of the proceedings.

Out of the Morrison Hotel schedule meeting went a committee composed of Amos Alonzo Stagg of the University of Chicago and George Huff of Illinois, athletic directors, and John L. Griffith, the Commissioner. Their apparent mission was to proceed to the North Shore Hotel in Evanston, Illinois, where the Conference Faculty Representatives were in session, and to report that the making of football schedules had been deferred. However, they also reported that "because of the growing practice of recruiting and proselyting the time has come for drastic action." Director Huff stated that "three Conference institutions have violated Conference rules and regulations, but such evidence seems conclusive against the University of Iowa." The faculty representatives appointed a committee from their group, composed of Thomas E. French of Ohio State, G. A. Goodenough of Illinois and James Paige of Minnesota to meet with the committee of directors.

From this meeting of committees came a hastily drawn report, written on hotel stationery, which was read into the minutes of the meeting:

"Your committee beg leave to report that they met with Messrs. Stagg, Huff and Major Griffith at 1:00 P.M. That the committee placed before your committee the evidence it had collected indicating a violation of Conference rules by Iowa University. That your committee carefully considered and duly weighed the evidence. That your committee after due and most careful consideration — Finds that Iowa University has violated the rule passed May 28, 1927, and General Regulation 6.

"We therefore recommend that the Conference sever athletic relations with Iowa University, this act to become effective January 1, 1930."

A copy of the evidence on which the committee had acted was not made available to the Iowa representative, nor did he attempt to defend the position of the University.

This was the "official" charge, although shortly thereafter one of the six director-faculty representatives commented that the major charge actually consisted in the conviction on the part of several of the directors that Dr. Belting's resignation had been brought about through a deal with the alumni in order to give them more complete control of the athletic situation at Iowa; that newly appointed director Lauer was a "stuffed shirt," and that his appointment would mean increased activity in proselyting.

Dr. Belting also issued a statement to the effect that in his opinion the Commissioner of the Conference shared Belting's opinion that his discharge meant surrender to the power of evil in athletics. It is worthy of note that two of the "six" were from the University of Illinois, also the school of the deposed Belting immediately prior to his Iowa association.

When word of the unprecedented action of the Conference reached Iowa City, the repercussions were spontaneous. Incensed students headed for the home of Dr. Belting and from there proceeded to the home of President Jessup. Signs demanding "We Want to Know" were prominent. One report said the student demonstration was stopped on Old Capitol steps by Dr. Lauer and George Bresnahan but Belting said otherwise. The Daily Iowan of May 27, 1929, quoted Dr. Belting as saying that the demonstration was by no means stopped at the steps of the Old Capitol — that his home had been hit with eggs, bricks and other objects during the night of May 26, 1929, and that he had to ask police to disperse the crowd. Some students had accused Belting of providing Major Griffith with the facts on which the Conference based its action.

University authorities asked Commissioner Griffith to visit Iowa City and discuss the severance of athletic relations. He arrived in Iowa City May 28, 1929, and conferred with President Jessup and the Athletic Council. He explained that one major accusation and four minor charges had been filed against Iowa, as follows:

A. Major charge:
   Fear on the part of the Conference faculty representatives that Iowa was losing faculty control of its Athletic Department.

B. Minor charges:
   1. The practice of giving a commission on the sale of yearbooks, which commission was said to have been given to athletes.
   2. The existence of a businessmen's slush fund for the purpose of subsidizing athletes.
   3. The practice of refunding tuition and using scholarships improperly to aid athletes.
   4. The failure on the part of the University registrar to certify athletes.

Following the Commissioner's report on the charges, University authorities drew up the following resolution:

"Be it resolved that the Athletic Council of the University of Iowa has had presented to it by Major John L. Griffith. . .the information upon which the faculty committee of the Intercollegiate Conference based its action regarding the University of Iowa. Having given earnest consideration to this information and feeling that the chief point at issue is faculty control of intercollegiate athletics, the Council hereby requests the President. . .to direct Professor Louis Pelzer. . .and Professor E. H. Lauer. . .to ask the faculty committee for immediate reconsideration of its action of May 25th because of its confidence that the appointment of Director Lauer gives fullest assurance of complete faculty control."

Minutes of the Athletic Council, May 28, 1929, disclose that at the request of President Jessup the Commissioner amplified the charges in correspondence, declaring that. . ."inasmuch as the recalcitrant alumni had openly boasted for a number of years that they were going to see to it that George Bresnahan was made Director of Athletics . . . when his appointment was announced they took this as prima facie evidence that the alumni had gained their point.

"I pointed out," Major Griffith's letter continued, "that you had made it clear that Dr. Lauer was in complete control but they were not convinced. They feel that George has been active in recruiting athletes and that he will not cooperate fully with them in their efforts. They further feel that although Dr. Lauer is head of the department that so long as Bresnahan is the Director of Intercollegiate Athletics, even though he may not represent Iowa in the Directors' meetings, that the alumni gained their point and that Lauer, who is unknown to the Conference men, will be unable to guarantee that Bresnahan will not keep up his relationship with the alumni that have caused Iowa all this trouble.

"As I suggested to you it is not proper for me to propose what should be done but I do feel that it is my duty to pass this information on to you. I have not and will not give the press any detailed information regarding the charges. However, since at least thirty men know the details, it is unreasonable to believe that the story will not ultimately get out. Tremendous pressure is being brought to bear on Goodenough, who is the only one who has any right to speak for the Conference. I cannot predict what he will or will not do. . .

Yours very sincerely,
John L. Griffith"

Commissioner Griffith was more specific about some of the charges two days later when he again corresponded with President Jessup. His letter, preserved in the University files, reviewed facts he had discussed in an appearance before the Iowa Athletic Council shortly before. It said, in part:

"First, it was charged prior to 1924 that the Faculty Board had authorized the diversion of monies accruing from the sale of student year books to the alumni fund, to be used in subsidizing athletes. You and Professor Pelzer told me that you knew about this matter and one of the men, I think it was Mr. Kuever, in the meeting stated that he knew that was true and Mr. Horack in the discussion touched upon this also. Since so many of the Council knew the facts I did not deem it necessary to submit any additional proof. I further reported that when Dr. Belting went to Iowa he was told that it was customary for the Athletic Board to turn over a certain amount of money yearly to the alumni fund and that he refused to do so.

"Second, I stated that it was charged that a fund had been in operation in Iowa City for a number of years and that the money in this fund was used to aid athletes. I stated that while it was probably true that not so much money had been collected in the last five years as formerly, yet it appeared that there had been renewed activity along these lines in the last twelve months. Certain newspapers have recently stated that in the last year individuals in Iowa City have contributed five dollars a month to the upkeep of football men.

"I reported the case of Tom Stidham. As you will recall, the details were these: namely that an Iowa alumnus had given the boy transportation to Iowa City where he was met by Mr. Goltman of the Iowa Supply Company. Stidham was taken to the Kappa Sigma fraternity house where he met Dr. White who appraised him relative to his athletic ability and the group was later joined by Mr. Williams of the supply firm. These men offered Stidham $75.00 a month but he said he expected $100.00 so it is reported he was paid $100.00 a month in checks signed by Mr. Williams. You will recall that I suggested further that Mr. Williams was reported to have made arrangements at the business office relative to Stidham's fees and tuition and that Stidham did not sign any notes or pay any money at the University Treasurer's office. Mr. Bates, the University Treasurer and a member of the Athletic Council, was present when I presented this charge regarding Stidham's tuition and fees and did not deny the validity of the statement.

"Further, I called your attention to the fact that the University Auditor had written Mr. Mercer suggesting that many of the athletes had not paid their notes, which had been guaranteed by coaches and others and that the Auditor had stated that if an investigation were made it would cause embarrassment. . .

"As a part of my general talk on recruiting I pointed out that a small group of Iowa alumni had for five years been attacking you and the athletic administration, that these men had been reported several years ago as having boasted that they were going to make Mr. Bresnahan the Director of Intercollegiate Athletics and had recently claimed that the Legislature had insisted that Mr. Bresnahan be placed at the head of athletics.

"I suggested that a great deal of Iowa's trouble was possibly due to the fact that this small group of alumni wished to dominate the Iowa athletic situation and to dictate athletic policies and that some of the men in the Conference felt that sovereignty resided in this small group of alumni, rather than in the University heads. Reasoning from this, I suggested to the Council that the most serious problem in connection with our intercollegiate athletics related to the matter of sovereignty in athletics in our various institutions. I did NOT say that in my judgement this was the sole problem at Iowa but as suggested above I spent a great deal of time in outlining the methods that were reported to have been used in connection with the recruiting and subsidizing of athletes.

"By way of a summary I reported that it was generally believed:

1. That at one time Athletic Association money had been diverted to an alumni fund.
2. That an athletic fund controlled by alumni and business men had been in operation in Iowa City for a number of years.
3. That the University business office had allowed coaches and business men to suggest that certain athletes have their tuition fees waived and that individuals in some cases had paid for certain athletes' fees, such payments being made direct to the University business office.

"Some of the men in the meeting of the Council the other day said that they knew that these first two charges were true and Mr. Cobb's letter would possibly indicate that the third charge likewise was true. . .

Yours very sincerely,
John L. Griffith"

With the athletic affairs of the Hawkeyes under investigation, the University was busy with its own probe. Information was volunteered and requested. E. T. Petersen, associate professor of education at Iowa, wrote President Jessup June 3, 1929, to inform him of an incident that took place the preceding fall. He referred to "a representative of Major Griffith's office," who, in company with "Mr. Simmons, assistant director of athletics, joined Dean Packer and Petersen at the luncheon table.

". . .The question was raised as to whether any Big Ten institution was entirely free from such (recruiting) abuses. Mr. Griffith's man stated definitely that, in his opinion, Chicago was the only institution with absolutely clean hands. He indicated that he regarded Iowa as far from the worst offender and further stated specifically that the evidence gathered and on file in Major Griffith's office indicated that the worst offenders in the Conference were Wisconsin, Northwestern, Indiana and Ohio.

"In the light of the foregoing statements, which represent substantially the comments made by Mr. Griffith's representative, you can imagine my surprise at Iowa's being singled out for specific attack on these issues. I could not refrain from calling this conversation to your attention.

Very truly yours,
E. T. Petersen
Associate Professor of Education"

Regardless of possible infractions by other schools of the Conference, only Iowa was openly confronted with charges. In its effort to answer the charges, all phases of the infractions were investigated by the University. The matter of the existence of funds in Iowa City and known disbursements from the funds brought a letter from R. H. Fitzgerald to President Jessup under date of June 3, 1929, which included this report:

". . .About a year and a half ago a group composed of Mr. White, Mr. Bremer, Mr. Updegraff, Mr. Brown, Mr. Welt and Mr. Weidner got together and planned a fund which would provide work for athletes. Mr. Cannon became a member of the group later. Dr. Fieseler of the athletic department was quite prominent in this matter and Mr. Bresnahan sat in at some of the meetings. This group raised a fund of about $4,000 a year. It was administered by the above committee to athletes for work they did in certain business concerns around the city. I am told that the single athletes received $7.00 a week, and for the most part were justly compensated for the work performed.

"The man who gave me this data stated that the one exception to this was the Indian, Mayes McClain, and in this connection I learned of another fund which the Chicago alumni provided and paid to Mr. Williams of Iowa Supply, who in turn paid it to the Indian. This Chicago fund was administered for one year by Mr. Williams, which was the first year that Mayes McClain was here. Due to a bad football season the Chicago alumni did not kick in the second year for Mayes McClain and those in charge of the Labor fund were approached and asked to keep the Indian in school. They decided that he would be handled by Mr. Welt, who, by the way, was chairman of the committee. Mr. Welt assigned the Indian the job of taking a real estate census of the city and he was paid $60.00 a month out of the Labor fund. While he reported to Mr. Welt, I am told that this matter was looked upon as a joke by the committee.

"I am told that Pape, who is married, also received $60.00 a month from the Labor committee.

"I am told further that Mr. Belting informed the athletes that they were to sign tuition notes and that they would be given work so that they might pay them. When Mr. Cobb, the University Auditor, began riding the athletes to make payment of their notes Dr. Fieseler took the matter up with Mr. Belting and then the matter of paying tuition came before the Labor Committee. The Labor Committee instructed Dr. Fieseler to tell Dr. Belting that they would not pay tuitions with the money they had.

"Soon after the Labor fund was organized Mr. Welt and Mr. Weidner went to Dr. Belting and Mr. Simmons and explained to them the work of the Labor Committee and stated that they felt the business men and alumni who were helping with this fund should receive special seats at the Homecoming and Dad's Day games. Mr. Belting and Mr. Simmons agreed and the best seats on the field were reserved for these men who had provided the funds.

"While digging up this matter I learned of another fund which I have investigated. I am told that the Lions Club, about one and one-half years ago, voted approximately $250.00 for helping needy athletes. This fund was disbursed by Mr. George Frohwein upon the recommedation of coaches.

"I believe that the publicity which has come out, together with our present predicament, has caused these men to give me the truth in regard to the above matters.

Very truly yours,
R. H. Fitzgerald"

Professor Pelzer and Director Lauer of Iowa arranged a meeting June 4, 1929, with members of the faculty committee of the Conference — French, Paige and Goodenough. President Jessup also appeared at the meeting, without having disclosed such an intention to the University's two representatives. In this meeting at Hotel Sherman in Chicago, President Jessup made a personal plea for reinstatement of the University to good standing but the faculty group voiced the view that such reinstatement would be premature until such time as Iowa had demonstrated to the Conference that "she can correct present abuses."

The docket outlining the official charges had been withheld from Iowa eyes. Commissioner Griffith had suggested that the major charge against the University was the fear that Iowa was losing faculty control. At the June 4 meeting Iowa based its plea for reinstatement on its assurance of faculty control, but the petition was denied. The faculty committee of the Conference issued this statement:

"The petition of Iowa to the Western Intercollegiate Conference asking the Conference to reconsider its action of May 25, 1929, has been duly and carefully considered. The committee's opinion is that it is premature to grant this petition at this time. Time must elapse. This will afford Iowa an opportunity to demonstrate her ability to make the resolutions of her governing bodies effective and to demonstrate to the Conference that she can correct present abuses.

Signed: G. A. Goodenough (Illinois)
Thos E. French (Ohio State)
James Paige, chairman
(Minnesota)"

The Conference had read the brief containing the charges to University representatives but it had not formally provided Iowa with a written copy of the charges. With the University striving to meet Conference requirements, it once more sought a copy of the charges in order that it might proceed along two lines: (1) To investigate the charges as contained in the docket, and (2) To proceed so as to be in position to give assurance that it had done all in its power to meet the demands of the Conference on faculty control. Dr. Lauer succeeded in obtaining a partial and unofficial copy of the charges, although Commissioner Griffith, in answer to Dr. Lauer's request for the official charges, wrote in a letter June 13, 1929:

". . .there is a rather long story connected with this which I would like to tell you about when I see you."

There were many such "stories" in the ensuing weeks, along with many rumors and a great deal of baseless speculation. But the University worked diligently, first to discover exactly what it was accused of, and then in an effort to correct the evils as they were uncovered.

Progress appeared to be piecemeal, but advances were made. An early development was the agreement of divided alumni forces — the Alumni Association of the University of Iowa and the newer Federation of University of Iowa Alumni Associations — to join forces and support the University.

President Jessup appointed Professor Paul C. Packer and R. H. Fitzgerald to look into the affairs of the department of Physical Education with the aim of uncovering any irregularities upon which Conference action had been based. On May 27, 1929, Mr. Fitzgerald had issued a report that centered some of the attention on Athletic Director Belting. The report:

"In examining the files of the Athletic Department in the Secretary's office, I find an athletic voucher signed by P. E. Belting, dated January 30, 1928, transferring $1,037.50 to a trustee fund.

"As I understand it, the athletic department made recommendations to Mr. Bates, Secretary of the University, and he in turn O.K.'d the loans to the trustees. The trustees then made the loans to the athletes." This was the first formal reference to the so-called "Belting Fund."

In testimony before a State University investigative committee in 1931, Commissioner Griffith said he had not been informed of this fund until May 28, 1929 — three days after the suspension action by the Conference. Armed with the "fund" findings of Mr. Fitzgerald, the University proceeded with its effort to correct existing ills. It had been customary for the director of athletics to fill the added role of chairman of the Athletic Council. Dr. Lauer suggested a discontinuance of this practice and recommended that a faculty member with no athletic department connection be appointed chairman, with the same man to serve as Iowa's faculty representative in Conference matters. This recommendation was adopted and on August 3, 1929, Dean C. C. Williams of the College of Engineering was appointed.

Dean Williams assumed his duties as chairman of the Athletic Council and faculty representative on September 10, 1929. On this date the Athletic Council adopted a measure stating that henceforth it would be known as the Board in Control of Athletics, to serve as a University Senate committee on athletics, to have control of all athletics subject to the University Senate while acting as an advisory council on matters of physical education and intramural athletics. In line with the new effort to emphasize faculty control, the Board in Control of Athletics recommended the appointment of four permanent committees — one on eligibility, another on grounds and public property, a third committee on finance and audit, and a staff committee. It also was recommended that all purchases by the Department of Physical Education be made through the University purchasing office. These recommendations were approved by the State Board of Education on October 8, 1929. Iowa was preparing its case of appeal which would be acted upon by the Conference in December.

Minutes of the meeting of the Board in Control of Athletics for October 10, 1929, disclose that "Mr. Fuhrman and Mr. Kelsh had been declared ineligible because of participation in professional football before matriculating at the University, but in the case of Mr. Fuhrman the committee had decided to ask for his reinstatement to amateur standing." It also was disclosed that the eligibility committee "wished to bring up for discussion by the whole Board the question of eligibility of certain students owing notes at an Iowa City bank, which notes had been given by them in order to pay notes for tuition originally held by the University." The minutes stated that it "was the sense of The Board that there was not sufficient basis for declaring such students ineligible." Fourteen Iowa players who had previously been declared "tentatively ineligible" by the Hawkeye eligibility committee were thus reinstated.

In the minutes of the Board meeting, October 28, 1929, the name of "Mr. Pape" was mentioned in an informal discussion regarding eligibility. At this meeting, also, it was voted that a letter written by the Board Secretary, E. H. Lauer, to the Conference Commissioner acquainting him with certain decisions of the Board be made a part of the minutes of October 10. This letter expressed the view that no man on the University's eligibility list should be ruled ineligible "on the basis of evidence furnished." The letter, in part:

". . .The Board received a report from its eligibility committee relating to the list of athletes certified as eligible to compete in intercollegiate football this season. This report was made by the chairman of the eligibility committee, Dean C. C. Williams, who is at the same time chairman of the Board.

"The committee reported that it had received from the director of athletics numerous letters giving information regarding a number of men, said information having been transmitted by the Commissioner of Athletics. The committee reported that in conjunction with the director they had reviewed these matters and had concluded that no man on the eligibility list as prepared should be declared ineligible on the basis of evidence furnished. . .

"The committee reported further that it had received from the Commissioner information regarding alleged participation of certain men in professional football. The committee reported that the director had been asked to investigate these charges. On the basis of this investigation the committee reported that:

1. None of the three athletes mentioned had participated in professional games after matriculating in the University.
2. That one man mentioned, Pape, had not participated in such games while in high school.
3. That the two other men, Fuhrman and Kelsh, had participated in such games and had been declared ineligible by the committee.
4. That in the case of Fuhrman, because of the circumstances of his infraction of the rules, and since he played openly under his own name, the committee had asked his reinstatement to amateur standing by the Conference.

"The eligibility committee further brought to the attention of the Board a matter which had come to its notice while investigating the information transmitted. It learned that a number of athletes now enrolled at the University, of whom five are members of the present football squad, had been advanced sums of money on their personal notes, from a fund set up by the former director of athletics, Dr. Paul E. Belting, and administered by an official of an Iowa City bank as trustee. These notes were all made in January and February of 1928, are due at dates ranging from 1931 and 1932, and therefore at this date not legally due, and hence have not been paid.

"The Board entered on a careful discussion of the situation presented. It recognized the unethical character of this fund. However, after careful deliberation the Board agreed that since these notes were drawn at a time when the practice of taking notes from students for tui-

tion was an accepted University policy and inasmuch as there was no evidence that men now in school had executed these notes in bad faith and because of the fact that the Board was convinced that there was no culpability on the part of the men concerned. . .and finally since the Board was faced with a set-up of legal contracts to be neither annulled nor revoked but to be lived through, therefore, there was not sufficient ground for action against individual men involved. . ." The significance of these decisions was to be made manifest later when, on December 6, 1929, the Conference was once again requested to resume athletic relations with Iowa.

Tucked away midway in the minutes of a meeting of the Board held November 26, 1929, was this information:

". . .The committee on staff made a report suggesting certain policies and changes in the organization of the division. The Board took action as follows:

1. It was voted not to have any assistant director.
2. It laid on the table the matter of a director of intramural sports.
3. It voted to abolish the office of director of intercollegiate athletics, Mr. Bresnahan to be retained as head track coach at his present salary.

The Board entered into an extended discussion of a petition to the Conference," then adjourned to meet at 7:30 p.m.

This meeting was resumed that same evening, with Mr. Fred Pownall in attendance "to advise in the matter of publicity," concerning the petition of appeal which would be presented to the Conference the following week. It was voted that the chairman, Professor H. C. Horack, and the secretary prepare the brief of Iowa's arguments, send a copy to each faculty representative and the Commissioner, as confidential, and to the press associations, to be held for release. The brief of approximately 3,000 words was entitled "Athletic Conditions at Iowa." It summed up a report on the Conference charges in this fashion, with the Board's answers listed in parenthesis following each charge:

A. That the Registrar of the University. . .has not for some years complied with the Conference rule that the Registrar shall certify on the eligibility blanks as to the scholastic eligibility of the athletes. That this matter was taken out of the hands of the Registrar by the President of the University of Iowa to permit greater freedom of certifying athletes for Conference competition.

(That the Registrar had not certified to the eligibility of the athletes is true, but this function was taken over by the athletic board during the directorship of Howard H. Jones as a result of personal difficulties between Jones and H. G. Dorcas, the Registrar, and not at the instigation of President Jessup. According to B. J. Lambert, this had been done with the approval of the Big Ten faculty committee.)

B. Athletic Fund for Athletes. That an athletic fund to subsidize athletes existed at the University of Iowa during the period that it had its championship football team, and that approximately $10,000 was expended yearly from this fund, which was administered by Judge R. P. Howell, Henry A. Walker and Willis Mercer.

(That this fund existed was true, but the amount never exceeded $5,000 annually according to the testimony of Mr. Mercer. Furthermore, Mercer stated that the fund was administered legally and that the athletes were required to sign notes for the loans with the understanding that they were to be paid. Some notes were paid; some were renewed, and others went unpaid.)

That during the early part of the administration of Dr. P. E. Belting as Director of Athletics at Iowa this fund was discontinued or allowed to dwindle to small proportions if it existed at all.

(The investigation of Mr. Fitzgerald proved this assertion to be false. In fact, letters produced at the hearings of the State University of Iowa Investigating Committee reveal that the fund was very much in existence in 1927, although it had dwindled somewhat.)

That members of the coaching staff and alumni of the University of Iowa have been insistent that athletic moneys of the University be diverted into this fund to aid athletes.

(The investigations of Mr. Fitzgerald proved this to be true.)

That about two years ago this Athletic fund was revived and last year amounted to approximately $3,500.

(There is no basis for this assertion, but during this time there did exist a so-called labor fund, discovered by Mr. Fitzgerald. However, this fund was used to subsidize merchants and businessmen in Iowa City who provided work for athletes. In all cases except one the athletes performed specific duties and were paid at an hourly rate. The exception was one man who was hired to take a "real estate census in Iowa City.")

That the present administrator of the fund in Iowa City is Mr. Willis Mercer of the Economy Printing Company. That the fund has existed and exists now is known to University of Iowa officials.

(The letters from W. H. Cobb to Messrs. Belting and Mercer proved point two, while the investigation of Mr. Fitzgerald established point one.)

The attached letter from the Jefferson Hotel, Iowa City, pertains to this fund.

(This charge was denied in the brief itself on the basis that the Jefferson Hotel never contributed to the fund.)

That in 1927 Coach (Bill) Kelly, of Cedar Rapids, Iowa High School, was employed to raise money for the above mentioned fund and to procure athletes for the University of Iowa.

(Mr. Kelly was employed by the sponsors of the fund. However, due to the unpopularity of Coach Burton Ingwersen and Director P. E.

Belting he was scarcely able to raise sufficient money to pay his own expenses.)

C. That the Board in Control of Athletics at the University of Iowa prior to 1924 permitted the diversion of some of the funds arising from the sale of year books to the unofficial alumni athletic fund; that Mr. Mercer in 1924 requested Dr. Belting to continue this practice, which request was refused.

(During the early twenties the job of selling yearbooks on a commission basis was given to a member of the athletic loan organization. The amount of commission ranged from two and one-half to four per cent, with an increased commission of six per cent for sales of books above two thousand. Using athletes as salesmen, the loan organization realized about $2,500. This practice was discontinued on September 12, 1923, about seven months before Dr. Belting took office. During his administration, Dr. Belting had permitted athletes to sell yearbooks for a commission.)

D. That the University was billed for athletic goods in excess of the price and value and the balance was used unofficially in connection with the University athletics. In August, 1927, Mr. John Goltman of the Iowa Supply Company is reported to have suggested to the assistant director of athletics (Mr. Orville Simmons) that athletic supplies be purchased through the Iowa Supply Company so that the University Athletic Department could be charged in excess of the value of the goods and the money thus obtained might then be used to help the football players.

(The brief flatly denied charge one and suggested that charge two cannot be substantiated by concrete evidence.)

E. That the existence of the above mentioned athletic fund and its official administrator is known to the University of Iowa officials is indicated by the. . .letter from Mr. W. H. Cobb, Auditor of the University of Iowa, to Mr. Willis Mercer, administrator of the fund, under date of September 29, 1927.

(University officials explained the Cobb letter as an attempt to collect, rather than an attempt to hide the notes of the athletes.)

F. There is no section F. in this memorandum.

G. Notes to athletes. It is reported that prior to 1924 athletes were permitted to sign notes for tuition at the University Treasurer's office and those who administered the alumni athletic fund took up the notes when necessary. In the case of athletes who graduated, their notes frequently remained unpaid. During the years 1927-28 and 1928-29 when it is reported that the alumni athletic fund totaled approximately only $3,500 it was impossible to reimburse the University in the case of notes signed by athletes. In the years 1927-1929 inclusive it is reported that the University of Iowa business office accepted notes from athletes to the extent of $6,097 not including remission of tuition. Some of this indebtedness has been paid by the athletes themselves or by sponsors. The reports of the business office of the University of Iowa for 1926-1927 and 1927-28 indicate that Coaches Bresnahan and Barry guaranteed a large number of these notes.

(These charges are true, but misleading. It was the general policy of the University to allow students to sign notes for tuition at this time, regardless of their status as athletes or nonathletes. Furthermore, it was a policy to require faculty approval for all student loan applications, therefore the actions of Coaches Bresnahan and Barry are not to be considered as guarantees, but as approvals.)

H. During the summer session of 1924 Mr. Everett Case of Frankfort, Indiana, high school attended the University of Iowa. In 1925 and 1926 Justin Barry, Basketball Coach at the University of Iowa assisted Mr. Everett Case with the coaching of the Frankfort, Indiana, high school basketball team in the Indiana championship tournament. Mr. Everett Case needed to have certain university credits to have his Indiana teaching license renewed for 1926-27. Mr. Everett Case went to Iowa City for a day or two at the opening of the summer session at the University of Iowa and registered in the regular way for certain courses. He then returned to Frankfort where he was employed as a playground athletic director during the period that the courses for which he registered at Iowa were in session. He was given credit by the University of Iowa for these courses and on a basis of these credits his teaching license was renewed.

(The Dean of the College of Liberal Arts, in a report to President Jessup, clarified the policy of the College of Liberal Arts by stating that it was not unusual to allow a former student in good standing to register for work at the University without attending classes, provided the student agrees to submit to a special examination at the close of the session. The only discrepancy that Dean G. F. Kay found in this matter was that the instructor in charge of the class had apparently overlooked the matter of proper approval from the Dean of the College of Liberal Arts for Mr. Case's special examination. After reviewing the matter Dean Kay assured President Jessup that Mr. Case's credits had been legitimately earned.)

In the fall of 1926 Robert Spradling and Doyal Plunkett, ex-members of the Frankfort, Indiana, high school basketball team, entered the University of Iowa as freshmen. The question then arose in Frankfort as to whether there was any collusion or connection between the fact that the Frankfort high school coach had received the credits he needed from the University of Iowa and the fact that two star athletes from Frankfort high school went to the University of Iowa.

(The University had been appraised of this suspicion by Major Griffith on April 27, 1927. Thereafter, an investigation of the situation proved to the satisfaction of Major Griffith that there was no connection between the enrollment of the two athletes and the credits received by their coach.)

The matter was raised by the Indiana Board of Education early in 1927 as to whether that body should not bar future acceptance of credits from the University of Iowa, since it was learned that Mr. Everett Case had not taken the work at the University of Iowa as he had stated in a letter to the Indiana State Board of Education and as to the transcript of credits from the University of Iowa indicated. The President of Iowa was informed of all phases of the situation. The President of the University of Iowa

sanctioned the credits in work done in absentia.

(The matter was clarified by investigation to the satisfaction of the Indiana State Board of Education. It was only natural that President Jessup should take action regarding matters affecting the accreditation of the University of Iowa.)

I. That Coaches Justin Barry and George T. Bresnahan of the University of Iowa have been active in proselyting athletes and that they have worked closely with leaders in the movement to bring about greater freedom in recruiting for, and subsidizing athletes at the University of Iowa.

(The Board in Control of Athletics in December, 1929, assumed the position that the failure of Director Belting properly to enforce Conference regulations at the University of Iowa affected the actions of the coaches under his command and therefore the reported activities of Coaches Barry and Bresnahan are but a reflection of the policy rather than independent efforts to proselytize athletes and gain greater freedom in recruiting. The replacement of Dr. Belting by the new director was suggested as assurance by the Board in Control of Athletics that such activities would henceforth cease.)

J. That Coach Bresnahan has recently been appointed Director of Intercollegiate Athletics at the University of Iowa.

(The ruling of November 26, 1929, abolishing the office of Director of Intercollegiate Athletics invalidated this charge.)

The extensive brief and the vast effort put forth by Dean Williams, Dr. Lauer and Professor Horack were wasted. When the December 6, 1929, petition of the University came up for Conference attention, it was rejected by a six-three vote. The suspension, effective on January 1, 1930, would stand.

Upon returning to Iowa, Williams, its faculty representative, and Director Lauer reported in detail on the meetings which proved so disheartening to Iowans. Originally the two groups,

The handwritten resolution which prompted Iowa's censure and subsequent suspension from athletic participation within the Big Ten Conference.

faculty representatives and directors, met separately. According to Lauer, Huff of Illinois and Yost of Michigan argued strongly against the Iowa position. The Friday meting of directors was summed up by Huff when he said he was "not convinced that Iowa has set her house in order." Specifically, according to Lauer, he charged:

1. There has been no radical change in the Board.
2. Mr. Bresnahan was still on the staff.
3. No athletes had been declared ineligible.

At the same time, faculty representatives were meeting at Chicago's University Club. Dean Williams reported "there were many questions and several points of argument, but the chief obstacle to a favorable consideration of the petition obviously concerned the disqualification of athletes 'who had been improperly financed.' Paige, Minnesota's representative, vigorously raised the question of Pape's eligibility, contending that he had played profes-

sional football and that Mr. Griffith's evidence was conclusive that he had so played."

The evening session concluded at 3 A.M., to reconvene jointly with the Directors at 9 that morning. Lauer, in his "Memorandum of the Meeting," detailed the results:

"Mr. Huff again brought up the matter of Mr. Bresnahan, Mr. Stagg the matter of the personnel of the Athletic Board, whereas Mr. Yost hammered away on the eligibility. It was evident that the general opinion was that conditions at Iowa were very bad, in fact so bad that it seemed inconceivable that no athletes should be found guiltless."

At 11:30 A.M. the directors withdrew to another room to "render a judgment." Dean Williams, in his "Report of the Hearing," stated:

"After about half an hour Mr. Yost appeared and reported a unanimous vote, with the Iowa director not voting, to this effect:

1. Athletic conditions at Iowa are still unsatisfactory.
2. The directors recommend that the petition be not granted."

The Conference agreed that whatever action should be taken should be unanimous. After considerable discussion, Professor Aigler of Michigan moved that Iowa's petition be denied. Such was the verdict.

Approached by the press for his views on the refusal of the Conference to reinstate Iowa, a disheartened Dr. Lauer said:

"Iowa. . .was not willing to sell its soul, in order to gain the world." The Hawkeyes were now in the paradoxical position of still being a member of the Conference but being unable to engage in athletic competition with any of its members.

On December 11, 1929, the Iowa Board again convened. A series of resolutions were proposed and discussed and one was brought to a vote. It reiterated the belief that individual athletes should not be disqualified "for the sins of a past athletic administration in which the Board believes their participation was innocent" and suggested that the individual cases be referred to the eligibility committee of the Conference. The motion was lost.

With a suggestion of desperation, perhaps, the Board, in a night session of the December 11 meeting, capitulated to Conference demands. It accepted all conditions laid down by the faculty representatives, declared the individual athletes ineligible, but asked the Conference to send a committee to Iowa City to determine "whether essential justice due these men may not warrant their reinstatement." The minutes of the meeting disclosed:

The Board in Control of Athletics at the University of Iowa, believing that Iowa's proper field of competition lies within the Conference, is of the opinion that it should continue its membership and will conduct the administration of athletics in conformity with the principles established by the Intercollegiate Conference.

The Intercollegiate Conference denied the Iowa petition for reinstatement in large measure because the Athletic Board at Iowa certified as eligible certain athletes who had borrowed money from a fund which was unethical in its inception. The Board again affirms that its decision was based in good faith on the principle that it was not fair or just to the individual athlete to penalize him for innocent participation in an irregularity of a past athletic administration.

Recognizing the superior authority of the Conference to reverse the eligibility findings of any member institution, the Board in Control of Athletics at Iowa accepts the decision of the Conference and declares the athletes in question ineligible. The Board will request the Conference to send a committee to Iowa City within the near future to review the situation for the purpose of ascertaining whether essential justice due these men may not warrant their reinstatement.

Regarding questions which were raised at the Conference meeting concerning the personnel of the staff and of administrative organization at the University of Iowa, the Board in Control of Athletics can not recognize the right of the Intercollegiate Conference nor any other body except the regular constituted authorities of the State of Iowa to interfere in matters of such sovereign jurisdiction.

Every athletic team at Iowa suffered. Rollie Williams, head basketball coach, was faced with the necessity of replacing four regulars in mid-season. Football captain-elect Mike Farroh, along with stars Oran Pape and Irving Nelson, was lost to Coach Burt Ingwersen. Indeed, Ingwersen would find himself with only three major letter winners when the 1930 campaign opened.

The University, shorn of its Conference competition and faced with the necessity of arranging a football schedule for the next season, discussed procedure in the matter of scheduling games. The Board advised Director Lauer:

1. Not to schedule football games with state teams.
2. To use his judgment in scheduling games in other sports with state teams.
3. To abide by Conference regulations regarding post-season games and games on fields other than the home fields of the institutions played.

The following week it was announced that the Big Ten Committee on Eligibility would come to Iowa City early in January for a first-hand study. In advance of the arrival of the Conference committee the Iowa Board, at a meeting January 6, 1930, authorized its chairman to express to the committee the willingness of the Board to place at the disposal of the commitee any phase of the Iowa situation, if the committee so desired. The Conference sent its eligibility committee to Iowa City, the group including W. J. Moenkhaus of Indiana, J. F. Pyre of Wisconsin and Thomas E. French of Ohio State. The group did not interview the individual athletes who reportedly had borrowed money from the "unethical" fund. Instead, the committee satisfied itself with interviews in which some Iowa City businessmen were questioned about loan funds.

The Board's minutes of the regular meeting on January 21, 1930, disposed of the visit of the committee by stating: "The chairman reported on the visit of the Conference committee invited to consider the eligibility of certain Iowa athletes." That Iowa still was shackled by the Conference suspension was reiterated in another paragraph of the minutes of that meeting:

"The director reported on various matters regarding the scheduling of football games. In the face of difficulties in this connection the Board voted to ask the Conference that Iowa be exempted from certain restrictions imposed by Conference regulations. It instructed the chairman and secretary to prepare such a request, to transmit it to the chairman of the Conference, and asked for immediate action.

"The secretary was instructed to hold and investigate further all charges regarding irregularities at other Conference schools."

The foregoing paragraph may have been in reference to the extensive investigation of college athletics carried on by the Carnegie Foundation for the Advancement of Teaching, which made public its findings in October, 1929. In that investigation Iowa was by no means alone when the Carnegie group looked into the affairs of the Big Ten, as well as other schools. Only the Universities of Illinois and Chicago were missing from the list of schools charged with irregularities. Upon reading the report Dean C. C. Williams, chairman of the Board in Control of Athletics remarked: "That an investigation of such unbiased and authoritative character should find only minor offenses at Iowa is gratifying." The report referred to an Iowa fraternity as "a clearing house for subsidized athletes."

Harrassed Iowa, at long last, saw the beginning of the end of its trying period. The suspension action taken on May 25, 1929, was rescinded in its entirety on February 1, 1930, following the report of the Conference committee which had visited the University. With the announcement of reinstatement the Conference released a statement saying, in effect, that it was not yet thoroughly satisfied that Iowa had corrected all of its abuses. The University was told it would be unwise to repeat its request for a review of the cases of the 14 athletes rendered ineligible on December 11, 1929.

The official statement of Big Ten faculty representatives read:

"Whereas the conference is satisfied that the athletic authorities at Iowa have re-established the principle of faculty control and are earnestly endeavoring to correct the conditions which led to the suspension of athletic relations,

"And, whereas, although there is reason to suspect that certain forces outside the administration are still resorting to improper methods of aiding athletes, the conference has confidence in the ability and determination of the Iowa authorities to ascertain the facts and to deal effectively with such abuses as may be found to exist.

"Therefore resolved that athletic relations with Iowa be resumed effective at once."

The supplementary statement:

"It was moved, seconded and carried that it is the sense of this meeting that Iowa authorities be informed that it would be inadvisable to apply for the reinstatement to eligibility of those athletes disqualified December 11, 1929."

The Conference pardon was effected without a formal request from Iowa. Some sources linked the school reinstatement to the Carnegie report and its suggestion that infractions were commonplace. Still without knowledge of the complete charges on which the Conference had acted when it suspended the Hawkeyes, Chairman Williams of the Iowa Board requested information on the charges on which the faculty representatives had based their suspension action. As part of a letter from Thomas French of Ohio State and Professor Ralph W. Aigler of Michigan on March 26, 1930, he was told:

"The Conference never has, nor does it now, take the position that it is the duty of the Commissioner's office to prove or disprove the charges that may be made against a Conference college. His office acts on information and belief, leaving it to the college affected to clear up all doubts."

Dean Williams, on behalf of the Board, also took occasion on February 6, 1930, in the wake of the reinstatement action, to dispatch a letter to Professor W. J. Moenkhaus of Indiana, the Conference chairman, which said in part:

I, as well as my colleagues, resented the statement of the Conference that "there is reason to suspect that certain forces outside the administration are still resorting to improper methods of aiding athletes." It seems to me that to make such a statement at this dramatic occasion was unfair, to express it mildly, unless the alleged "reason to suspect" amounted almost to a certainty. We had not been informed that the Conference had any basis for such a suspicion that had not been probed. May I ask that you have the secretary, or other qualified Conference official, transmit to us at once the evidence which caused the Conference to have a "reason to suspect" so that we may investigate it thoroughly.

Meanwhile, although reinstated, Iowa was by no means out of its schedule difficulties. The 1930 schedule had been completely disrupted when the Big Ten broke off relations. The University went outside the Conference in an effort to continue its football program and negotiations were carried on with such schools as

George Washington University, Oklahoma A. and M., Boston University and others. With the lifting of the suspension, Purdue offered the Hawkeyes a place on its 1930 schedule and the offer was accepted. The Boilermakers were the only Conference team to oppose Iowa that fall.

The University had not given up its effort to gain reinstatement for the 14 individual athletes who had been suspended. On April 1, 1930, minutes of the meeting record, "It was voted that a committee consisting of the director and Mr. Horack be asked to prepare a brief for presentation to the Conference at its May meeting with a view of securing the reinstatement of athletes made ineligible by this Board because of infraction by the Iowa Conference rules." The University made its final effort in behalf of the individuals at the May meeting. It was rejected.

References to the individual athletes who fell under the eligibility ruling were numerous but it was not until December of 1930 that their names were disclosed. At that time the identity of some of the men charged with borrowing from the "fund" and signing notes for the loans was made public. Several others who had come under the ruling went undisclosed, faculty spokesmen having said there was no point in divulging their names, since they had completed their eligibility. In this category was the name of Marvin H. Schmidt of Moline, Illinois. The average amount borrowed by the ineligibles was $45.00 which, it was indicated, was approximately the amount of tuition. Several of the men participated in more than one sport.

Among the men listed was Oran (Nanny) Pape, a blond halfback whose touchdown runs had been instrumental in the defeat of Minnesota two years in a row. It was charged that Pape had played professional football under an assumed name. A University investigation in the fall of 1929 revealed no such evidence and Pape's eligibility remained in good standing. On April 15, 1930, in a letter to President Jessup, Dean Williams of the Board said: ". . .our findings were incorrect, as Pape's subsequent admissions showed. This error on our part was unfortunate at this particular time, for the Conference incorrectly construed our failure to declare Pape ineligible as an unwillingness to do so. . .There was at no time any disposition to do otherwise than to probe each charge honestly. The weight of the evidence that we could find certainly indicated that Pape was clear. . ."

The names of the ineligibles included:

Football
Mike Farroh, Michigan City, Indiana
Oran Pape, Dubuque
Irving Nelson, Omaha
Pete Affree, Quincy, Illinois

Basketball
Doyal Plunkett, Frankfort, Indiana
Seward Leeks, Independence, Missouri
Floyd Mitchell, Highmore, South Dakota
Laurence Benson, Michigan City, Indiana

Track
F. O. Wilcox, Fort Madison, Iowa

Baseball
Homer B. Musgrove, St. Louis, Missouri

Swimming
Boyd Liddle, Davenport, Iowa
Charles M. Stewart, Iowa City, Iowa

Iowa's Athletic Board chairman closed his April, 1930, letter to President Jessup by writing: "I am confident that athletic conditions at Iowa are not only 'relatively clean' but 'absolutely clean,' the latter condition constituting the objective of our Board. There is no aspect of our present athletic procedures that would not pass satisfactorily the closest scrutiny. Moreover, since I have been chairman of the Board, I have observed no disposition on the part of anyone connected with athletics at the University to do otherwise than to conduct intercollegiate athletics at the University in a manner wholly above reproach."

George Bresnahan, subject of heated attack by certain conference members, served on the athletic staff at Iowa without interruption for 26 years. Known for his friendly manner, Bresnahan gained universal respect for his ability as a track coach and as the author of numerous periodicals which have long been used as a basis of track and field instruction.

The fund from which the Iowa athletes made loans was referred to frequently as the "Belting fund." The former director was specifically accused of responsibility for the University's troubles in an editorial in the Mason City Globe-Gazette of December 12, 1929. The three column heading over the editorial read:

"Thank Paul Belting For This!
"An Explanation of the Situation at Iowa Which Made Compulsory the Brand of Ineligible on 22 Athletes Who Are Without Blame.

"The old saying that 'There is no fury like that of a woman scorned' may have to be revised a bit to make room for a former university athletic director.

"This observation is prompted by the action of the Iowa Board in Control of Athletics Wednesday by which 22 innocent victims of the system conceived and put into practice by one Paul Belting were temporarily, at least, and permanently, possibly, placed on the ineligible list.

"The Big Ten conference in its action last week denying reinstatement to schedule-making rights made these men and their status the cardinal point in its case. From the highest court of appeal Iowa stands convicted of sanctioning the participation in athletics of ineligible athletes.

"Doubtless many will take the position that Iowa should have elected to stick to the boys, as it has in the past. But an intelligent understanding of the situation discloses that the action taken was the only one left, irrespective of whether Iowa sticks to the Conference or goes it alone.

"It was both wise for the University and kind to the students affected for the reason that the request for reinstatement is the only way to remove from the athletes a taint which isn't in any way deserved. If there is even a spark of reasonableness in those who have judged Iowa, restoration to unquestioned eligibility will be granted straightaway.

"Without such action the Hawkeyes would be confronted with this open verdict of 'unclean' in every game that is played. Nebraska and Penn State, to be played on Iowa Field next year, would with propriety inquire:

"'How about these men the Big Ten conference says are not qualified to play?'

"It is to be noted that there is no surrender to principle involved in the Iowa stand. It believes now as it believed last fall when it reviewed the matter that the athletes in question deserve no such stigma as has been fastened upon them. Iowa clung to this belief in full knowledge that a retreat was the one way to insure reinstatement.

"The fund in question bears the soiled fingerprints of Mr. Belting, the former athletic director, who squealed when he lost his job because of the many stupid things he did. Without the knowledge or consent of anybody he diverted funds from his department and established the loan fund in an Iowa City bank.

"Needy athletes were directed by him to sign a note at the bank. It was a straight-out business transaction as far as they knew. The students had no other idea than that the notes constituted a regular legal obligation. Nobody but Paul Belting was at fault and his irregularity was by far the gravest uncovered at Iowa.

"But here's the real irony of it. The Conference had no knowledge of this fund or practice when it, without a hearing, dumped the Hawkeyes out of the circuit. The unceremonious action was taken on the assumption that Mr. Belting's story was unequivocally true and that his hands were spotlessly clean.

"It was Iowa itself that dug up the facts about the Belting fund. And now the discovery, voluntarily reported, comes back in the form of a curse. This in spite of the fact that the cause of the trouble — Mr. Belting — and the trouble itself have been eliminated forever.

"What fair-minded judge or jury would continue the taint that the situation has left both upon the institution and upon the boys? If justice is a sincere objective of the Conference, there will be prompt action on the question referred to it."

There were other references to Dr. Belting and the Iowa situation in publications in various sections, including this excerpt from an article by Westbrook Pegler in the Chicago Tribune of June 5, 1929:

"It develops that President Jessup made an unfortunate choice of demeanor in conducting his university's appeal for reinstatement. He came in without his hat in his hand and not only was he a little too unwilling to let bygones be bygones, but he blamed Prof. Paul Belting, whom he removed from the post of athletic director at Iowa some months ago, for the evils set forth in the bill of complaint.

"In fact, he said, there had been a letter from Belting to him not long before Belting's dismissal, assuring him that Iowa's ethics were in good health and fit for inspection. Thus he would have cast upon Belting most of the responsibility for the subsidizing and proselyting which was a serious error he will presently apprehend.

"The point of the matter just here is that Prof. Belting is a member of the right-minded element of the Big Ten, of which Alonzo A. Stagg of Chicago is the most right-minded, and Maj. John L. Griffith, the Big Ten athletic commissioner, and George Huff of Illinois are tied for the position of next most right-minded. Moreover, Prof. Belting used to teach of his learning at the University of Illinois and lived no further from Prof. Goodenough than you could walk to borrow a cup of sugar. Mr. Stagg, Maj. Griffith and Huff instigated the original complaint against Iowa.

"All this makes Prof. Belting a man of singular merit with the Big Ten and if Iowa's boys are not allowed to compete in the Big Ten for a period of one year it will be equally because Iowa trifled with the rules and because President Jessup tried to run the good professor down to his friends.

"It had been supposed that Iowa University, suspended from the Conference nine days ago, would send in a team of penitents and if the president had evinced the proper contrite spirit the suspension would have been lifted next January 1.

"There was a special hue and cry for George Bresnahan, a popular young man at Iowa University and a very good track coach, too, whom the right-minded element regard as the least right-minded person in the whole Iowa problem. But President Jessup apparently felt some personal loyalties of his own and his reflections on Belting were intended as a defense of Bresnahan, the two being placed in opposite positions in this row. President Jessup wants to retain Bresnahan and the Big Ten, while disclaiming any intention to name the personnel of a fellow member, has become a sort of posse, determined to keep Iowa out of the conference unless Bresnahan is humbled and Belting, by inference, is vindicated.

"The other members of the Iowa delegation, who came in proud but like emissaries of a beaten nation after a war, were Prof. Edward Lauer, the general athletic director, and Prof. Louis A. Pelzer, a tall, Lincolnian figure. For hours they sat at a long board composed of several kitchen tables set in a row and covered with sheets from the linen locker, arguing the distinction between tweedle-dum and tweedle-dee.

"To be sure, there had been a jingle of unauthorized small money in the locker rooms of the Iowa varsity squads, but — and I imagine the thick-built Iowa president hoisted an eyebrow just about here — but was that jingle in the locker rooms of the other varsities of the Big Ten? Could that have been nothing but the boys' keys clinking innocently in their pants pockets?. . ."

There were many facets to the suspension of 1929, and possibly not much satisfaction to any of the parties concerned.

The Suspension — Memoirs of Professor F. G. Higbee

The most intimate, and perhaps the most personal account of the suspension of Iowa from participation in athletic affairs of the Conference was included in the memoirs of F. G. Higbee, a University engineering professor and member of the athletic council. Professor Higbee's treatise, entitled "Athletic Board Matters and The Reorganization of the Alumni Association" is a part of University Archives and is preserved in the University library. We present here, in detail, his account of the athletic department situation covering the period leading to and spanning the time of the suspension:

* * *

At the time of this memoir physical education and athletics at the State University of Iowa were under the supervision of Director Paul E. Belting. Faculty control of intercollegiate athletics, as required by Big Ten regulations, was vested in an Athletic Council appointed by the President of the University, with representatives from each undergraduate college.

Professor Louis Pelzer, representing the College of Liberal Arts, served as Chairman of the Council and also as the University's faculty representative in the Big Ten Conference. Dr. Belting served as Secretary of the Council, and W. H. Bates served as Treasurer. The other

members of the Council were Claude E. Horack, of the College of Law; Howard L. Beye, the College of Medicine; Ralph A. Fenton, the College of Dentistry; Burton P. Fleming, the College of Engineering; Rudolph A. Kuever, the College of Pharmacy; Rush C. Butler, W. Earle Hall, and Professor F. G. Higbee, ex officio, representing the alumni.

When President Jessup appointed Dr. Belting in 1924, he placed full responsibility for intercollegiate athletics and physical education in his hands and notified the faculty committee, which up to then had been the Board in Control of Athletics, that the Board's function would now be advisory and the Board would be known as the Athletic Council. This appointment and action incensed the Board and left them in doubt about their responsibilities and somewhat concerned about faculty control.

With the approval of the Board of Education, the athletic administration had built a fieldhouse and a stadium. Revenue bonds had been issued to raise the money for these facilities, and, at the time of this memoir, the fieldhouse had been partially paid for and the approximately half million dollars in stadium bonds had just been subscribed. The stadium was dedicated in the fall of 1929.

By this time, for reasons best described as a singular flair for antagonizing people — students, faculty, associates, alumni and friends of the University — Dr. Belting had become a *persona non grata* and the target of widespread criticism. There was no compensating success in athletics to neutralize the genuinely vituperative resentment which came from all over the state demanding his removal.

Dr. Belting was a highly trained specialist in physical education and came to Iowa with superior recommendations. In appointing him with so much authority and control in physical education and intercollegiate athletics, President Jessup looked forward to an improvement in Iowa's athletic status in the Big Ten, and relief from the intolerable nagging to which his office had been subjected. For reasons not evident to even close advisors, the President seemed deaf to the criticisms of Dr. Belting.

When in 1929 President Jessup finally yielded to both the external and internal demands for Dr. Belting's removal, he conferred with Dr. Belting and reached an amiable understanding. Dr. Belting would remain as Head of Physical Education (for both men and women) and would resign as Director of Intercollegiate Athletics. This agreement was reached late one afternoon and Dr. Belting left the President's office to prepare his resignation.

On the following day, however, Dr. Belting called at the President's office in a towering rage and declared he would not accept the arrangement agreed upon the day before. When advised that the arrangement was the only one available, Dr. Belting resigned and left the University.

Later it was discovered that, upon leaving, Dr. Belting had stripped the files in his office of all records concerning actions during his administration, and that he visited all the Directors of Athletics in the Conference advising them he had been fired. He also stated that President Jessup, in firing him, had caved in to alumni pressure and that faculty control at Iowa was doubtful.

Recognizing that an unpleasing personality coupled with conspicuously unsuccessful public relations had contributed to Dr. Belting's failure, President Jessup naturally sought replacements of demonstrated success in these characteristics. He therefore announced the appointment of Dr. E. H. Lauer, then Director of Iowa's Extension Division, as Director of Phys-

Athletic Director — 1929-1934
Edward Lauer

ical Education, and of Coach George H (sic) Bresnahan, Iowa's track coach, as Director of Intercollegiate Athletics.

In conveying this information to the Athletic Council (and the Council had not been previously consulted about the merits of the appointments) the President indicated that hereafter the Council was to be known as, and to act as, a Board in Control of Athletics.

Such was the administration and organization of intercollegiate athletics just prior to the Big Ten action suspending Iowa from athletic competition in the Big Ten.

At the spring meeting of the Big Ten conference in May, 1929, a meeting which included coaches, directors and faculty representatives, an action was taken suspending athletic relations between Iowa and other members of the conference effective January 1, 1930.

To correct a common misunderstanding, it should be recorded that Iowa was not expelled or suspended from the Big Ten conference. The conference action was to deny Iowa the privilege of competing in all intercollegiate athletics with other members of the conference. Iowa continued to hold membership in the conference and continued to have faculty representation in the conference.

In those days the Rock Island railroad operated a sleeper between Chicago and Iowa City which reached Iowa City about eight in the morning. It was on this train a large number of the Iowa delegation returned from the conference meeting with more news of the action. It was on this train my close personal and professional friend, Thomas Ewing French, who was Ohio State's faculty representative and who also was chairman of the committee recommending this punitive action against Iowa, came to Iowa City for his usual spring visit with the Higbees. I met him at the railroad station, hurried him away because the place was crawling with newspaper men, and took him home to breakfast. The only comment made relative to the crisis Iowa faced was made by French, who ruefully stated he doubted if he should have come to Iowa at this time for a visit. But he explained his main purpose was to have me check some proposed revisions in his text on engineering drawing, and this needed to be done at once.

Breakfast was over and a check on the revision had just been started when President Jessup telephoned: "Was French there?" In spite of my suggestion that he was here on professional business of considerable importance, President Jessup asked me to bring him over to the President's house. When I asked, and really urged him to go, French very reluctantly consented. On our way over, French again indicated a reluctance and asked me what attitude he should take. I urged him to be frank, not to evade or soften his answers to questions, and to remember President Jessup was honestly trying to learn what this conference action was all about.

This conference between Jessup, French and Higbee lasted without interruption most of that Sunday morning. It was carried on in a relaxed, friendly and informal fashion. Jessup appeared to be making a sincere effort to learn the background and causes of the action; French appeared to be somewhat sorrowfully, but none the less frankly, informational; Higbee acted as a sort of promoter to be sure no points were overlooked. Questions were asked and answers were given; the discussions following were in the nature of clarifications and amplifications. These were the facts brought out:

1. The Conference for some time had been investigating alleged infractions of Conference regulations. Three institutions had been found about equally guilty. Iowa was chosen for disciplinary action because more documentary evidence against Iowa was available.

2. These infractions consisted of illegal and irregular recruiting practices; the subsidizing of athletes; the certification as eligible, and the playing of athletes who were scholastically and otherwise ineligible under Conference rules.

3. Iowa had been warned by the Commissioner of the Big Ten that irregularities were practiced in Iowa's conduct of intercollegiate athletics. This warning was in the form of a letter from Commissioner Griffith to President Jessup (dated December 6, 1927). (Author's note: The Warning Letter, never specifically identified by Commissioner Griffith, may well have been from Griffith to Director Belting, dated June 11, 1924.)

4. When asked why Iowa was not given an opportunity to be heard on this matter before action was taken, French again referred to the letter of warning, and stated that, before a vote was called for, Iowa's representative was asked if he wished to be heard. His reply was that 'This is something you just have to take on the chin."

5. The final fact which was brought to light was that faculty control of intercollegiate athletics was gravely in doubt. When attention was called to the appointment of Lauer as Director of Physical Education and of Bresnahan as Director of Intercollegiate Athletics, French commented that no one in the Conference knew Lauer and that Bresnahan was well and unfavorably known for his recruiting activities.

Both the Lauer appointment, which was referred to as a "stuffed shirt appointment," and the Bresnahan appointment served only to reinforce the belief that faculty control at Iowa did not exist.

6. When pressed for the background of this belief, French stated that the whole Iowa picture gave the impression that alumni pressure was so severe that the President of the University had yielded to it.

7. When asked what Iowa should do to get reinstated, French replied that the first step would be to have a conference with the Commissioner, become acquainted with all the charges in detail, correct the irregularities and violations, and ask for reinstatement.

On the way home from the conference French assured me he would help Iowa all he properly could and would be willing to work with me, personally, toward a reinstatement. This explains the main reason for my many personal activities which were without Board sanction and without official portfolio.

The meeting with Major Griffith, the Conference Commissioner, was held at the request of the Iowa Board in Control of Athletics in the Board Room, Old Capitol. With the exception of Alumni member Rush C. Butler, all members of the Iowa Board were present.

Major Griffith reviewed the violations and irregularities of which Iowa was considered by the Conference to be guilty and referred again to his letter of warning to President Jessup, which had, according to Major Griffith, called attention to these. Major Griffith offered to lay before the Board the documentary proof with which his fat briefcase seemed to be stuffed.

To most members of the Board Major Griffith's report merely reiterated what was already known and added little to the distressing realization that Iowa was indeed "guilty as charged." In fact, many on the Board at this meeting knew that additional official misbehavior had already been uncovered so reprehensible as to make Major Griffith's charges relatively unimportant.

The Herculean task confronting Dr. Lauer, the new Director, can be roughly measured by the fact that he found his office stripped of current records. He had been assigned responsibility which was made uncertain by the appointment of George Bresnahan as Director of Intercollegiate Athletics, and he was given a mandate to clean house. Dr. Lauer set about this duty with courage and determination.

The first major change came about quietly and without anyone knowing just how it was accomplished. Bresnahan was eased out of his new appointment and Lauer was made Director of both Physical Education and Athletics. In the turmoil going on about athletics, not very much attention was given to this change. Bresnahan probably could have done an excellent job, but with his reputation as a recruiter of athletes, in the Conference, it was thought to be inexpedient to retain him in such a responsible position during a period of house cleaning.

In a relatively short time Dr. Lauer had made and verified the following with respect to intercollegiate athletics:

1. The certification of the eligibility of athletes for Big Ten competition was a "rubber stamp" procedure. Louis Pelzer, chairman of the Board, seemed to approve all lists submitted to him for approval without further or personal verification.

2. There was evidence that a member of the Physical Education staff had allowed credit for a summer session course to a high school coach in return for the "delivery" of an outstanding high school athlete. The high school coach had registered for, but had not attended, classes in the course.

3. There was evidence that Dr. Belting had withdrawn a sum of money from athletic funds and had deposited this money with the president of a local bank with instructions to loan the money only to men who had certification from Dr. Belting. The loan record showed some fifteen (more or less) loans in trifling amounts only to athletes on the eligibility lists. This violation of Conference rules was not known to the Conference at the time of the punitive

action, but was made known to the Conference as soon as discovered by Iowa.

The distressing and disturbing knowledge of the defection of her trusted officials claimed Iowa's major attention. Nevertheless, efforts were continued to discover proof of the ineligibility of a number of athletes as charged by the Conference; further information was collected about a "slush fund" for subsidizing athletes which was managed by an Iowa City business man; and plans were made to present a statement to the Conference claiming a house cleaning and asking for reinstatement.

Toward the accomplishment of this purpose, Dean C. C. Williams of the College of Engineering was appointed as Chairman of the Board in Control of Athletics and Iowa's faculty representative in the Conference.

Before Iowa had completed its own internal study of possible deviations from Conference regulations, and at a time when Iowa's only claim for reinstatement was a knowledge that she had "sinned" and was determined to reform, President Jessup met with faculty representatives in Chicago, at a meeting called at his request, to consider reinstatement.

Against the insistent and vigorous protests of his closest faculty advisors, President Jessup had determined on this move and carried it out.

My friend, Professor French, reported to me that his colleagues in the Conference resented President Jessup's plea as premature and as resembling the attempt of an executive accustomed to having what he wanted given to him. The faculty representatives could discern no evidence of reformation at Iowa. Iowa was still playing ineligible athletes and, beyond a verbal assertion that Iowa was cleaning house, there was no indication on which to base claims for reinstatement.

The Conference turned President Jessup's plea for reinstatement down and stated no consideration would be given to a subsequent plea without evidence of a thorough "house cleaning."

Following the unfortunate and unsuccessful request for reinstatement by President Jessup,

Director Lauer and Chairman Williams, with the assistance of faculty persons who were called upon for advice and help, continued their investigations and reformations. The plan was to ultimately prepare a brief to submit to the Conference which would set forth in detail how Iowa had dealt with each of the specific conditions warned by the Commissioner which were considered violations.

Deserving of mention is the fact that the climate in which this work was carried on was not only critical but hostile. The sports pages of the newspapers were filled with articles calling for changes in management, condemning actions by the Board and its officials, and expressing the conviction that there was no hope for a successful athletic program at Iowa so long as conditions remained as they were. Letters and comments were received daily from alumni, faculty members, students, and alleged "supporters" expressing anger, irritation, and lack of confidence.

During this period some time was spent investigating a Conference claim that a certain athlete had played football under an assumed name, and for money. Two separate investigations failed to prove these charges. Later it was learned that the athlete had played for money and under an assumed name, but not at the time, or under the name, or at the place set forth in the Conference charges. Hence Iowa's investigation failed to prove these charges.

Iowa notified the Conference in detail about the loan fund established for athletes out of athletic funds, and also stated in detail the thinking of the Board in Control of Athletics about the eligibility of the athletes who had borrowed from this fund. It can be correctly assumed that many long and difficult sessions were held on this matter.

The final conclusion of the Board was the recognition, of course, that the establishment of, and the participation by athletes in, this loan fund was a clear cut violation of Conference rules. But the fifteen (more or less) athletes who borrowed from this fund did so in ignorance of the source of the funds, and innocently believed they were making a bank loan. They should not, therefore, be punished by being declared ineligible since a University official had led them astray. The Board gave guarantees that steps now were completed to make such misuse of athletic funds impossible in the future.

When Iowa's brief was completed (it was a lengthy document explaining how changes and corrections in manageemnt and procedure would make similar violations impossible in the future) a Conference meeting was called to ask for reinstatement. This meeting was held December 6 and 7, 1929.

Since Iowa's brief was lengthy and detailed, Iowa's public relations advisor recommended that the brief be mimeographed and distributed in advance to the newspapers with a release time to be given by the Conference. The Chicago *Tribune* published the brief in full under a Lafayette, Indiana, date line on the morning the Conference was to meet in Chicago to consider it.

Suffice it to relate here that the Conference was incensed, and later that day denied Iowa reinstatement. Reasons advanced were:

Iowa was trying her case in the newspapers.

There was no satisfactory guarantee of faculty control.

Iowa was still allowing ineligible athletes to compete.

There were persistent rumors of athletes' being paid.

My own personal feeling, as a member of the Board in Control of Athletics and as Executive Secretary of the Alumni Association, had been up to this point that, even if Iowa had been guilty of violations due to the default of University officials, and negligent in allowing illegal and irregular practices to exist, now that she had been punished, and had established the administration of athletics in responsible officers of known integrity, she would be allowed her rightful place in the Conference.

This refusal to recognize these patent facts was an affront to Iowa's institutional integrity which made me angry and determined to take a more personal part in bringing about reinstatement.

In refusing to reinstate Iowa in the Conference, considerable emphasis was placed on the fact that Iowa continued to allow athletes who had participated in the so-called "Belting loan fund" to compete, and had not declared ineligible a certain athlete who had played for money under an assumed name.

Concerning the thinking of the Iowa Board about the fifteen (more or less) athletes who had borrowed from the Belting fund, there is a document on file in Archives at the Library describing this entire situation in some detail. Since I wrote that document I can vouch for it. Suffice it to record here that on December 11, 1929, the Iowa Board reversed itself and declared all these athletes ineligible. The Board believed, by so doing, a good case for reinstatement to eligibility could be made for these athletes as is recorded in the document referred to.

The uproar which followed this action of the Board is a notable example of the extremes to which sports pages are allowed to go. Anyone interested in this athletic affair should, by all means, read the newspapers that cover that period. The administration of the University, the Alumni office, the members of the Board in Control all received letters of condemnation and criticism of a very heated nature. If it can be said the climate in which University athletes had to operate before this action was unfavorable and hostile, it could be said that hurricane conditions prevailed after the action.

Upon notifying the Conference that these athletes were now declared ineligible, the Iowa Board asked that a hearing be held — as was Iowa's right — before the Conference eligibility committee on Iowa's plea for their reinstatement to eligibility. The Conference notified Iowa that its eligibility committee would come to Iowa City on January 10, 1930, to review the matter and to hear Iowa's plea. Private information indicated favorable considerations unlikely.

The other eligibility problem facing Iowa concerned a star on the football team named Oran Pape. The Conference had claimed Pape played football for money in the area near Dubuque. Two separate and careful investigations "on the spot" had failed to disclose that

Pape had played under the false names, money claimed or on the dates claimed, or on the teams claimed. These facts were reported to the Conference. The Conference claimed, nevertheless, that Pape had violated Conference rules and was not eligible.

Personal letters from Thomas Ewing French, written long hand and in confidence, revealed the disturbing news that Pape's eligibility would have to be cleared before the Conference would consider further pleas for reinstatement.

More by accident than by design information came to me from reliable sources that Pape and his fraternity brothers were laughing at the Iowa Board. This information claimed that Pape had played under assumed names and for money but not under the names given or at the times claimed. Therefore Pape, when asked, had been able to deny the specific charges, and investigations had failed to prove specific charges.

At a called meeting of the Iowa Eligibility Committee, I stated that I had reliable information that Pape had violated Conference rules and demanded that Dr. Lauer call Pape in to tell him his last chance to remain respectable in the Iowa Board's eyes was to admit it; that if he did not do so, I was prepared to prove it, and thus discredit him. The committee demanded my proof and I refused to disclose it. Neither Lauer nor the other members of the committee were willing to proceed on such a basis to review Pape's case.

There resulted a rather violent and heated debate on the ethics of such procedure, but at long last Lauer agreed to ask Pape to confess. The committee and the Board were dumbfounded when Pape admitted he had played for money and under assumed names. When the committee demanded the proof I had I refused to give it on the ground that it was information given to me in confidence.

Pape was declared ineligible and the Conference so notified.

Shortly before the date, January 10, 1930, when the three members of the Conference eligibility committee were to be in Iowa City to hear our plea (see document on file in Archives for reason Iowa believed she could make a case for these ineligible athletes) for the reinstatment of the Belting fund athletes declared ineligible on December 11, 1929, a had written personal letter came from Thomas Ewing French telling me the belief that Iowa had a "work fund" for athletes just would not die out in the Conference, and that the committee (French of Ohio State, Moenkhaus of Indiana and Pyre of Wisconsin) had been asked, while they were in Iowa City on January 10, to conduct an investigation about such a fund.

I telephoned French I considered such an investigation an unwarranted and highhanded piece of impertinence, that Iowa would not subscribe to such snooping; but if they insisted we would endeavor to arrange a program for them and we would neither interfere nor sponsor.

When the committee arrived (they came from Chicago on the same train and had been in session thereon) they each had a list of people, business and professional men, they wanted to interview. I told Tom I would take him about and introduce him. The others said they could find the people they had to see. The committee agreed to meet at lunch and to convene later with the Iowa Board at 2 P.M.

French and I called upon Robert Whetstone; Harry Bremer of Bremer's Store; Updegraf of the Ford Motor Company; and there were others French talked to when I had to leave to meet a class. I was told later that everywhere these men went they were treated respectfully and were advised exactly about the employment of athletes. In some cases they were invited to look over account books. Their interest was to discover if athletes were on "clock winding" jobs, to what extent contributions were made, if any, to work funds, and so on.

The three members of the committee met for lunch, reported to each other what they had learned, and then at 2 P.M. met with the Iowa Board. They opened the meeting by stating they had found no irregular practices, the information (this was but further verification of the belief growing at Iowa that there were one or more local enemies systematically feeding "information" into Major Griffith's office. Moreover, the type of "information" furnished indicated the informants had access to "inside information") on which they based their "survey" was not verified and they would so report to the Conference.

With that out of the way, the committee heard Iowa's plea for the reinstatement of disqualified Belting fund athletes. The plea fell upon deaf ears. While no decision was reached, an atmosphere quite unfavorable was noticeable. The meeting adjourned with the statement the committee would report to the Conference, Iowa might well expect to hear soon that the Conference was ready to consider reinstatement, but that we must not expect much sympathy for the ineligible athletes.

Day after day passed after the January 10 meeting with no word from the Conference. The tension at Iowa was severe. Institutionally Iowa was suffering as an educational institution because of this disciplinary action. Important decisions and foundation grants were being held up. The educational world, as well as Iowa as an educational unit in that world, was waiting. The waiting became almost an unbearable strain. We had expected, as was promised by the Conference committee, an early call to present again our claims for reinstatement.

Late in January I received a handwritten letter from Thomas Ewing French almost begging me to take a hand personally. Pointing out that members of the Conference were not satisfied a work fund for subsidizing athletes did not exist at Iowa, and that Iowa was not able to discover what was going on under her very nose, French pointed out "you were able to settle the Pape matter" and asked if I could not do something about this work fund.

My answer was to call at once on French in his office at Ohio State University. There was no authorization for this call and very few at Iowa knew about it. I simply called Tom on the phone and asked if I could count on talking to him in the morning.

When I asked him next morning what was holding up Conference action, he replied that, in spite of the committee's report they could find no evidence of a work fund at Iowa, several members of the Conference were unconvinced.

I reminded French that he had had opportunity to investigate and had satisfied himself, that he had known me for many years and could trust me and that I was prepared to guarantee no such fund existed; and further, that I was ready to assure him that as long as I remained on the Board in Control of Athletics, the Conference could depend upon a clean administration of athletics.

French then asked me (he was most uncomfortable) what I thought should be done. I told him he should let Moenkhaus (the chairman of the Conference) know at once that his committee was ready to report favorably on the Iowa situation. French then said he would write Moenkhaus to that effect. I then demanded that he call up Moenkhaus and tell him he was writing such a letter and that I (Higbee) would deliver it to Moenkhaus personally. There was an argument and some objection to the procedure, but eventually French made the call, explained to Moenkhaus that I was there by his side, that he was writing this formal notice that Iowa had no work fund, and that I would deliver this letter to Moenkhaus in the morning.

Moenkhaus received me cordially the next morning, read the letter I delivered from French, and then asked me to help him word a telegram calling a meeting of the Conference. When this task was completed Moenkhaus looked at me with a twinkle in his eye and asked if I thought Iowa should participate in the meeting! We agreed it was like asking a defendant to sit on a jury, that Iowa had already made her case before the Conference, that maybe Williams (Iowa's representative) might not be welcomed by the other Conference representatives. Since Moenkhaus felt he could not ignore Williams, I suggested a special delivery letter of notification in place of a telegram. Together we figured out such notification would probably be delivered too late for Williams to attend the meeting. As soon as the telegram had been filed, I took leave of Moenkhaus and hurried to Iowa City. When I arrived there I took to my bed with influenza.

After I arrived home, and while I was still bedridden, Williams called me on the phone to say he had just received a special delivery letter from Moenkhaus calling a meeting of the Conference to consider Iowa's reinstatement and he was calling me to ask me what I would think of his not attending! I assured him that I thought it more appropriate for Iowa to leave the matter in the hands of the Conference without representation, that we had already said all we had to say. Williams was pleased I agreed with him and he did not attend.

The day following, about February 1, 1930, I believe, the Conference reinstated Iowa. The action included a sort of left-handed expression of doubt as to our ability to maintain faculty control.

The athletes for whom Iowa had asked reinstatement were not reinstated.

The reinstatement of Iowa to full standing in the Big Ten Conference did little to improve the attitude of the public and the newspapers toward the conduct of athletics at the University. The Board in Control of Athletics was most unpopular, the Director of Athletics was unpopular, and nothing about the conduct of athletics seemed satisfactory.

There was indeed an unhealthy situation prevailing. Many good athletes in several sports had been disqualified for competition; the football schedule was very uninteresting because reinstatement came too late to schedule most Big Ten teams; a new football coach was obviously needed; confidence in the administration of athletics had suffered severe internal shocks during the suspension and, finally, athletics was in bad shape. The interest on stadium bonds was defaulted, there were still some bonds outstanding on the field house, and money had to be borrowed for operating expenses for 1930-1931.

This concludes the memoirs of F. G. Higbee as they refer to the suspension of Iowa from athletic participation in the Big Ten conference as well as the allied problems confronting the University in its time of greatest distress.

❊　　❊　　❊

Nearly twenty years after the suspension of Iowa from Conference athletic participation, Howard Roberts, a Chicago newspaper man, wrote a book entitled: The Big Nine — A Story of Football in the Western Conference.❊

❊　　❊　　❊

Chapter 4 of the book, headed "Family Feuds," starts in this fashion:

Outside an unpretentious house in Iowa City, a muttering mob milled and mauled. Occasionally an arm was drawn back in anger and an overripe egg smashed against the siding, leaving a yellowish stain that trickled slowly downward. Inside sat a haggard man, a shotgun resting across his knees. He didn't want to use the gun even with a light load of buckshot and probably wouldn't have, regardless of the provocation, but it was comforting just to stroke its barrel and realize that it might scare someone.

The man's tension increased as the tumult outside swelled into a roar. He could see the reason for the mob's excitement. A rope had been flung over a low-hanging branch of a convenient tree and he was being hanged in effigy.

So did the townsfolk and students of the State University of Iowa react to the news that Iowa had been suspended from the Western Conference. It had burst upon them like a bombshell. The Hawkeyes out of the Conference! It was inconceivable. Someone had blundered — someone would have to pay for this smear on the school's fair name!

"Traitor!" came catcalls from the mob.

Within, Paul E. Belting, deposed a fortnight before as Iowa's athletic director, sat fondling the gun and praying the mob would disperse. He was the man the crowd held responsible. He was the traitor, they believed, who had sold Iowa into athletic bondage.

❊Courtesy of G. P. Puttman & Sons.

The mob did not exact vengeance against Belting that night or ever, and the former director always sidestepped blame for the ouster, charging that the responsibility rested on the shoulders of President Walter A. Jessup. Wherever the fault lay, the fact remains that on May 25, 1929, Iowa was dropped (sic) from the Conference, the suspension to become effective January 1, 1930. The school was restored to good standing a month after the suspension actually took effect.

The basis on which the Conference faculty committee took its action, which came without a preliminary warning rumble late on a Saturday evening, was the existence of a so-called alumni "slush" fund condoned by the University administration. Under this fund student athletes as well as others could receive limited financial aid, in exchange for signed promissory notes. The average loan ranged between fifteen and fifty dollars, and many of them had been repaid. Folks laughed about football "out where the tall coin grows" but the tall coin was pretty small potatoes.

Iowa representatives were informed that the ban might be lifted provided Iowa could prove satisfactorily these four points: (1) The school could effectively guard scholastic eligibility; (2) it could eliminate the subsidizing of athletes by funds of various kinds and by abuse of student notes; (3) it could restrain alumni activities and maintain full faculty control; (4) the athletic department was willing to disqualify all present athletes who had received improper financial aid.

Viewed through the sober, revealing eye of time it is obvious now that Iowa's offenses were not serious; that she was doing only what, as the famed Carnegie Foundation report disclosed, seven other members of the Big Ten were guilty of doing to some extent and most large colleges to a marked degree. Iowa's case gave obvious cause for investigation because its football team, which failed to win a Conference game in 1926, was a potent title contender only two years later and had among its stars Mayes McLain, the big Indian fullback who had spent two years at Haskell Institute.

Professor E. H. Lauer assumed the duties of athletic director in July of 1929, and in September he was succeeded as chairman of the athletic council and as faculty representative by Professor C. C. Williams. Not long afterward, the athletic council was changed from an advisory body to a Board in Control of Athletics to which the director was responsible, and at the same time the Board arranged for certifying eligibility of athletes.

These and other steps taken, Iowa applied for readmission to the Conference at its December 7 meeting. The plea was denied after two days of solemn deliberation on the grounds that, in its house cleaning, Iowa had overlooked certain pieces of furniture. The ruling, it was reported, was the result of adverse opinion expressed to the faculty representatives by the athletic directors, notably Fielding Yost of Michigan and George Huff of Illinois.

This brought a scathing denunciation in the press by Michael L. McKinley, of Chicago, an Iowa alumnus serving as judge in the superior court of Cook County. Said the judge:

"To my mind the most striking thing in connection with the 'ouster' of Iowa is the weak and spineless action of certain faculty representatives (who prate so much of complete faculty control) in asking advice and personal opinions of certain athletic directors who for years have been known as hostile to Iowa, so that the faculty representatives might divide responsibility and muster up courage sufficient to render a decision that is manifestly unfair.

"The action of these professors who voted for the 'ouster' is likened to a judge on the bench calling into chambers the prosecuting attorney and saying to him: 'I want your assistance and moral support in helping me find the defendant guilty.'"

It is impossible to measure the influence of the judge's blast, but on February 2, 1930, after a meeting of something more than four hours, Iowa's suspension was suddenly lifted and she was restored to good standing in the Big Ten effective immediately. The formal resolution ending the case was adopted by unanimous vote and (was effective at once).

Despite the tumult and shouting occasioned by its brief but effective "spanking," Iowa actually never missed a football season of Conference competition, although Purdue was the only Big Ten foe encountered in 1930. The cumulative effect of the ouster, however, was far-reaching inasmuch as it wasn't until 1939 that Iowa again fielded an eleven of championship contender caliber.

This concludes the comment of author Howard Roberts on Iowa's problems centering around its suspension.

*   *   *

One last point about the Hawkeyes and their troubles in the turbulent months of the suspension period:

A long time Iowa newspaperman, close to the Hawkeye situation, maintains a distinct recollection of a conversation he had with Major John L. Griffith, the Conference commissioner at that time.

"Iowa was not the school we started out to get," the commissioner declared. "The other school covered its tracks at every turn. We couldn't prove our suspicions." The Hawkeyes were, quite possibly, a substitute victim.

In the wake of the Big Ten ouster and subsequent developments, the report of an investigator for the Carnegie Foundation for the Advancement of Teaching was of timely interest. Some two years prior to the suspension of the University from active participation in Conference affairs, a letter from Howard J. Savage of the Carnegie Foundation was received by Iowa, accompanied by a brief on the findings of the Foundation's investigator, who had visited the University. Among the findings of the investigator was this comment: "No evidence of organized funds."

It was about two years after the visit of the investigator that Mr. Savage, on April 17, 1929, forwarded to the University the brief of the Foundation's findings. The brief was prefaced by this letter from Mr. Savage:

Dear President Jessup:

We send you enclosed an excerpt of data collected at the University of Iowa on the occasion of the visit made by the field agent of our inquiry concerning American school, college and university athletics in which you so kindly cooperated.

Although it is not our present intention to publish this material all together in any one part of our report, we anticipate that much of it will find place in our discussions of various phases of athletics. The data are not released for publication. These considerations, however, need not prevent your making such confidential and administrative use of the information as you may wish.

The report is now approaching a final version, and we shall make sure that you receive a copy immediately upon publication. We shall hope, later, to be able to supply any reasonable number of copies that you may wish to have sent to your colleagues.

Permit me again to thank you for your cooperation in the inquiry.

Very truly yours,
Howard J. Savage

The letter from Mr. Savage was accompanied by this brief:

University of Iowa   Visited by H. W. Bentley
    February 15-17, 1927
Enrollment: 3,522   Tuition: $90.00
    State Institution

I. Organization and Control:
    A. Theoretical: 1. An Athletic Council of 9 faculty members appointed by the President (advisory only). 2. A Director over all activities.

    B. Active — lies with the Director and the President. Regular departmental responsibility placed on the Director.

II. Facilities: 3 gymnasiums including an enormous, modern, well-equipped field house; adequate playing fields; tennis courts; one 18-hole golf course; 3 swimming pools; favorable facilities for rowing; grand stand not adequate; expansive program.

III. Finances: Accounts kept by the Treasurer of the University; audited by State.

Ticket sales are recorded in athletic office by means of a cash register. Whole system economical and efficient. Figures for 1925-26; total receipts, $378,035.36; total expenditures, $364,958.09. Expenditures include savings account — $10,000, notes paid — $10,000, construction — $144,639.64, interest — $10,940.75; football receipts, $180,283.16; expenditures, $61,087.58 including $36,069.53 guarantees. Various items: scouting: football — $873.47, basketball — $727.17, track — $33.23; football equipment, $7,284.03; pre-season expense, $200.

IV. Intramural: Program is supervised by an instructor of orthopedics by a graduate student. 2 years required physical training; credit given; sports may be substituted; 4 years of required physical training being sought by the Director; intramural sports program not fully developed; competition inter-fraternity; intramural sports are self-sustaining through entry fee charged.

V. Eligibility: Rules are made by the Conference. Eligibility lists are checked by faculty member. Entrance requirements uncertain; 16 hours in course; passing grade in 10 hours; students with high school conditions permitted to play; scholastic check not carefully made; one-year residence rule; summer baseball enforcement strict.

VI. Coaching Information: Coaches are selected by the Director and appointed by the President. Head coaches are members of the faculty on full-time basis; they teach some theory courses in regular session and summer school; salaries $6,000. Two head coaches in past 10 years.

VII. Recruiting and subsidizing information: Coaches and assistants and alumni solicit promising high school athletes. Some campus jobs and fraternity jobs given athletes. Needy athletes are assisted financially by alumni. No evidence of organized funds.

VIII. General: Careful medical attention given to athletes and students in general. A major course in physical education and coaching is provided. This institution has no major and minor honor awards; all are of the same distinction. Printed records of the physical education department a distinctive feature.

Late in the afternoon of October 23, 1929, the Carnegie Foundation made public the elaborate results of its searching and in some respects sensational investigation into American college athletics, particularly football.

The 383-page document ran the gamut of methods, practices and conditions but focused principally upon what the investigators characterized as "the deepest shadow that darkens American college and school athletics" — the widespread practice of recruiting and subsidizing athletics.

The Foundation report, given page one space in newspapers throughout the country, placed the responsibility squarely upon the shoulders of college presidents. Of particular interest was the disclosure that only two of the Big Ten conference schools, Illinois and Chicago, were given a "clean bill" in the Carnegie bulletin. Wisconsin, Northwestern and Michigan were found to have an "intensely organized system of recruiting which utilized or coordinated numbers of agents on or off the campus."

The detailed, highly specific study, released less than five months after Iowa had been notified of its discretions by the Conference, lent further credence to the nationwide public sentiment that "Iowa was made the scapegoat, paying for the sins of all conference schools."

CHAPTER

15

A Fieldhouse,
A Stadium,
Nearly
a Championship

Apart from the internal confusion and unrest which involved Iowa during the Paul Belting era, the Hawkeyes under Burt Ingwersen continued to field football teams, some of which challenged mightily for the conference championship. There were still other developments on the Iowa campus, principally the construction of a new fieldhouse and the building of a new stadium.

WORLDS LARGEST FIELDHOUSE

The printed program covering the ceremonies when the Iowa fieldhouse was formally dedicated in January, 1927, carried a photograph of the newly completed structure. Accompanying the photograph was this statement:

"No finer or larger building of its kind has ever been erected in the world."

Indeed, this all-encompassing statement could have been more than a mere boast as a study of the vast edifice and the facilities it provided would indicate. The vital statistics of the building, presented in the program under the heading "Figures to Prove Immensity" revealed these basic specifications: length 464 feet (north and south); width 430 feet (east and west); space content 5,500,000 cubic feet; average height, 60 feet; ground covered, three acres; seating capacities: fieldhouse proper, 15,000; around swimming pool, 3,500.

Through the years there has been reason to challenge the seating capacity figures quoted, although the 15,000 maximum probably was reached, if not surpassed, on infrequent occasions in basketball, when even standing room has been exhausted and hundreds urged to "stay away."

There can be no challenging the statement that the fieldhouse was, and still is, one of the most spacious ever erected. When Dr. Paul E. Belting was appointed director of athletics and physical education in 1924, he made a quick appraisal of athletic department property and reached the conclusion that new and enlarged facilities were a necessity that must be arranged for immediately. From a period that dated from about the turn of the century, the old gymnasium on the east bank of the Iowa river had served the needs of students in both intramural and varsity activities. Just outside the gymnasium doorway, a few feet to the west, was the arch that marked the entryway to the football field. Today the University band practices on autumn afternoons at the site where memorable football games of an earlier day were fought. Beyond the Iowa river, to the west, little or nothing was available in the way of University facilities.

It was on April 15, 1925, that Dr. Belting put himself on record concerning physical expansion of the athletic department. He made a statement to the press that day, prophesying that the University of Iowa would, sometime, build the largest fieldhouse in the world. The prophesy was followed by prompt action. On October 15, 1925, the night before a homecoming game, announcement was made that the Iowa State Board of Education had authorized the Athletic Council to begin construction of a fieldhouse on the hilltop west of the river, said structure to incorporate the armory, which had been in use since 1922.

Within 15 months after the approval of the project, the sprawling structure was ready for dedication. During the three-day ceremony spread over January 13, 14 and 15, Michigan met Iowa in basketball, Wisconsin engaged the Hawkeyes in a wrestling dual, and Illinois opposed Iowa in a brand new swimming pool that was described as "the equal in size of any in the world." The great building was erected in approximately 12 months. Structural steel was ordered in December, 1925. Scores and scores of men ripped into the frozen area with winter at its height, preparing for the concrete footings which were poured in February, 1926. By March, the raising of the steel skeleton had begun.

The general contractor was the A. H. Neuman Construction Company of Des Moines. Through the late winter, the spring, summer and fall, work progressed at a rapid rate. The vast arena was virtually completed on December 4, 1926, when the Iowa and St. Louis University teams met in the first basketball game ever played in the fieldhouse. The crowd of 3,497 was announced as the largest ever to watch an opening game at Iowa.

In the University's bulletin of Physical Education and Athletic Coaching, dated May 21, 1926, some interesting claims were made in citing the need of this fieldhouse which had now materialized. These claims included statements that 4,000 people played tennis on 11 University courts during the month of October; in the winter 1,000 men used the gymnasium facilities daily; 40 intramural basketball teams played a regular schedule of games; 35

indoor baseball teams were in organized competition; over 300 men participated in about 20 events constituting a test of all-around efficiency; wrestling, swimming and indoor golf tournaments attracted relatively large groups of students, while intercollegiate baseball, basketball, football, track, swimming, wrestling, gymnastics and fencing engaged the time of approximately 500 more.

This claim for improved and expanded facilities which preceded the building of the fieldhouse cited the inadequacy of the existing area for every sport on the Iowa program. It said: "The new Armory was pressed into service at the close of military drill every day. Approximately 225 track candidates, 60 basketball players, 25 baseball men and 30 football competitors used this space simultaneously after four o'clock in the afternoon."

Whatever the validity of the claims presented, it is a matter of record that efforts were made to provide for extensive facilities in the new arena. It was composed of four sections — the gymnasium to the north, the swimming pool to the south, the fieldhouse proper between these areas with a lengthy exhibition hall for trophies and two levels of offices and classrooms stretching along the front. More than 25 years after the fieldhouse was formally opened, a new athletic department office building connecting with the fieldhouse was constructed immediately east of the basic structure.

The original seating for basketball claimed accommodations for 7,000 in the double-decked stands. When the Big Ten basketball schedule of 1927 opened, the 7,000 seat arena was ready. Later, the facilities were increased when steel bleacher seats from old Iowa Field were installed to form the third deck in the fieldhouse.

A six-lap track was laid out, claimed at the time to be the largest indoor track in the nation. The new 500,000 gallon swimming pool, 60 feet wide and 150 feet long, flanked by double-decked bleachers on the north, attracted the interest of the National Collegiate Athletic Association, which awarded its 1927 swimming championship tournament to Iowa.

Space for eight regulation-sized tennis courts, a football field of standard dimensions, a regulation baseball diamond, and a soccer field is contained in the three acre fieldhouse enclosure.

No public funds were expended in the construction of the fieldhouse. The original bonded indebtedness of $300,000, carrying interest at 5 per cent, brought the original cost of the vast arena to $381,250 when interest to maturity was included. Net income from athletic receipts was used to retire the bonds. In approximately 10 years after completion, the building was reported to be free of debt.

In the winter months following the 1926 football season the Rules Committe of the Football Coaches Association adopted significant legislation calling for the replacement of goal posts from the goal lines to the rear of each end zone. The committee explained that the change was made "to avoid possible injuries and interference with the play, and also to make the try-for-point after touchdown more difficult."

1927

The 1927 football season at Iowa, although an improvement over the previous year, again left the Hawks in ninth place within the conference, this time with a 1 — 4 record. Even a five-hundred over-all season record, four wins against four defeats, failed to satisfy the thinking of many hypercritical alumni who measured accomplishment only in terms of Big Ten performance.

Iowa opened with an easy 32 — 6 victory over Monmouth, uncovering a brilliant sophomore sensation, Bill Glassgow, who ran for three touchdowns and kicked two extra points in the second period. The twenty point outburst in one quarter has never been duplicated by an Iowan.

Ohio State inflicted the first of four conference defeats on the Hawkeyes, 13 — 6, the others all being shutouts at the hands of Minnesota, Illinois and Northwestern. Iowa also supplied the whitewash three times during the season, defeating Wabash, 38 — 0, Denver, 15 — 0 and Wisconsin, 16 — 0. Lloyd Grimm and Paul Armil starred against the Badgers, Grimm intercepting a flanker pass on his own five and dashing 95 yards to score the final touchdown.

1928

Perhaps the finest season under Burt Ingwersen at Iowa was 1928. Conference title contenders until the final gun sounded ending the season, the Hawks thundered through six straight games before facing defeat. Bill Glassgow returned to head a backfield trio which included blond speedster Oran (Nanny) Pape and the hard driving Oklahoma Indian, Mayes McLain. Pape, destined to rank with Ozzie Simmons and Willie Fleming, along with Willis Edson and Leo Dick of earlier eras, as one of the most exciting players ever to play for the Hawkeyes, also would become a central figure in the ultimate suspension of Iowa from athletic participation within the Conference. McLain, third of Ingwersen's "torrid trio," had enrolled at Iowa after setting an all-time intercollegiate scoring record in 1926 while playing for the famous Haskell Indians. The powerful "Maze" notched an incredible 253 points as the Haskell eleven met and defeated such recognized teams as Tulsa, Bucknell, Wichita and Michigan State.

After an opening 26 — 0 victory over Monmouth, the formidable Chicago Maroons were met and defeated, 13 — 0. It was the first Iowa triumph over Chicago since 1900. A week later Ripon was crushed in the wake of a furious Hawkeye ground attack which gained 398 yards from scrimmage. Pape, who did not play in the first quarter, ran for four touchdowns and 139 total yards. Iowa, with 26 points in the second quarter, led by 40 — 0 at halftime, and won, 61 — 6. The quartet of scores by "Nanny" Pape marked the last time such a feat has been accomplished at Iowa.

Minnesota, with crushing 33 — 0, 38 — 0, and 41 — 0 victories over the Hawkeyes in 1925-6-7, journeyed to Iowa City for the 1928 Homecoming game. Gone from the Gopher attack were Herb Joesting and "Shorty" Almquist, but in their place was conference scoring leader Fred Hovde and a man named Nagurski.

Both teams were undefeated and battled on even terms through three bruising but scoreless periods. Iowa's defensive line and the punting of Glassgow had thwarted every potential Minnesota advantage. Then, early in the final quarter, Glassgow punted over the head of Hovde, deep in Gopher territory. The Minnesota safety man raced back, scooped up the ball at his nine, and raced 91 yards to score. The extra point was missed, but Iowa now trailed, 6 — 0. Glassgow was hurt trying to catch Hovde on his touchdown dash and Ingwersen substituted his speedster, Pape. Paul Armil returned the kickoff to the Iowa 32 and Pape added seven yards on the first play from scrimmage. With second and three from the 39 Pape

again was called upon. He responded with an electrifying 61 yard dash for the tying touchdown. Glassgow was hurt and unable to return, forcing Coach Ingwersen to call upon an inexperienced sophomore dropkicker, Irving Nelson, for the extra point. Nelson had never before appeared in an Iowa game and he inadvertently dashed on the field without his helmet. Confusion soon became pandemonium, however, as Nelson's kick cleared the crossbar and Iowa had won, 7 — 6.

South Dakota was next to fall, 19 — 0, and Ohio State became the sixth straight Iowa victim a week later, 14 — 7. After Iowa had lined up in field goal formation, Mayes McLain smashed for the game winning touchdown as the game ended. The big Indian notched both Hawkeye scores, but Glassgow's 153 yards rushing paced the winners. Cold, mud and rain combined with a determined Wisconsin effort to defeat the conference leading Iowans in a nationally broadcast game the following Saturday in Iowa City. The Badgers garnered only

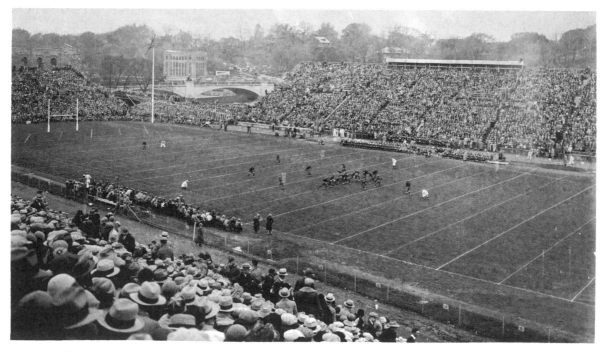

The Hawkeyes shock Minnesota, 7 — 6, in 1928, the last year Big Ten games were played on old Iowa Field.

three first downs to four for Iowa, but ten Hawkeye fumbles proved disastrous, Wisconsin winning, 13 — 0.

A victory over Michigan in the final game would still give Iowa a share of the Big Ten title. Midway in the first period Glassgow put the Hawks ahead with a sparkling 55 yard dash to pay dirt. The Wolverines countered with a field goal and the score remained 7 — 3 late in the fourth quarter. Here the Yostmen dusted off Michigan's most famous play, "old 83," designed to fake an off-tackle plunge by the half-back into the strong side of the line, and handing instead to a loose or trailer back who skirted the weak side end. Iowa was unable to stop the perfectly executed attack. Michigan scored in the final minutes, the Hawkeyes were unable to retaliate, and Ingwersen's charges suffered their second straight defeat, 10 — 7.

Some comfort was derived from the fact that the Dickinson rating system, which took the degree of games' difficulty into account, awarded the Conference championship to Iowa. As a result, the Rissman trophy, given annually to the champion, was presented to Iowa by the University of Illinois professor who invented this method. Percentagewise, the Illini won the Big Ten title.

Five Hawkeyes were honored following the season with selection on various honor teams. Willis (Bill) Glassgow, all Big Ten, all-Western and all-American gained most consistent recognition, with Mayes McLain given a second team all-Western backfield position by both Walter Eckersall and Knute Rockne. Guard Pete Westra was a 1st team all-America pick of N.E.A., while tackle Vince Schleusner was similarly honored by the New York Herald Tribune and N.A.N.A. service. Center Dick Brown gained first team all Big Ten from Eckersall.

Bill Glassgow led Iowa ground gainers with 546 yards, but Pape, used primarily as a substitute was just fifteen yards behind, averaging nearly seven and one-half yards on each of 72 attempts. The Dubuque flash also finished second to Minnesota's Hovde in points scored within the Conference during the season.

A NEW STADIUM

But the football campaign alone failed to provide all of the interest and excitement at Iowa in 1928. Athletic Director Paul Belting, already a headline-maker of much disputed talents, prepared to make another. Whatever else marked the tenure of Belting, his regime

Willis A. Glassgow

must be recognized as one of advancement in the expansion of the University's athletic facilities.

The glittering newness of the fieldhouse had not worn off before plans were announced for construction of a new stadium. Dramatically, and unexpectedly, Dr. Belting arose during a massive pep meeting in Iowa Union and made the announcement. It was October 26, 1928, the night before the Homecoming football game with Minnesota.

"Within a year, the University of Iowa will have a new football stadium, designed to seat between sixty and eighty thousand fans when fully completed," Belting said. An Iowa City paper, which featured the story on its front page, said that recommendations would be presented to the state board of education for approval, and if forthcoming, work would begin immediately to have 50,000 seats ready for occupancy by Homecoming in 1929.

Surprising as Belting's announcement may have been, it stood up. On March 7, 1929, the Iowa Athletic Council presented a resolution to the Board of Education proposing the construction of a stadium and pledging the net proceeds of athletic income to retire the bonded indebtedness. The Board of Education approved the plan, stipulating only that the general progress of the work, and supervision of the stadium when completed, be subject to the authority of the State Board of Education in the same manner as other improvements on the campus.

It was specified that the stadium was to be built on land owned by the State, "the approximate location being on Finkbine Field, 910 feet directly west of, and on the same axis as, the fieldhouse (with plans for expansion when the need arises)." Present at the meeting at which financial arrangements for the construction were discussed, were W. Earl Hall, Rush Butler, L. Pelzer, H. C. Horack, R. A. Kuever, W. H. Bates, F. G. Higbee, Paul E. Belting and President W. A. Jessup.

Behind the plans for the new stadium was the growing interest in football at Iowa, and the inadequacy of the old stadium on the east bank of the river. In that arena, in the Homecoming game of 1925, a total of 25,721 spectators had watched the Hawkeyes defeat Illinois and the unforgettable Red Grange, 12 – 10, in one of the all-time great games of Iowa history. The crowd, with some of the onlookers forced to stand, was the greatest ever to watch a game at Iowa up to that time.

On instructions from the Iowa Board of Education, the athletic director asked for bids on the new stadium. Plans had been drawn by Proudfoot, Rawson, Souers and Thomas, Des

Moines architects who had provided plans for the fieldhouse (and the general hospital). The authorized cost of the stadium was $500,000, with Metcalf, Cowgill & Company of Des Moines purchasing the bonds for construction. Bids for the general construction were opened on February 20, 1929, with bids for heating and plumbing and for electrical construction following. President Jessup then recommended approval of construction and the sanction was forthcoming at the meeting of March 7, 1929.

Ground for the stadium actually was broken on March 6, 1929, according to a program of the dedication, which said:

"Aided by the natural contour of the terrain, the excavation went smoothly forward, inexorable and unceasing, hour after hour as the day and night shifts succeeded each other. Carpenters erected forms. Concrete, made from 64,000 bags of cement, was poured into them. The twin stands took form. At the peak of the job a force of about 250 men drew paychecks, and it was not until the 1st of July that good progress enabled contractors to abandon night work. And so, step by step, work progressed until, on September 20, the stadium itself was declared complete. The time of construction was just three days over 28 weeks."

Al Grady, sports editor of the Iowa City Press-Citizen, provided this comment as he reviewed the history of the stadium:

"The cost of the entire project was what now seems like the incredibly low figure of $497,-151.42, especially when compared with the almost equal cost of $490,628.62 for the mammoth press box alone, built in 1958. But it was a sizable amount then, and, because of many dark days in the Iowa Athletic Department which followed the suspension of 1929-30, the last of the indebtedness was not retired until 1948." Financial reports of the department of athletics point out that with the addition of the press box, the purchase of and erection of the south bleachers and rest rooms in 1956 at a cost of $317,684.41, the annual improvements in the matter of paving, rest rooms, dressing facilities, field cover, fiberglass seat covers and water proofing which have cost $134,146.83, the University has a total investment in the stadium of $1,439,611.28.

The Iowa stadium is regarded as one of the better structures of its kind. Its 79 rows of seats on either side include 41 rows set on a gradual incline with the last 38 rows set at a steeper slope. Critics have said that there is not a poor seat in the regular stands. The excavation for the stadium went down 30 feet. The distance from the ground level to the top of the brick walls is 50 feet. The Hawkeye football arena gained distinction in 1963 when it became the first in the nation to install permanent plastic coverings over all seats in the regular stands. The permanent stands include an estimated 12 1/2 miles of seats. Rated as one of the 15 largest college-owned football arenas in the United States, the stadium has provided capacity accommodations for more than 60,000 fans in recent years.

1929

Although the new structure was virtually completed, the 1929 season opened in the old Iowa Field, with Carroll College absorbing a 46 − 0 defeat. The next week, October 5, 1929, the first game was played in the new stadium with the Hawks dishing out another 46 − 0 defeat, this time to Monmouth College. Bill Glassgow had the honor of scoring the first touchdown, on a 32 yard run in the opening period.

The official dedication ceremonies were saved for the Homecoming game with Illinois on October 19. Unfortunately, it began to rain on Friday and continued with a steady downpour throughout the game on Saturday. Doug Mills, currently athletic director at Illinois, but touchdown maker for the Illini that afternoon, wrote: "That game was played under weather conditions which were the worst in my playing career."

Illinois won the toss but chose to kick off to Iowa. Brice Thomas received the kick and brought it back to the 22-yard line. The first scrimmage play was an off-tackle slant, designed for Captain Bill Glassgow to shoot be-

tween tackle Harold Ely and end Lawrence Reedquist. Glassgow received the ball from center, found a hole, dodged the Illinois fullback and safety man, and dashed 78 yards to score. His place kick for the extra point hit the crossbar, bounced, and fell over the bar for the point.

Iowa maintained the 7 − 0 lead into the second period. Mills later related the story: "We had the ball and it was second down. The play called was for Judd Timm to sweep left end on a direct pass from center. The interference all went to the left, but the center passed the ball to me by mistake. There I was with the ball, the interference already on its way. It was too late to hope to complete the play as the signal called. Therefore I faked to Timm, then ran to the right. The Iowa left tackle and end had cut in to meet the interference which left me a clear field except for Glassgow the safety man. He cut to the corner to head me off, but when he tackled me in the southwest corner, I was across the line. It was the most unusual play in which I ever figured. Of course it was a most fortunate break to have a missed signal converted into a touchdown."

It was said later that the naked reverse was born on that play against Iowa. Frosty Peters kicked the extra point for Illinois and the game wound up tied, 7 − 7.

The Hawkeyes were now one loss and a tie in conference play, having dropped a heart-breaking game to Ohio State the week prior to the Illinois game. A blocked Iowa punt, recovered in the end zone by Buckeye Dick Larkins, current athletic director, wiped out a 6 − 0 Iowa lead and gave State a 7 − 6 victory. It was the third straight game in which Iowa was unable to complete a forward pass. Wisconsin fell 14 − 0, and a week later Minnesota journeyed to Iowa City for the second year in a row. Another of the memorable games in Iowa football resulted. A second quarter Bill Glassgow field goal gave the Hawks a 3 − 0 lead which held up through three periods of play. Then, early in the final quarter, Bronko Nagurski crashed through the entire Iowa team, powering 41 yards to the end zone. The Gophers led, 7 − 3.

Late in the period Iowa began a final drive. It culminated, dramatically, as Nanny Pape, a Minnesota jinx two straight years, dashed six yards for the game winning touchdown just thirty seconds before the final gun. Iowa had won, 9 − 7, and Pape led the two day victory celebrations which followed. It would be the last such occasion at Iowa for ten years.

Purdue, enroute to its first Big Ten title in thirty seasons, faced a stiff challenge against the Hawkeyes. The Boilermakers scored only once, on a 17-yard pass play, Harmeson to Woerner, but it was enough to notch a victory, 7 − 0. The Iowans again had been in contention for the conference championship until the Purdue loss. After the game, and with the suspension of Iowa already scheduled, Irving Vaughn wrote this tribute to one of the Hawkeyes in the Chicago Tribune of November 17, 1929:

"If Iowa needs any consolation for its failure to create more havoc in the Big Ten circle from which it is to be banished, it can find it quite easily. The Hawkeyes have Captain Bill Glassgow. No halfback ever revealed himself in a brighter light. He ran off the tackles, he ripped into the line and he passed. He literally carried almost the entire Purdue team with him at times. When tougher and more willing backs are built, they will have to make the model from the stocky lad from Shenandoah, Iowa."

Iowa closed its season against Michigan, a scoreless tie. The brilliant Hawkeye defensive line had permitted only 28 points in eight games, with none of the opposition able to score more than a single touchdown. Yet, the season record showing four victories was dampened by two losses and a pair of ties. For the third straight year Bill Glassgow was the leading Hawkeye ground gainer. That record has not been equalled since. Glassgow became the first Iowan to win the coveted "Silver Football" award, given annually to the most valuable

The new Stadium, as it appeared in 1929 when a last minute touchdown by Nanny Pape gave Iowa a 9 — 7 victory over Minnesota and Bronko Nagurski.

player in the Big Ten conference. Named the "finest back in the country" by recognized critic George Trevor in the New York Sun, he was selected on the first all-America team of Grantland Rice and Collier's, and was a unanimous all-Western choice.

Pete Westra and Fred Roberts, outstanding bulwarks in the Iowa line, were again accorded high mythical honors. Westra received all-Western and all conference rating, while Roberts, Big Ten first team selectee of both Associated Press and United Press, was also given second and third team all-America mention.

Two weeks after the season closed, when Iowa's December 7 plea for conference reinstatement was denied, Albon Holden, a writer for the Chicago Herald-Examiner, began his account of the denial:

"The Big Ten is dead; long live the Big Nine."

BEST OF THE DECADE — 1920 - 1929

Ends	Lester C. Belding	1918-1919-1920-1921
	Max Kadesky	1920-1921-1922
	Lowell Otte	1922-1923-1924
	Richard E. Romey	1923-1924-1925
Tackles	Emerson W. Nelson	1925-1926-1927
	Fred W. (Duke) Slater	1918-1919-1920-1921
	George D. Thompson	1920-1921-1922
Guards	Paul Minick	1920-1921-1922
	Fred E. Roberts	1927-1928-1929
Center	John C. Heldt	1918-1919-1921-1922
Quarterbacks	Aubrey A. Devine	1919-1920-1921
	Leland C. Parkin	1922-1923-1924
Halfbacks	Willis A. Glassgow	1927-1928-1929
	Nicholas A. Kutsch	1925-1926
Fullbacks	Wesley L. Fry	1923-1924-1925
	Gordon C. Locke	1920-1921-1922

The fourth decade of football at Iowa was over. More victories (52) and less defeats (22) were recorded, two conference titles were won

and no less than seventeen Hawkeyes had been selected to first, second or third all-America teams by nationally recognized syndicates and writers. However, the decade of the twenties also produced heartbreak, disappoinment and internal difficulties which reverberated throughout the nation and signalled the beginning of nine years in which Hawkeye football would reach an incomparable low in despair and frustration, winning only six of 43 conference games during the period.

1930

Although Iowa was actually suspended from athletic relations within the Big Ten conference for only 31 days, gaining reinstatement on February 1, 1930, its athletic program and its ability to compete successfully within the conference had been dealt a paralyzing blow. Only one Big Ten opponent could be scheduled in 1930, other games being arranged with teams which generated little interest in Iowa fans. As a result, income from football fell from an all-time high which exceeded $200,000 in 1929 to only $42,000 in 1930.

Knute Rockne, analyzing Western Conference prospects for the season, wrote in the Chicago Herald-Examiner, September 12, 1930:

"Poor Burt Ingwersen at Iowa is really in a tough spot. Practically all of his good material has been declared ineligible and with a makeshift schedule there isn't a great deal of nourishment in store for the Iowa rooters. However, Burt is a thoroughbred and is taking his medicine standing up. Exuding no squawks or alibis, he is preparing to dig in and do the best he can."

After an easy opening game victory over Bradley, Iowa lost two tough decisions, to Oklahoma A & M, 6 — 0, and to Centenary of Shreveport, Louisiana, 19 — 12. Purdue provided the opposition in the only Big Ten game, and the Boilermakers, on the strength of two touchdown runs of more than seventy yards, shut out Iowa, 20 — 0. Undefeated Detroit, coached by Gus Dorais, hosted the Hawkeyes early in November and a 52-yard touchdown dash by Jack Warrington on the first play of the fourth period enabled Iowa to win the game, 7 — 3. After a 7 — 0 loss to Marquette the following week, Ingwersen's band closed a surprisingly successful campaign with two victories. Penn State invaded Iowa City for Homecoming and was defeated 19 — 0, and Nebraska was throttled 12 — 7. Junior halfback Randahl Hickman literally shocked the Cornhuskers in the finale by rushing for 162 yards in 26 attempts.

Harold Ely was the only Iowan honored at the close of the season, being selected to the United Press all-Western second team, but more important, the Hawkeyes had managed to stand off eight opponents, winning four and losing four.

On February 16, 1931, President Walter Jessup nominated eleven men to formally incorporate into an organization known as The Board in Control of Athletics of the State University of Iowa, Inc. The business and object of the corporation was "to carry on intercollegiate sports and other athletic activities of the University, to promote athletic interests among the students, and to manage the finances and business of athletics at Iowa."

The newly incorporated athletic board consisted of seven faculty members representing the different colleges of the University, athletic director E. H. Lauer, the alumni secretary, and two Iowa alumni. In effect this same group had served in previous years, although since 1924 it had officially been only "advisory" in capacity, and was known as the "Athletic Council." Henceforth, the Board in Control of Athletics would legislate, execute and adjudicate all matters pertaining to athletics at the University. . .substantially as set forth in the 1931 Articles of Incorporation.

1931

Football reached the depths of depression and despair that fall. Iowa was the lowest scoring team of 156 major schools playing the game in 1931. The team was shut out in seven of eight games. So inept was the Iowa offense that the team averaged less than six first downs a game throughout the season. Pittsburgh and Texas A & M, winners by 20 — 0 and 29 — 0 scores in the opening two games, held the Hawkeyes to a total of five first downs.

George Washington University succumbed to Iowa in the fifth game, 7 — 0. The four yard touchdown smash by Hickman and extra point kick by Oliver Sansen were the only points scored during the season. Ironically, the defeat suffered by George Washington was its only loss of the year.

Burt Ingwersen had completed eight years as head football coach at Iowa. His over-all record showing 33 victories, 27 losses and 4 ties was creditable. However, in Western Conference competition between 1926 and 1931 Iowa teams were able to produce but six wins against 18 defeats and three ties. In the face of alumni discontent and dismal football prospects in the immediate future, Ingwersen submitted his resignation to the Board in Control of Athletics on December 10, 1931, stating that he did not "care to fight the critics who are now or will be asking for a new coach at Iowa. . ."

Two days later the Board in Control of Athletics accepted the resignation and the search was under way to find a replacement. Following is a detailed chronology of the efforts which the Iowa Board expended in trying to find one football coach:

Jan. 4, 1932—Scott McIntire appeared before the Board to recommend appointment of Irl Tubbs to the football vacancy.

Jan. 16, 1932—Board recommended that Jim Crowley, Michigan State coach, and George Little of Wisconsin be invited to visit Iowa City to confer about the football vacancy. It recommended also that negotiations be inaugurated with Coach Bill Roper of Princeton and Ike Armstrong of Utah. Meetings with Crowley and Little were held.

Jan. 21, 1932—Crowley, in a telegram to Athletic Director E. H. Lauer, requested that his name be withdrawn from consideration.

Jan. 23, 1932—Board met and decided to take more active steps to interest Crowley in the Iowa job. He was contacted by telephone and informed that Iowa would like to send a delegation to East Lansing to confer with him. Crowley asked that he be given 24 hours to consider the request.

Jan. 24, 1932—Crowley telegraphed Iowa authorities saying he had definitely decided to remain at Michigan State, hence a visit by an Iowa delegation would be pointless.

Jan. 25, 1932—The Iowa Board met and decided to send Chairman Williams and Mr. Phillips to East Lansing to consult with Crowley. A salary of $9,000 a year was mentioned.

Feb. 1, 1932—Board met and arranged to invite Ossie Solem, Drake University Coach, to meet with it. It decided also to communicate with Bo McMillin of Kansas State and to invite Frank Murray of Marquette and Maddy Bell of Texas A and M to visit with the Board in Iowa City.

Feb. 8, 1932—Mr. Kuever reported on a telephone conversation with Howard Jones of Southern California. Kuever was authorized to meet with Coach Jones in Chicago and did so. Jones indicated a lack of interest in a return to Iowa.

Feb. 20, 1932—The Board voted that an attempt be made to confer with Jim Crowley in Chicago and offer him a salary of $10,000.

Feb. 22, 1932—Board Member Phillips met with Crowley in Chicago, then returned with him to Ypsilanti, Michigan.

Feb. 24, 1932—The Board agreed to pay Crowley $10,000 for the school year, plus $750 for the summer session. He was offered a five-year contract and given until Feb. 27 to make his decision. Shortly before noon on Feb. 27 Crowley telephoned that he had decided to remain at Michigan State.

Feb. 29, 1932—The Board authorized Mr. Phillips to telephone Coach Harry Stuhldreher of Villanova to inquire if he were

interested in the Iowa position. He indicated interest and said he would give Iowa a definite answer the following day. Stuhldreher telephoned on March 1, 1932, saying he was no longer interested but would complete his contract at Villanova.

March 2, 1932—The names of Maddy Bell, Ossie Solem, Frank Wickhorst, Mike Hyland, Gus Dorais, Frank Murray, Irl Tubbs and Harry Stuhldreher were considered and their availability discussed. Telephone contact was made with Wickhorst and arrangements made to confer with Dorais in Detroit. An interview with Stuhldreher in Philadelphia also was planned.

March 11, 1932—Higbee and Lauer of the Board reported on meetings with Stuhldreher, Dorais and Elmer Layden of Duquesne. Following the report, the Board voted to discontinue its negotiations and to select Ossie Solem of Drake as the new head coach. The vote in Solem's favor was 7 to 2.

March 12, 1932—Coach Solem was formally offered the Iowa post and a three-year contract calling for a salary of $8,500 for the

Head Football Coach — 1932-1936
Athletic Director — 1934-1937
Ossie Solem

first two years and $9,000 for the third. Negotiations were concluded March 13, 1932, when Solem visited Iowa City.

Iowa had a new football coach, but other problems continued to mount. Indiana University, playing in Iowa City in 1931, lost $8,563.18, its share of the proceeds of the football game, when the school failed to cash Iowa's check of December 31, 1931, and the First National Bank of Iowa City, on which it was drawn, failed shortly thereafter.

CHAPTER
16

Years of Despair

Early in December of 1931, at an Athletic Board meeting, a motion was made and seconded to the effect that the decline in receipts made it impossible for the Board to meet interest and bond payments falling due. The motion, subsequent to discussion, was withdrawn, but later that month the Board voted to direct the treasurer to pay the $3,750 interest payment on the fieldhouse bonds due on December 31, 1931, on the condition that members of the athletic staff would agree to take notes for the deferred payment of salary to the foregoing amount, in case the interest payment created such a deficit at the close of the fiscal year.

"I don't know of anyone who stepped into a more unfortunate situation," Solem said long after his career at Iowa had ended. "I got my first paycheck and it was just one half a check. So I said: 'Gee, what's this all about?' and they said, 'Well, you know the athletic fund is exhausted; hasn't been able to meet expenses in over a year.' It was a pretty discouraging thing, I'll tell you."

Solem, a University of Minnesota alumnus, had filled coaching assignments at Luther College, East Des Moines High, South High of Minneapolis and had served a highly successful eleven-year stretch at Drake University. A large part of Solem's Drake tenure saw him filling the dual role of head football coach and director of athletics, a prelude to the combined duties he would later assume at Iowa. As an opening step he invited his top assistant at Drake, Bill Boelter, to accompany him to Iowa. Boelter, long regarded as one of the foremost halfbacks in Drake history, had served there as head basketball coach in addition to his football duties. He followed Solem to Iowa.

1932

After an opening 31 — 7 victory at the expense of Bradley, the 1932 Hawkeyes failed to win another. Wisconsin belted Iowa, 34 — 0, and Indiana followed with a 12 — 0 triumph. The Hoosiers scored a safety, field goal, touchdown and extra point in gaining their first win in history over the Hawks. Minnesota, led by all-American "Pug" Lund, pasted a 21 — 6 defeat on the Iowa record and a week later George Washington won by an identical score. The game was played in Washington, D.C., and was the first night game ever played by Iowa. Momentary optimism was generated against Nebraska a week later when the Hawkeyes battled the Huskers all the way, only to lose, 14 — 13. More defeats followed, including an 18 — 0 loss to Purdue and a jarring 44 — 6 windup against

Northwestern. Duane Purvis riddled the Iowa line in the Boilermaker game, averaging more than eight yards rushing with each of 23 attempts. Iowa had won only the Bradley game, lost all five Big Ten encounters, and finished last in the conference. It was the third year in a row without a Big Ten victory.

Early in 1933 another blow was administered to Iowa when the Conference decreed that two stars of the Hawk basketball team were ineligible. This decision, made in January, caused statewide repercussions. In December, the Eligibility Committee of the Board in Control of Athletics, consisting of Dean C. C. Williams, F. G. Higbee and Henning Larson, had declared the two basketball players ineligible.

Unable to understand the technical grounds which the Eligibility Committee had used, the complete Iowa Board on January 3 reversed the ruling of its Committee, and declared the two players eligible until the case could be investigated more thoroughly. The immediate result of this action was the resignation of Larson, followed shortly by the request of Dean Williams to be released from his duty as chairman of the Board in Control.

Just four days after the two players were declared eligible by the Board, the Iowa basketball team was to meet Michigan in the first conference game of the season. Twenty minutes before game time the Iowa athletic director received a telegram from Ohio State's Thomas E. French advising him to withhold the two athletes in question from competition pending a decision by the Conference Eligibility Committee.

Two days later, on January 9, the Western Conference overruled the Iowa Board in Control of Athletics by declaring the two athletes ineligible for further conference competition. Immediately students, alumni and "friends" voiced their discontent. The Davenport Democrat and Leader editorially stated that the Board in Control of Athletics was "driving athletes away from Iowa by its vascillating policy."

Sportswriter Dick Cullum, writing in the Minneapolis Journal, commented:

"Iowa is not getting a fair break. Either the Conference has got into the habit of persecuting the Hawkeyes or Hawkeye officials are too timid or contrite.

"In any event, Iowa is getting much the worst of it for, in spite of the fact that it is as clean in its athletic administration as the average in the league and always was less defiant of the rules than some of the worst offenders, it has been the butt of more than its share of disciplinary action.

"Whether through dictation from the Conference or choice of its own, Iowa has put men in charge of its athletics whose attitude it is to cringe before Conference authority, and the Conference, not unnaturally, shows the bully in its nature when it is approached subserviently.

"Justice is not being administered evenly. The Conference should either put Iowa at its ease or go after some of the other offenders."

Four months after the original Conference ruling, in May, 1933, one of the two players was declared eligible through reinstatement by the Big Ten.

Still another problem faced Iowa, and particularly football coach Solem, during 1932 and 1933. It was charged by the coach and others that discrimination was used in the employment of student help. Solem stated that conditions made it difficult for many athletes to stay in school because of the scarcity of jobs. "I was unable to find a single job for a football player at the hospital where several hundred students are employed," said Solem. "This situation has arisen from the fear of Mr. Fitzgerald, supervisor of the employment bureau, and the administration that giving too many athletes jobs would bring about the ire of the Western Conference. Maybe we aren't fighting enough; perhaps it is because we take a spineless and backward attitude about everything."

Solem's attack was partially sustained when an investigator of the North Central Association of Colleges and Secondary Schools reported in 1932 that there was "reason to believe that there is some discrimination against athletes as a group at Iowa."

1933

Hopes were not high as the 1933 season opened. Northwestern, having pounded the Hawkeyes 44 — 6 the year before, was the first opponent. But Iowa got its revenge. Joe Laws ran 31 yards late in the game for the only touchdown in the 7 — 0 victory, and Dick Crayne, appearing in his first game, smashed the Wildcats for 139 yards rushing.

A week later Bradley journeyed to Iowa City only to be shut out, 38 — 0. The Braves never penetrated Iowa territory, were held without a first down and surrendered 437 yards to a potent Iowa ground attack. Wisconsin was next and the Hawks again won decisively, this time, 26 — 7. New names were assuming prominence — Crayne, Russ Fisher, Tom Moore, Bill Secl, Fred Radloff, Dwight Hoover, George Teyro. Bernie Page was impressive also, as he had been the year before. Joe Laws had one of his great days against Minnesota but Iowa could not match the over-all strength of the Gophers and went down, 19 — 7. No other team could score more than once on the 1933 Hawkeyes, however.

In a somewhat historic resumption of relations with Iowa State, which had not been met in more than a decade, Crayne powered for three touchdowns and the Hawks raced in with a 27 — 7 victory. They traveled to Michigan and gave the Wolverines a fight for the full distance only to succumb, 10 — 6. Purdue was next and the Iowa line dominated the play, providing the openings for the biggest conference upset of the season, 14 — 6. The Boilermakers had been unbeaten in twenty games before Iowa snapped the streak. Joe Laws scored both Hawkeye touchdowns, one on a 27 yard run from scrimmage and the other on a 55 yard punt return.

The season ended in frustration, again at the hands of Nebraska. A freak torrential gale was blowing through the Husker stadium that day and it aided the Iowa downfall. The Hawkeyes won the toss, but by mistake the Iowa captain said: "We'll receive and take the wind." The

referee disagreed: "You can't have both, and you said you would receive. It's Nebraska's choice of goals." The Huskers took the wind,

Joe Laws

scored a lone touchdown and kicked the goal to gain a 7 — 6 victory. Bernie Masterson, later an Iowa assistant coach, notched all of the Nebraska points.

Joe Laws, completing his brilliant career as a Hawkeye, was selected to the first all-Big Ten team of both Associated Press and United Press. He also was a second team all-America honoree of Grantland Rice and Collier's magazine. Laws, leading Big Ten scorer in conference games, was further honored by winning the Chicago Tribune Silver Football Award, emblematic of his recognition as the Big Ten's most valuable player in 1933. Francis (Zud) Schammel, rated by Ossie Solem as "the finest guard I ever coached," was a consensus all-America pick, being given first team honors by both the Associated Press and by the football coaches for United Press, the first time an Iowan had been so honored by the two wire services.

Minnesota, according to Conference record keeping at the time, shared the Big Ten title with Michigan. The Gophers won only two of

Francis Schammel

six conference games but maintained a 1,000 percentage when each of their other four games ended in a tie. Iowa, with a 5 — 3 season record and a 3 — 2 Conference mark, gained fifth place in the Big Ten.

The contract of Ossie Solem was rewritten in January, 1934, to extend until July 1, 1938. The original salary figures which had been agreed to when Solem came to Iowa in 1932 had been reduced according to the scale of salary reductions adopted by the State Board of Education. The Hawkeye coach would be paid $8,000 for the 1934-35 year, $8,000 for the 1935-36 year, and $8,500 for each of the two calendar years beginning July 1, 1936, and extending until July 1, 1938.

The matter of wages may have been of less concern to Solem, however, than the lack of cooperation he received from other schools of the Big Ten in schedule meetings. Each member of the Conference was guaranteed five

games with member schools, but the problem of scheduling the five games was at best difficult for Iowa. Coach Solem described his scheduling problems after he had left Iowa.

"I'll never forget. We were sitting in Chicago at a schedule meeting. In those days, when they made the schedules, they had all the coaches and athletic directors in the room and they had a big blackboard. I'm sitting there and I've got three games. It was getting on toward noon and somebody said: 'Well, let's adjourn. Everybody has his schedule.' And I said: 'No, now let's start to work on the Iowa schedule. I've got three games. I'm going to get five.' They kind of hemmed and hawed and finally I said: 'You know, it's a strange set of circumstances. Here I represent Iowa and I've got three games. Here's Elmer Layden (Notre Dame football coach). He's not in the Big Ten but he has more games than I have.' I went up to Major Griffith and said, 'Major, I'm going to get five games.'

"Pretty soon Elmer Layden walked out of the room with Dr. Clarence Spears (Wisconsin coach) and when he came back he went to the blackboard and rubbed off the Notre Dame-Wisconsin game. So I got a game with Wisconsin, and I had four games. And somebody said: 'Well, you satisfied now, Ossie?' and I said: 'No, I'm going to get five games.' And nobody would yield. Finally, before we adjourned for lunch Harry Kipke of Michigan came to me and said that the 'old man,' meaning Fielding H. Yost, was calling Lou Little at Columbia University. Kipke said that if it was agreeable with Columbia, Michigan would cancel that game and give Iowa a game. I remember I asked Stagg (Amos Alonzo Stagg) if he would give Iowa a game and he answered: 'Me play Iowa? Chicago will never play Iowa.' Anyway, we went to lunch and it was during that time that Kipke came to me and told me that the Iowa-Michigan game was on. So I got my five games."

The salary reduction and the schedule-making did not constitute all of the supplementary problems.

"I had been asked to do some writing for the Des Moines Register," Solem recalled. "I did it, thinking that maybe I could do some good in creating good will for the University. Right away I had Earl Hall (Mason City editor) on my neck. He started blasting. I told him I was doing a series of articles and that next year I'd be glad to talk about doing it for him. Well, the next year came and I didn't hear from Hall. Sec Taylor came down from Des Moines and, since I had not heard from Hall, I told Sec I'd write one more year for the Register. Then Hall started in again. He even wanted to prohibit us from allowing newspaper men to officiate in any of our games. Finally, the third year, I just didn't write again."

Ossie Solem was assigned new duties before the start of another season. Early in June Dr. E. H. Lauer resigned as director of athletics to become dean of liberal arts at the University of Washington. A month later, acting President Eugene Gilmore announced that Solem would assume the twofold duties of athletic director-football coach, effective August 1, 1934.

1934

The situation appeared to be promising as the 1934 campaign began. There was more squad depth and more individual promise in sight. The opening 34 — 0 decision over South Dakota raised no eyebrows but the 20 — 7 conquest of Northwestern that followed put Iowa in the limelight from coast to coast. The Hawkeyes had introduced a brilliant new star named Simmons — Oze Simmons he was, or Ozzie, depending on the whim of the writer describing him. His ball carrying against Northwestern was electrifying, 304 total yards gained by rushing, kickoffs and punt returns. It earned him the nickname "the Ebony Eel" and led one unprejudiced writer, Ralph Cannon of the Chicago News, into rave assertions about this "new comet in the western skies."

"Inevitably, the comparison goes back to Grange," wrote Cannon on October 7, 1934. "But this slithery, rubbery, oozy flyer with his gyrating balance, cool, masterful mental poise, sleek, smooth, fluid weaving hips and the most perfect open-field pivot probably in the game today, can make his legs talk more languages that even Grange's could when he was a sophomore.

"The arrival of a football entertainer like Simmons is a valuable asset to middle western football and a great break for the fans. He is a master, a finished big-league runner like Eddie Mahan of Harvard or Eddie Kaw of Cornell, who knows all of the tricks of open-field progress. Most of it seems to come naturally to Simmons, as such things must come to the genius of any line. . ."

Simmons earned a sensational reception in his first Big Ten game. Alas for the Hawks, his tremendous possibilities never reached full stature. The very next game, with Simmons in the lineup, the Hawks dropped their third straight frustrating one-pointer to Nebraska, 14-13. Instead of Simmons, the plaudits went to Russ Fisher, Dick Crayne and Ted Osmaloski, a young center of promise. The glory that had been anticipated for Iowa was dimmed, but even greater distress lay ahead. The Hawks had Iowa State as their next opponent and more than a quarter of a century later this meeting with the Cyclones brought pangs to Iowa followers.

The Hawks, it had been assumed, could win as they pleased. Iowa State was hardly likely to contain the advances of the dangerous Hawkeye backfield. There may never have been a more astonishing upset on the Iowa record. Iowa State not only won but smashed the Hawkeyes, 31 — 6. The crowd, reportedly 18,000, was far from record size but it was the largest ever to watch a game in Ames. It witnessed an unbelievable reversal. Tommy Neal, a 155 pound halfback whose home was in Sioux City, scored three Cyclone touchdowns. Simmons scored none for Iowa. Fred Poole punted a dozen times for Iowa State in the course of the game, for the sensational average of 54.5 yards. Harold Miller, State's big ground gainer, accounted for 85 yards on 16 carries. Dick Crayne, the Iowa leader, made 50 yards in 17 tries. The winners were in front at the half, 17 — 0.

The shock of this loss was great. There was no effort to minimize the great achievement of the Cyclones. Their play was appraised as vastly superior to Iowa's. The inevitable suggestion of dissension within the Hawkeye ranks followed — rumors that grew in volume a week later when soon to be National Champion Minnesota smothered Iowa, 48 — 12. It was Homecoming in Iowa City, but the Gophers unleashed a relentless fury which all but annihilated the Hawkeyes under a ground attack which rolled for a record breaking 595 yards. The largest crowd to witness a game in Iowa Stadium up to that time, 53,000, watched Minnesota hit for 34 points by halftime. Three Gophers, Julius Alphonse, Stan Kostka and Pug Lund, each gained more than 100 yards rushing, while the entire Iowa team was held to 70.

The season that had opened on such a high note of hope was regarded as a vast disappointment even before the concluding games against Indiana, Purdue and Ohio State. The Hoosier contest, played with a wet ball on a drenched gridiron, was memorable for one particular kick. Dick Crayne of Iowa, standing deep in his own end zone, kicked the ball out of bounds on the Indiana 5-yard line. The punt, traveling more than 90 yards past the scrimmage line and 102 yards from Crayne's foot, was the longest in Iowa annals. But the sodden game ended scoreless. Purdue stopped the Hawkeyes in the season's seventh game, 13 — 6. Only a 69 yard pass play, Crayne to Frank Jakoubek, brightened the Iowa day. It was the Hawkeyes' longest completed pass up to that time, and set the stage for Crayne to score from the Purdue 11 on the following play. Ohio State buried Iowa, 40 — 7, to close the season, resorting to a devastating passing attack to bewilder the Hawks. An 80 yard touchdown run by Simmons, following an intercepted pass, put Iowa on the scoreboard. The team finished 2 — 5 — 1 for the season and 1 — 3 — 1 in the Big Ten. Four Iowa opponents held the Hawkeyes without a yard gained by passing.

As the season advanced complaints had taken various forms. The "What's the Matter with Iowa" contingent was heard. Some critics, following the drubbing by Minnesota, charged that the Gophers were "determined to put Ozzie Simmons out of commission right off the bat, and they did it." Alarm was voiced over the "uncurbed drinking" by spectators at Iowa games. One week later some 300 ushers were deputized in an effort to halt the bottle tippers. But for all the disappointments and distress of the 1934 season, gate receipts re-

Dick Crayne

bounded upward and athletic staff members were compensated for the overdue portions of their salaries. Junior Dick Crayne received highest post season honors among Hawkeye players when he was named all-Western and all-Big Ten for his 1934 play.

Coach Ossie Solem had opportunity to leave Iowa and thus walk away from some of his problems.

"Northwestern wanted me to come there and coach," Solem said at a later date, "but I told Tug Wilson (athletic director at Northwestern) that I was trying to work things out at Iowa. I wanted to get the situation straightened out if I could.

"I went to see Commissioner Griffith and I asked him if it was all right to let kids sign notes for tuition, to be paid later. He said that was the way to do it. So we started in. We had some good kids coming in. I was up at camp and started getting letters from some of the kids. They said they had gotten letters saying they would have to pay their notes before they could enroll in the fall. I told them that that was wrong and that when I got back to Iowa City I would see Cobb (University treasurer) and Updegraff (athletic board chairman.). When I saw them they reiterated that the kids could not enroll until they paid up the tuition notes. Two days before our first game with Bradley (1935) we didn't have a kid enrolled. In the meantime I got in touch with those incoming freshmen and told them to go home. I told them to go to some other school; I couldn't live up to what I had promised.

"We were sitting in a meeting in the President's office with the Athletic Board and some of the faculty. And Bill Boelter and Frank Williams, unbeknown to me, went out and knocked on doors to raise money to keep 25 kids — practically the whole varsity — in school, so that we could put a team on the field against Bradley. The funny thing about it all — Updegraff and Cobb were the guys who originally gave me permission to do this note business. And I told them I knew the procedure was right because I had talked with Major Griffith about it. But it was Cobb and Updegraff who wrote the letters to those kids the following summer, telling them they had to come up with the money before they could enroll again. . .Well, it was an experience. I've never seen such double-crossing."

1935

In a setting clouded by such numerous problems, Coach Solem moved into the 1935 campaign. With the tuition matter settled, he had a promising squad, including the Simmons brothers, Dick Crayne, Johnny Hild, Dwight Hoover, Homer Harris, Jim Kelley, Floyd DeHeer, Connie Walker, Bill Secl, Ted Osmaloski, Bush Lamb, Bob Lannon, Rudy Leytze, Floyd McDowell and others. Bradley went down in the opening game, 26 — 0, and South Dakota absorbed a 47 — 2 beating the next week. On came a Colgate team in charge of the veteran Coach Andy Kerr, with eastern writers associating a possible Rose Bowl berth with Colgate. Nationally known football experts had publicly predicted a Colgate victory. Grantland Rice wrote: "You will find few football players as good as Dick Crayne. But I have an idea Andy Kerr's dipsy-doos will be slightly more than Iowa's defense can stop." John Kieran of the New York Times was equally outspoken: "The Red Raiders of the Chenango will try their now-you-see it and now-you-don't football on the Skeptics' Society of Iowa dressed in football uniforms. If the tricks fall flat so will Colgate. Until then, one vote for the slight-of-Handy-Andy magicians from Colgate." Iowa won, 12 — 6, with Ozzie Simmons twice breaking away for touchdowns.

If Simmons ever had a day that rivaled his sensational start against Northwestern as a sophomore, it was against Illinois in the fourth game of the 1935 season. That afternoon he rushed for 192 yards, intercepted an Illini pass, returned three punts for 33 yards, returned two kickoffs for 54 more yards and scored one touchdown. Iowa notched an impressive 19 — 0 victory and was recognized as a threat in the Big Ten.

Indiana was next and the icy field gave neither team a chance to show to its best advantage. The game ended in a 6 — 6 tie. Hopes were high against Minnesota but in spite of remarkable line play by the Iowa forwards, the Gophers came from a 6 — 0 halftime deficit and prevailed in a rugged 13 — 6 go. Minnesota again won the national championship. The first trophy at stake in an Iowa football series went into competition that November day in Iowa City, however. Tension between representatives of the two schools had been increasing and it reached a peak in 1934, when Minnesota routed the Hawkeyes, 48 — 12. With the 1935 game approaching, Governor Floyd B. Olson of Minnesota and Governor Clyde Herring of Iowa made a friendly wager on the outcome of the game. The bet was regarded as a diplomatic move to lessen the friction between followers of the two teams. As a result, Floyd of Rosedale was declared to be the "spoils of victory" — awarded to the possession of the winner of each Iowa-Minnesota game.

The original Floyd was a full-blooded champion hog, a litter mate of "Blue Boy," a hog featured with Will Rogers in the motion picture "State Fair." Governor Herring, following the 13 — 6 defeat of Iowa by Minnesota in the 1935 game, forwarded the live hog to Governor Olson. The Minnesota governor, in turn, presented it to the University of Minnesota after commissioning Charles Brieschi, a St. Paul sculptor, to create a bronze likeness of the hog. (See page 197 for photograph.)

The trophy, 21 inches long and 15 1/2 inches high, weighs 94 pounds. It was first awarded in 1936, after the Gophers had taken possession of the "in the flesh" trophy a year earlier.

Against Purdue Ozzie Simmons departed from his ball carrying role long enough to fire a touchdown pass to Homer Harris but the Boilermakers came on to win in the final thirty minutes, 12 — 6. The 1935 campaign ended against Northwestern and Dick Crayne, in his final game, played so brilliantly that his mates carried him off the field after the scoreless battle. Crayne had battered the Wildcats for 140 yards. Iowa closed with a 4 — 2 — 2 season record, holding eight opponents to a total of 39 points. Throughout his coaching career Solem held to the view that his 1935 Iowa team was one of the best in college football, "although awfully short of reserves in key spots."

Five Hawkeyes, Ozzie Simons, Dick Crayne, Floyd DeHeer, Ted Osmaloski and Bob Lannon gained all Big Ten, all Midwest or all-America recognition following the season. Simmons was given a first team all-America berth by The Sporting News and was a second team pick of Associated Press and N.E.A. Crayne was a third team all-America selection of both the United Press and Associated Press. The 20 touchdowns and 122 total points scored by Crayne during his Iowa career were the most since the days of Aubrey Devine and Gordon Locke in the early twenties and only George (Dusty) Rice, playing in the fifties, would top the marks in later years.

Mindful of the tuition situation that had left him virtually without a team on the eve of the 1935 Bradley game, Coach Solem called upon President Gilmore at the close of the season. He requested permission to take over the janitor service in the fieldhouse and in other facilities in that area. Gilmore granted the request, with the understanding that jobs thus created would cover only unskilled labor.

"I was able to recommend 45 good legitimate jobs, I think it was, none to exceed $40 a month in compensation. Waddy Davis had just returned to Iowa City, from St. Louis. He had been on the staff at Washington University. I asked him to take charge of the janitor service in the fieldhouse and in the other facilities around there. He accepted."

With the help of the janitor jobs Iowa attracted "the finest group of freshmen during my tenure" in 1936, Solem recalled. Nile Kinnick, Erwin Prasse, Dick Evans and others were in the group and replacements were beginning to appear for the graduates of 1935 and 1936.

1936

The effort to raise football at Iowa to the Big Ten level was proving to be extremely difficult, nevertheless. Coach Solem in 1936 sent his team against Carleton College in the opener and the valiant fight of the Midwest Conference team forced Iowa to settle for a 14 — 0 victory. Ozzie Simmons was a senior. He had an able backfield mate in Bush Lamb of Newton, a versatile athlete who later gave his life in World War II. The two backs were standouts in the Carleton game.

On their next appearance the Hawks were stopped by Northwestern, 18 — 7, but rebounded the following week by racing past South Dakota, 33 — 7. A scoreless tie was played with Illinois, the impotent Iowa offense being held without a first down in the second half. After the Illinois stalemate, the Hawks lost to Indiana, 13 — 6 and prepared to meet Minnesota. It was a rout; the Gophers, slashing through the Hawkeyes for a 33 — 0 halftime lead, won as they pleased, 52 — 0. In the wake of that game Ozzie Simmons turned in his suit, but he soon rejoined the squad. Iowa's luckless Hawkeyes went against Purdue and lost, 13 — 0, and reports were heard that Coach Ossie Solem soon was to leave Iowa for a new coaching berth. The Hawks, aware that they had only one more game to play for Solem, slammed through a favored Temple University team in the windup to win, 25 — 0, with Lamb, Simmons and Frank Jakoubek the standouts. Temple, coached by the immortal Glenn (Pop) Warner, had been heavily favored to win the Philadelphia game. Warner went to the extreme of starting his second team but the experiment backfired as Iowa scored twice in the first six minutes on perfectly executed 70 and 74 yard scoring dashes by Bush Lamb and Ozzie Simmons.

Simmons had closed his brilliant although sometimes controversial career at Iowa with a record of more than 1500 yards gained from scrimmage. Eight times during his three years of play he thrilled Iowa partisans with touchdown runs of more than fifty yards.

Coach Solem recalled the play of Simmons by saying:

"He was one of the two or three greatest backs I've ever coached and the best halfback I've ever seen. One thing has been overlooked in connection with him — he was a terrific defensive back as well. He had one weakness, if you want to call it that. Like so many great runners, he seemed to lack the ability, or the intuition, to take advantage of his interference. Sometimes he would think a little faster than his interference and get away from his blockers and get himself in trouble. But he had so many

Ozzie Simmons

great qualities that he could overcome that. He had a great stiff arm, a great change of pace, unlimited courage, and I've never seen a better tackling halfback, or very few others who could tackle better than Ozzie."

Ossie Solem left Iowa after the 1936 season to assume new duties at Syracuse University. During his stay, the Hawks won 15, lost 21 and tied 4.

Among the other men who played under him at Iowa were four whom he cited for their exceptional ability. More than 25 years after they had played for him, Solem spoke of them as follows:

Dick Crayne — I would certainly put Dick in a class with the greatest fullbacks I've ever seen. We had to do a little juggling when we had those two (Simmons and Crayne) because they were both exceptionally good backs. We didn't have quite the support and the blocking and the speed to take full advantage of all of their potential. Dick was a great kicker. You won't find a better punter today, or anytime. I can say without any question of doubt that I've never had two kids on the same team to compare with those two boys.

Joe Laws — I would put him right in the same classification with Simmons and Crayne. Later events proved that. He was with the Green Bay Packers for 11 or 12 years after he left us. Joe wasn't what you would call a real clever back, and he couldn't throw, but he had a terrific heart. He developed speed — more of it than I thought he had initially. And he was very smart. He was an excellent quarterback.

Zud Schammel — He was one of the great guards. As fine a guard as I've ever seen. He was the perfect guard. And the amazing thing was that all during his season with us he had a leg infection and was in the hospital practically every week from Saturday night until about Wednesday of the following week. There's no question about it. He was the greatest guard I've ever coached.

Bob Lannon — He was a great end and a great kid. After my first year at Syracuse I brought Bob out there to be on my coaching staff.

Another Solem assistant at Syracuse was Bud Wilkinson, who was to establish a fabulous record as a coach at the University of Oklahoma later in his career. Wilkinson made his bow into coaching under Solem.

"I had known this kid Wilkinson just slightly when he was at Shattuck," Solem explained. "And he played for Minnesota all the time I was at Iowa. The more I saw of him the more impressed I was with him, as a great fellow to have around. So when I was moving to Syracuse I went to see Bud in Minneapolis. I didn't know where to look for him but I ran into George Hauser of the Minnesota staff and I said, 'George, where can I get hold of Bud Wilkinson?' And he said, 'You mean Bud Svendson, don't you?' and I said, 'No, Bud Wilkin-

son.' So Hauser found him in class and I met him and I said, 'Bud, are you interested in coaching?' and he said, 'Well, I think I would like it but I don't think my parents would permit me.' So I told him I wasn't trying to persuade him to go into coaching but if he would like to do so I was moving to Syracuse and would like to have him join us. And he did. Incidentally, I have never seen a quarterback call a more perfect game than Bud called against us in 1936. And, as far as that one day was concerned, I am doubtful if I have ever seen a team any better than Minnesota."

Two of Ossie Solem's greatest players gave somewhat parallel impressions of him. One of them wrote: "He was the fatherly type. He had imagination and played more wide-open football, believing in more finesse with spinners, reverses and passes mixed in with power."

Another reflection of Ossie Solem: "I feel that he was a better offensive coach than he was a defensive coach. He did not have too much material to work with. He was a fine, clean living man, and was very well thought of in athletic circles."

During his stay at Iowa Ossie Solem had many problems, a few unpleasantries, and numerous frustrations, as have coaches everywhere. But he returned to Iowa City for a football game long after he had resigned as coach and later wrote:

"I went down to Iowa City for the Iowa-Minnesota game, the first time I had been on the campus since the year after we left Iowa. As I sat there watching the game and admiring the beauty and growth of the campus, recalling the many friends we had in that lovely town, I could not bring myself to have any feeling of dislike or hate, but rather a feeling of regret. and gratefulness for having once been a part of that great institution."

The resignation of Ossie Solem left vacant the athletic directorship, as well as the football coaching post. The Board in Control of Athletics took care of the first vacancy on Jan. 18, 1937, with the recommendation that Ernest G. "Dad" Schroeder, who had been called the father of intramural athletics at Iowa, be appointed to the directorship. The recommendation was approved. Action on the coaching vacancy also was prompt, although it followed a pattern that brought criticism to the Board and to the University.

Athletic Director — 1937-1947
E. G. (Dad) Schroeder

With the departure of Solem many names were mentioned as possible successors, some by the Board itself but most by writers commenting on the vacancy. Prominently mentioned, and in some cases contacted by the Board, were Gus Dorais, of Detroit University, Jim Kelly of DePaul, Eddie Anderson of Holy Cross, Arthur (Dutch) Bergman of Catholic University, Irl Tubbs of Miami and Maddy Bell of Southern Methodist University. One newspaper printed a table of approximately 100 college football coaches, suggesting that the name of the new Iowa coach was somewhere on the list. It was not. In the midst of widespread discussion of possible appointees the Board indicated that the more prominent candidates were Tubbs, Bell and Bergman.

The Board held an afternoon meeting in the Old Capitol on February 4, 1937. A motion was passed that a football coach be appointed before the meeting ended. Members present were asked to choose between two final candidates, Tubbs and Bergman. Eight of the 10 members voting favored Tubbs and it was agreed that he should become the head football coach, but a proviso was attached: The Board wanted assurance that Tubbs would bring with him from Miami University of Flor-

Head Football Coach — 1937-1938
Irl Tubbs

ida his line coach, Pat Boland. Assurance was forthcoming and Tubbs was signed to a one-year contract, effective March 1, 1937.

Criticism followed, not of Tubbs, but of procedures followed in filling the coaching vacancy. Not all of the criticism stemmed from Iowans. A Detroit sportswriter, W. W. Edgar, began his comment in this fashion:

"The University of Iowa has hired a new football coach and reached an all-time high — or low — in the process. The other day there was occasion to point out that those in charge of athletics at the Hawkeye institution could do worse than take a course in better business methods. After reading the tactics employed in the hiring of Irl Tubbs, head man of Miami University, to take over the gridiron duties, it becomes increasingly apparent that more harm than good was done by the transaction.

"In the first place, when Ossie Solem resigned to become the football coach at Syracuse, Iowa immediately rushed into print with a list of coaches whom they would invite for interviews regarding the vacated position. As soon as those names were published, the coaches directly concerned were put on the spot at the schools where they hold contracts. At first thought, it was only human to feel that the coach whose name appeared on Iowa's preferred list was dissatisfied at the school at which he had been working. And this might have been true. But no coach wants to jeopardize his own job until he is reasonably sure of another. . . .

"After announcing the list of preferred coaches, Iowa rushed into print each time it interviewed a candidate. This, too, had a damaging effect. Any coach who consented to an interview at Iowa's expense found that he had only half a job when he returned home. . .And more than one coach has had to do a lot of explaining since the day Iowa singled him out. . .

"All these tactics were crude enough. But the all time high — or low — was reached in the final act of signing Irl Tubbs for the position. The choice, according to officials, had dwindled to two men — Dutch Bergman of Catholic University and Tubbs. Both were invited to Iowa City for luncheon and interviews. Iowa made no pretense at keeping its actions secret. Both candidates sat at the same luncheon table and talked over terms. Then, they were asked to wait until the officials went into a closed conference to weigh all matters and make a decision. Meanwhile, Bergman and Tubbs waited outside — two puppets in a whirl of self-importance on the part of the Iowa officials. . . Finally, the door of the meeting room opened. The Iowa athletic officials filed out— like a jury that had just reached a momentous decision — and announced that they had decided to hire Irl Tubbs on a year-to-year contract. Dutch Bergman was left standing there — spurned and tagged as an 'unwanted coach.' It was a crude way of doing business. . ."

Charles Johnson, writing in the Minneapolis Star, saw no long range solution of Iowa's problems in the hiring of Tubbs. He wrote: "Irl Tubbs' appointment as head football coach at Iowa may not solve this school's problem except for the time being. This is one sport that requires more than one season at any institution for a coach to make a showing. . .Iowans wanted a big name. They didn't get it in Tubbs, even though they may have a sound football strategist. If the new gridiron boss doesn't turn out a reasonably good team next fall, the Hawkeyes will find themselves worse off than ever. Tubbs unquestionably got the job over Dutch Bergman because of his abundance of confidence. He was willing to take it on a make-good-or-get-out basis after one year. . .Tubbs knows little or nothing about play in the Western Conference because he has been away from this section for a few years. It will take him at least one full season to get acquainted with his opposition. That's not all. It will take him and Pat Boland several games to learn what their own squad has in the way of material. . .Ability to coach isn't the first requisite of the new football boss at Iowa. He must get harmony among the many factions that have made things miserable for Ossie Solem in recent years. . ."

At the time of his appointment Tubbs was quoted as telling the Iowa Board: "I don't need a contract. Pay me on the basis you pay your professors. If you are not satisfied with my work after one season, I'll move along." The Board gave Tubbs a one-year contract at a $6,500 salary — a figure somewhat lower than the University had been paying. This was occasioned, perhaps, by the understanding that Tubbs, a man with numerous inventions to his credit, had a private income from royalties on such inventions as improvements in athletic equipment including an inverted valve for the ball, special cleats and an elastic insert in football pants.

With the hiring of Tubbs, the Athletic Board turned its attention to heading off any movement which might lead to difficulties such as had been experienced at the time of its ouster from athletic participation in the Western Conference. Word had come to the Board that a group of alumni planned to form a club composed of former lettermen of the University. Action was prompt. On March 15, 1937, the Board, on the promise that its own cooperation would insure the interests of the Board and eliminate the possibility of any authority outside of it, went on record as saying that the proposed organization should be planned and sponsored by the Board in Control of Athletics.

A committee was appointed by the Board to arrange a dinner at which the matters of organizing an 'I' Club were to be discussed. As a result, an earlier 'I' Club at the University was revived, under the auspices of the Board. The purpose of the organization was to persuade athletes to enroll at the University, legitimately and legally. The Board took a stand against the granting of awards to athletes by any agency other than the Board itself. In an effort to pump life into the ailing athletic picture, a group of Chicago alumni had, in 1936, provided four scholarships to athletes from the Chicago area. Investigation disclosed that these awards did not, at the time, conflict with Conference rules, but Major John L. Griffith, the Conference commissioner, told the Iowa Board in January, 1937, that the low scholastic averages of two of the men suggested that the scholarships could hardly have been awarded for anything other than athletic ability.

With some alumni striving to bolster the athletic prospects of the University and the Board striving to thwart any action that might endanger the status of the University in the

Conference, Irl Tubbs moved onto the Iowa scene. The Board had seen fit shortly before his arrival to recognize the activities of John Goltman, who was interested in attracting athletes to the University. By way of emphasizing the fact that Goltman was not acting with the sanction of the Board in Control of Athletics, the Board, on January 18, 1937, adopted a resolution:

BE IT RESOLVED that this Board at this time goes on record as disapproving any action of John Goltman or any other ambitious individual. . .

"BE IT RESOLVED that this Board goes on record at this time as emphatically condemning any such solicitation on the part of any individual or group of individuals and recommending to the alumni and friends of this institution that they support no individuals seeking to raise funds for such purpose (assisting athletes through the University.) This Board and the Athletic Department of the University have never approved of any such solicitation and at all times condemn and disapprove the same."

1937-1938

A FOOTBALL DEPRESSION

The football atmosphere at the University was not exactly grooved to success when Irl Tubbs took charge. Ossie Solem's last team had had its problems in 1936, defeating only Carleton, South Dakota and Temple. Tubbs' team started with its own problems. It opened against the University of Washington at Seattle, lost 14 — 0 and came home to beat Bradley, 14 — 0. Six consecutive defeats followed. Most difficult to accept was a tight 7 — 6 defeat at the hands of Michigan. Neither team had won a conference game since 1935. Sophomore Nile Kinnick returned a punt 74 yards for the Hawkeye score, but the Wolverines equalled the touchdown and added an extra point to gain victory. Minnesota again trimmed Iowa, 35 — 10, but not before overcoming a surprising 10 — 0 Hawk advantage. Wisconsin, Purdue, Indiana and Nebraska all defeated Iowa, the latter three teams shutting out the Hawkeyes. Only one victory had been registered, and only 36 points scored during the season, although six of the eight opponents were limited to 14 points or less.

Bob Lannon was given a first team berth on the Associated Press Conference honor eleven, while Kinnick earned not only all-Big Ten recognition but was selected on the all-America third team of N.E.A. Iowa as a team led the nation in punting, kicking 70 times for a brilliant 43 yard average.

In 1938 the Hawkeyes again took to the road for their opening game. They lost to U.C.L.A. in Los Angeles, 27 — 3. Wisconsin beat them 31 — 13 the next time out. It was the eighth straight defeat for Iowa, an all-time record for consecutive losses. Only a fortunate schedule making move enabled the Hawks to snap the streak a week later. Chicago, like Iowa with no Conference victories since 1935, was the opposition. The Maroons, soon to give up football, fell by two touchdowns, 27 — 14. It was the second triumph, and the last one, of the Tubbs regime.

After a disappointing 14 — 0 loss to Colgate, an Iowa paper commented editorially:

"Iowa's football hopes, such as they were, painfully passed away yesterday afternoon, a victim of brutal grid assassins from the east — Colgate's Red Raiders.

"Interment ceremonies will be held on almost any Iowa City street corner at almost any time you suggest. The sooner the better, however."

In two seasons the teams of Irl Tubbs compiled a 2 — 13 — 1 record. The Hawks scored only three points in the last five games of 1938 and only 82 in the 16 games they played under Tubbs. They were shut out in one-half of the games.

With his second season not yet behind him, Coach Tubbs appeared before the Board in Control of Athletics on November 15, 1938. He presented his views of the football situation at the University. The preliminaries to that meet-

ing were explained years later by Walter L. (Stub) Stewart, a board member:

"I went down to a Board meeting and they told me Tubbs wanted to meet with the Board. And the Board didn't want to meet with him. They told me to talk to him. So he came over and he said we ought to have all the (football) boys living in a house, with a housemother to take care of them. He said we also ought to have a training table. I told him that according to Big Ten regulations we couldn't do any of these things. So I told him I guessed there wasn't anything for us to do but look for another coach. He agreed. . ."

On the financial side, football receipts for the 1938 season were $64,986.45, lowest since 1932. Expenses were $38,751.59. The athletic department as a whole had a deficit in 1938 of $10, 641.19.

Tubbs was 49 when he took the Iowa job. He had been a successful coach who worked largely with small squads. A graduate of William Jewell College where he played quarterback and end, Tubbs coached for two seasons in Missouri high schools, moving then to Superior, Wisconsin, where he coached for five seasons. His record included a nine year stay at Wisconsin State Teachers College, where his career was interrupted by an attack of malta fever. He was convalescing in Miami, Florida, when he first was approached about the coaching job at the University of Miami. Upon accepting the post, he coached there for two years, winning 11 games, losing 6 and breaking even in two. He had won 70 per cent of his career games when he came to Iowa. With the Hawkeyes he won 2, lost 13, tied 1. Among the notable players he coached elsewhere were Ernie Nevers, later an All-Time All-American at Stanford; Pat Boland, who coached the line at Iowa, and John Hancock and Scott McIntyre, members of Iowa's undefeated 1922 squad.

Football at Iowa had reached such a low point at the end of the 1938 season that The Chicago Tribune took note, with a bit of sarcasm. With the tongue-in-cheek assumption that education prospers as football fortunes falter, The Tribune of December 8, 1938, said: "Nearly every Saturday afternoon the gridiron enhanced scholarship and endowed it with new luster" at Chicago and Iowa.

Further, it was proposed that Robert M. Hutchins, president of the University of Chicago, be "first all-American prexy" and President E. A. Gilmore of Iowa be "second all-American prexy." Chicago, like Iowa, had known far better days in football. Indeed, the Maroons would give up the sport within another year.

The Ironmen and Nile Kinnick

Friendly pokes at the Hawkeye football level of accomplishment were supplemented by hard facts. Iowa, from 1930 through 1938, won only 22 of 50 games. During five of the nine seasons the Hawks went without a conference victory, and only once during the period did they win more than one Big Ten game. Vast expanses of empty seats were noted in the stadium on game days. As gate receipts fell, bond interest could not be met and the financial situation in the Department of Athletics became acute. The Board in Control of Athletics reached a quiet decision to change coaches. Chairman Karl Leib, who had succeeded Clarence Updegraff early in the year, commissioned Walter L. Stewart, Des Moines attorney and long time alumni member of the Board, to make personal contact with several potential new coaches. Stewart, a nine-letter man as an undergraduate at Iowa, had in mind the names of Jim Crowley of Fordham, Maurice (Clipper) Smith of Villanova, Jock Sutherland of Pittsburgh and Dr. Edward N. Anderson of Holy Cross as he headed east on his mission. One contact was sufficient.

Stewart's first approach was to Dr. Anderson, who was at the crest of a spectacular six-season stretch at Holy Cross. His teams had met only seven defeats in 58 games with four ties. A former chairman of the Iowa Board,

when Anderson's name was mentioned as a coaching possibility, said the Holy Cross coach was not interested in Iowa. However, a telephone contact by Stewart brought the word

**Head Football Coach — 1939-1942 and 1946-1949
Eddie Anderson**

from Dr. Anderson that this was not the case. He was interested. Stewart had been given full authority to offer Anderson a contract. Indeed, Dr. Ernest G. (Dad) Schroeder, Iowa athletic director, had suggested that Stewart throw in the directorship as an added inducement, if he thought Anderson might be available.

A secret meeting in Boston was arranged. Holy Cross still had a game with Boston College before it concluded its 1938 season. Anderson invited Stewart to go with him to Worcester, under an assumed name, to watch the Holy Cross team practice. After the workout they visited Anderson's home, conferred with Mrs. Anderson, and went back to Boston to continue their discussion. Stewart drew up a contract on Plaza Hotel stationery, Dr. Anderson signed it, and his connection with Iowa began. The contract, covering three years, called for a $10,000 salary but the athletic directorship was not involved.

It was November 29, 1938, when Anderson and two of his assistants, Joe Sheeketski and Jim Harris arrived in Iowa City and conferred with the Athletic Board. Their contracts were approved and the way opened for the highly successful coach to return to his native Iowa. Anderson was born in Oskaloosa, Iowa, November 13, 1900. He played his high school football at Mason City, graduating in the spring of 1918. He enrolled at Notre Dame in September and gained immediate varsity eligibility under the wartime emergency rule permitting freshmen to engage in intercollegiate competition. Anderson learned his football under the famed Knute Rockne, captaining the 1921 Irish, and earning all America consideration at the end of his four-year playing career. He promptly was given an opportunity to coach football at Columbia College (now Loras) in Dubuque, Iowa, and accepted it. He coached Columbia for three years starting with an undefeated season and establishing a record of 16 victories, six defeats and two ties. Anderson taught the Notre Dame style of football at Columbia as he did later at Iowa, but in between he filled a coaching stay at DePaul University and played Sunday professional football with

the Chicago Cardinals while qualifying for a degree from Rush Medical College. He proceeded to Holy Cross in 1933.

A tinge of regret at leaving Holy Cross where his success had been exceptional must have been tempered by the zest of the challenge to coach Big Ten Conference football at the University of his native state as Dr. Anderson signed the improvised contract handed him by emissary Stewart. It was in Iowa City, 18 years before, that Anderson had played in one of his most memorable games as an undergraduate. Notre Dame had visited Iowa City backed by a string of 20 consecutive victories and a reputation as one of the nation's great teams. The Hawkeyes, coached by Howard Jones, were expected to be the twenty-first victim, but such was not to be. In one of the all-time great games played by Iowa, the record was broken by a 10 — 7 Hawkeye victory. It was the only defeat Notre Dame suffered during Eddie Anderson's sophomore, junior and senior seasons.

1939

When Dr. Anderson called the Hawkeyes together for the first time he met with holdover players from the Irl Tubbs regime and sophomores who were to fill big roles for Iowa. Included were veterans of ability, whom success had evaded. There was one, Nile Kinnick, who would become legendary in Iowa football. Erwin Prasse and Dick (Whitey) Evans, ends; Floyd (Buzz) Dean, halfback; Ray Murphy, fullback, and Mike Enich, Bruno Andruska and Herman (Ham) Snider, who had won letters under Tubbs, met with Anderson. The sophomores included Al Couppee, Bill Diehl, Bill Green, Bill Gallagher, Max Hawkins and Jim Walker. These men, with Kinnick, were to form the nucleus of a team that sprang up literally from nowhere to achieve national success and become a landmark in Hawkeye football history. Anderson's 1939 squad, his first at Iowa, became known as the "Ironmen" through the physical durability of its members — a true "Cinderella" team.

The ultimate appeal of the 1939 team was an unknown factor at the outset, however, and there was not much factual basis for nurturing optimism. Joe Sheeketski, who had accompanied Eddie Anderson to Iowa from Holy Cross, returned to the Worcester school when he was offered the head coaching position there. Sheeketski would rejoin Dr. Anderson at Iowa in 1946, but a vacancy had already been created in 1939. Frank Carideo, an all-time great quarterback at Notre Dame who led the Irish to national titles under Knute Rockne in 1929 and 1930, agreed to join the Iowa staff as backfield coach.

Bill Osmanski, perhaps Eddie Anderson's finest player at Holy Cross, spent three weeks in Iowa City aiding the new Hawkeye staff in spring football practice. Upon his return to Worcester late in April, Osmanski was quoted in the Worcester Daily Telegram, saying: "Of 5,000 male students at the University of Iowa, there are only five real football players."

Painting even further gloom, Osmanski continued, "Right now Iowa would love to have next fall's Holy Cross team, face any Big Ten opponent, and not fear one of them."

However, Dr. Anderson and his two chief assistants, line coach Jim Harris and backfield coach Frank Carideo, approached the season with enthusiasm coupled with restrained optimism.

The crowd of 16,000 that showed up for the opening game against South Dakota was somewhat larger than many games had drawn in previous seasons but it hardly reached Big Ten proportions. Nile Kinnick, scoring three touchdowns and five extra points, paced Iowa to an easy 41 − 0 victory. Kinnick's 23 points rank as the best single game effort since 1928, when Nanny Pape scored four touchdowns against Ripon.

The first great Hawkeye stand in 1939 was to be made the following week at home against Indiana. The Hoosiers had a gifted forward passer named Harold Hursch. They had not lost to an Iowa eleven since 1921. Further,

Iowa had not won a Big Ten football game in Iowa City since 1933.

Both jinxes were smashed in the aftermath of an offensive show which reached spectacular proportions. George Strickler, writing of the game in The Chicago Tribune, waxed prophetic when he commented: "The renaissance arrived at Iowa, borne triumphantly on the shoulders of Nile Kinnick and fleet-footed Erwin Prasse. Coming from behind twice, the Hawkeyes marched and passed their way to a 32 to 29 conquest of Indiana to rest, virtually hysterical with joy, at the top of the Big Ten championship race."

The lead had surged back and forth, from a 20 − 17 Iowa lead at halftime to a 29 − 20 Hoosier advantage as the fourth period began. An Iowa touchdown narrowed the margin to three points, 29 − 26, but time was running out. A final Hawk drive moved deep into Hoosier territory, placing the ball squarely in front of the goal posts on fourth down. Kinnick was a talented dropkicker and a field goal would tie the score. But Iowa scorned the three points and gambled on victory. Kinnick fired his third touchdown pass to Erwin Prasse and thrilled onlookers headed for the exits loud in their praises of the courageous "new" Hawkeyes. Word went out in the Big Ten to keep an eye on Iowa.

For the moment, however, the warning was premature. Iowa traveled to Michigan, where the Hawkeyes had been served virtually nothing but a diet of defeat. They started strong. Kinnick sped a pass to Buzz Dean who went all the way on a play that covered more than half the length of the field. With Kinnick passing, Iowa moved deep into Michigan's end of the field again but this time Tom Harmon, all-America halfback for the Wolverines, speared an angling toss and raced 90 yards to score his first of four touchdowns that afternoon. Michigan came on with more than Iowa could match and one of those who put power into the Wolverine attack was a quarterback named Evashevski — Forest Evashevski, a man destined to fill a top role in Iowa football history but who, just then, was bent only on flattening Hawkeyes to clear the way for his back-field mates. Evashevski, one of the great blockers of his time, helped lead the assault that spilled Iowa, 27 — 7. Harmon scored all of the Michigan points. That was to be the only defeat of the year for Iowa. It dulled the earlier glitter of the Hawks briefly, but they quickly renewed their advance.

It was in the very next game that the nickname Ironmen was applied to the Hawks. They wore the tag proudly and justified it to a degree that the name was still being used to describe the team a quarter of a century later.

Iowa was playing at Wisconsin. Thin in manpower at best, the players were at a season's low physically. One, Wally Bergstrom, had never played football — high school or college — until 1939, his senior year. But so lacking in personnel were the Hawks that he started against the Badgers and had to play the full 60 minutes. "He finished a college football course in one afternoon," Kinnick said after the game. Bergstrom got the call to start because Jim Walker, the regular tackle, was injured and out of action. There was no experienced replacement. Four and a half consecutive games without substitution would be the Wally Bergstrom contribution in 1939.

The Wisconsin game was furiously fought. Four Iowans, Max Hawkins, Mike Enich, Charlie Tollefson and Nile Kinnick, joined Bergstrom as 60-minute players.

Center Bill Diehl was lost for the season before the Badger game ended. But Kinnick's touchdown passes to Couppee, Evans and Bill Green were more than Wisconsin could match and Iowa won, 19 — 13.

This was a day when Iowa was content to schedule more than its share of road games, because big home crowds were not assured. So, for the third straight week in 1939 the Hawkeyes went afield for their opposition. They played at Purdue and when the gruelling match was over Iowa had another victory, by the rare score of 4 — 0, two safeties representing the entire scoring. Aboard the train on the homeward trip Jim Harris, the Iowa line coach, made a long remembered remark. "Shucks," said Har-

ris, "we didn't even need that last safety. We just wanted to make it decisive." Mike Enich took extra bows after that game. The strapping Iowa tackle twice broke through to block Boilermaker punts and in each case Purdue downed the ball in its end zone for a safety. Eight of Iowa's starting eleven, Erwin Prasse, Wally Bergstrom, Ken Pettit, Bruno Andruska, Mike Enich and Dick Evans in the line, and Al Couppee and Nile Kinnick in the backfield, played the full 60 minutes.

At the halfway mark in the season Iowa had a 3 — 1 record. Notre Dame was next. The Irish had not played in Iowa City since Dr. Anderson's playing days when the Hawkeyes won a memorable victory. This Notre Dame team, like its earlier predecessor, was unbeaten when it arrived in Iowa City and, like its predecessor, it went away a loser. This, too, stands with the great Iowa games. Notre Dame's speed and power piled up big yardage. But sixteen Kinnick punts, averaging nearly 46 yards, drove them back. Up and down the field the teams surged until Notre Dame fumbled and Ken Pettit recovered for Iowa, on the Irish four yard line. Kinnick strategy helped produce the Iowa touchdown that followed. He switched halfback positions with Buzz Dean, who had been at right half. Improvising, Kinnick took a direct pass from center and bolted into the hole opened by Dean and the Iowa line for the score, then dropkicked the extra point. Notre Dame's savage retaliatory onslaught brought a fourth quarter touchdown but the conversion failed. The Irish got no additional chance for in the waning moments Kinnick boomed one of the mightiest clutch punts on record in Iowa stadium, putting the ball out of bounds on the Notre Dame 5-yard line. Iowa won, 7 — 6, with eight Hawkeyes again playing 60 minutes.

Hawkeye stature was increasing game by game but every start meant another furious back-to-the-wall fight and the Minnesota game that followed was like the others. The Hawks were at home and their following increased day by day. Fifty-thousand jammed the stadium as the Gophers came and, as they so often did, put pressure on Iowa until one wondered

More than 50,000 fans jam Iowa Stadium to cheer the famed Ironmen.

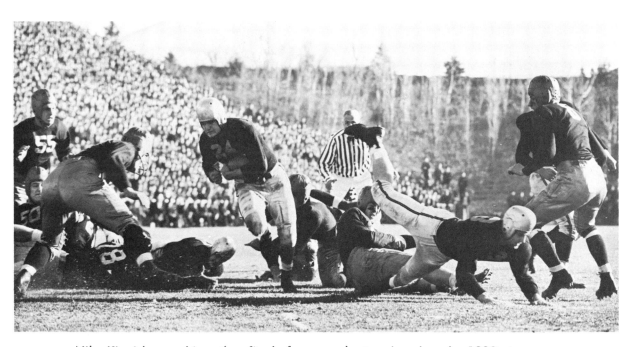

Nile Kinnick smashing the final four yards to give Iowa's 1939 team a
stunning 7 — 6 victory over previously undefeated Notre Dame.

why the Hawks did not break. Outweighed,
outpowered, outscored, Iowa went into the
fourth quarter trailing, 9 — 0. Minnesota's Joe
Mernik had kicked a 16-yard field goal in the
second quarter for a 3 — 0 lead at the half, and
George (Sonny) Franck, a Davenport native,
had sped seven yards for the only Minnesota
touchdown in the third period. With one quarter to go, a nine point deficit and a history of
not having beaten Minnesota in 10 years, Iowa's
outlook was black. But the indomitable Ironmen refused to concede. Minnesota punted

into the Iowa end zone. The Hawks put the ball in play on their 20-yard line and in four plays moved 80 yards to score. Passes, Kinnick to Dean for 18 yards on first down; then Kinnick to Dean again, for 15. A variation. Kinnick plunged for two yards, and then, on the next play, he went back to pass, maneuvering just out of the reach of crashing Gophers while Erwin Prasse sped downfield. Prasse took the pass for a touchdown and Kinnick drop-kicked the extra point. The score was 9 — 7, Minnesota, with 11 minutes to go. The ball changed hands a couple of times before Harold Van Every of Minnesota punted to Kinnick, who caught it on the Iowa 10 and ran it out to the 21. The goal was 79 yards away. Kinnick threw an incomplete pass, then one to Dean for 17. A throw to Prasse was too strong but an official called Minnesota for interference on the play and Iowa had first down on the Gopher 45. Bill Green ran for seven, and Kinnick picked up ten more. Green raced for the end zone on the next play while Kinnick faded for a pass. Newton's Bill caught it deep in the end zone, just a step away from the frenzied Iowa fans who swarmed over him a second later. Iowa won, 13 — 9. Six of Iowa's starting linemen, along with Kinnick in the backfield, played 60 minutes.

A Chicago writer began his account of the game: "Nile Kinnick 13, Minnesota 9; tersely that tells the story of the most spectacular football game in modern Big Ten history."

And a Minnesota editor opened his story: "Iowa's team of destiny and its man of the hour, Nile Kinnick, are still marching forward in the most amazing bid for the Western conference football championship in memory."

The fabulous Ironmen were in the stretch. Undermanned, undaunted and courageous, they had yet to face Northwestern. Bruno Andruska, who replaced Bill Diehl at center after the latter's injury, had played the last half of the Minnesota game with a fractured wrist which he never got around to mentioning. But he could go no further. George (Red) Frye, the last of the Iowa centers, played against the Wildcats in his first conference

Nile Kinnick

Erwin Prasse

game. He took fearful punishment but went all the way. Kinnick's shoulder was torn and battered and he was lost after 402 minutes — nearly seven straight games — without relief. The Hawks were all but spent but they had just enough left, even in their battered condition, to salvage a 7 — 7 tie at Northwestern. Ray Murphy scored the Iowa touchdown and Buzz Dean kicked the point. A victory would have given the Big Ten title to the Hawkeyes. The tie was not enough to win the championship but it was huge in the eyes of the football world.

Dr. Eddie Anderson, in his first season at Iowa, was acclaimed as Coach of the Year, and to Nile Kinnick, the durable, versatile Hawk went the greatest of all the player awards — the Heisman Trophy. No other Hawkeye has won it.

Kinnick was named on every major all-America team selected, topping the voting in both

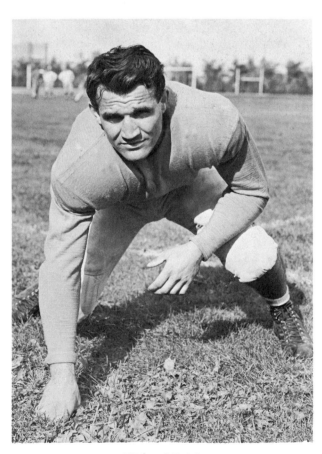

Michael Enich

the Associated Press and United Press polls. He was the most overwhelming winner of the Chicago Tribune Silver Football Award since the inauguration of the trophy in 1924. Kinnick was also selected as the outstanding male athlete of 1939, beating out baseball great Joe DiMaggio for the honor.

He scored or passed for all but 23 of the points tallied by Iowa during the 1939 season. He led the nation in two categories: runback of kickoffs with 377 yards, and defensive pass interceptions with eight. The Hawkeye immortal ranked among the nation's top ten in total offense, although the opportunist Iowa team was out-rushed, out-passed and out-first downed by its opposition during the season.

At that, no team in the Big Ten could equal the Iowa record of only a single loss in eight games through the '39 campaign.

Deserved national recognition was accorded two other Hawk heroes. Captain Erwin Prasse was a unanimous all Big Ten selection as well as a member of the United Press all-America second team.

Mike Enich, although only a junior, was given a first team all Big Ten berth and third team all-America honors by the N.E.A.

The Iowa Board in Control of Athletics was quick to recognize the success of Dr. Anderson and his staff. The 1939 season had barely ended when, on November 22, 1939, the Board voted to enter into a new contract with Anderson, with a period of six years and a salary of $12,000 involved. The Board went one additional step. It voted, at a special meeting on December 4, 1939, that Dr. Anderson be paid an additional $1,000 for his work with the 1939 team.

The Athletic Board had ample reason to recognize the contribution of Coach Anderson and his squad. Iowa's football receipts in 1938, the year before Anderson's arrival, had totaled $64,986.45, with football expenses listed at $38,751.59. Under Anderson in 1939 the football receipts climbed to $158,168.70, with expenses $44,249.09. Athletic Department figures placed the net loss to the department of $10,-

641.19 in 1938, and a net operating profit of $85,741.56 in 1939.

With the new financial success, the Board took note of semi-annual interest installments to stadium bond holders, which had gone unpaid for five years. On January 8, 1940, the Board authorized payment of $60,000, covering five of the overdue semi annual installments.

Iowa's 1939 "Ironmen" of Football.

FRONT ROW — Left to right: 63. James J. Walker, South Bend, Ind., tackle; 12. Lloyd R. Dean, Atlantic, Ia., halfback; 60. Russell H. Busk, Clinton, Ia., halfback; 16. Jack V. Edling, Moorhead, Minn., center; 39. Kenneth J. Pettit, Logan, Ia., end.

SECOND ROW — Left to right: 52. Herman Snider, Iowa City, Ia., guard; 24. Nile C. Kinnick, Jr., Omaha Nebr., halfback; 37. Erwin T. Prasse, Jr., Chicago, Ill., end; 33. Mike Enich, Boone, Ia., tackle; 35. Richard J. Evans, Chicago, end; 25. William B. Gallagher, Oskaloosa, Ia., quarterback; 21. Jens A. Norgaard Iowa City, Ia., end.

THIRD ROW — Left to right: 65. Joseph L. Moore, Ida Grove, Ia., end; 31. Robert J. Otto, Fort Dodge, Ia., tackle; 23. Carl C. Conrad, Fonda, Ia., tackle; 36. Matt S. Miletich, Chariton, Ia., tackle; 50. Burdell Gilleard, New London, Ia., halfback; 49. Henry L. Vollenweider, Dubuque, Ia., fullback; 64. Max S. Hawkins, Philadelphia, Miss., guard; Coach Eddie Anderson.

BACK ROW — Left to right: 27. Charles W. Tollefson, Elk Point, S. D., guard; 43. William C. Green, Newton, Ia., fullback; 69. James R. (Ray) Murphy, Great Neck, N. Y., fullback; 19. George D. Frye, Albia, Ia., center; 29. William F. Diehl, Cedar Rapids, Ia., center; 44. Wallace W. Bergstrom, Winfield, Ia., tackle; 11. Gerald E. Ankeny, Dixon, Ill., back; 30. Albert W. Couppee, Council Bluffs, Ia., quarterback.

BEST OF THE DECADE — 1930 — 1939

Ends	Robert Lannon	1935-1936-1937
	Erwin T. Prasse	1937-1938-1939
Tackles	Michael Enich	1938-1939-1940
	Fred Radloff	1932-1933-1934
Guards	Francis (Zud) Schammel	1932-1933-1934
	Charles Tollefson	1938-1939-1940
Center	Marcus J. Magnussen	1929-1932
Quarterback	Joseph R. Laws	1931-1932-1933
Halfbacks	Nile C. Kinnick	1937-1938-1939
	Ozzie Simmons	1934-1935-1936
Fullback	Richard Crayne	1933-1934-1935

1940

While Iowa gained national plaudits for its 1939 gridiron accomplishments, the University of Chicago also gained football notoriety, but of another kind. Chancellor Robert M. Hutchins, long an opponent of the game, formally announced that Chicago, winner of six conference championships under Amos Alonzo Stagg, would henceforth drop intercollegiate competition in football. Reverberations were heard throughout the country even though the Maroons had not had a winning season since 1929, and were outscored 192 — 0 within the conference in 1939.

It was announced by Hutchins that his school was giving up football because a winning team could not be produced without subsidizing players. On the heels of Hutchins' blast came the disclosure of Big Ten commissioner John L. Griffith that Chicago "which abandoned football because of a general overemphasis of the sport at other schools, led the entire conference in financial aid to athletes."

Chicago's two-year total was $75,943.90. It was first in total value of scholarships to athletes, fourth in student loans and third in total salaries for campus jobs. Iowa ranked third with $47,878.68, leading in total salaries paid athletes for campus jobs — $16,665.

Stagg Field, once the scene of national championship football classics, was left to weeds, desolation and later a housing development. But it was not until March, 1946, that the Maroons withdrew entirely from the conference they had helped establish.

President E. A. Gilmore of Iowa reaffirmed his support of football by stating: "If a boy is properly disposed he can derive immeasurable benefit from football. The game brings out endurance, stamina, the spirit of cooperation, the ability to take it on the chin — all of which are important in later life."

Not since 1921-22 had Iowa known success to match that of 1939. The Hawkeye realm would not experience a season of matching brilliance for 17 more years, until the first of Forest Evashevski's greatest teams marched at the front of the Big Ten parade.

The year 1940 opened auspiciously. The fans foresaw a great season. Many of the Ironmen were on hand once more but Nile Kinnick was no longer a player, nor were the pass-grabbing ends, Prasse and Evans. The Hawks opened against South Dakota as they had the year before, and the 46 — 0 victory was greater than the 1939 verdict. In the course of the game, with the Hawkeyes completely dominating, the South Dakota quarterback, Bob Burns, after trying just about everything without success, called across the scrimmage line to the Iowa quarterback:

"Couppee, you're a Big Ten quarterback. What would you call?"

Wisconsin was measured for a 30 — 12 trimming, Jim Walker racing 66 yards with a blocked punt for a score and Bill Green racking up three touchdowns. Jim Youel, a sophomore, gave indication of promise as a passer. Iowa's followers were sky-high in enthusiasm, but the Big Ten had not forgotten the Hawkeye forays of 1939. Indiana, out to avenge the 32 — 29 loss of the year before, succeeded 10 — 6, with "Oops" Gilleard scoring Iowa's points. Minnesota, still burning from the 13 — 9 loss in Dr.

Anderson's opening year, played host to the Hawks most energetically, Coach Bernie Bierman's powerhouse winning, 34 — 6. George (Sonny) Franck riddled the Iowa defense with four touchdowns. Purdue came for the Iowa Homecoming and belted the Hawks, 21 — 6 and Nebraska deepened the gloom by sacking up the Hawkeyes, 14 — 6. There was little reason to hope for the return of better things against unbeaten Notre Dame but, borrowing a page from the book of the Ironmen, the Hawkeyes played another of their unforgettable games and won, 7 — 0. Thus Notre Dame's record took strange form — three meetings with Iowa, three Notre Dame defeats — each breaking an Irish undefeated streak.

Line and backfield men of Iowa shared the roar that went up across the state but the bulk of the tributes went to Mike Enich, Bill Green, Ross Anderson, Bill Burkett, Jim Walker and Ken Pettit. Enich, at one point, captured a loose ball and stampeded more than 50 yards to eliminate an Irish threat. Bill Green, in one of his greatest games, rushed for more than 100 yards and scored the Iowa touchdown. Only Illinois remained and the Hawks took charge in that game to win, 18 — 7. It was a standoff season, 4 — 4, with the glamor of the Ironmen still a treasured memory. Gate receipts enabled the Board to pay off $96,000 more in overdue payments to bondholders, thus clearing obligations to September 15, 1940.

Ironman Mike Enich merited high honors for his play in 1940. In addition to consensus all conference selection, the Iowa tackle was named to the first all-America teams of both the New York News and The Sporting News.

Bill Green, although only a junior, was all midwestern at fullback. The speedy Green would join an exclusive group of 1000 yard ground gainers at Iowa before his career would close.

1941

Prior to the 1941 season the football rules committee legislated in favor of free substitution, a far-reaching enactment. A player could henceforth be substituted for at any time, and communication between players was legalized for the first time.

A year before, the committee after lengthy deliberation added a negative clause which said simply: "Female cleats without an effective locking device are prohibited."

Couppee, Diehl, Green and Walker formed the basic nucleus of the 1941 team but the squad included 15 letter winners from the 1940 season and a few newcomers of promise. Success was elusive, however. The Hawks, in their last meeting with Drake, were 25 — 8 winners. Bus Mertes, later to coach the Bulldogs, led Iowa with two touchdowns, one a 59 yard jaunt from scrimmage. Anderson's team defeated Indiana, 13 — 7, and Illinois, 21 — 0, but were shut out by Michigan, 6 — 0, and by Wisconsin, 23 — 0. The Badgers held Iowa to a minus 87 yards rushing. The Hawks lost to Purdue, 7 — 6; to national champion Minnesota, 34 — 13, and to Nebraska, 14 — 13, thus experiencing one of the least successful seasons of the Anderson regime.

CHAPTER
18

War Once Again -- 1942-1946

On March 7, 1942, the Big Ten waived certain conference rules because of wartime restrictions and conditions, permitting a ten-game football schedule in 1942 and permitting games with teams that "do not observe conference rules."

In the 1942 opener Washington University was unable to match the Hawks and lost, 26 – 7. Next came Nebraska and a chance for vengeance by Iowa. The Hawks made the most of it, Tom Farmer firing three touchdown passes in the course of the 27 – 0 victory. World War II was on and the Great Lakes Naval Training Station was in athletics in a big way. The Sailors belted the Hawkeyes, 25 – 0, and Camp Grant followed with an Army challenge the following week, but Iowa downed the soldier trainees, 33 – 16.

In the give and take season Iowa played Illinois and lost, 12 – 7, but won a 14 – 13 squeaker from Indiana. Purdue, with Chuck Uknes playing his finest game, was defeated, 13 – 7, and on came Wisconsin, with its sights on the national championship. In the lineup of the undefeated Badgers were such notables as Elroy (Crazylegs) Hirsch, Pat Harder, Dave Schreiner and others. On the last play of the first half Iowa stopped the Badgers on the very goal line and fought off every Wisconsin challenge in the last half. For Iowa, Tom Farmer

hurled a scoring pass to Bill Burkett and the upset of the year was Iowa's, the Hawkeyes winning, 6 – 0.

Five Hawkeyes, Tom Farmer, Jim Youel, John Staak, Bob Penaluna and Bob Yelton played sixty minutes. The resulting victory, which deprived Wisconsin of the national title, was the last Big Ten triumph by Iowa for more than three years.

The Hawks faltered in their remaining games, losing to Minnesota, 27 – 7, and to Michigan, 28 – 14. Iowa registered only two first downs, one by rushing and one by passing against the vaunted Gophers. Dick Hoerner, a powerful fullback who played only a season before entering military service hit a high spot of his Iowa career when he raced 89 yards with the second half kickoff to score against Michigan. Hoerner would return in 1946 to receive all Big Ten honors. Tom Farmer gained national recognition for his brilliant passing, being chosen third team all-America by sportscaster Bill Stern and named to the Big Ten first unit by Central Press Association.

The 1942 season was unusual in that war, and pending military service, vied with football to claim the attention of players and coaches everywhere. As the men reported for military duty Dr. Eddie Anderson entered the Army medical corps as a major and Frank Carideo, the backfield coach, won a lieutenant's commission in the Navy. The Hawkeyes were to see no more of these coaches until 1946, when the war was over. Meanwhile, three seasons of hopelessly undermanned football were ahead, with the Hawkeye 'teen-agers sometimes going against seasoned teams manned by rugged service trainees. Few schools escaped a wartime sag of some sort, however.

Dr. Anderson was in his fourth season as head football coach when he made the decision to seek a leave of absence in order that he might add his services to the Army medical corps. Under date of November 18, 1942, he announced to the University's Board in Control of Athletics his intention to enter the armed forces. He wrote:

"I believe that I shall shortly take steps to enter the service of the United States, as I feel that it is my duty. I realize that I have an obligation to the University of Iowa but at this time I feel, and I think that you will agree with me, that I have a more important obligation to our country. . .

"If I go into the service," Dr. Anderson continued, "the compensation which I would receive would be inadequate to carry out the program which I have before me, largely in the nature of life insurance. . .I would like to have my present contract with the University remain status quo. . .I would like to have my contract take up when I return at the same place it is when I leave.

"Also, I would like very much to have the Athletic Board. . .pay me $200.00 a month while I am in service. The salary I would receive, that of Captain or Major in the Army, or its equivalent in the Navy, would not permit me to carry my insurance program. When I return they can deduct from my salary the sum of $200.00 monthly until the amount which has been advanced, plus reasonable interest . . .has been paid. If, in the interim, anything happens to me, the money would be paid out of my insurance."

The Board in Control of Athletics approved Dr. Anderson's request for a leave of absence but, not wishing to set a precedent, denied his request for compensation during his absence.

As interest lessened in intercollegiate athletics, the State University's athletic facilities hummed with the activities of pre-flight trainees and Seahawk athletic teams. The attempt to keep major athletic programs of two institutions going simultaneously on one campus strained the available facilities. The Navy's Pre-Flight School had control of most of the Athletic Department fields and facilities. Problems frequently arose regarding their use. In these jurisdictional discussions, spokesmen for the Pre-Flight School were known to inform representatives of the University that the Navy Department had authority to declare any part of the fieldhouse or the playing fields a naval reservation during such time as these facilities were in use by the Pre-Flight School. Any resulting tension was quieted by the authorities of the University and the Pre-Flight School.

The combination of problems centering around the departure of students for military duty, the hiring of interim coaches and the attempt to maintain an intercollegiate athletic program in the same area occupied by the Iowa Pre-Flight School had its discouraging aspects. At one stage, presidential correspondence files indicate, President Virgil M. Hancher might have favored a moratorium on intercollegiate sports for the duration of the war had he not yielded to the recommendations of some newspapers and conference officials.

With the heavy drain on its manpower due to departures for the service, freshmen were made eligible by the Conference as an emergency measure. The Big Ten did not suspend its athletic program. Indeed, some schools gained greater strength when service trainees were assigned to the campus for special training programs. For Iowa, however, the start of hostilities in Europe was a tremendous blow to any athletic hopes it may have had.

Interesting events were occurring on the campus, however. The Board in Control of Athletics, at a meeting November 10, 1942, recommended the employment of Paul Brechler as freshman basketball coach for the 1942 season.

He was to serve from November 1, 1942, to February 28, 1943, at a monthly stipend of $75.00 — a total of $300 for the season. Brechler, at a late date, was to become the University's director of athletics at a substantial salary.

With the departure of Dr. Anderson, the necessity of appointing an active head football coach arose. Minutes of a Board meeting on February 15, 1943, record the appointment of Jim Harris as acting head coach. Harris had served as line coach under Dr. Anderson. Minutes of another Board meeting, on April 19, 1943, disclosed the resignation of Mr. Harris, which was "accepted with the stipulation that his connection with athletics at Iowa be permanently terminated."

Dr. E. G. Schroeder, the director of athletics, was given instructions at a special Board meet-

Head Football Coach — 1943-1944
E. P. (Slip) Madigan

ing one day later to interview Maurice (Clipper) Smith of Villanova about assuming the coaching duties at Iowa until the return of Dr.

Anderson. It was May 24, the records reveal, when Director Schroeder reported to the Board that Smith had accepted a commission in the Marine Corps and would be unavailable for duty at Iowa. Hawkeye authorities looked elsewhere in the field of men who had been trained in the Notre Dame system of football and on June 18, 1943, Director Schroeder recommended the appointment of Edward (Slip) Madigan as acting head coach. Madigan, widely known earlier as the coach of Santa Clara's Galloping Gaels, received the appointment and with it compensation of $5,000 for the period from July 1, 1943, through December 31, 1943.

A month before Madigan's term was to begin, the University, the state and the nation were shocked to learn that Ensign Nile Kinnick had been killed in the Caribbean Sea while attempting to crash land his disabled fighter plane.

The soft-spoken, unassuming Kinnick, not yet 25 years old, has no parallel in Iowa sports history. His bearing as an all-American on the football field, and as a Phi Beta Kappa scholar in the classroom, were only indications of the way he lived his whole life.

Within two months following his death President Virgil Hancher had given considerable thought to a Kinnick Memorial, under University auspices, which would "keep alive the memory of his qualities and ideals."

Three ideas were advanced: 1) naming the Stadium for Kinnick; 2) collecting a fund for the building of a Kinnick memorial on the campus; and 3) collecting a fund for scholarship awards to bear Kinnick's name.

Mr. and Mrs. Nile Kinnick Sr. wrote President Hancher expressing their feeling that "if the Stadium is rededicated that it be in the names of all men and women of the University who made the last sacrifice in the war."

By 1945 a scholarship memorial bearing Kinnick's name but in memory of all Iowa men who died in service during World War II was a reality. It has provided seventy-seven worthy young men the opportunity of attending the University to perpetuate the ideals, scholastic achievements and sportsmanship typical of Iowa men as exemplified by Nile Kinnick.

Frank Bloomquist, Burt Britzman, Bill Fenton, Andy Houg, Lynn Lyon, Kenny Ploen, Roger Wiegman and Ralph Woodard are among the football recipients of Nile Kinnick grants who have been outstanding scholar-athletes.

1943

The team of "schoolboys" which greeted interim Coach Slip Madigan in the autumn of 1943 was in odd contrast to the rugged array of manpower on the nearby Iowa Pre-Flight squad. Madigan's lot, from a coaching standpoint, was nearly hopeless. Even Bill Hofer, the freshman coach, had reported for military duty. Except for players of tender age, or men permitted to remain at the University for medical or dental training, the playing personnel changed week by week.

Coach Madigan brought no assistants with him but called on Maury Kent, Glen Devine and Waddy Davis of the athletic department to complete his staff. In spite of the unusual conditions, Madigan's team made a creditable start. It held a strong Great Lakes team to a 21 — 7 score and lost a 7 — 5 game to Wisconsin, the Hawks scoring on a safety and a 45-yard Bill Barbour field goal. The powerful Iowa Seahawks, featuring some of the great names of college football, marked up a 25 — 0 victory over Iowa. The undermanned Hawks tied undermanned Indiana, 7 — 7, and for three quarters led a Purdue team that was heavily bolstered by service trainees. However, the Boilermakers scored three times in the final twelve minutes to subdue Iowa, 28 — 7. Tony Butkovich made three Purdue touchdowns. He was called into active service after only four conference games, but notched thirteen six pointers against Ohio State, Illinois, Wisconsin and Iowa to establish an all-time Big Ten mark. The previous record of twelve touchdowns had been set by Iowa's Gordon Locke in 1922.

Illinois added further dismay in 1943 by downing the Hawks, and so did Minnesota, on the strength of four touchdowns scored and one thrown by Gopher "Red" Williams. But Madigan's men had enough left to finish out with a 33 — 13 victory over a Nebraska team that was also having its wartime manpower troubles.

The largest crowd to view the Hawkeyes in Iowa City was 11,200 for the Illinois game. Their biggest thrill, perhaps, came when Illini Eddie McGovern intercepted an Iowa pass and raced 95 yards to score. It was the second longest touchdown ever made against Iowa, exceeded only by a 98 yard scrimmage dash of Indiana's Mickey Erehart in 1912.

Gross football receipts were $35,562.15, lowest such figure since 1918 with the exception of the depression year of 1932. In less than twenty years, income from radio broadcast rights and football program sales alone would match the 1943 gate receipts.

1944

The Board in Control of Athletics gave its reaction to Madigan's effort by offering him a new contract. On December 6, 1943, the Board proposed an eight-months agreement, for which Madigan was to receive $7,500. The proposal was passed and Madigan signed for the 1944 season.

But 1944 was a repeat of 1943, except that manpower was at an even lower ebb and defeats higher in margin. Iowa opened at Ohio State and lost, 34 — 0. In succession it bowed to Illinois, 40 — 6, to Purdue, 26 — 7, and to Indiana, 32 — 0. Discouraged, Madigan notified friends that night at Indiana that he was through. Whether this report helped spur the players is not known but they came through with a 27 — 6 victory over Nebraska, then faded against more superior opposition and lost to Wisconsin, 26 — 7; to Minnesota, 46 — 0, and to Iowa Pre-Flight, 30 — 6.

It should be noted that the plucky Hawkeyes held Nebraska without a first down by rushing, but two weeks later Minnesota permitted Iowa only 19 yards total offense, and the following week, against the powerful Seahawks, Iowa's ground game was able to notch but one first down.

Gross income from the Iowa-Seahawk game amounted to $290.42. However, the cost of policing and hiring of ticket sellers came to $360.27. An additional $348.84 was paid to the officials and $248.43 was the Seahawks' share of receipts. Scouting and other expenses totalled $200.56, leaving Iowa with a net loss of $867.68 in addition to the 24-point defeat.

On November 20, 1944, the Iowa Board once more considered the coaching situation and agreed to offer Madigan compensation of $1,000 per month to coach the 1945 team. He declined and the Hawks were forced to search anew for another interim coach. At a March 5 Board meeting, Athletic Director Schroeder reported having contacted several possible candidates, among them Clarence (Biggie) Munn, then line coach at Michigan, and Hugh Devore, line coach at Notre Dame. The lack of permanency surrounding the position caused Munn to indicate a lack of interest. Devore was to be named to a similar interim post at Notre Dame the next day. The Board, consequently, authorized the athletic director to proceed with his search for a coach and to offer a contract not to exceed $9,000 in salary. Schroeder's next nominee was Clem Crowe, another exponent of the Notre Dame system. Crowe visited Iowa City and met with the Board on March 15, 1945. He was offered a two-year contract at $9,000 salary annually and accepted. Thus Iowa's second interim coach of the war period was hired.

Meanwhile, others who were to stand squarely in the spotlight in the Iowa athletic picture of subsequent years were on the Hawkeye campus. On the Iowa Pre-Flight scene Forest Evashevski, a Michigan graduate and a man who had won wide acclaim as a block-ing back, was one of the many athletic greats training on the campus. Evashevski was a quarterback for the Pre-Flight football team and an instructor in hand to hand combat as it was taught to the Air Force pilots in the training program.

Paul Brechler, too, was a man who cast only a nominal shadow on the Hawkeye scene in the early stages of World War II. He had been a coach at University High in Iowa City. The University had appointed him freshman basket-

Head Football Coach — 1945
Clem Crowe

ball coach late in 1942. A year later he, too, was in uniform and he, like Evashevski, served in the Navy. There is no crossing of their paths on record during their service days. In the postwar days they were to serve in close proximity at the University of Iowa. Some of the University's greatest athletic progress was to be made during their tenures and days of wide disagreement were to be known.

Kenneth L. (Tug) Wilson, long time athletic director at both Drake and Northwestern, was appointed Commissioner of the Big Ten Conference in March, 1945. Wilson succeeded John L. Griffith who had held the position since 1922. Griffith died on December 7, 1944.

1945

Clem Crowe left an assistant's post at Notre Dame to take over the Iowa team of 1945. He brought with him as new staff members Bud Boeringer, a one-time varsity center for the Fighting Irish, and Charles Jaskwich, a former Notre Dame quarterback. He reportedly equipped the Hawks with plays identical with those employed by Notre Dame, but the men who were to execute the plays for Iowa were a shade less efficient, or gifted, than their Irish counterparts. In short, Clem Crowe's experiences, with one great exception, were much the same as those of Slip Madigan.

Jerry Niles, a quarterback who specialized in passing, had returned to Iowa for the 1945 season, after having first appeared on the scene as a center under Irl Tubbs seven years before. Niles and his mates instilled a trace of hope in Iowa circles when the Hawks edged Bergstrom Field, a service team, 14 — 13 in the opener. But the faint optimism was blotted out on the next start, a 42 — 0 trimming by Ohio State. Then, in succession, Iowa was trampled by Purdue, 40 — 0 and by Indiana, 52 — 20. The Hoosiers led 52 — 0 after three quarters, but strangely Iowa outrushed, outpassed and out-first downed the winners by wide margins. Notre Dame shook off the jinx created by earlier Iowa elevens by smashing the Iowa team coached by Crowe, the former Notre Dame assistant coach, 56 — 0. It was the first victory ever earned by the Fighting Irish over the Hawkeyes, and the most decisive on record. Iowa made only two first downs against 55 Notre Dame players, 44 of whom were used before halftime.

The ill-fated Hawkeyes moved next against Wisconsin and went down, 27 — 7. Illinois overwhelmed them, 48 — 7, and on came Minnesota. Iowa had gone eighteen straight conference games without a victory and had been outscored 278 — 48 in its first six games of 1945, so if the Gophers treated themselves to a bit of complacency, it was understandable. Minnesota started impressively enough, but the astonishing surge by Iowa in the latter stages

was entirely unexpected. The Hawks came roaring from behind, scored three touchdowns, and waylaid the Gophers, 20 — 19. Iowa's winning touchdown came on a screen pass, Niles to Nelson Smith, who took the ball at midfield and went all the way.

Floyd of Rosedale, the prized bronzed pig was returned to Iowa City after a five year stay in Gopherland. It was only the second Hawkeye triumph since the porker had first been vied for in 1935.

An Iowa sportswriter waxed a poetic tribute following the upset victory:

> Iowa Hog With Fancy Name
> Was a Trophy of the Game.
>
> Minnesota's Head is Achin'
> Iowa Won the Castiron Bacon.

Hawkeye morale was high going into the final game at Nebraska. The team had its chances, failed to capitalize, and lost 13 — 6. Jerry Niles broke two Iowa single season passing records, for yards gained and pass interceptions thrown. The latter, 16, remains an all-time school high. Clem Crowe had served one year of his contract, but he served no more since Dr. Eddie Anderson had been discharged from his medical post after military service at Churchill Hospital near London, England, and returned to the University.

Within a few weeks after the close of the 1945 season the Iowa Board forwarded to President Virgil M. Hancher a recommendation that Anderson be given a new five-year contract as head football coach and on February 13, 1946, the president announced the new contract, approving at the same time one-year contracts to Frank Carideo and Joe Sheeketski, assistant coaches.

The University of Chicago, not having fielded a football team for six years although still technically a part of the Big Ten Conference, formally and completely resigned as a member institution in March. For the next three years the Big Ten would be known unofficially as the Big Nine.

PAUL BRECHLER

Paul Brechler, returning from naval service, moved toward a more prominent spot in the athletic department picture. Charles S. Galiher, the University's business manager of athletics, announced his resignation to enter the insurance business in Iowa City. Brechler was on duty at University High in Iowa City when the vacancy loomed in the post of business manager of athletics. The Board had accepted Galiher's resignation "with regret," the records disclosed. Dr. Karl E. Leib, then chairman of the Board in Control of Athletics and faculty representative to the Big Ten conference, made a call on Brechler. He was accompanied by E. G. (Dad) Schroeder, the athletic director.

They wondered if Brechler might be interested in the position of business manager of athletics. Brechler thought not, and the University's emissaries departed. They returned in a week, however. They informed him, Brechler later disclosed, that Director Schroeder was nearing the retirement age and that Brechler most certainly would be given consideration for the directorship, providing he accepted the business manager's post and handled it creditably. There was no definite commitment involving the directorship, Brechler said, but the possibility was of interest. He accepted the offer of the business manager's job and assumed his duties on July 1, 1946.

In the meantime other names were offered to President Virgil Hancher as possible considerations for the soon to be vacant directorship. Among them were Bill Boelter, Leonard Raffensperger, Wes Fry, Lawrence (Pops) Harrison and Willis Glassgow. Boelter, one of Drake's all-time great athletes, had served as assistant coach at both Iowa and Syracuse. Raffensperger, later to be Iowa's head football coach, was a highly successful high school coach and teacher in Waterloo. Wes Fry, star of Hawkeye teams in the mid-twenties, had spent most of his coaching years as an assistant to Lynn (Pappy) Waldorf, first at Northwestern and later at California. Pops Harrison was then coaching the defending Big Ten champion Iowa basketball team, and Willis Glassgow,

the nation's outstanding gridder in 1929, was a Cedar Rapids businessman.

Hancher himself felt that Eddie Anderson would be an excellent choice if 1) he would be willing to devote his life to athletic work and discontinue medical work, and 2) he would not consider the financial sacrifice too great for him to make. Anderson himself negated the possibility of pursuing the idea.

Dad Schroeder retired on schedule, and more names popped up as possible candidates to succeed him as director of athletics. The name of Tom Hamilton, who had headed the Navy's Pre-Flight program, was mentioned. Rollie F. Williams, Iowa's head basketball

Athletic Director — 1947-1960
Paul Brechler

coach from 1929 until 1942, was a strong possibility. He had returned to duty at Iowa shortly before, after assignments in the Navy which included a high post in the athletic program of the Great Lakes Naval Training Station. Even the name of Dr. Leib, the Board chairman and faculty representative, was suggested as a candidate for the directorship.

Brechler, however, won the appointment of the Board and on July 1, 1947, one year from the day he had assumed the post of business manager of athletics, he stepped up to head the department as director of athletics. His starting salary was $6,500, an increase of $2,000 over the salary for the post he was vacating.

CHAPTER

19

1946-1952:
From Anderson
Through
Raffensperger

The business of readjusting the athletic department to a peacetime footing after its shaky wartime operations provided difficulties but most of them were met as they arose. In football Dr. Anderson resumed command and the Hawkeyes promptly moved up to the Big Nine level, bolstered as they were with added maturity and experience represented by men returning from the service. His 1946 team rapped North Dakota State, 39 — 0 in the opener and along the way they defeated Purdue, 16 — 0; Nebraska, 21 — 7; Indiana, 13 — 0, and Wisconsin, 21 — 7. The Badgers were held to one first down during the game. But the Hawkeyes took their lumps too, as the 14 — 7 loss to Michigan, the 41 — 6 pounding by Notre Dame and the 7 — 0 loss to Illinois suggest. The Hawks won four of their first five games but finished with a 5 — 4 record and a 3 — 3 mark for a fifth place tie in the conference.

Financially the season was the most successful in history. Football receipts totalled more than $245,000, the most since 1929. In addition the 52,300 on hand for the Notre Dame game was the largest crowd in ten years.

Individually three Hawkeyes gained mythical post-season honors. Earl Banks, squat Negro guard, became the first and only Iowan ever to receive all conference recognition in his freshman year. Banks was named on the United Press first team.

Dick Hoerner, returned from service duty, made the Associated Press all-conference first team at fullback, and junior Bill Kay was given a third team tackle berth on the Central Press all-America eleven. Bob Smith, another service veteran, became the first Hawkeye since Ozzie Simmons to rush for more than 500 yards in a single season.

Far-reaching, high level discussions were being held by athletic and academic administrators of the Big Nine and Pacific Coast conferences in the fall of 1946. Announcement came early in September that the Big Nine had voted affirmatively to enter into a five year agreement with the coast organization permitting appearance in the Rose Bowl. The Big Nine requested action by the Pacific Coast "as early as possible," the pact to take effect on New Year's Day, 1947.

Faculty representatives of the coast schools were to meet in November. Their decision, although not supported by U.C.L.A. and Southern California, was to solidify the agreement immediately.

The Los Angeles Times presented the story to its readers:

In Memoriam. . . . .

THE ROSE BOWL

Born. . . . . .January 1, 1916
Died. . . .November 20, 1946

May It Rest In Peace

It had been hoped that unbeaten and untied U.C.L.A. would host undefeated Army, featuring touchdown twins Glenn Davis and Doc Blanchard. The immediacy of the Pacific Coast-Big Nine merger thwarted such an opportunity. Instead, twice-beaten Illinois, one touchdown victors over Iowa, was the reluctant but mandatory choice. The underdog, unrated and unwelcome Illini responded vehemently, winning, 45 − 14.

Came 1947 at Iowa, with Brechler in the director's chair. Karl Leib, for nine years chairman of the Board in Control of Athletics, and later president of the N.C.A.A. between 1947 and 1949, resigned his duties on the Board. His place was filled by Paul Blommers, named Iowa's faculty representative to the conference and elected Board chairman. Within a year, Rudy Kuever, dean of the School of Pharmacy, would also resign from the Board. Kuever played a significant role in the legislation and execution of Iowa athletic policy for 32 years — longer than any faculty or alumni board member.

1947

The 1947 Iowa football team opened by pasting North Dakota State, 59 − 0, smashing for 27 points in the final quarter. The winners notched 28 first downs and rolled up an impressive 566 yards total offense. Thoughts were quickly turned to a California trip and a meeting with U.C.L.A. A 22 − 7 loss resulted before 90,910 fans, most ever to see a regular season Iowa game, and on their next time out Illinois slammed past the Hawkeyes, 35 − 12. The readjustment problem was mentioned at Iowa and at other schools. Young men with wartime experiences, many of whom had become accustomed to giving rather than taking orders, now comprised the athletic squads. As players they had problems, as did their coaches. Iowa, losing its first two major games, seemed to indicate that its readjustment would be slowed appreciably. Suddenly the team reversed itself and conquered Indiana, 27 − 14. Emlen Tunnell, one of Anderson's finest all-around players, caught a record-tying three touchdown passes from quarterback Al DiMarco. Tunnell's 155 yards gained as a pass receiver that day established a single game record which would last for ten years.

A 13 − 13 tie with Ohio State followed and the Hawks were all square for the season at 2 − 2 − 1. Another relapse set in — three more losses on successive Saturday's and by decisive scores. National champion Notre Dame, led by Johnny Lujack, defeated Iowa, 21 − 0. Purdue won by the same score and Wisconsin smashed the Hawkeyes, 46 − 7. Dissatisfaction with the showing of the team became widespread and the unrest reached a quick climax.

Minnesota was about to arrive for the final game of the season and Dr. Anderson, quite aware of the shortcomings of the Hawks and noting the increasing unrest among the fans, took action. He filed his resignation. It was submitted on the eve of the Minnesota game, Anderson having been unable to contact President Hancher until late in the evening of Friday, eighteen hours before the game. President Hancher accepted the resignation conditionally, since it had not yet been presented to the Board in Control of Athletics. Announcement of the resignation reached the public the morning of the Minnesota game. President Hancher called for a quick conference with Brechler, the athletic director, and Jim Jordan, director of the University News Bureau. Dr. Anderson's contract had been written to include the 1950 season, at a $12,500 salary.

Meanwhile, the Hawks had a football date with Minnesota. It was cold and windy and the slush of a recent snowstorm covered the stadium seats. The crowd poured in, however, and the general subject of conversation was not the football team or its losses but the sudden and unexpected resignation of Coach Anderson. Temperature dropped to freezing as the game began. A record equalling crowd of 53,000 jammed the stadium. Some Minnesota partisans suggested that Iowa was going to great lengths in trying to win a football game — having its coach resign the day of the game. Coach Anderson's squad knew there was nothing rigged about the resignation, however, and they responded with a powerful effort. The Hawks fought off the Gophers, scored twice on a pass to Hal Schoener and a smash by Ron Headington, and won the game, 13 — 7.

Iowa fans, sensing the fury of the team that was turning back the Gophers, reacted to every decision unfavorable to the Hawkeyes. Sometimes their reaction took the form of a shower of snowballs. When the Hawks retained their aggressive fury all the way and won, more than a few casual onlookers wondered why the team had not played at such a tempo against Notre Dame, Purdue and Wisconsin. Floyd of Rosedale, the game trophy, came home to Iowa and satisfaction over the victory mounted, as did suggestions that Anderson withdraw his resignation. Reports, lacking confirmation, had it that the coach might be inclined to reconsider.

Word went out to the members of the Board in Control of Athletics setting a meeting for the following Monday and urging the presence of the full membership. On the Board were Dr. Paul Blommers, chairman; Dean Mason Ladd, Prof. J. W. Jones, Dean Chester Phillips, Business Manager of the University Fred N. Ambrose, Dean Bruce Mahan, Dr. Stuart Cullen, Prof. Fred Higbee, Dr. R. A. Fenton, Dr. Paul Brechler and Walter L. (Stub) Stewart and Dr. Wayne Foster, alumni members. The meeting began with dinner at the Jefferson Hotel but the night's action only produced a postponement, since Board members considered it advisable to confer with Dr. Anderson before reaching a decision. A three-day period was agreed upon before the resumption of the meeting.

Just before the session reconvened, three Board members met with Coach Anderson — Chairman Blommers, Director Brechler and Alumnus Stewart. Their discussion was thorough and Dr. Anderson apparently was agreeable to a suggestion that he remain at the University, for out of the continuation of the postponed meeting came this unanimous action by the Board:

"The Board in Control of Athletics, after careful consideration of the circumstances leading to the resignation of Dr. Edward N. Anderson as head football coach at the State University of Iowa, and in accordance with the recommendation of Dr. Paul W. Brechler, director of athletics, unanimously recommends to President Virgil M. Hancher that, in the best interest of the State University of Iowa, the resignation be not accepted." President Hancher approved the recommendation of the Board and expressed the hope that "everyone will work together." Anderson said he was "thankful things had been straightened out."

Before the unexpected resignation had been submitted, the Board, acting on the anticipation of sustained drawing power of Iowa teams coached by Eddie Anderson, had mapped a financial campaign designed to free the stadium of a debt of long standing. On March 7, 1946, it had negotiated a loan aimed at retiring some $300,000 in bonded indebtedness. Approximately one year later, Director Brechler was authorized to pay off $100,000 of the loan. Within six months an additional $50,000 was paid, and finally, on March 11, 1948, following a football season in which receipts exceeded $300,000 for the first time, the Board voted that the total remainder of the stadium debt, the sum of $152,000, be paid off. Athletic income from all sports would top one-half million dollars in the 1947-48 school year, a new high. With the athletic department thus relieved of a financial burden of nearly 20 years' standing, the way was cleared for physical expansion and improvement of the athletic department property.

Football income, having increased tenfold in the four years between 1943 and 1947, had been further augmented by an increase in the price of individual game tickets from $2.75 to $3.00 in 1946, and up to $3.50 prior to the 1948 season.

A new Iowa mascot, first since the short, ill-fated tenure of "Burch," the bear-cub, in 1908 and 1909, was born on an artist's drawing board in 1948. Dick Spencer, a member of the journalism staff created "Herky the Hawk" in answer to a plea by the S.U.I. athletic department to find an emblem for the teams.

Spencer submitted several life drawings and added, as an afterthought, a caricature which became "Herky." He has since been featured on many homecoming badges, has been highlighted countless times in feature stories throughout the state and in official university publications. Revered whether from the artist's pen or alive on the football sidelines, "Herky" became an Iowa tradition overnight.

1948

Eddie Anderson still had Frank Carideo as his backfield coach, with Pat Boland handling the line as thoughts were turned toward the 1948 season. The head freshman coach was Leonard Raffensperger. The Hawks had Marquette as an opening opponent; Indiana, Ohio State, Illinois and Boston University as opponents away from home, and games with Purdue, Notre Dame, Wisconsin and Minnesota in the stadium. The victories fell just short of offsetting the defeats, with Iowa winning four while losing five, and finishing 2 − 4 for a fifth place tie in the conference.

Home fans were treated to one of the fine comeback performances by an Iowa team when the Hawks struck for three second half touchdowns to erase a 13 − 0 Badger halftime lead and win, 19 − 13. In the season finale against Boston University, Al DiMarco, completing an abbreviated two year career, threw passes totalling 246 yards, 151 of which were received by Jack Dittmer. DiMarco ran his season passing yardage to more than 1,000, the first time the feat had been accomplished.

Bill Kay and Dick Woodard also closed their Iowa careers. Kay again was named to the all-conference first team, and was further recognized by the Associated Press with a position on its second all-America team. Woodard, a four year performer, was the Hawkeye passing leader in 1944, spent a year in service, and returned as a center to bulwark Iowa lines from 1946 thru 1948.

The Big Nine added its own bit of history on December 12, 1948, when it was voted that Michigan State College be admitted to membership following faculty representative certification. Such action came on May 20, 1949, and the Big Nine once again became the Big Ten.

1949

Coach Anderson's final season at Iowa was 1949 and it was something of a duplicate of the 1948 campaign in the matter of victories and defeats. Three of the four wins, however, were over conference opponents. Through the Oregon game, sixth contest of the season, Iowa had a 4 − 2 record and a team strong enough to average 26 points a game against such opponents as U.C.L.A., Purdue, Illinois, Indiana, Northwestern and Oregon. The closing games did not follow that pattern. All three were lost and the opposition stacked up a combined total of 118 points. Minnesota beat Iowa, 55 − 7, rolling for 27 points in the fourth quarter; Wisconsin won, 35 − 13 and Notre Dame won, 28 − 7. And yet there were thrilling highlights, particularly against Northwestern and Oregon. Jerry Faske, a high school all-American from New York, set a modern era rushing record which has remained unbroken in regular-season play, when he ran for 183 yards in 20 attempts against the Wildcats. However, it was a brilliant 63 yard fourth period scoring pass, Fred Ruck to Jack Dittmer, which capped the Hawkeye victory, 26 − 21.

A week later the most exciting comeback effort in Iowa history was unfolded before 38,000 fans. Late in the third period, with the

Hawks trailing Oregon, 24 — 6, Bob Longley fielded a Webfoot punt on his own six and raced 94 yards to score, the longest punt return in S.U.I. football. Moments later a 21 yard touchdown toss, Faske to Dittmer, brought the Hawkeyes close, 24 — 20. But Oregon retaliated, pushing the margin to 31 — 20. On the ensuing kickoff sophomore Bill Reichardt dashed 99 yards to score, once again leaving the Iowans four points short. After holding Oregon for downs a final Hawk drive was climaxed with Reichardt smashing into the end zone. Iowa had scored 28 points in 9 minutes and 47 seconds, winning 34 — 31, and throwing back Oregon in the final minute after the invaders had gained a first down on the Iowa four.

Jack Dittmer, one of the great pass receiving ends to play for the Old Gold, finished his career the holder of five school reception records, including most passes caught in a career, most yards gained during a season and career, as well as most touchdown passes caught over the same stretch. Dittmer's record of six scoring passes in a season has never been exceeded, although tied, and his thirteen career six-pointers remains an all-time school record.

BEST OF THE DECADE — 1940-1949

Ends	Jack Dittmer	1946-1947-1948-1949
	William Parker	1940-1941-1942
Tackles	William Kay	1945-1946-1947-1948
	James Walker	1939-1940-1941
Guards	Ross Anderson	1940-1941-1947
	Earl Banks	1946-1947-1948-1949
	Robert Liddy	1942-1943-1946
Centers	William Diehl	1939-1940-1941
	Richard Woodard	1944-1946-1947-1948
Quarterbacks	Al DiMarco	1947-1948
	Thomas Farmer	1940-1941-1942
Halfbacks	William Green	1939-1940-1941
	Emlen Tunnell	1946-1947
Fullback	J. Robert Smith	1946-1947

Jack Dittmer

Dr. Eddie Anderson had been gone from Holy Cross eleven years when he concluded the 1949 season. He had been active as head coach at Iowa during eight of the seasons, winning exactly half of seventy games. Holy Cross had never forgotten the coach who had moved the Crusaders to the front row of football with the prominent success that crowned his efforts before he left Worcester. Now indications began to appear that Holy Cross wanted Dr. Anderson to return. Aware of this, and also of the fact that Ohio State University had just given a rare concession of faculty tenure to its football coach, Wes Fesler, Anderson voiced a request for tenure at Iowa. Director Brechler and the Iowa Board expressed sympathy with the request, but informed the coach that tenure could not be gained immediately. A certain amount of time was necessary. Dr. Anderson told Brechler that Holy Cross had asked him to make a decision by a given date. The Iowa Board was unable to guarantee tenure by the specified date and Anderson submitted his resignation on January 28, 1950, to return to the Holy Cross post he had left after the 1938 season. With his resignation began the search by Director Brechler and the Board for his replacement.

LEONARD RAFFENSPERGER

There was widespread interest in the next man to be selected as head coach and in his background. Attention was centered by some on the advisability of placing an Iowa graduate in charge of the University's football fortunes. Those most interested in the selection of an alumnus as coach were particularly active in their recommendations and, while Iowa graduates were comparatively rare on the major coaching front, there were several to be considered. One was Dennis Myers, a guard between 1927 and 1929, who was coaching at Boston College. Another was Moray L. Eby, a great player half a century earlier at Iowa, who had a long and successful coaching record at Coe College. Still another was Wes Fry, a backfield standout during the Burt Ingwersen regime at Iowa, but then assisting Lynn Waldorf as backfield coach at California. Leonard Raffensperger, a Hawkeye lineman who had graduated in 1927, already was at the University, having been appointed head freshman coach under Anderson two years before. The search for a new coach was not entirely limited to graduates but the clamor for an alumnus seemed to be increasing. After a study of the available candidates, the needs of the University and the desires of spokesmen among the fans, the Board chose Raffensperger as its new head coach. He was given a three year contract and a salary of $10,000 a year, the first graduate to head the football staff since John G. Griffith in 1909.

Raffensperger, born at Victor, Ia., on November 6, 1903, was 46 when he took over as head coach. He had played under Burt Ingwersen, although not extensively. He played no high school football and a knee injury in the

Head Football Coach — 1950-1951
Leonard Raffensperger

Homecoming game against Illinois ended his collegiate career as a junior in 1925. He won a basketball letter at Iowa as a sophomore and took on a coaching job at Reinbeck, Ia., high school following his graduation. As a high school football coach, he was a success from the start. Between 1927 and 1930 his Reinbeck teams won 20, lost 7 and tied 6. East High of Waterloo hired him and in 17 seasons with that school his football teams won 90, lost 41 and tied 8. He had an all-time high school success record of 110 — 48 — 14, for a .680 average. Raffensperger was big, powerful (6'2" and 225 lbs.), determined and sincere.

1950

The new coach assembled his staff. He retained Pat Boland as line coach, signed Bernie Masterson, former Nebraska star, as backfield coach; Bob Fitch of Minnesota as end coach, and Ben Douglas of Grinnell as varsity assistant. The 1950 Hawkeyes opened auspiciously with an impressive 20 — 14 victory over Southern California in Los Angeles, but two touchdown defeats at the hands of both Indiana and Wisconsin, the latter a 14 — 0 shutout, dampened the premature enthusiasm. Lou D'Achille and Bob Robertson had combined on a record-breaking 91 yard touchdown pass to feature the Indiana triumph. It was the longest scoring pass ever made against Iowa.

Purdue was next. The Boilermakers had already scored the biggest upset of the season when they handed Notre Dame its first defeat in 40 games, 28 — 14. Little trouble was expected from Iowa. However, the inspired Hawkeyes, led by quarterback Glenn Drahn's three touchdown passes, scored in every quarter and gained a 33 — 21 win. The following week a football avalanche in the form of Ohio State's Buckeyes buried Iowa under a twelve touchdown onslaught, 83 — 21. All-American Vic Janowicz paced the winners offensively and kicked a conference record ten extra points in eleven attempts. Ohio State blasted to a 35 — 0 first quarter lead, largest ever against Iowa, and increased their advantage to 55 — 14 by halftime.

Just seven days later the inconsistent but determined Iowans rebounded with a vengeance, shutting out Minnesota, 13 — 0. It was the last Big Ten triumph of the Raffensperger regime, and the final win of 1950. Losses to both Illinois and Miami were taken, although lofty football heights were reached once more before the season ended when Iowa notched a deserved

14 — 14 tie with Notre Dame. Only an 80 yard touchdown march in the final five minutes enabled the Irish to escape defeat. A sixth place mark in the conference and an over-all 3 victories, 5 losses and a tie proved comparable to Iowa performances of most previous seasons.

Glenn Drahn closed his career having established a record of seventeen touchdown passes thrown during only two seasons. The mark, since eclipsed by Randy Duncan, remains second best in the Hawk record book. Bill Reichardt, rushing for 585 yards, most since 1936, was named to the all-Big Ten first team by United Press.

Financially, although football expenses exceeded $100,000 for the first time, net income from the sport also reached a new high, topping $400,000. Total income from all athletics during the 1950-51 year would hit $616,411.50, another Iowa mark.

As the 1950 playing season closed the last notes were being written to a new song which shortly would catch the interest of all Iowans and soon become the official "Iowa Fight Song."

Composer of both the words and music was an Iowan by birth, but one who never attended the University of his beloved state. Meredith Willson, formerly of Mason City, but always a Hawkeye, answered a somewhat disguised challenge which originally appeared in the Cedar Rapids Gazette, and his response was another smashing success.

In October, Les Zacheis, a former bandman who wrote a popular and jazz record column for The Gazette, reviewed a newly released Percy Faith album of college songs in which the "Iowa Corn Song" was used. Zacheis wrote:

"Putting it bluntly, the University of Iowa and its fine football teams deserve a better rouser than the rickey-tickey tune that fate wished upon them. The 'Corn Song' may have been hot stuff in the days of the silver cornet band but its strictly from hunger today.

"Maybe if Meredith Willson keeps hammering away, he'll turn out a spirited, swingy state song fit for a university some day."

Shortly thereafter the editorial writers of The Gazette seconded the plea:

"Some talented and resourceful musician (should) get to work and compose a better state song than the 'Iowa Corn Song'. . .

"Corn has taken on some new connotations in the last generation and there are some kinds which a state shouldn't brag too much about producing.

"Iowa is a wonderful place. . .Surely it must have something to spur creative musicians to write a stirring state song that doesn't fall in the Mickey Mouse bracket."

Mr. Zacheis bundled the two pieces together, added an accompanying letter, and sent them on to Mr. Willson.

Less than a month later a telegram from Meredith Willson announced that a new song was written and was in the mail. "I hope the Iowa boys will like it," he said, "but if not, I'll try again."

The song was aired nationwide on the NBC network late in December. It was first played in Iowa City as a halftime feature of the Iowa-Indiana basketball game on February 12, 1951.

Response from university authorities, students and alumni was immediate. Could Iowa use the new tune as an addition to "On Iowa"? Meredith Wilson not only assented, he turned over all rights to the words and music to the University. Iowans have adopted the song, and Iowa athletic teams have prospered since its adoption.

In the spring of 1951 the Big Ten again recognized the difficulties made manifest by the outbreak of the Korean War. The conference voted that for the ensuing school year the one year residence rule be suspended for new freshmen entering in the summer or fall of 1951. Beginning freshmen thus immediately became eligible for varsity athletics. The Big Ten also legislated in favor of renewing the Rose Bowl agreement for a three year period, no team being allowed to appear more than once in a two year span.

1951

The 1951 season found the Hawkeyes winning two early season non-conference games, against Kansas State, 16 — 0, and Pittsburgh, 34 — 17. There were no other victories. Purdue, Michigan, Ohio State, Illinois and Wisconsin defeated Iowa, while 20 — 20 tie games were posted against Minnesota and Notre Dame.

It was a season of contrasts which left Iowa followers highly elated at times, although more often deeply disappointed. Wisconsin, 34 to 7 victors, dominated every phase of play, picking up 26 first downs and holding Iowa to a minus 18 yards from scrimmage. Earlier Ohio State had again crushed the Hawks, this time 47 — 21, largely on the strength of four touchdown passes thrown and 308 total yards gained by quarterback Tony Curcillo. In addition Minnesota's might mite, Paul Giel, had one of his greatest days at the expense of Iowa. His 179 yards rushing led a vicious Gopher onslaught which rocketed the Norse into a 20 — 0 advantage in the fourth period. The lethargic Hawkeyes had offered little resistance and were at that point the object of critical outbursts from partisan Iowa fans. Raffensperger's charges, their pride shaken, retaliated with a reckless abandon. Bill Reichardt crashed from eight yards out to score with just over ten minutes remaining. Six minutes later Burt Britzman hit Hubert Johnston with a ten yard touchdown pass, bringing the score to 20 — 14. Reichardt then bulled his way for 37 yards in the final two minutes to knot the game, 20 — 20, and send 40,000 fans home limp from the excitement.

Three weeks later Notre Dame returned the compliment with a furious last period effort which produced 14 Irish points in the final minutes and another 20 — 20 deadlock.

Individual accomplishments were notable throughout the season. The Hawks, although 34 — 30 losers to Purdue, scored in every period. Dusty Rice, versatile junior halfback, raced 102 yards for an early Iowa touchdown, followed with a 69 yard dash from scrimmage for another score, and caught a 55 yard pass from Burt Britzman for a third. The Oelwein speedster scored nine times during the season, including a record tying six touchdowns on passes from Britzman.

Britzman's eleven touchdown passes thrown were the most since Nile Kinnick connected on a like number in 1939. The unheralded junior either scored or threw for fourteen of the twenty-three touchdowns tallied by Iowa during the season.

Fred Ruck, a converted quarterback, set a new single season pass receiving record with 25 caught for the year, bettering the mark of 22 made by Bob McKenzie in both 1948 and 1949.

Bill Reichardt, capping a brilliant three year career, gained national recognition for his 1951 accomplishments. The burly fullback was unanimous all conference of both Associated Press and United Press. Perhaps his greatest tribute came when it was announced that Reichardt was winner of the Chicago Tribune Silver

William Reichardt

Football Trophy, emblematic of his play as the most valuable player in the Big Ten. Iowa had not won a conference game in 1951.

Reichardt, who rushed for more than 150 yards against both Michigan and Minnesota, gained 737 yards from scrimmage, the most since Cowboy Nick Kutsch ran for 781 in 1926. His 1,691 career yards rushing has been exceeded only by Aubrey Devine and Gordon Locke, backfield all-Americans in the early twenties. Reichardt also kicked a record 51 of 63 extra points, breaking the old mark of 50 conversions set by Joe Warner of the 1899 and 1900 championship teams.

Center John Towner, a three-time football letter winner, and a 1952 graduate of the university, became the seventh Hawkeye gridder to give his life in the service of his country. The others were Bush Lamb of the 1935-6-7 teams; Nile Kinnick, 1937-8-9; Burdell "Oops" Gilleard, 1940; and Bob Yelton of the 1942 eleven. Fred Becker and Frank Grubb, both members of the 1915 team, were killed during World War I.

Leonard Raffensperger's game chart through two seasons showed five victories, ten defeats and three ties. Noteworthy on his record is this fact: Minnesota and Notre Dame, arch rivals of the Hawkeyes, never beat his teams.

One of those closest on the Iowa scene during the Raffensperger years felt that his two biggest problems were in the area of recruiting and over-all handling of his squads. As a high school coach he had very little experience in recruiting, knew little about it, and didn't like to recruit. Because he lived in Iowa most of his life, his contacts limited his ability to recruit successfully in the tough Big Ten league. Raffensperger also found it difficult to control his players under certain conditions. One of his better players said of him: "Raff was one of, and still is, the finest gentlemen I have ever known. This was probably his biggest weakness; he was not hard enough on us."

Suggesting that a lack of depth in manpower may have been an allied problem, as it had been under so many Iowa coaches, was the frequent prominence of individuals of unusual ability. Over-all squad strength was missing, however. The possibility of dwindling gate receipts may have further agitated the thinking of the Iowa Board when the 1951 season was over. In addition, alumni group and general fan reaction was such that a revaluation of the football situation became necessary.

A SEARCH BEGINS AND ENDS

First concrete explorations into the problem occurred on December 8, 1951. That evening, in a dimly lit corner of Gibby's, an exclusive restaurant on Chicago's near north side, three men, two from Iowa and one from Michigan, discussed the Iowa football picture. Athletic director Paul Brechler and Board Chairman Paul Blommers were the Iowa twosome, while H. O. (Fritz) Crisler, athletic director and long time head coach at Michigan, was the invited guest. Iowa had not decided to change football coaches, officially or unofficially, but both Brechler and Blommers were interested in discussing the over-all situation with the knowledgeable and highly respected Crisler. During the course of the evening the name of Evashevski was introduced by Crisler as a "fine, young football coach." He had played quarterback for him at Michigan, attaining all-conference recognition. "He's a tough, stubborn Polack, and you might have to put reigns on him," said Crisler. "I found that out when he was playing for me; but he was a great player, and I have the highest regard for him today as a person and as a football coach."

Brechler and Blommers returned to Iowa City. The situation was discussed further, but no concrete Board action was taken. However, a staff committee of the Board was authorized to "talk with Evashevski" if it was deemed desirable and if Evashevski would agree. In the fall of 1951 he had concluded a highly successful season at Washington State College. His accomplishments had attracted the attention of the University of Indiana. Evashevski had conferred with Dr. John Mee, the faculty representative there, and with "Pooch" Harrel, the

director of Hoosier athletics. "Evy," as he was widely known, was interested not only in the Indiana offer but in the opportunity to launch a coaching career in the Big Ten conference.

A call was made to Pullman, Washington, shortly before Christmas, 1951. It was Paul Brechler asking if Evashevski would be willing to meet with Iowa representatives. Evashevski, hesitant at first because of the Indiana discussions, agreed to a meeting in Denver, Colorado, on December 28. Paul Brechler, Paul Blommers and Dr. Stuart Cullen, all of the Iowa athletic board, arranged for the secret session to be held in a private home in Denver. Both parties arrived by train, the meeting was held, and Evashevski was "unofficially" offered the Iowa position.

The coach found the Iowa proposition interesting, although hardly more interesting than Indiana's proposal. Terms were quite similar. Each school mentioned a $15,000 salary and a five year contract, but the Indiana discussions had listed a projected salary increase not mentioned by Iowa. Evashevski had two interesting offers to ponder and he still had a job at Washington State.

The impressionable young coach returned to Pullman, Washington. Iowa's emissaries flew back to Iowa. A special meeting of the Board in Control of Athletics was held on the morning of December 31 in order to have "a complete review and discussion of the present football coaching situation and a further discussion of the several alternatives suggested for consideration."

According to minutes of that board meeting, these alternatives were:

1. To renew and extend the contract of Leonard Raffensperger.
2. To do nothing — which would indicate that Coach Raffensperger would continue as head football coach for one more year according to his contract which had one year to go.
3. To continue with the present football coaches and add additional assistants.

4. To remove Coach Raffensperger as head football coach and replace him with a new coach.

After a long and lengthy discussion, there was no formal action taken at the meeting.

In the meantime, Raffensperger was in Montgomery, Alabama, and New Orleans, Louisiana, attending the North-South game and the Sugar Bowl game. He had read in the papers that Iowa was thinking of replacing him as football coach. Raffensperger had left Iowa City before the meeting with Evashevski and could not be contacted, but, as the board minutes of December 31 confirm, he had not been relieved as football coach.

According to most Board members actively a part of the discussions, Iowa would change coaches only if a "top man" could be hired. Evashevski was considered that man.

During this period Evy had picked up the telephone and communicated with Crisler at Michigan. He has since confirmed the fact that it was Crisler who sold him on the advantages of coaching at Iowa. The factor that convinced Evashevski that Iowa would provide the best opportunity was the realization that it would be easier to attain statewide support in Iowa than in Indiana, where Notre Dame and Purdue were potent forces in football. Being a split-state, it would be difficult to congeal much more than southern Indiana, whereas in Iowa the recognition and support would encompass the entire state if the job could be done successfully.

On January 3 he conferred with athletic authorities at Washington State. Three days later, Sunday, January 6, the soon to become Iowa coach phoned director Brechler in Iowa City. He agreed to accept the Hawkeye coaching position on the basis of terms expressed in Denver nine days before.

Raffensperger by this time had returned to Iowa City. He was informed by the Iowa Board that he would receive his full salary for the unexpired portion of his contract and be retained on the staff in a different capacity. Twelve years later he was still a member of the Iowa athletic department.

Evashevski's appointment was hailed throughout the state. This young man, who had gained his individual fame as a field leader and blocking back at the University of Michigan, had his coaching reputation well under way when he elected to cast his lot with the Hawkeyes. In his second season after assuming the coaching of a steady loser, he had built Washington State into the surprise team of the Pacific Coast Conference by winning seven of nine games. An excerpt from a Washington State football program said of Evashevski: "Behind the present 32-year old football coach at Washington State College is a story of continued success and determination." That appraisal of Evashevski held good throughout his coaching career.

Born in Detroit, February 19, 1918, and deprived of almost all of his high school football career by an injury, he had come out of a Ford Motor Company factory where he had played on an amateur football team to enter the University of Michigan. A center originally, he was transformed into a blocking back by Michigan's Fritz Crisler, under whom Evashevski played during the seasons of 1938, 1939 and 1940. As a senior he captained the football team, was president of his class and won the Big Ten medal for excellence in scholarship and athletics.

Such is a partial view of the background of the man who was to move abreast of Howard Jones as the most successful of the coaches in the University's football history. There was more. He was outspoken, dedicated to success and not inclined to curry favor at any time. Early in his career he told a group of Iowa alumni: "The kind of a football team we have at Iowa the next five years depends on you. If you're the kind that gives up and growls when we lose a few games, then to hell with you. I've got a rich father in law and I may get fed up with coaching anyway. . ."

On another occasion Evashevski said: "Regardless of what the educators may say, the main reason for putting on a football uniform is to win. If I ever go on the field with any other idea, I will quit coaching. When these kids leave me, I want them to be winners. The desire to win is the greatest thing a young man can have."

Evashevski treated his players like men. He rarely if ever dropped a man from his squad for a training violation but he was a disciplinarian nevertheless. "If you even get up slow after a play," one player declared, "he'll slap you back on the third team."

This description of Evashevski is taken from an article by Jim Zabel in True Magazine:

"He can build team morale to a savage pitch for a game, yet remain the calmest man on the field himself. A gifted speaker, he can break up a student pep rally with a sly remark or a bit of self ridicule, but can hold an audience for an evening with a serious discussion of the value of athletics. He is a fierce competitor and a perfectionist on the football field; a devoted father and husband off the field. . ."

Such was the man the University hired early in 1952. Evashevski's first appearance as an Iowa representative took place in Cincinnati that January, at the Coaches-NCAA convention. He asked the first question — inquiring about a certain Iowa tailback he might use to head up the single wing system he employed at the time. "I'll run 70 per cent single wing," he told newsmen, "and 30 per cent 'T' formation, just to keep the alumni happy."

CHAPTER

20

Forest Evashevski-- The Beginning of an Era

Coach Forest Evashevski's first concern after committing himself to Iowa and its football fortunes was that of assembling a staff to go with him into this venture in Big Ten coaching. He had planned to bring with him from Wash-

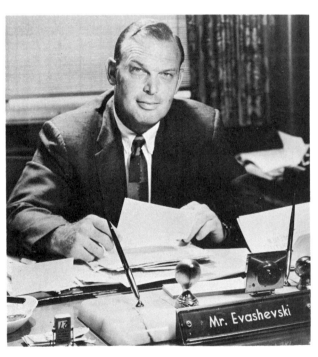

Head Football Coach — 1952-1960
Athletic Director — 1960-
Forest Evashevski

ington State Al Kircher, who had been his top assistant, Dan Stavley, and Bob Flora, who had played with Evashevski at Michigan. In the end, only Flora of his Washington State staff accompanied him to Iowa. In assembling a staff he scanned the football horizon. He surrounded himself with men who literally had grown up in successful football administrations and whom he thought well equipped to instill in the struggling Hawkeyes the foundation of the winning tradition Evashevski considered vital.

Archie Kodros, another former Michigan player who had been coaching at the University of Hawaii, joined Evashevski. So did Henry (Whitey) Piro, who had played at Syracuse under Ossie Solem, former Iowa coach. From the Oregon staff he signed Chalmers (Bump) Elliott, an all-American halfback at Michigan in his playing days. Wally Schwank, a Coe College graduate who had served under Raffensperger, was retained as freshman coach. The new staff moved quickly into the planning of the 1952 campaign, the search for recruits capable of strengthening future teams and the many problems associated with the advent of a new football administration.

Evashevski had played and coached the Single Wing. He brought it with him to Iowa. It was evident almost at once, however, that

Iowa needed much more than a system. Evashevski found not only a losing team but a losing tradition. The 1951 Hawkeyes, with a 2 — 5 — 2 record, had not won a Big Ten game. More than a few of the alumni were disinterested. The upcoming football squad was confronted by a schedule which was to open with Pittsburgh, close with Notre Dame, and include seven Big Ten opponents in between. There was not much optimism at Iowa, even with a new coach.

Early in September, Wilfrid Smith, writing in The Chicago Tribune, said: "There isn't a Hawkeye player on the practice field who can block with Evashevski, run with backfield coach Bump Elliott, or play like center Archie Kodros.

"All of which leads to the conclusion that if Iowa escapes last place in the 1952 Western Conference standings, the state should declare a holiday."

Four weeks into the season found the Hawkeyes without a victory. Pittsburgh, Indiana, Purdue and Wisconsin had averaged better than 32 points a game in smashing the Iowans. Most exciting play, perhaps, had been a booming 96 yard punt which Wisconsin's George O'Brien had registered during his team's 42 — 13 win at Iowa City.

The need for a quick revitalizing of Iowa football was obvious, but the suddenness with which the revitalizing was to set in was not. Within a week the Hawks had shaken the nation's football front with a colossal upset. A strong Ohio State team had been charging toward the top as lowly Iowa took its early assortment of beatings. This game was to signal the rise of the Hawkeyes, a soaring climb that was to bring them to the top in football in the ensuing years, although the Ohio State victory was only an isolated start in the climb.

The two teams met in the fifth game of the Evashevski tenure at Iowa and the shock of that upset victory has yet to wear off. The date was October 25, 1952. It was Iowa's Homecoming. A total of 44,659 fans sat stunned as the inspired Hawks held Ohio State to only 42 yards rushing. The Buckeyes never got closer

than Iowa's 28 yard line, while a second period safety and fourth quarter touchdown provided the Iowa points and an 8 — 0 victory. An Associated Press poll named the Hawkeye win the third most startling upset in sports during 1952.

Tactics, psychology and philosophy, along with a thorough indoctrination in basic football had their places in Evashevski's coaching. He accomplished his first great feat on the Big Ten front largely with tactics, but of course psychology figured in. Long after that first victory of his Iowa career, Evy told the story of the game.

"We had scrimmaged Tuesday before the Ohio game and we didn't look good at all," he recalled. "I went to bed tired that night and was drawing circles and x's diagramming play possibilities. I knew we lacked the speed to run outside and I was trying to figure how we could get an inside attack going. I decided that the only thing we could do was to try to spread Ohio State out as far as possible. With the wingback left, by shifting our backfield we could put the core of the offensive strength about three yards over to the right. This would be hard to cope with, from a defensive standpoint.

"We gave the offense to our squad on Wednesday and that was one of the few times I've ever scrimmaged a squad on Wednesday. It was the first time we had scrimmaged the offense. We used it on Saturday and beat Ohio State."

Evashevski's chart of accomplishments had grown long and impressive before he discarded his coaching togs, but that game stands with the great milestones. Ohio State was not prepared for the ammunition employed by an upstart Iowa team. No team, collegiate or professional, had faced that particular type of wide line spacings at that time. Years after the 1952 season had blended in with others, one who helped Evy with his coaching had some recollections:

"All the conniving and scheming we did to keep that 1952 bunch going. I can remember trying to pick a kickoff team. You couldn't get eleven guys to stick their hands up. We were playing platoon football, we were all banged up, and we practically had to draft people to run down on the kickoff.

"We had a bunch of fellows who just couldn't run. We had no tailback. Dusty Rice (George Rice) had been our big hope but he was out for the season with a knee injury. We had lost four games when Evy came up with his offensive changes. What it amounted to was throwing out the Single Wing and putting in the unbalanced Split-T, with splits of a yard — in some cases four feet. All of our plays were called at the line. Our quarterback, Jerry Reichow, was a big, strong fellow capable of making three or four yards at a shot. By splitting our line all the way along we figured we had a chance to move the football and give the defense some problems. Ohio State set up a standard defense and split right with us. They just couldn't seem to adjust to what we were doing. We gave them problems they had not anticipated, offensively."

If there was one key game in the 83 played by Evashevski's teams at Iowa, the 1952 Ohio State game could have been it. It was the springboard to later successes. Until that time Evashevski had been making a desperate effort to lift the Hawkeyes — fans as well as players. He had made no secret of his views that "The Big Ten had to be made conscious that Iowa was in the league." He had told the Iowa athletic authorities that he might say a few things and do a few things that might seem somewhat out of character until the team gained adequate strength on the football field.

Convinced after the Ohio State game that they could win, the Hawks went to Minnesota the next week for the Gopher homecoming. An incident occurred. There had been a time when the Hawkeyes seemed to be about ready to go out and congratulate their opponents before they played them, but that day was gone. At Minnesota an overflow crowd jammed the entire stadium, including temporary bleachers along the sidelines. From the bench, the Iowa coaches and players had only a limited view of the field because the stands were nearer the field than the players' bench. The Iowa players, seeking a better vantage point, left the bench and crowded the sideline. Minnesota fans objected. They demanded that the Iowa coach restrict the players to the bench. Evy refused. There was a momentary flurry of action on the sideline but it subsided, and the Iowa players retained their positions just outside the sideline. But Minnesota, with 17 fourth quarter points, won, 17 — 7.

After the game, when Gopher players entered the Iowa dressing room demanding the coveted game trophy, "Floyd of Rosedale," Evy authorized his student manager to hand over the bronzed pig with the remark, "Okay, give 'em the hog — but make sure you hand it to 'em hind-end first!"

The business of demonstrating that Iowa was "in the league" was on. When Illinois played at Iowa City the following week Evashevski did one of the "brassy" things he had said he might have to do. He marched onto the field to demonstrate his dislike of an official's ruling. His object was to show his players he would fight for them. In effect, the incident seemed to arouse the crowd to heated support of Iowa and before the game was over some of the spectators let fly at the Illinois players with apple cores and similar articles of ammunition. Following the game, in the heat of the moment, an Illinois player struck an Iowa student, breaking his jaw. The incident possibly figured in a lapse of more than a decade in the football meetings of the two schools.

The Illini won from Iowa, 33 — 13, and Evashevski called the passing performance of Tom O'Connell "one of the great individual efforts I have seen." O'Connell completed 22 of 34 tosses for 306 yards, while end Rex Smith caught 11 for 190 yards. Both yardage marks remain Big Ten conference records.

When Iowa and Northwestern met late in the 1952 season the record stood 1 — 6 against Iowa, but 46,000 spectators turned out for the game with the Wildcats. A fighting team and a fighting coach had centered attention on the Hawkeyes and they responded with a convincing 39 — 14 victory, largest Iowa margin over a Big Ten foe in thirty years. Only Notre Dame remained on the Hawkeye schedule, and the fact that Iowa was held scoreless was, in itself, a memorable feat. No other Iowa team coached by Evashevski was to be shut out and 78 consecutive games were to be played before the Hawks again went scoreless, this time during the tenure of Evashevski's successor.

The first season was over for the new regime. The count stood two victories, seven defeats. The figures failed to indicate, however, how an undermanned team with virtually no "future" had fought its way up to a sixth place tie in the Big Ten standings. The team and the coaches were the toast of the Hawkeye realm.

Only captain Bill Fenton received all Big Ten recognition, being named to the first team defensive unit of Associated Press. However, other individual Hawkeyes, notably Jim Hatch and Dan McBride, gained deserved plaudits. Hatch raced 78 yards from scrimmage against Illinois to record the longest such dash at Iowa since Bill Glassgow turned the identical feat at the stadium dedication in 1929. It, too, was against the Illini. McBride set a school single game pass receiving mark which still stands when he caught nine aerials against Wisconsin. The 29 receptions for 448 yards by McBride were new school marks at the time, since broken. Oddly, McBride had never caught a pass for Iowa prior to his senior season.

The philosophies of Forest Evashevski were already apparent. As he built his teams he drilled his theories into his players. He urged them to have pride in themselves, their team and their University. He told them that losing was no disgrace, providing they had given everything they had on the field. He reminded them, however, that it was the rankest kind of shame to be outfought. He told his men he placed great emphasis on winning, but the victory had to be one to which they might point with pride. He told them he never wanted them to win a game for him.

"I have always hated the thought of a game being won or even played for something that was artificial, such as for the coach. I told them that coaching was my profession and that winning was a part of it and losing was a part of it.

I told them I never wanted them to win a game for me, or any other coach."

Evashevski also had a sense of humor — a sense of humor which was deep-rooted. After one rugged practice session he spent ten minutes trying to lock his backfield coach, Bump Elliott, in his locker. When spring practice drew toward a close in 1953, Evashevski called the press and radio contingent together a few days before the annual intra-squad game and said:

"You coach the two teams in the spring game. I will sit in the press-box and write the story." On the afternoon of the game the coach and his staff withdrew from the field, leaving the divided squad and its nonplussed "coaches" to await the kickoff. When the contest was over Evashevski, as good as his word, wrote this account of the proceedings:

"In spite of sloppy play and the disgusting employment of antique, two-platoon football, 1,600 fans left Iowa's Stadium happy that there will be more to cheer about when they get their coaching staff back in the harness. Both teams failed to impress. . .sloppy coaching from both staffs. . .was evidenced by the failure of the backs to run through the proper apertures. . .After witnessing this exhibition, I know why the newsmen ask so many questions in the locker room. . ." Evashevski's "reporting" had one glaring inadequacy. He mentioned neither the score nor the winner.

Also in the spring, faculty representatives of the Conference voted to renew the Rose Bowl agreement for three years, in response to an invitation received from the Pacific Coast Conference. Before another football season drastic changes were adopted as part of the Official Football Rules. The American Football Coaches Association had voted 4 to 1 for retention of free substitution or "two platoons."

At that point the NCAA Council drafted a resolution which recommended that the two-platoon system be killed. The NCAA convention passed the resolution and the NCAA's Football Rules Committee followed the recommendation. The nation's football coaches were caught by surprise and were forced into drastic reorganization of their programs. The new substitution rule stated that players removed from the game during the first and third periods could not return to action in those periods. Players withdrawn before the final four minutes of the second and fourth periods could go back into the game in those last four minutes.

1953

Came the autumn of 1953 and Iowa's second season under Evashevski. Some promising newcomers who had arrived on the campus in 1952 moved up to the varsity. Among them were the "Steubenville Trio" composed of Frank Gilliam, end; Eddie Vincent, halfback, and Calvin Jones, guard. Jones actually visited Iowa as sort of a lark, to see how his friends Gilliam and Vincent would fare at their new school. He had made plans to enroll elsewhere. Jones decided to stay at Iowa, became one of its all-American stars and, a few years later, met a tragic death in an airplane crash in Canada.

Evashevski and his staff worked overtime perfecting a multiple offense style of attack, feeling that it would most effectively meet the problems which were presented by opponents switching and changing defenses. The Iowa team in 1953 retained the single-wing, but they also ran the split-T offense from an unbalanced line as well as the tight-T unbalanced line series.

Defending national champion Michigan State offered the first season challenge, holders of a 24 game winning streak when they arrived in Iowa City. Iowa met the test statistically, gaining more first downs and more yards rushing, but the Spartans prevailed on the scoreboard, 21 — 7. Washington State, coached by Forest Evashevski two years previously, became the first Iowa victim a week later. The Hawkeyes smashed existing offensive records with 538 total yards, including 396 on the ground, to crush the Cougars, 54 — 12. Next, Michigan spoiled the return of graduates Evashevski, Flora, Kodros and Elliott by earsing a stunning 13 — 0 Iowa lead with two seven point salvos and a 14 — 13 victory. Wyoming and Indiana

were Hawk victims but Wisconsin lay in ambush to overhaul the Iowans, 10 — 6, scoring the winning points midway in the fourth period on a deflected 38 yard touchdown pass.

Purdue was no match for the now respected Hawkeyes, falling, 26 — 0. The game, orderly until the closing minutes of the third period, was broken wide open when Iowa exploded for three lightning-like touchdowns in only 2 minutes 23 seconds to gain the win. Their next start brought Minnesota and its all-American halfback, Paul Giel, to Iowa City. The Hawkeyes, playing before a record crowd of 53,355, were ready in a furious way.

Preparations for the game were based on the Evashevski philosophy of forcing the opposing team to do what it didn't want to do. In the games preceding its meeting with Iowa, Minnesota had built its attack around Giel, to a degree that he carried the ball, or passed, on nearly 75 per cent of the Gopher plays. Iowa knew, consequently, that it had to stop Giel and force the other Minnesota halfback, or the fullback, to carry the ball. The Gophers indicated that they had not wanted to do that, because they keyed everything around Giel. So Evashevski devised the Iowa defense to overbalance for Giel.

Henry (Whitey) Piro, a long time member of the Iowa staff, had made an interesting observation about Giel while scouting the Gophers. When the Minnesota all-American was going to run with the ball, he always faked a pass. When he was going to pass, he faked a run. Giel's procedure seemed to be unquestioned and, as Evashevski later pointed out, "It was a strong enough tendency to base our whole defense on it."

Two Iowa linebackers bore the brunt of the defensive assignment. One drifted out to cover the flat and the other stayed put until Giel made his move. If Giel raised his arm the linebacker shot in on him. If he threatened to run, the defense sagged back, confident that he actually intended to pass.

Paul Giel was one of the great halfbacks of his time. Ten years after his graduation he still held two Big Ten and nine Minnesota offensive records. Against Iowa in 1953, however, he had no chance. The Hawks swarmed in. They simply engulfed him. Mates who tried to block for Giel, or protect on his passes, were flattened. The Gophers were overmatched by the defensive fury they were up against. When the battered but courageous Giel left the field he had netted only 13 yards in 14 running plays.

Floyd of Rosedale

Awarded annually to the winner of the Iowa-Minnesota game.

His passing was nullified as well. Minnesota completed only three tosses all day, totalling 22 yards. Dusty Rice notched three Iowa touchdowns and the 27 — 0 victory, biggest conference win since 1922, was another memorable milestone.

The Hawks had shut out Purdue, 26 — 0, and Minnesota, 27 — 0, on successive Saturdays. Meanwhile, Notre Dame, with one of its greatest teams, had stormed across the land, crushing seven straight opponents. Iowa was next in line and the Fighting Irish had just been selected the most overwhelming choice as the nation's number one team in the history of a major wire service poll. Evashevski and Iowa were unshaken. So keen for the battle were the Hawkeye players that they began keying themselves for the South Bend game before leaving the stadium following the Minnesota victory. Evashevski, sensing the premature emotional rise, applied the psychological brakes by minimizing the importance of the Notre Dame game. As he said later: "At times you have to hold the boys down and play the game down a bit. Too much of an emotional build-up dissipates energy."

Neither Iowa nor Notre Dame is likely to forget that 1953 game. It was virtually beyond belief that the Irish managed to avert defeat. Twice during the game, as each half ticked away, Notre Dame employed desperate clock-stopping maneuvers to pass for last-second touchdowns and gain a 14 — 14 tie.

Iowa had scored in the first quarter, on a 13-yard run by Eddie Vincent. Jim Freeman kicked the extra point. The Hawks maintained the lead, 7 — 0, going into the final minute of the half. Notre Dame, with the ball in its possession and time running out, "had players dropping here and there" after it had exhausted its allotted time-outs, to force the stopping of the clock. Only two seconds showed on the scoreboard clock when Ralph Guglielmi, the Notre Dame quarterback, went back to fire a scoring pass to end Dan Shannon in the end zone. The kick was good, and the half ended, 7 — 7.

Again in the last half Iowa, with Binkey Broeder playing his finest game, went ahead. Broeder, driving for 127 yards through the Irish line that day, led the Hawks to the Notre Dame four. Left hander Bobby Stearnes was rushed in to toss a surprise pass to Frank Gilliam for the touchdown. Again Freeman converted on the extra point try. Two minutes and six seconds remained, but in that scant stretch of time the Irish may have reached the height of ruthless desperation. Starting from their own 41-yard line, firing passes, Coach Frank Leahy's charges moved. Seven times the passer connected. The throws were short, but they found their mark. The clock does not stop automatically on completed passes, so Notre Dame had to husband the fleeting seconds in other ways. Again, one, two or more Irish were stretched on the turf.

The clock was stopped. Finally, with just six seconds of the game remaining, Guglielmi once more passed to Shannon, this time from the 9-yard line and, with Don Schaefer's extra point, averted defeat. The final score, 14 − 14, marked as frenzied an effort as the Irish had made to escape defeat and a new high in frustration for Iowa. The Hawkeyes did not win, but the tie dulled the shiny Notre Dame record and Iowa was named the ninth ranking team in the nation in the final Associated Press poll. Veteran sportswriter Grantland Rice, speaking to the New York Football Writers luncheon on Monday following the Iowa-Irish game said, "I consider it a complete violation of the spirit and ethics of football and was sorry to see Notre Dame, of all teams, using this method. Why, in heaven's name, was it allowed?"

Discussions of the "fainting" tactics went on for days. In one of them Forest Evashevski was moved by the muse. Paraphrasing the immortal words of Grantland Rice, he said:

"When the One Great Scorer comes
    To write against our name,
He won't ask that we won or lost,
    But how we got gypped at Notre Dame."

The 1953 football season at Iowa, showing a 5 − 3 − 1 record, was the finest since the "Ironmen" of 1939. Sustained football strength was beginning to assert itself. Spectator interest in the Evashevski brand of football was not confined to Iowa. Net income to the Hawkeye athletic department from the Notre Dame game was $92,916.15, most ever realized by Iowa from an athletic event.

Forest Evashevski received his first of many coaching honors when the Detroit Times selected him as Coach of the Year, and his players also gained post-season honors. Jerry Hilgenberg was named by Grantland Rice and the Football Writers Association to the first all-America team. The Iowa center-linebacker was also a first team all-conference pick of both the Associated Press and United Press. Ends Bill Fenton and Frank Gilliam were both rated third team all-Americans by The Sporting News and Central Press respectively. Guard Don

Chelf was a first team all-midwest selection of Collier's and The Chicago Tribune, while sophomore guard Calvin Jones, an Associated Press first team all-conference award winner, also was the recipient of various all midwest and all-America team honors.

Dusty Rice, completing his illustrious career at Iowa, closed with 21 touchdowns scored during three seasons of play, the most since Gordon Locke more than three decades before. Rice, slowed by injury during his junior and senior seasons, gained more than 1,000 yards rushing for Iowa and is recognized as one of the top pass receivers the school has had.

The years of the Evashevski regime were unfolding. Crowds and gate receipts were increasing. Iowa's board in control of athletics took note. Hawkeye football had come off the scrap heap to take a place among the nation's leaders. Only two years of the five covered by Evy's original contract had expired but the Board, in December of 1953, handed him a new ten year pact, which was to have extended into 1964. Evy, reversing procedure in which he had tossed his original Iowa contract into a desk drawer without signing it, affixed his signature to the new one.

Assistant coaches Bob Flora and Bump Elliott had salary increases to $8,700, and before another season a young man named Jerry Burns arrived quietly on the Iowa scene, assuming the duties of freshman coach. His addition to the staff carried no great significance at the time. It developed later that he carried the tag of destiny.

1954

In April, 1954, Evashevski was honored by an appointment as assistant coach of the College All Stars in their annual August engagement against the champions of the National Football League. And there was another Iowa team to be readied for a schedule of rugged opposition. As holdovers from the 1953 squad Iowa had 20 lettermen. There was a handful of players practicing as sophomores who might help, among them a youthful looking quarterback, Kenny Ploen, a center named Don Suchy and a halfback named Dobrino.

The schedule, with Michigan State, Michigan and Ohio State to be met in the first four weeks of the season, was far too severe to permit a realistically confident approach to the season. A shortage of line strength suggested no possible opportunity for preparing two units of anything of equal strength, as Evashevski had done in 1953. The 1954 campaign began with a promising backfield outlook and a questionable line situation.

In the percentage table, Iowa did not fare too badly, winning four of its seven Big Ten games. The story was not told in the percentages, however. The Hawks lost to three conference teams by a total of nine points. Iowa, then in the process of becoming one of the nation's high scoring teams, could have won the Big Ten championship that fall with 12 properly placed additional points.

With Michigan State as the opponent in the tough opening game, on a sultry September afternoon in Iowa City, the Hawkeyes gained a first half lead on a 33-yard touchdown run by Earl Smith and an extra point by Jim Freeman. Michigan State struck hard in the third quarter, scoring on a short touchdown burst by Leroy Bolden and a 23-yard field goal by Jerry Planutis. The Hawks were 10 — 7 short-enders going into the fourth quarter. An Iowa drive carried to the Spartan 13 and was stopped. Michigan State punted out and Eldean Matheson caught the ball on the Iowa 44. He raced 53 yards on the return before a desperation tackle felled him three yards from the goal. From there the Hawks bit off ground in small chunks, Jerry Reichow scoring and Freeman adding the point for a 14 — 10 victory.

Iowa sailed past Montana next, highlighted by a 94 yard touchdown run following a pass interception by Bobby Stearnes. The team then made one of its usual trips to Michigan. It was there that the Hawkeyes had lost a 14 — 13 heartbreaker in 1953, and it was there that they were to lose another by the same score. Duplicating its 1953 feat, Iowa had slammed ahead to a 13 — 0 first half lead, scoring quickly after Michigan fumbles. This time, however, the Hawks did not maintain the margin through the half. After Jerry Reichow had smashed a yard for one touchdown and Earl Smith added another from eight yards out, Iowa had a 13 — 0 advantage. Then Michigan made its move, scoring once in the first and again in the second quarter, and the two successful conversions by Ron Kramer decided the 14 — 13 struggle.

The first of the 1954 heartbreakers was in the record. Another followed shortly. At Ohio State the following week Earl Smith speared a Buckeye pass and sprinted 66 yards to score for an Iowa lead. The Bucks tied it late in the first quarter and went ahead in the second. In the third Smith fairly took the breath of the 82,141 spectators by fielding a punt and racing 75 yards for his second great scoring run of the game. But Ohio State countered with a scoring pass, Leggett to Brubaker, and a 20 — 14 deficit was Iowa's. The fact that the Hawks twice were almost within arm's length of the goal in a maddening fourth quarter effort frightened Ohio State supporters but only added to the ultimate Iowa heartbreak. By season's end the Buckeyes were national champions.

It was two and two for the season the next time out, at Indiana. And there was nothing easy about the 27 — 14 Iowa victory, except at the start. The Hawkeyes stacked up a 21 — 0 halftime lead, scoring three times in the second quarter, then held on to win, 27 — 14.

Coach Evashevski seemed to have a particular appreciation of Dad's Day games, and he was able to transmit that thinking to his players. "I often reminded the squad," Evashevski said, "that their Dads were in the stands; that through them their father's image was being projected on the gridiron, and that one of the many joys a father received was living his own life through his son." The philosophy was well taken.

It is noteworthy that Evashevski closed his coaching career at Iowa with eight straight Dad's Day triumphs.

Wisconsin came to Iowa City for the 1954 game. Rugged previous encounters had left the

Hawkeyes on the battered side but they arose to the challenge as their fathers watched. In the fiery duel Iowa had the edge in running and the Badgers had it in passing. But Iowa sent Jerry Reichow and Bobby Stearnes over the goal line at the end of touchdown marches, and Wisconsin counted only on a score by Alan (The Horse) Ameche. More than 52,000 saw the Hawks win, 13 — 7.

An alumnus once took Coach Evashevski to task, charging that he did not consistently produce outstanding punters. Evy explained that he did not like to coach punting because "the thought of giving the other team the ball makes me sick." It may be recalled that during one stretch of years Iowa was among the nation's foremost teams in making the fewest punts in a season.

It was another phase of the punting game that added a brilliant chapter to Iowa football in the 1954 season, however. The Hawks were playing an explosive Purdue team with Leonard Dawson fingering passing dynamite all afternoon. Sweat and toil and a final yard by Eddie Vincent produced an Iowa touchdown late in the first quarter. It came hard. A couple of minutes elapsed before the Boilermakers failed their yardage requirements and had to punt.

Purdue was the toughest team in the Big Ten in defending against punt returns. It could boast that no player had returned a punt for a touchdown in years. This fact may have bothered Evashevski because the week of the Purdue game he had his men work on a punt return designed to draw Purdue down one side of the field so that the other side was virtually clear. The maneuver was not successful even once in practice. When the Boilermaker punt came down the field late in the first quarter, however, the Hawks gave the maneuver one more try. A fake, placing Jerry Reichow deep, pulled

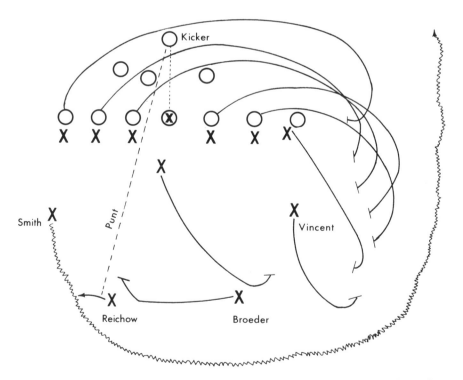

The long discussed, perfectly executed punt return was completed without a hand being laid on Iowa's touchdown maker, Earl Smith. The line of scrimmage was the Purdue 30 and the kick was received by Reichow at his own 32.

Purdue over just a step or two and cleared the way for Earl Smith to race back, take the ball from Reichow and dash 68 yards for a touchdown.

Perhaps because of that startling play, Iowa split the Boilermakers apart. The team ran up a 25 — 0 first half lead, with Bobby Stearnes notching a second quarter touchdown as a preliminary to another sensational Iowa play. On this one Eddie Vincent took a handoff on his own 4-yard line and, with mates clearing the way, raced 96 yards down the east sideline for

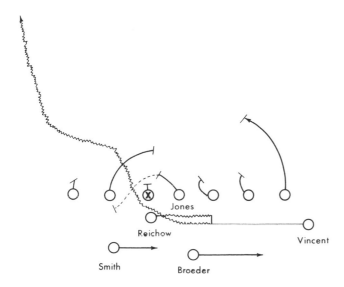

Eddie Vincent's record-breaking 96 yard scoring dash from scrimmage was successful because of the good faking of backfield decoys Smith and Broeder, coupled with precision blocking by the Iowa linemen. Particularly noticeable was the work of guard Calvin Jones who moved his Purdue opponent out of the play, across the line of scrimmage, and into the path of a second Boilermaker who was driving for the tackle from the rear.

a score. It remains the longest touchdown run from scrimmage in 50 years in the Big Ten. Dawson's passes hurt Iowa. He completed a dozen, including a throw to John Kerr, the bristling end, for an 80-yard touchdown. Iowa did not score in the last half, but won, 25 — 14, rushing for 368 yards, most ever against a conference opponent.

A week later came the Minnesota game. The Gophers to this day hold a decisive superiority over Iowa in football, but no victory in the record was sweeter to Minnesota hearts, or more disappointing to Iowa, than the 1954 game. It was mid-November. The Hawkeyes had a 4 — 2 record in the conference and were the favorite. The game, however, was one of maddening futility for Iowa, with a Hawkeye statistical edge only increasing the frustration. Minnesota, playing at home and honed to a perfect edge emotionally, sprung Bob McNamara for a 36-yard touchdown run with the game barely two minutes old. In two more minutes the fiery Gophers again broke McNamara loose and he sprinted 89 yards for another score. Every Iowa player had a shot at McNamara somewhere in the play. Saddled by a two-touchdown deficit in the first five minutes, the Hawks struck back. Jerry Reichow scored before the first quarter was over. Earl Smith's short touchdown tied the score but Minnesota stormed ahead again on a 27-yard pass, Swanson to Don McNamara. Iowa earned another touchdown early in the third quarter and erased the Gopher advantage. The score stood at 20 — 20.

For just an instant, the sun broke through for the Hawkeyes. Earl Smith streaked away and ran a Gopher punt 81 yards to the goal, bringing uncontrolled joy to the Iowa side. It changed to deep gloom an instant later when the play was called back and Iowa charged with clipping, setting them back to the three. It was a costly decision and led to a study of the game films as an aftermath. The clipping was not located in the Iowa films. A newspaper printed what purported to be photographs of the clipping incident but the published sequence could not be found in the game films. The ruling stood. The fire was gone from the Hawk attack and three plays after what had appeared to be the winning touchdown run Iowa fumbled and Eddie Vincent fell on the ball in his own end zone. The resulting safety gave Minnesota a 22 — 20 victory. Vincent, second leading ground gainer to play for Evashevski at Iowa, picked up 154 yards rushing against the Gophers and averaged more than ten yards on each of 28 attempts during Iowa's two game set with Purdue and Minnesota.

Another campaign was ending. Notre Dame, with its memories of the 14 — 14 tie in 1953 and its resentment over the "fainting" allegations, was the final opponent. The Irish came in with their guns loaded and their fingers on the trigger. The Hawkeyes were driven back twice on Notre Dame touchdown drives in the second quarter before an Iowa score was registered. It was 14 — 6 for Notre Dame after Jerry Reichow's 44-yard scoring pass to Frank Gilliam late in the second quarter, but the Irish margin mounted to 28 — 6 before Iowa scored again. In the fourth period Don Dobrino threw a pass to Earl Smith for a 76-yard scoring play, longest on record at the time, and farther along Bobby Stearnes went the last nine yards on another Iowa scoring drive. The Hawkeyes went down, 34 — 18, and the last Irish point, a conversion after the final touchdown, was made by Paul Hornung, later to become one of the greats of professional football with Green Bay.

As the 1954 season ended on a 5 — 4 record, Calvin Jones, powerful Iowa guard, was chosen on 15 different all-America teams and lesser honors were won by the Iowa halfbacks Earl Smith and Eddie Vincent, by Frank Gilliam, a big contributor both on offense and defense, and by tackle John Hall. Smith, one of Iowa's most exciting runners, notched 11 touchdowns during the season, and his 54 points in Big Ten games earned the talented junior the conference scoring title. It was the first time since 1933 that an Iowan claimed the honor. Captain Binkey Broeder, a four year varsity performer at Iowa, closed his career rated the top punter for the Hawkeyes since Nile Kinnick. Broeder had led the Big Ten in that department in 1953.

Net income from Hawkeye athletics, perilously low at $33,354.45 in 1952-53, reached an

all-time high of more than $300,000 during the 1954-55 school year. Gross receipts from foot-

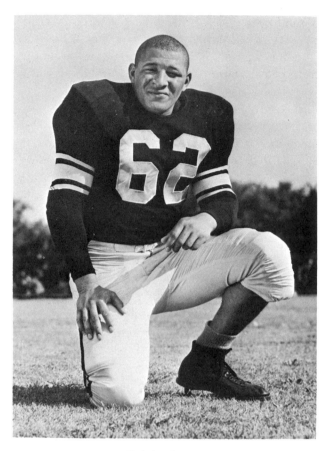

Calvin Jones

ball in 1954 exceeded $875,000, a figure $200,000 above any previous season.

As Coach Evashevski put his third season behind him, a movement designed to express the appreciation of the followers of the Hawkeyes was under way quietly across Iowa. It reached a climax in early November, 1954, at a mass meeting in front of Old Capitol, on the campus. Evashevski was presented with the keys to an expensive automobile. Within a week a member of the University faculty. Professor Charles Tanford, was on record in a "letter to the editor," protesting such a gift to a football coach.

Dissenting voices were heard only rarely, however, as appreciation of the accomplishments of the coach and the football team was sounded. Rumors also were started. One of the first that Evashevski might leave Iowa was heard in 1954, when reports were noted that he might succeed Bennie Oosterbaan as head coach at Michigan. Another was that he might run for governor of Iowa. Both rumors proved groundless. Stories linking Paul Brechler with a possible departure from Iowa proved to be more solidly based.

Director Brechler came to a meeting of the Board in Control of Athletics on December 20, 1954, with some questions: Did the University wish him to continue as Athletic Director? Had he, in effect, reached a salary ceiling, insofar as his future at the University was concerned? These questions were the aftermath of discussions Brechler had engaged in with the University of Indiana. The Board, in a private meeting, declared its "unanimous desire" to have Brechler remain as Director and assured him that it did not feel that his current salary necessarily represented a ceiling. The Board said, however, that it did not feel that a salary adjustment should be made at the time.

The Board's answers apparently satisfied Brechler and the Indiana approach was not in further discussions for some time to come. Instead, in April of 1955, the Board recommended a salary increase to $13,500 for Brechler, covering the 1955-56 period.

1955

Evashevski had coached for three seasons at Iowa. He had instilled great confidence in his players. Optimism was voiced that the 1955 team might be his best. There was a veteran at every line position; an effective passing and running quarterback in Jerry Reichow; speed at the halfbacks with Eddie Vincent and Earl Smith; Frank Gilliam was at one end and Cal Jones, all-American guard, was the captain. Sophomores Frank Rigney, Jim Gibbons, Bill Happel and Alex Karras appeared promising. In addition, the four conference games won in 1954, the most credited to Iowa since the conquests of the famed 1939 team, added to the optimism.

The high hopes appeared to be justified when the Hawks opened with an easy 28 — 7 win over Kansas State. Playing before 44,500, the largest opening crowd ever to attend a non-conference game, Iowa piled up big yardage, holding the Wildcats without a pass completion and only four first downs. A trip to Wisconsin followed, and that engagement probably affected the entire season.

Wisconsin was ready for Iowa's spread formation and quick line splits. Not many opponents were outgaining the Hawkeyes, but Wisconsin did. The Badgers did it after the Hawks had punched home a touchdown in the first two and one-half minutes. Vincent completed the march and Freeman kicked the point but Iowa's lead was offset almost immediately when Jim Haluska of Wisconsin passed to Dave Howard for a touchdown. That was the start of a Wisconsin surge of vast proportions. Before the game ended the Badgers had rapped Iowa with five touchdowns, four extra points and a field goal. Three of the touchdowns came on Haluska to Howard passes for 42, 16 and 33 yards. Iowa, which had gained a 14 — 13 lead in the second quarter on Kenny Ploen's five yard "keep," ended up battered and beaten, 37 — 14.

From a Wisconsin official, in the wake of the game, came the word that the Badgers had spent a great part of their spring practice building a defense to stop the Iowa attack and generating the emotional steam to stop the Hawkeyes. The suggestion that Iowa was not as ready mentally as Wisconsin came from Coach Evashevski of Iowa when he said: "When a team has so much more desire than its opponent on a particular day, you can take a good physical beating." Iowa did. Most battered of the Hawks were Capt. Calvin Jones and Eddie Vincent. Some of the injuries lasted throughout the season.

From the Wisconsin game the Hawkeyes went against Indiana at Iowa City, and a 20 point first half accumulation was sufficient to win for Iowa. Ploen threw to Don Dobrino and Jim Gibbons for touchdowns, with Dobrino getting a second score on a short run. There was significance in the touchdown pass to Gibbons, although it was not apparent at the time. Gibbons was a sophomore. Before completing his career he would become one of the Big Ten's great pass receivers and an all-American end. Against Indiana, however, Gibbons and his teammates settled for a 20 — 6 victory.

Purdue was next, with the Hawks at home once more. This one was gruelling. Leonard Dawson's passes for the Boilermakers offset everything the Hawkeyes could do. Even with Iowa leading, 20 — 13, and only seven seconds left to play, Dawson came through with a pass to third string end Steve Chernicky from 14 yards out to save the game. When the same Dawson kicked the extra point only four seconds remained. Dawson passed for all three Purdue touchdowns and kicked both extra points. The game was a 20 — 20 stand-off, although Iowa led, 13 — 7, at the half on touchdowns by Roger Wiegmann and another Ploen to Gibbons touchdown pass. Reichow's three yard sweep in the last six minutes helped the Hawks gain the tie.

The over-all strength expected of Iowa just wasn't there. From the Purdue game the Hawks journeyed to Los Angeles for a meeting with U.C.L.A. The Iowa coaches had quietly believed they could win, but they couldn't do it with their patchwork lineup. Injuries had taken their toll. Cal Jones still was out of action. Vincent was back in the lineup for the first time since the Wisconsin game. A talented halfback named Sam Brown got the Bruins off in the lead in the first quarter but Mike Hagler scored for Iowa before the period expired. Onto the scene came Ronnie Knox of U.C.L.A., one of the widely publicized players of his time. Knox put the Bruins ahead when his eight yard run capped a touchdown march. Late in the second quarter Iowa drove deep — and lost the ball on downs at the one-yard line. Twice that day the Hawks were stopped just short of a score. They had the guns to outgain the Uclans in total yardage but on the scoreboard they took a 33 — 13 pasting.

The Hawkeyes of 1955 were not the clutch team some of their predecessors were. When the first four games of the season were over

the lack of "finishing fury" was readily noted. In the four games Iowa had scored a total of only 13 points in the last half. Four opponents had made 47. More of the last half inadequacy was in evidence against Michigan the following week. Iowa, which had lost 14 — 13 heartbreakers to the Wolverines the two previous seasons, went into this one with a 14 — 0 lead at the half and came out at the finish beaten, 33 — 21. Two outstanding Michigan ends, Tom Maentz and Ron Kramer, snatched Jim Maddock passes out of the hands of Iowa defenders too often in the last half. The Hawkeyes, with 72,096 onlookers watching, moved through the first three quarters with a 21 — 13 lead, then were mangled under a 20 point Michigan onslaught in the fourth quarter. It was the sixth game of a season that started hopefully, and Iowa had two victories, a tie and three defeats.

The Hawkeyes had one winning effort left, and they exploded it against Minnesota. The emotional buildup that preceded the game is not in the record but it must have been effective. The Hawks mixed new ammunition with great desire for a 26 — 0 victory. They started with a previously unused weapon, Eddie Vincent making his first appearance as a passer. The innovation caught all hands by surprise, including the Gophers when Vincent tossed an 18-yard scoring pass to Jim Gibbons. That first quarter effort was followed by two Vincent touchdowns in the second period, each from inside the 10-yard line. Kenny Ploen wrapped it up with a 25-yard touchdown run in the third.

Two games remained for the ill-fated team of 1955, both defeats. Howard (Hopalong) Cassady and his Ohio State mates took care of one, 20 — 10, and Paul Hornung engineered the other for Notre Dame, 17 — 14. Cassady, near the end of a brilliant career, saved one of his great games for Iowa. The customary capacity crowd of more than 82,000 saw the racing redhead carry the ball 26 times, score all three Ohio State touchdowns on runs of 45, 10 and 3 yards, and gain 169 yards from scrimmage. Jim Freeman's 18-yard field goal and his touchdown following a five yard pass from Jerry Reichow kept Iowa in the game, but trailing 13 — 10, through three quarters. With five minutes remaining, Cassady's third touchdown clinched it.

Iowa made a determined try to close the season with a victory at Notre Dame. This was one of many rugged games in the series and it went into the fourth quarter tied, 7 — 7. The record crowd of 59,995 in the Notre Dame stands saw Iowa stopped on the six-inch line once, then come relentlessly back to score on a short pass, Don Dobrino to Jerry Reichow. The Hawks were ahead, 14 — 7, with five minutes gone in the fourth quarter. Notre Dame sledged its way back with Hornung rifling passes to his mates and fullback Dick Fitzgerald slamming out yardage. On second down from the Iowa 15 Hornung, trying to find a receiver, was driven back to the 30. Still eluding his rushers he ran, then leaped and hurled a pass to Jim Morse. Morse jumped and caught the ball in the end zone. The game was tied, 14 — 14, with about eight minutes remaining.

Notre Dame broke the tie with a shade more than two minutes left when Hornung drilled a field goal between the posts from 28 yards out. Iowa's season was over, a disappointing 3 — 5 — 1 in the record book. The Hawkeyes had played hard, tough football, but they encountered more frustrating experiences. Before another season, Forest Evashevski would make vast and widely heralded changes in his offense.

For the third year in a row Calvin Jones received all-America recognition, being a con-

sensus selection again in 1955. Coach Evashevski paid ultimate tribute to his finest lineman when he announced that Jones' number "62" would never again be worn by a Hawkeye while he was coaching at Iowa. The Board in Control of Athletics officially retired the number and Calvin Jones' jersey would henceforth rest alongside number "24," that of Nile Kinnick.

Eddie Vincent again was named to various all-midwest and all Big Ten first teams and completed his three years at Iowa as the top career season ground gainer under Evashevski. Jerry Reichow, unheralded in many quarters while a Hawkeye, wrote his name with distinction in the Iowa record book. In 1955 the Decorah product exceeded 1,000 yards in total offense. Only four others, Aubrey Devine and Nick Kutsch in the twenties, Nile Kinnick in 1939 and Randy Duncan have accomplished the feat. Further, Reichow, in three years at Iowa, rushed and passed for 2,177 total yards. Only Devine and Duncan have bettered that career mark. Although not known as a great passer, Jerry Reichow led Iowa in passing three straight seasons, a consistency of performance shared only with Nile Kinnick and the incomparable Devine, who was Iowa's rushing, passing and scoring leader in 1919, 1920 and 1921.

A record 545,025 fans saw Iowa play in 1955, and athletic income for the school year topped one million dollars. Iowa's net football receipts from the Notre Dame game, played at South Bend, exceeded $100,000, the first time such a figure was reached for a single game.

Championship Dreams Reach Reality

Thursday, April 5, 1956, was an unrecognized but notable day in State University of Iowa football history. That afternoon marked the first meeting of the Hawkeyes and the Wing-T, balanced line attack that was to bring them from the Big Ten obscurity of 1955 to the top of the football heap in 1956. That was the day Coach Evashevski explained the offense to his players and gave them their spacings, starting count and formations. Four days later they scrimmaged.

The development of the 1956 team is told in the records. It won the Big Ten championship for the first time since 1922, it earned a Number 3 rating nationally, and it won the Rose Bowl game. It was the first Iowa team in 51 years to win more than eight games in a season. It was the first Iowa team in 16 years to defeat Notre Dame, and it was the team that shattered Ohio State's unmatched string of 17 consecutive conference victories. Evashevski was named Coach of the Year by the Washington Touchdown Club, the Los Angeles Times and the Kansas City Rockne Club. His goal of making Iowa "respectable" in football had been accomplished in stunning fashion.

When the 1956 football prospectus was issued by Eric C. Wilson's Iowa Sports Information Service, it carried a line in a preview of the season:

"It appears that Iowa will use mostly the Single Wing with balanced line, instead of the multiple offense of recent years, with unbalanced line."

The Hawks did use some features of the Single Wing, notably the blocking, but the tactics were different than anything the Big Ten had seen previously. Iowa became an efficient demonstrator of the new Wing-T. The radical change in attack was to establish Evashevski's team as a fast, razor sharp attacking force, loaded with deception. The 1956 season became a milestone in the school's football history.

The story of the switch in offenses began with Dave Nelson, head coach at the University of Delaware, a close friend of Evy and his teammate at Michigan. Nelson, employing a multiple offense against Delaware's opponents, decided that his Single Wing type of blocking was inadequate in meeting the defenses employed against his team. This was primarily because the exchange of the ball preceding the fake left an offensive blocking weakness which it was not possible to plug effectively. So he installed the T formation where the fake preceded the actual exchange of the ball. Therefore, anytime a man was faking he could plug a hole created by a pulling lineman and not get leaking defensive men into the play situation. In this way Nelson was able to open up new offensive innovations and at the same time retain the advantages of single wing blocking. The result was highly effective.

When the 1955 season was over Evashevski reviewed his own situation and appraised the material he expected to have available for 1956.

"I could see coming up an entirely different type of lineman than we had had," Evy explained. "So I sat down with Dave after the 1955 season and told him I was real interested in his attack. I could see an entirely different group of boys on our field. I could see Frank Bloomquist and Gary Grouwinkel and Bob Commings, three very maneuverable guards. I could see big tackles like Alex Karras and Dick Klein and Frank Rigney, who were not especially good movers. Then I could see our ends, who had good maneuverability — Jim Gibbons and Frank Gilliam, who also had speed enough to pull. We had an explosive type

backfield and we had the guy who could make the big play in Kenny Ploen.

"We had to find a way to utilize Kenny to the best of his ability. He was not a really good Split-T man. He was poor on the option. You knew how Jerry Reichow could go on that play but when you put Ploen in he liked to get back and look things over. Well, this is how we came to change. So I conferred with Davey about this type of attack. I had felt for a long time that he was one of the finest coaches in the game.

"We put in the Wing-T in spring practice. We tried to improvise and improve upon the offense and I think we did. We featured the bootlegs. We made a study of football that went back into the '20's and found that with the Single Wing in vogue it actually was just aiming at one point. This was one dimension of football, as I called it. When the Notre Dame

1956 Team

box came in it provided a two-dimension at-tack, based on the buck lateral and the Harlow series of shifts and spinners at Harvard. Imme-diately after the second dimension came in the scores kept going up. This went along until once more the defense was catching up and Don Faurot came in with the Split T at Mis-souri.

"I took that apart and tried to find out why the Split T was an immediate success and de-cided that it was because a third dimension had been introduced into football. The quar-terback either gave the ball to a halfback, or threatened to keep as his second dimension, or to pitch out to a fellow trailing as his third. We tried to work this into an offense where we always had the three dimensions but where we also added a fourth dimension. With it we could threaten the middle with the fullback, threaten both flanks or go off tackle with the halfbacks, and the quarterback, by virtue of a bootleg, could fake the pass or endanger either flank. The fourth dimension always provided the pos-sibility of threatening a different area.

"That's what I think made the Wing-T a real successful offense. But I have said a number of times that it was very definitely Davey Nel-son's offense. I've said that in all my clinics and I would be guilty of plagiarism if I failed to recognize the man who had the basic idea. I think we put an individual touch to it. A lot of teams have tried the Wing T and every one of them has taken part of the Iowa offense or Delaware offense and used it. It became one of the most copied offenses outside of the Split T."

The significance of Iowa's switch to the Wing-T, and the ability of the Hawkeyes to adjust to and most effectively execute their new offense, made no great impact in advance of the season. Iowa generally was consigned to seventh place in the Big Ten previews. Perhaps the "how wrong can you be" cliché originated just about then for the Hawkeye team made extremely bad guessers of most analysts.

The year 1956 was, without question, one of the most fabulous in Iowa football history. The season started at Indiana. As the new attack be-gan to roll, with Kenny Ploen at the controls, Iowa ground out two first quarter touchdowns on 82 and 69 yard scoring marches. Bill Happel and John Nocera got the six-pointers with Ploen and Gene Veit adding second half scores to give the Hawks a 27 — 0 victory. Perhaps the most significant thing about the game was the balance demonstrated by Iowa. On attack the team rolled up 242 yards rushing and 24 through the air. Defensively they limited the Hoosiers to only 76 yards on running plays and 73 on eight completed passes.

Game Number 2 had its historic aspects, but this fact was obscured until the season had ended and the identity of Iowa's Rose Bowl opponent was known. Oregon State came to Iowa City. Its appearance generated most pain-ful moments for the Hawks, who seemed to have exceptional difficulty gearing themselves to meet the challenge of the West Coast team. Oregon State's great halfback, Joe Francis, was establishing the reputation he later achieved but the Iowa players may not have been aware of it. Just 1 minute and 10 seconds after the first kickoff Francis threw a pass to Earnel Dur-den for a 30-yard touchdown play. The extra point was blocked by Iowa's Frank Bloomquist. The Hawkeyes tramped off the field trailing 6 — 0 at the half, and were shaken by a new jolt in the third quarter when Paul Lowe raced 49 yards for a touchdown. Only after they trailed 13 — 0, did the Hawks make a move toward victory.

Shut out until the fourth minute of the fourth quarter, and forced to play with number one quarterback Kenny Ploen on the sidelines nurs-ing an injury, the Hawkeyes broke through for the first time when John Nocera, in an unex-pected move, threw a 10-yard pass to Frank Gilliam in the end zone. It was Nocera's only pass of the season, but it brought Iowa within reach of the Beavers, 13 — 7. Less than two min-utes later sophomore Randy Duncan passed to Jim Gibbons for 33 yards and the tying touch-down. When Bob Prescott's second successful conversion spun between the goal posts, Iowa had a 14 — 13 victory to compensate for an all afternoon scare.

Wisconsin played at Iowa in the third game of the campaign. Once more the Hawkeyes had their new ground gaining machinery oiled adequately, although the Badgers were a rugged defensive club. Late in the second quarter a 78 yard drive was climaxed when Ploen passed to Mike Hagler for 11 yards and a touchdown. One second remained on the clock when Ploen attempted the extra point and missed. In less than four minutes of the third quarter Iowa concluded another march, covering 50 yards in seven plays. The payoff was launched from the 1-yard line, with Ploen scoring. Bob Prescott kicked the point. Wisconsin scored on a fourth quarter pass of 23 yards, Carlson to Melvin, but a fierce Iowa defense, spearheaded by Alex Karras, Bloomquist and Frank Gilliam, thwarted any further scoring. The Hawks had won, 13 – 6, the first time in more than twenty years that Iowa had won its initial three starts.

A favorable schedule in 1956 fitted into the business of perfecting the new attack. Adjustments needed after the Wisconsin game, particularly the need to strengthen a rushing offense, were made a week later against an overmatched team from the University of Hawaii. The Hawkeyes, far too strong for the Islanders, were able to get 42 men into the contest and win, 34 – 0. Play was generally ragged, Iowa losing the ball four times on fumbles, but it outgained the visitors, 331 yards to 78.

The Hawaii game put an end to any experimenting. The rest of the way was over the rockiest kind of road, with Purdue, Michigan, Minnesota, Ohio State and Notre Dame ahead as regular season opponents. In the Purdue game at Lafayette, the Hawks again had to contend with the exceptional passing of Leonard Dawson, along with the receiving of giant Lamar Lundy, among others. It was a 7 – 7 standoff in the first quarter, Mel Dillard of the Boilermakers matching an early Iowa score when Ploen threw a 14-yard touchdown pass to Jim Gibbons.

Bill Happel raced the last six yards of an Iowa march in the first minute of the second quarter and Dawson countered for Purdue with a scoring pass to Tom Fletcher from the 18-yard line. Again they were tied, this time at 14 – 14. Still in the second quarter Iowa came on again and once more Happel climaxed the move with a 30-yard run to the goal. Kenny Ploen's conversion, along with two earlier by Bob Prescott, gave Iowa a 21 – 14 lead at the half. The scoring slowed in the last two periods, but not the pace. Purdue stopped every Iowa threat. Dawson engineered a passing blitz for Purdue but not until the fourth quarter was about half gone, when he fired a throw to Lundy, did the Boilermakers score again. That pass, from 20 yards out, threw fear into Iowa but Dawson missed the extra point. There still was time for Purdue to threaten again and threaten they did. Starting from their 4-yard line the Boilermakers advanced to Iowa's 21 where a pass was fumbled and Iowa recovered. Ninety seconds remained and the Hawkeyes ran out the clock to win their second one-point victory of the season, 21 – 20. Purdue gained 405 yards, 242 of it on 17 completed passes. Iowa moved the ball 349 yards, including 290 on the ground. Bill Happel gained 99 Hawkeye yards in 12 carries and Don Dobrino 94 in 15 trips with the ball. The Hawkeyes had won five in a row for the first time since 1928, and stood as the only undefeated, untied team in Big Ten ranks.

Game Number 5 of the season was in the record, but opponent Number 6 was Michigan. The game was played at Iowa and for once an Iowa victory appeared to be in the making. It was Homecoming and Coach Forest Evashevski had never tasted defeat at a homecoming, either as a coach or player. Further, the Hawks had not lost a game on their home field in more than three years; but, the Iowa coach never had won from his alma mater in three previous games.

A record stadium throng of 58,137 watched the Hawkeyes bounce back brilliantly from an early Ron Kramer field goal to score twice and hold a 14 – 3 halftime lead. Hawkeye followers, encouraged by the advantage, nursed fond hopes for the first Iowa victory over the Wolverines in thirteen games.

Michigan killed that hope. Grinding it out on the ground and superior in passing, the

Wolverines scored a third quarter touchdown then applied the customary heartache by consuming much of the fourth quarter with an 80-yard march which ended behind the Iowa goal line with 66 seconds left to play. The 17 — 14 defeat was the only blot on the Hawkeye record, and John Herrnstein could take the bows. Six times on the fateful, last minute Wolverine march, he crashed out first downs by inches to keep the drive going.

The loss to Michigan, acknowledged by Evashevski to be the most bitterly disappointing of his coaching career, was compounded when it was learned that seven of his first twenty-two men had received disabling injuries. The problem of defeating upcoming Minnesota seemed almost insurmountable. The Gophers were undefeated; they had beaten the same Michigan team by two touchdowns, and a victory over Iowa would send them Rose Bowling on New Year's Day. The technical preparation of the Hawkeyes was good during most practice sessions. University President Virgil Hancher, visiting a mid-week workout, commented: "Some of the best teaching in the University is done on this field."

The tension and tedium on the morning of the Gopher clash was electric. Out of the Curtis Hotel in Minneapolis and into the raw November day trooped the Hawkeyes, to board their team buses for the ride to Memorial Stadium. Coach Forest Evashevski described the ensuing minutes:

"As we were riding in the bus I was still concerned about the attitude and mental buildup of our squad. I felt that it wasn't just right; that we needed something more than the normal incentive. This was provided for us when we arrived at the stadium.

"As our squad left the buses and went to the pass gate they were stopped by the Minnesota gatekeeper who wouldn't permit them to enter the dressing room without their pass tickets. I had been given the passes but by the time I got there the boys were all standing around trying to get in. The gatekeeper was properly insistent and as I walked up, ready to hand him the tickets, he turned to me and said, rather

harshly, 'You know better than this. You know you were given tickets and that you can't get in without them.'

"The light went on in my head immediately. I pushed the tickets back down in my pocket and told him: 'Well, I'm sorry, but I guess there won't be any game if you aren't going to let our squad in.' So I never did produce the tickets, and by that time they were calling for the athletic director and various other officials. I think we were kept there fifteen minutes, and this incensed our squad to no small extent. It was a very cold day and by the time they allowed us to go in anyway, our boys couldn't wait to get out on the field to meet the Gophers. By this time they were no longer concerned about their injuries or the great rating of Minnesota. It was a psychological windfall which doesn't happen often, but it was placed right in my lap."

The 1956 Minnesota team was the finest the Gophers had had since the days of Bernie Bierman. Its followers had already reserved all Western Airline bookings from Minneapolis to Los Angeles between Christmas and New Year's. Iowa was a seven-point underdog. The game, played before a nationwide television audience, was a meeting of two tough teams that could move the ball or stop an opponent. The Gophers received the kickoff and marched quickly for a first down. Then on the fourth offensive play of the game a Minnesota back fumbled and two Hawkeyes pounced on the ball at the Gopher 38. The aroused Hawks began a drive, rammed their way to the one-yard line, highlighted by a clutch 7-yard toss from quarterback Ploen to reliable Jim Gibbons. Fred Harris was called upon and he stampeded into the end zone. Bob Prescott kicked the extra point. More than 55 minutes of playing time remained but there was never another touchdown. Iowa's defense was furious. The Hawks caught fire. They helped force six Minnesota fumbles, and recovered half of them. Three times they captured Minnesota passes, Bill Happel snatching one just a yard from the Iowa goal and another in the final two minutes when the Gophers were making a desperate try for a score. The Hawks left the field with their coach on their shoulders, and a Sunday newspaper headlined the story: "Iowa Unpacks Minnesota's Bags, 7 — 0." Don Suchy was named national "lineman of the week" by one wire service, but 21 other Hawkeyes shared in the post game accolades. Any decision over Minnesota is cherished by an Iowa team. That one was doubly so, and most disheartening to the Gophers and their Coach Murray Warmath.

Iowa's record was 4 — 1 in the conference when Ohio State arrived at Iowa stadium on November 17, 1956. The proud defending champions, possessors of seventeen straight Big Ten victories, were favored to add an Iowa scalp to their impressive, record breaking string. Hawkeye experience had been that ominous business threatened whenever the Buckeyes provided the opposition. Coach Forest Evashevski posed a penetrating challenge to his

team when he told them: "You have sixty minutes to play — and the rest of your life to remember it."

The manner in which the Iowa team rose to the occasion has become a story of the pride, the desire and the unselfish sacrifice which Evashevski expected and received from his players. After a bruising, scoreless first half Iowa got the ball on its own 37 to start the third quarter. The Hawks went on the march, covered 63 yards in 10 plays, including a climactic 17-yard scoring pass from Kenny Ploen to Jim Gibbons. Bob Prescott missed his first extra point of the year, but Iowa had a 6 — 0 lead. That was the final score.

So ferocious was the Hawk defense that it permitted Ohio State no advance beyond the Iowa 32-yard line. It permitted only two pass completions for 18 yards, and it limited the Ohio ground attack, which had rushed for a

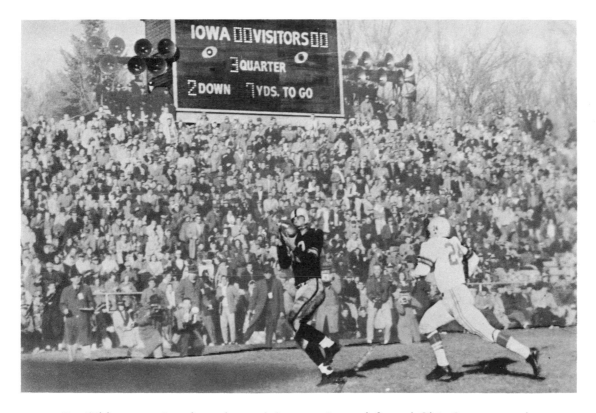

Jim Gibbons scoring the only touchdown as Iowa defeated Ohio State, won the Big Ten title and a Rose Bowl invitation in 1956.

modern conference record of 465 yards the week before, to only 147. The Bucks were out-first-downed, outrushed and outpassed. More importantly, they were outscored and stripped of their Big Ten title in the wake of the most important victory ever witnessed on the turf of Iowa Stadium.

Kenneth Ploen

The Hawkeyes had earned a Rose Bowl trip. That night, at a victory celebration in the Memorial Union, university provost, Harvey Davis, solemnly advised 2,000 cheering students that there would be two additional days of Christmas vacation.

"An excellent victory deserves one day," he said in measured academic voice, "and an extraordinary one deserves two."

Amid the echoes of celebration came further accolades. Alex Karras became the second Hawkeye in two weeks to earn national "lineman of the week" honors. Kenny Ploen was named Midwest "back of the week," and Forest Evashevski received his first 1956 coaching honor: Midwest Coach of the Year, by the Chicago Football Writers Association.

Following is a diagram of the all-important pass play, Ploen to Gibbons, which beat Ohio State, gave Iowa the Big Ten title, and sent them to the Rose Bowl.

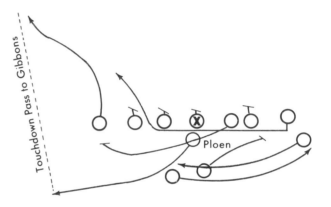

This dramatic 16-yd touchdown pass, Ken Ploen to end Jim Gibbons, gave Iowa its 6 — 0 victory over Ohio State, the Big Ten championship, and a trip to the Rose Bowl. The play, featuring the bootleg keep by Ploen, came off the counter criss-cross action of the Winged T offense.

There was reason to suspect that Iowa, basking in the glory of the first championship claim a Hawkeye team had filed since 1922, might not be capable of reaching the necessary peak required for a victory over Notre Dame. That fear was wasted. The Hawks slammed into the Fighting Irish with one of the most ruthless running attacks ever employed by an Iowa team. An impressive total of 409 yards was gained on the ground, and 50 more on four completed passes. The Iowans scored the first five times they had the ball. A 28 — 0 halftime lead was increased in the final two periods.

Three touchdowns, by Ploen, Mike Hagler and Fred Harris, were made on runs of more than forty yards.

Not since 1940 had the Hawkeyes beaten a Notre Dame team and in the 11 intervening games three ties had provided Iowa its only consolation. This time the most decisive victory ever wrested from the Fighting Irish was Iowa's, 48 — 0. Forty-two Hawkeye players took part in the seven touchdown onslaught. Only once before in more than 50 years had Notre Dame surrendered more points to an opponent. Even before the game was over word was flashed to Hawkeyeland that Michigan had beaten Ohio State. Iowa's championship was undisputed — the first such title since 1921.

With dash and dazzle, the trim and talented State University of Iowa band swung smartly up the field in the Rose Bowl stadium in Pasadena, Calif., January 1, 1957. From the Iowa side of the vast concrete arena a roar welcomed the finely co-ordinated unit directed and beautifully readied for the occasion by Fred Ebbs, the Hawkeye bandmaster. Moments later Coach Evashevski's football squad jogged out from the dressing room, ready for battle in the most glamorous struggle ever engaged in by an Iowa team.

Across the field, tense and fidgety, the Oregon State players waited, the same men who had held the Hawkeyes without a point for nearly 50 minutes, some 11 weeks earlier. This was to be an historic rematch in the Rose Bowl of two teams that had fought each other to a standstill in the regular season. No such principals had been paired in the Rose Bowl before. Iowa's indecisive 14 — 13 edge in the earlier meeting provided great doubt as to which team would prevail in the classic post-season game. More than 10,000 Iowans journeyed to California and were part of the 97,-126 who jammed Pasadena's famed stadium.

The game began. For the first four minutes it was crashing, mashing give and take. Iowa had the ball in midfield. Suddenly, with the Wing-T threatening to strike almost any point of the Oregon State defense, Kenny Ploen bolted through an opening into the secondary

and raced away. He ran 49 yards for the first Iowa touchdown, with less than five minutes gone. The Hawks came right back in that first quarter, raging downfield once more with that speedy, deceptive attack. A 37 yard blast by Don Dobrino put the ball on the Beaver 9 yard line. From there Ploen called on Mike Hagler, who swept on in. Iowa had two touchdowns with the first quarter only half gone. Adding Bob Prescott's extra points, the Hawks held a 14 — 0 lead. That was as many points as they had scored in the full 60 minutes of the regular season game between the two clubs.

Oregon State slammed its way back into contention. With little more than two minutes gone in the second quarter it moved to a touchdown but missed the extra point. Iowa, leading 14 — 6, widened it to 21 — 6 before the half when Bill Happel's five-yard romp capped another drive. At that particular stage of the game Iowa was threatened with trouble. Kenny Ploen, who started brilliantly, had been carried off the field with what appeared to be an injury that would prevent his return. Quiet but fervent thanks was evident in the Iowa stands when Ploen returned for the second half and resumed his outstanding play.

His role as the game's most valuable player must have been obvious to all, but by way of clinching that honor he received an overwhelming majority of the votes of the writers who make such selections. Iowa had many standouts that day, including Mike Hagler. He streaked 66 yards for his second touchdown in the early minutes of the third quarter. With a 28 — 6 margin the ultimate winner was fairly well assured but Oregon State was not ready to concede. The Beavers stormed back for a third quarter touchdown of their own, again missing the goal kick. Iowa went into the fourth quarter leading, 28 — 12.

The fifth and last Iowa touchdown came in the first 13 seconds of the fourth quarter, with Ploen passing to Gibbons for the final 16 yards of the drive. Six minutes later Joe Francis drilled home a 35 yard touchdown pass for Oregon State. The final score was 35 — 19, Iowa winning and giving thirty-nine players the experi-

IOWA WILL HAVE TWELVE MEN ON THE FIELD
IN THE 1957 ROSE BOWL GAME

CALVIN JONES

A Frank Miller cartoon tribute to the late Calvin Jones and Forest Evashevski's
1956 champions.

ence of participating in a Rose Bowl victory. The game ball was sent to Mrs. Talitha Jones, mother of Iowa's great Calvin Jones, to whom the Iowa team had quietly dedicated victory. Iowa's interior linemen, Alex Karras and Dick Klein at the tackles, Frank Bloomquist and Bob Commings at the guards and Don Suchy at center, helped jam the day with frustration

for Oregon State. They had notable help from John Nocera, Iowa's line-backing fullback. The ends, Frank Gilliam and Jim Gibbons, were invaluable.

The Rose Bowl game was featured by exceptional forward passing. Iowa's passers hit 11 of 15 for 107 yards and the Oregon State air attack accounted for 130 yards on 10 completions in 14 tries. In addition, Iowa raised its total yardage to 408 by gaining 301 on the ground. Kenny Ploen carried the ball seven times for 59 yards and completed 9 of 10 passes for 83 more. Important contributors were the starting halfbacks, Don Dobrino and Mike Hagler, who ran for 64 and 85 yards, respectively.

The Hawks flew home and packed away their equipment. Their heads were high. During the regular season they had been just 66 seconds away from an undefeated season, Michigan winning, 17 — 14, with only 1:06 to play. They had swept just about everything a college team could win — the Big Ten championship, a convincing Rose Bowl victory and recognition far and wide as one of the great teams of the nation. The Columbus (Ohio) Touchdown Club awarded the Robert C. Zuppke Trophy to Iowa as the outstanding college football team in the country.

Various groups handed Evashevski "Coach of the Year" awards. In accepting the accolades the Hawkeye coach passed deserved bouquets to his capable assistants Bob Flora, Chalmers (Bump) Elliott, Archie Kodros, Henry (Whitey) Piro, Jerry Burns and Jerry Hilgenberg. Kenny Ploen added the Big Ten's "most valuable player" trophy to the corresponding honor he had won in the Rose Bowl. The versatile quarterback led his team in rushing, passing and scoring, the only such triple leader at Iowa since Nile Kinnick 17 years before. Alex Karras won a place on the all-America team chosen by the Football Writers Association of America for Look Magazine as well as a berth on the Associated Press all-America first unit. Two other Hawkeyes, Frank Gilliam and center Don Suchy, were named to Number 1 all Big Ten teams, and both also were accorded all-America second team honors. Gilliam, recognized by his coaches as the finest defensive end to play at Iowa during the Evashevski era, also was presented the Virgil M. Hancher award for his over-all contribution to the team. Within a week after his return from the Rose Bowl, Evashevski was in Washington, D.C., receiving from the hands of his old Michi-

gan teammate, Tom Harmon, the Washington Touchdown Club's annual coaching award.

Not until he had put aside his coaching duties and assumed the athletic directorship did Evashevski reveal the place the 1956 team held in his affection. He said it was by far the best defensive team he coached at Iowa, although it was not up to the level of the 1958 team on offense. "If you had to evaluate which one was the better team, I would have to go along with the 1956 group because it had more ability to come through in the clutch."

Late in 1956 the Big Ten Conference endorsed legislation whereby financial aid could be given to athletes on the basis of proven demonstrated "need." The following spring the rule was modified to permit financial assistance covering basic educational costs on the basis of superior scholarship.

1957

These were golden days. As the 1957 season opened Kenny Ploen was gone but Randy Duncan was just entering his junior year. Frank Gilliam had played out the string at end. Behind him came Don Norton, a sophomore who also was to become an all-American. Gone also was assistant coach Chalmers (Bump) Elliott who had resigned early in the year to become an assistant under Bennie Oosterbaan at the University of Michigan. It was generally conceded that Elliott would succeed Oosterbaan as head coach of the Wolverines after a stint as chief varsity assistant. Coach Evashevski was going into his sixth season at Iowa. Seven starters from 1956 were returning and 21 lettermen were on hand. The outlook was good, and the stature of a defending champion was Iowa's.

The Hawks lived up to their promise. They campaigned through the first seven games without a loss, although tied by Michigan in a 21 — 21 thriller, then met their only defeat against Ohio State in a 17 — 13 game. Thus, in the seasons of 1956 and 1957 one loss by three points and one by four points were the only reverses charged against Iowa.

Utah State was out of its class in the opener, being swamped, 70 − 14. For Iowa, the highlights were many. Three Randy Duncan passes, to Jim Gibbons for 44 yards, to Don Norton for 47 and to Gene Sessi for 80, all went for touchdowns. Sessi handled the ball only three times, scored three times and picked up 131 yards. The 70 Iowa points were the most since State College of Iowa (then Iowa Normal) surrendered 95 in 1914. The Hawkeyes piled up a record-breaking 648 yards rushing and passing, with the 328 notched through the air setting another all-time mark.

In the next start, against Washington State, Ray Jauch made his first move toward prominence. A sophomore halfback, and one who belongs with the grittiest competitors in Hawkeye annals, Jauch steamed in for two short yardage touchdowns in the first half of a rugged go, enabling Iowa to attain a 13 − 7 first half lead. It ended with the Hawks winning, 20 − 13. Kevin Furlong scored for Iowa in the last four minutes of a game that saw the Hawkeyes vastly superior on the ground attack but a victim of Washington State passes that brought the Cougars most of their yardage.

The Hawks opened the Big Ten season at Indiana and found the Hoosiers woefully inadequate. In the 47 − 7 victory Iowa's defense swarmed all over Indiana, leaving it with minus 30 yards in running. Long Indiana passes functioned intermittently, one bringing 75 yards and a score. Iowa had a 34 − 0 halftime lead, with Bill Gravel counting twice, Duncan firing touchdown passes to Bob Prescott and Gibbons, and Ray Jauch belting one home on a 19-yard run. Hagler and Happel were last half scorers for Iowa, giving the Hawkeyes their most points against a conference opponent in 35 years.

Evashevski's charges won their second conference game of the season from Wisconsin. In a duel of offenses which saw the Badgers gain 160 yards on the ground and 154 on 13 completed passes, Wisconsin gained its only touchdown on a blocked punt recovered in the end zone late in the third period. Iowa, a 21 − 7 winner,

gained its touchdowns on a seven yard run by Hagler, a 35 yard advance by Don Horn and a late game sprint by Bill Gravel, who intercepted a pass and hauled it 45 yards to the goal.

With the elements at their worst, Iowa met Northwestern in a late October game at Evanston. For more than three quarters they sloshed and struggled through mud, snow, sleet and rain, to no avail. The defenses were better than the offenses. With five minutes gone in the fourth quarter the turning point came in the form of a pass, Duncan to Furlong, covering 31 yards for the only score. In the 6 − 0 contest Iowa's running brought only 121 yards and its passing 59 for one of the low points of the era in Hawkeye yardage. Northwestern ran for 107 and passed for 13.

The difference between a great offensive play and a lapse by the defense often is hard to detect. Iowa-Michigan games have abounded in such plays and the 1957 contest was no exception. Was a 65-yard punt return by Jim Pace of Michigan the result of strategy, as was Earl Smith's 1954 carry back for a touchdown against Purdue? It all depends on the viewpoint. On the Iowa side the temptation was to mention poor tackling. In any case the Hawkeyes, playing at Ann Arbor, moved out to a first quarter lead on John Nocera's touchdown, then sweltered under a barrage of Michigan touchdowns in the second. First it was Pace on his long punt return. Next Jim VanPelt hit Gary Prahst with a 31-yard scoring pass and finally Stan Noskin hit through for the final yard of a drive. The Hawks came on in the last half to recoup with Horn bucking for the score on one drive and Duncan smashing home on another. The Wolverines, winners of 11 straight from Iowa, were held to a 21 − 21 draw. A total of 90,478 fans, the most ever to see the Hawkeyes in a Big Ten game, jammed the mammoth Michigan stadium for the battle. It was also beamed to a nationwide television audience, the first football game to be shown in color.

Iowa coach Forest Evashevski, featured in a controversial article by Sports Illustrated magazine earlier in the year, again was the target of Henry Luce syndicate reporters when sister publication, Time magazine, accused Iowa of being "The Team That Quit" in its game against the Wolverines. The Hawkeyes had rebounded with two second half touchdowns to tie the score and then, with slightly more than three minutes remaining, stayed on the ground to run the clock out. Evashevski, playing to win the Big Ten title, knew that every other conference team excepting Ohio State had at least one loss on its record. If Iowa could enter the showdown battle with the Buckeyes, which was two weeks away, without a loss, the winner would claim the conference championship.

The Iowa-Minnesota game of 1957 was doubly notable because it marked the third straight Iowa victory over the Gophers and the largest total points the Hawkeyes ever scored against them. Not since the days of Howard Jones had the Hawks sustained an advantage over Minnesota for so long a stretch. The early November struggle at Iowa City saw Evashevski's team pile up yardage in great quantity, gaining 340 on rushing and 195 on passing. The 535-yard total was the highest on record in a Big Ten game. Iowa also broke an existing conference record by scoring in its forty-first straight Big Ten game, eclipsing the former mark of 40 held jointly by Michigan and Wisconsin.

The Hawkeyes, gaining a 7 — 0 first quarter edge against the Gophers, raced away to a 30 — 7 margin at the half and 44 — 13 after three quarters. The final score was 44 — 20. Iowa did not have to punt during the game and its 23 second quarter points were the most over a conference opponent since Jess Hawley's 1913 team garnered 28 against Northwestern in the opening period. Other highlights for Iowa were touchdown passes by Randy Duncan to Jim Gibbons for five and 52 yards. Duncan scored twice himself on sneaks. Bill Happel raced 48 for a touchdown and Bob Prescott, who kicked a 45-yard field goal at one stage, notched an easy touchdown by capturing a Minnesota fumble in the end zone. Gibbons, who was to set most Iowa single season and career pass catching records before the year ended, added two school single game

marks against the Gophers. His nine receptions tied the all-time high set in 1952 by Dan McBride, and the 164 yards gained broke the previous record held by Emlen Tunnell.

The Hawks went into the Ohio State game unbeaten but tied. They came out with a scar — small but vital — meeting a 17 — 13 defeat in their last Big Ten game of the year. The Buckeyes had a devastating sophomore fullback, Bob White by name, who immediately qualified on a select list of players who had established themselves as virtually unstoppable against Iowa.

Playing at Columbus before 82,935, largest crowd in Buckeye stadium history, climaxed an early drive with a scoring pass, Duncan to Prescott, for eight yards. Ohio State took up part of the 6 — 0 gap with a first quarter field goal by Don Sutherin, then went ahead when Frank Kremblas punched home from the one-yard line. Iowa regained the lead on a third quarter march, with Duncan smashing through from a yard out. The Hawkeyes held a 13 — 10 lead until late in the fourth quarter when White, bulldozing his way down the field, hammered the ball across from the five. The blasting Buckeye, who picked up 157 yards during the game, gained 66 of the 68 yards Ohio needed to notch the winning score. Less than four minutes remained. The Hawks could not retaliate, lost the Big Ten title and their first game in twelve starts. Iowa had one of its big yardage teams in 1957 but Ohio State led in total gains when the two teams met, 332 to 249.

Only Notre Dame remained as the windup drew near. Both teams were ranked in the nation's top ten. Iowa made the trip to South Bend, scored first when John Nocera blasted 36 yards through the Irish, and left the field at the half with a 14 — 6 lead. Duncan assumed a new role for Iowa, intercepting a pass for a 24 yard romp to the end zone. Bob Prescott scored two extra points for Iowa but Monte Stickles missed one for Notre Dame after George Izo had sped a 47 yard scoring pass to the same Stickles in the second quarter.

Notre Dame closed the gap to 14 — 13 in the third period, Steve Toth rambling 15 yards into the end zone, but Iowa clinched the decision in the fourth on a 21-yard Duncan to Don Norton pass. The final score was 21 – 13.

When the books were closed for the year, Bob Prescott led Iowa in scoring with three touchdowns, a field goal, and 21 of 27 successful extra point kicks. His 42 points stamped Prescott as the highest scoring lineman in Iowa history. Most recognized of all the 1957 Hawks was Alex Karras, broad and brawny tackle, who was selected on nine all-America teams, including all of the recognized listings. The durable tackle, second in balloting for the country's most coveted football trophy, the Heisman

Alex Karras

Award, was an overwhelming choice as the "outstanding interior lineman" of 1957, and recipient of the John B. Outland Award. Jim Gibbons, at end, won places on six all-America first teams. He closed a brilliant three year career at Iowa the holder of five Hawkeye pass re-

ceiving records and co-holder of another. Gibbons' marks include most passes caught in a game (shared), in one season and in a career, as well as most yards gained on receptions for each. In addition, his eleven touchdown passes caught ranks second to Jack Dittmer who caught thirteen over a four year stretch ending in 1949. Karras, Gibbons, Frank Bloomquist and Randy Duncan won berths on the All-Big Ten and Dick Klein, tackle, was a third team choice on the United Press All America.

Iowa, as a team, again placed high in the final wire service polls. Two, United Press and International News Service, had the Hawks in fifth place, while the Associated Press named Iowa sixth best team in the nation. The over-all record after two seasons of play under the Wing-T style of attack showed sixteen wins, two losses and a tie.

Football in 1957, as well as athletics generally, was the most successful in history at Iowa. Three games netted more than $100,000 each, topped by a record $129,453.50 as Iowa's share of the Michigan battle. Gross income from all athletics hit an all-time high of $1,113,576.67, and after expenses final figures revealed a profit of $359,436.15, also a new mark. Just five years earlier the net income from Iowa athletics had been only $33,354.45.

Before another season the Iowa Board in Control of Athletics had authorized construction of a large ultra-modern press box to replace the antiquated structure which had been in operation on both the east and west sides of the stadium since 1929. The new press box, to rise 100 feet above the top of the west stands, would be a three story facility, extending from one 25 yard line to the other. It was completed in time for the opening of the 1958 season at a cost of $490,628.62, approximately the cost of the stadium itself in 1929.

The Rules Committee of the American Football Coaches Association adopted two changes prior to the 1958 season which were to have a noticeable effect on play.

The substitution rule was further tightened by the provision allowing a player to re-enter the game only once during any quarter of play.

The first change in scoring since 1912 was made a part of the rules with inclusion of the "two point conversion rule." Two points were to be earned if the conversion were successful as a result of a running or passing play. One point was made if a kick were successful. The scrimmage line for conversions was moved from the two to the three yard line.

1958

On the gridiron the Hawkeye sweep contined. Evashevski's leadership had lifted Iowa high in the football world as the 1958 season came on. In the two previous seasons his teams had ranked among the nation's top five. The 1958 team was destined to earn an even higher standing, being rated second in the nation in both wire service polls.

There was no such outlook at the start of fall practice, however. Possibly because the prospects did seem bright, the squad appeared to be assuming the attitude that the offense would carry the team without particular effort. Jeff Langston, an end who had missed the entire 1957 season because of an automobile accident at the first Rose Bowl game, was back and ready for duty. The 1957 backfield was largely intact. A sophomore coming on, named Willie Fleming, was rated far above average. These factors, perhaps, helped instill the feeling that the 1958 team would roll along with only a minimum of effort. Such, at least, was the appraisal of squad attitude as interpreted by Coach Evashevski.

Highly rated Texas Christian University of the Southwest Conference was the opening opponent. The coach could see trouble ahead of the Hawks. As the week of the game began a scrimmage was ordered. Evashevski described it like this:

"It wasn't how they executed the Wing-T. They were impressed with it. Seemed to think it was a sort of magic offense. They had scrimmaged about seven minutes when I called them together. I said to them: 'Gentlemen, you don't want to play and you are going to be unpleas-

antly surprised next Saturday. You're going to be disgraced. You are going to lose an important intersectional game, and there is nothing I can do about it. We've tried to give you the tools to work with and you are not interested in using them. So you might as well go in and think it over. I don't want to see you.

"'I wish you fellows would get together and decide whether or not you think it is worth playing. And if you decide that it is worth playing, I want only those fellows who will go all-out to report to the practice field tomorrow. Some of you apparently do not have the sand to stick your nose in heavy traffic, so I would like to have just those who want to play to report tomorrow. For the others, there will be no hard feelings. Just turn in your uniforms and we'll forget about it.'"

The mental jarring was effective and the Hawks played fine football against Texas Christian. After a scoreless first half Bob Jeter broke the scoring drought with a 41 yard touchdown run in the third minute of the last half. In the course of the spectacular run Jeter dropped the ball and recovered it without breaking stride. Still in the third quarter Randy Duncan passed to Don Norton for six yards and six points. The conversions, and Bob Prescott's 21-yard field goal, gave Iowa a 17 — 0 victory. The Hawks hit for 206 rushing yards and 139 on passing.

The sag that had been anticipated by Coach Evashevski was avoided, but only temporarily. It set in the following week in an Iowa City game against the Air Force Academy. In the biggest surprise of the Iowa season the newly founded academy fought the Hawkeyes to a standstill, matched them in yardage, outdowned them, outfought them, outhustled them and earned a 13 — 13 tie.

Iowa was quick to score at the outset and that fact may have given the Hawks confidence to a dangerous degree. After three minutes of the first quarter Duncan's pass was hauled in by Jeter for 23 yards and a touchdown. Not especially impressed, the Falcons swooped in for a touchdown of their own just four minutes later, an aggressive young man

1958 Team

(All Left to Right): ROW ONE: Dr. W. D. Paul, Hugh Drake, John Nocera (c), Gary Grouwinkel, John Burroughs, Mac Lewis, Kevin Furlong, Randy Duncan, Bill Gravel, Bob Prescott, Coach Forest Evashevski.

ROW TWO: Asst. Coach Bob Flora, John McMeekins, Don Horn, Bill Lapham, Bob Jeter, Don Norton, Curt Merz, Olen Treadway, Geno Sessi, Mitchell Ogiego, Ray Jauch, Asst. Coach "Whitey" Piro.

ROW THREE: Manager Bob Steele, Ralph Dyess, Tom Moore, Bill Ringer, Allan Miller, Mike Lewis, Jerry Mauren, Bernie Wyatt, Paul Lees, Charles Lee. Asst. Coaches Jerry Hilgenberg and Archie Kodros.

ROW FOUR: Don Tucker, Bob Moerke, Steve Turner, Don Zinn, Mark Manders, Roger Ewen, Bob Hain, Dick Clauson, Bill Scott, Manager Jack Grier, Freshman Coach Bill Happel.

ROW FIVE: Asst. Coach Jerry Burns, Eugene Mosley, Lloyd Humphreys, John Sawin, Gerry Novack, Doug MacKinney, Jeff Langston, Jim Spaan, Jess Vargo, Paul Karras, Fred Long.

ROW SIX: Trainer Doyle Allsup, Willie Fleming, Don Shipanik, John Brown, Al Dunn, Dick Clark, Al Sonnenberg, Bob Russo, John Leshyn, Tom DiNardo, Dick Gajda, George Harrell.

named Mike Quinlan going 23 yards for the score. Tied as the first quarter ended, the Air Force scored again in the second quarter on a 10-yard pass for a 13 — 6 halftime lead. Iowa trailed until the final minutes ticked away in the third period when John Nocera plowed the last three yards of a drive. Beyond that, there was a standoff. The Air Force made itself a big batch of history in that tie.

Later, discussing the tie, Coach Evashevski commented:

"If we had beaten the Air Force, we never in the world would have won the Big Ten championship." The tie, in a game in which the Hawks had been greatly favored, reminded the players with something of a shock that execution as well as system was essential, as the coach had tried to emphasize. The lesson was well learned.

Iowa banged down Indiana, Wisconsin and Northwestern and unloaded on Michigan. The team also defeated Minnesota to make it five Big Ten victories in a row. Against Indiana Ray Jauch raced 64 yards to score after less than 90 seconds of play. Don Horn scored in the first and Randy Duncan crossed the goal twice in the second quarter, once on a 20 yard run with a lateral from Bill Gravel. The aroused Hawkeyes had a 28 — 0 lead at the half, 34 — 0 after three quarters and ample cushion for the two touchdowns made by Indiana in the fourth. Jauch alone carried the ball 108 yards in seven carries. The Iowa team made more than 500 yards rushing and passing, along with a record equalling 28 first downs. It was in this game that Willie Fleming bowed in as an Iowa scorer. Although he played only one season, he earned ranking with the greatest of Iowa's halfbacks.

While still early in the season Coach Evashevski first intimated his high regard for Fleming when he said publicly:

"I am not saying that this boy will be the best halfback Iowa has had in 10 years. I am saying, however, that he could be." Fleming, in effect, was kept under wraps in the earlier games and not until the Michigan battle on November 1 did the former Detroit High school star come on with the sweep of a comet. First, however, the Hawks had meetings with Wisconsin and Northwestern.

They played at Madison and the Badgers slammed into them at the start. Paul Shwaiko opened Wisconsin's scoring with a 15-yard field goal in the first five minutes. Before the half was over Dale Hackbart drilled a 31-yard pass to Ron Steiner and Wisconsin led, 9 — 0. Iowa struck hard and fast as the last half opened. A Hawkeye drive culminated with Duncan ramming through for the last yard. Later in the third quarter Don Norton of Iowa put such a furious rush on Hackbart, the Wisconsin passer, that Hackbart fumbled. Jeff Langston, playing the end opposite Norton, grabbed the fumble in mid-air and raced 21 yards to put Iowa ahead. Bob Jeter iced the game in the fourth, sprinting 68 yards to score on a screen pass from Duncan and Iowa won, 20 — 9.

Northwestern, fired by an earlier 55 — 24 overwhelming of Michigan, reached Iowa City on October 25, unbeaten and with high hopes. Writers had assigned the Wildcats the title "Cinderella" team, in a complimentary salute to their potency. Potent they were, as another

record Iowa crowd which exceeded 59,000 attested. The Hawkeyes ran up a 14 — 0 first half lead on Randy Duncan's passes to Curt Merz and Don Norton for 18 and 21 yards, respectively, and closed out the game, 26 — 20, in spite of a rugged late surge by the opposition. The passing of Dick Thornton of Northwestern, always dangerous, was more than offset by Duncan's shots through the air. He completed 14 of 18 for 174 yards and three touchdowns. Iowa ran its lead to 20 — 0 early in the third quarter when Merz went high for a 22-yard touchdown pass from Duncan. The Wildcats countered quickly with a Thornton to Elbert Kimbrough pass for a score, another by Fred Hecker, who plunged for the final yard of a 34-yard drive, and another on a 35-yard pass, Thornton to Ron Burton. Iowa, accumulating a 402 to 267 margin in total yardage, already had clinched the game, however, on Don Horn's short run early in the fourth period.

The Hawks moved into November of 1958 undefeated, with three for three in Big Ten games and with Michigan dead ahead. The game was at Ann Arbor and neither there nor elsewhere had the Hawkeyes won from the Wolverines in 34 years. This game made history. Iowa not only won by an uncontestable 37 — 14 score, but it took the wraps off one of the greatest backs to enter the Big Ten scene in some time — a very long time, as far as Iowa was concerned.

The first quarter was ticking off its final seconds when Willie Fleming came in. He was back in the safety position when Michigan punted. "Willie The Wisp" fielded the ball and took off. He raced 72 yards on that punt return for the first Iowa touchdown. Just two minutes later Ray Jauch rocked the Wolverines with another long touchdown run, going 74 yards for the score. Michigan countered with a drive that ended when Bob Ptacek flipped a 4-yard pass to Darrell Harper only seconds before the half ended.

Bob Jeter scored twice and Curt Merz once, on a pass from John Nocera, before Fleming sprinted away again. This time he sailed 61 yards through the Wolverines to contribute to the Iowa cause two of the most spectacular scoring runs made by a Big Ten sophomore in years. Michigan made big yardage through the air but Iowa was the superior team with 385 total yards against 263. Fleming, although not a starter, picked up a grand total of 240 yards — 86 rushing, 41 as a pass receiver, 72 on a punt return, and 41 more with a kickoff.

Victory Number 4 in the conference was in the record and Minnesota was next.

The Hawks met the Gophers at Minneapolis on November 8, and defeated them, 28 — 6. Before the half was over Willie Fleming had threaded his slippery way 46 and 63 yards for touchdowns. Duncan set another Iowa touchdown in motion with a pass on which Jeff Langston scored from 11 yards out. Another Duncan toss, to Norton, brought Iowa its fourth score, with Minnesota counting its only points on a 30-yard pass late in the third quarter.

Minnesota coach Murray Warmath called the Iowa backfield quartet of Jauch, Fleming, Jeter and Kevin Furlong "the best halfback foursome I've ever seen on one football field." Gopher athletic director Ike Armstrong was even more laudatory when he said: "Iowa is the best football team I've ever seen in the Big Ten."

Evashevski's remarkable ground gaining outfit covered 466 yards against the Gophers, 305 of them on the ground. Duncan's part of the passing attack accounted for 148 yards on nine completions. Fleming again paced the rushers, averaging more than 15 yards on each of 9 carries. The Hawkeyes used 33 men, racked up their fifth straight in the conference, and went home to get ready for Ohio State, already having clinched the Big Ten title and another Rose Bowl trip.

Long after the Buckeye game was played, with Ohio administering the only defeat of the year by a 38 — 28 margin, the rugged duel continued to be mentioned as the greatest offensive game ever played in the Iowa Stadium. It was a sensational meeting of two highly geared attacks. The game was 7 — 7 at the quarter, 21 — 21 at the half and 28 — 28 after three quarters. Through it all the ruthless slams of durable Bob White, Ohio State fullback, were leaving their imprint on Iowa. When he struck into the line as fear-somely in the fourth quarter as he had in the others, the Hawks hadn't quite enough fury for a last counter assault.

White, heading up the defeat of Iowa for the second straight year, carried the ball 33 times in one of the most strenuous assignments ever handled by a conference back. He went 71 yards for one of his three touchdowns and gained 209 yards all told. Halfback Don Clark, also a devastating dervish, added 152 more on only 15 attempts. He tallied the other two Buckeye touchdowns. A 12-yard field goal in the final moments was merely frosting on the Ohio State cake. When the sensational struggle was over Iowa had run for 178 yards, gained 249 more on 22 completed passes and registered four touchdowns and 427 yards in gains. It was not enough. Ohio State, relying almost entirely on the unstoppable rampages of White, gained 397 yards on runs alone, and 65 more on a single completed pass. Iowa made its touchdowns on a one-yard punch by Duncan, a gain of corresponding length by Fleming, a Duncan to Fleming pass for three yards and a 21-yard burst by John Nocera.

The defeat brought the only blot of 1958 but even the diehards stood in admiration of the tremendous try made by the Hawkeyes. They fought until they could fight no more and then, as if in reward for the effort, were praised by Ohio coach Woody Hayes for the part they played in "the greatest game I have ever seen."

There was to be no rest for the Hawkeyes, however. With the Notre Dame squad on its arrival in Iowa City for the final game of the regular season were a quarterback named George Izo and a pass receiver named Monte Stickles. Against one of Iowa's finest teams this Notre Dame pair provided nothing but trouble, although they never quite succeeded in catching the Hawks who won, 31 — 21.

Fleming of Iowa was first to score, on a 6-yard dash with only six seconds gone in the second quarter. Within five minutes he scored again, covering 36 yards with a pass from Duncan. Notre Dame was down, 13 — 0, before Izo moved the Fighting Irish into the battle. From his own 31-yard line he hurled a long pass to Stickles, who stormed to the Iowa goal on a 69-yard scoring play. Farther along he hit Joe Scarpitto with a pass for 52 yards and a touchdown, then scored one himself on a 3 yard run. Iowa kept the game under control, however, on Nocera's short touchdown in the third and scores by Norton (53-yard pass from Duncan) and Mitch Ogiego, the latter on a 1 yard run.

Iowa's furious onslaught produced 456 yards, including 260 on 15 completed passes. Notre Dame was almost as potent, accounting for 387 yards, of which 247 came on 11 passes. As the Hawkeyes jogged away to their dressing room the schedule had been played out but the season was far from over. The squad had a stretch of five weeks ahead before they would face California, the Pacific Coast representative, in the Rose Bowl.

As the regular season ended, honors were bestowed upon Forest Evashevski, his Iowa team, and many individual Hawkeyes. Evy was again named Coach of the Year by the Columbus (Ohio) Touchdown Club, by the Los Angeles Times, and by the Detroit News. Iowa placed second in the final Associated Press and United Press polls. The Hawkeyes became only the third Big Ten team to rank in the top ten for three consecutive years. Randy Duncan, consensus quarterback on the 1958 all-America team, was the second Hawkeye in two years to place runner-up in the balloting for football's Number 1 individual award, the Heisman Trophy. Duncan ranked first in the nation in forward passing percentage, first in yards gained passing, and tied for first in touchdown passes thrown. He ranked second in the nation in total offense, but first in average yards per game.

Curt Merz, acknowledged by many to be the finest all-around end to play in the Evashevski era when unhampered by injury, was given a first team all-America berth by the Football Writers Association and Look Magazine. Ray Jauch, a rawhide halfback of modest proportions, was all-Midwest first team of the New York Daily News. He led the nation in average gains on rushing plays, picking up more than

seven yards on each of 72 attempts during the season. Sophomore Willie Fleming, recognized on the all Big Ten first unit of the Associated Press, ran for nine touchdowns during the regular season and added two more in the Rose Bowl.

The Iowa team in 1958 scored a rare statistical double by ranking within the top ten in

Willie Fleming

the nation in both rushing and passing offense. No team since Oklahoma A & M in the war year of 1945 so dominated both rushing and passing nationally. Further, the Hawks were ninth in scoring for the year, with an average of 26 points a game, and they rated first of all teams in defense against punt returns, permitting kicks to be returned a total of only 36 yards during the season.

Such were the records of accomplishment as the 1958 regular season closed. The most important game, however, remained to be played.

The long drudgery of preparation for the Rose Bowl game came to a glamorous end on January 1, 1959, when Iowa smashed Cali-

The Rose Bowl, scene of two New Year's Day Hawkeye victories.

fornia's game but overmatched squad, 38 — 12. The Golden Bears had neither the class nor the versatility of the Hawkeyes who rewrote the Rose Bowl record book with five new marks, along with 24 first downs which equalled still another.

Bob Jeter, Iowa halfback, set the first new records by racing 81 yards for a touchdown and by singlehandedly accumulating 194 yards on nine carries. His average of more than 21 yards each time he carried the ball was a third all-time high. Jeter was chosen the game's most outstanding player and awarded the Helms Rose Bowl Trophy emblematic of the honor.

The post-season game was one of the easiest assignments faced by the 1958 team. Willie Fleming, for the fifth straight game, scored two touchdowns, one on a 36 yard run. Iowa scored five of its six touchdowns on a running game that simply ate up the defense. The lone score on a pass came when Randy Duncan threw seven yards to end Jeff Langston. Among the 98,297 spectators who watched, there were many who were disappointed California followers, but none who were unconvinced of the Hawkeye superiority.

Iowa ran for the remarkable total of 429 yards and added 87 more on passing to accumulate a combined figure of 516 yards. Both the rushing and total offense marks established new Rose Bowl standards.

With the commanding January 1 triumph the Hawkeyes concluded an 8 — 1 — 1 season. That brought the three-year record since the advent of the Wing-T to 24 victories, three defeats and two ties. In 50 years of Big Ten play only Michigan's teams of 1947, 1948 and 1949, with a 25 — 2 — 1 total, had a better three season performance mark.

At the conclusion of the Bowl games the Grantland Rice Award, symbolic of the National Championship, was voted to the University of Iowa by the Football Writers Association of America. Those were precious days to followers of the Hawkeyes. In the years before Forest Evashevski came to Iowa only one Big Ten team (Michigan, 1947) had averaged as many as 400 yards a game in total offense. Iowa erased that record with its 417 yard average. Not between 1922 and 1956 had there been an Iowa team to score as many as 200 points in a single season. The year 1958 marked the third straight year for the accomplishment, and the 272 points notched was the most any Hawkeye team had managed in 45 years.

Iowa continued a consecutive game scoring streak which by now had reached 56 games, by far the longest active string in the nation. During the period dating from the final game of the 1952 season, Evashevski coached teams averaged almost four touchdowns a game (23.19 points).

When Randy Duncan hit Jeff Langston with a touchdown pass in the Rose Bowl game, it marked the twelfth time he had thrown for scores, and the all-time Iowa record of 11 touchdown passes, first set by the immortal Nile Kinnick in 1939, was surpassed. Duncan closed his brilliant three year career following the 1958 campaign. His 24 career touchdown passes thrown exceeded the previous

National Champions — 1958

Randy Duncan

record by seven, and his career passing yardage topped the previous mark by more than one thousand yards. The 1,462 yards Duncan amassed by rushing and passing in 1958 was the most ever by a Hawkeye, and his career total offense yardage of 2,799 ranks second only to the more than 3,000 yards piled up by Aubrey Devine in the early twenties. The Chicago Tribune Silver Football Award, given annually to the player selected as most valuable in the Big Ten Conference, was presented to

Duncan for his play in 1958. He became the sixth Hawkeye to receive the award, following Willis Glassgow (1929), Joe Laws (1933), Nile Kinnick (1939), Bill Reichardt (1951) and Kenny Ploen (1956).

Bob Prescott also ended his career in 1958, having kicked 66 extra points in three years. The mark broke the former record of 51 established by Bill Reichardt between 1949 and 1951. Prescott's 24 conversions in 1956 (in 26 attempts) were the most at Iowa since durable Joe Warner notched a high of 26 back in 1900.

Indicative of the unparalleled explosiveness and ground gaining ability of the Iowa backs in 1958 is this fact: since 1919 only sixteen Hawkeyes have rushed for 500 or more yards during a single season. Three of them, Jauch, Fleming and Jeter accomplished the feat in 1958. Not since Bill Glassgow and Nanny Pape teamed together in 1928 had even two Hawks exceeded the 500 yard figure in one season.

It was a golden era for the Hawkeyes and 1959, in the long range previews, carried suggestions of being as good or better. These indications were sustained in the opening game of the season when the University of California was again submerged, this time, 42 — 12. Heavy clouds were in sight on the Iowa horizon, however.

1959

Unrest might be termed the keynote of 1959. Big personnel changes were in order as Coach Evashevski went into his eighth season at Iowa. Gone with the 1958 team were Randy Duncan and John Nocera, veteran backs, Bob Prescott, the most effective extra-point kicker in Iowa history; huge MacLewis and John Burroughs, tackles, and Gary Grouwinkel and Hugh Drake, dependable guards. Gone also, after a single season of competition, were the great running halfback, Willie Fleming, and highly regarded quarterback, Mitch Ogiego.

The Hawkeyes faced 1959 with personnel depleted by graduation and ineligibility, yet with the football world touted to expect great things of them. There was reason to hope. Starters in several positions were men of proven ability. A couple of spots were in question. Depth was inadequate but among the newcomers up from the freshman team were Bill Whisler, end; Al Hinton, tackle; Sherwyn Thorson and Bill DiCindio, guards; Wilburn Hollis, quarterback, and Larry Ferguson, halfback.

The football Rules Committee again altered the highly controversial substitution rule for 1959, this time allowing the free substitution of one player from each team when the clock was stopped. The group also widened the goal posts by five and one-half feet in an attempt to encourage more field goal kicking.

The season had opened in Berkeley, California, in a replay of the Rose Bowl game. Stunned for an instant when California scored on a 56-yard pass play immediately after the opening kickoff, the Hawkeyes came on to smother the Golden Bears even more decisively than they had in the Rose Bowl. The count was 42 — 12. Iowa stacked up 475 yards running and passing and yielded 319 to California, but after the first minute there was little doubt. Don Horn, John Brown, Gene Mosley, Ray Jauch, Bob Jeter, Olen Treadway and Wilburn Hollis all had big roles for Iowa. Of significance was the first touchdown scored for Iowa by Hollis, the deceptively powerful back from Boys Town, who had two great seasons before an injury deprived him of most of his senior year.

The Hawks opened the 1959 conference campaign against Northwestern and for some distance the game appeared to be under control. Don Norton's 47 yard run following an intercepted pitchout put Iowa in front in the third quarter and Tom Moore's field goal made it 10 — 0 for the Hawkeyes. In something of a duel between Iowa's running and Northwestern's passing, the game began to swing late in the third quarter when a pass, Chip Holcomb to Ron Burton, capped a Wildcat drive for a touchdown. The clincher came in the fourth quarter when Ray Purdin of Northwestern captured an Iowa pass and raced 42 yards to the

Iowa Stadium today, with the modern Press Box rising high above the west stands.

goal. Northwestern won 14 – 10 after losing its star quarterback, Dick Thornton, on the opening kickoff.

Off to a losing start in the conference race, the 1959 team came back with a victory. Michigan State played at Iowa and went down, 37 – 8, the worst coaching defeat of Spartan Duffy Daugherty. Back in stride, the Hawkeyes moved the ball 401 yards on runs and passes with Bob Jeter accounting for 104 rushing and Olen Treadway passing for 154. Treadway threw twice to Don Norton for touchdowns, the plays covering 31 and 17 yards. The scoring included a 22-yard field goal by Tom Moore, a 31-yard touchdown run by Jerry Mauren and 1-yard slams by Hollis and Don Horn.

Iowa took a 1 – 1 conference record to Wisconsin in the third Big Ten game of 1959, ran and passed like a winner but handled the ball poorly and lost, 25 – 16. The Badgers advanced to the Iowa 25-yard line in the first

five minutes, bogged momentarily, and called on Karl Holzwarth to drive home a field goal for the opening points. Twice in the second quarter Wisconsin racked up touchdowns, the first on a 1-yard keep by Dale Hackbart and the other on a 2-yard buck by Ken Wiesner. As they left the field for the half Iowa trailed, 17 – 0.

Olen Treadway broke the Big Ten record for pass completions in the game, hitting 26 of 41 for 304 yards. The yardage mark, passes attempted and number of completions all established new Iowa marks. Don Norton equaled an Iowa record by catching nine of Treadway's throws, but the Hawks could manage only two touchdowns. Their first came with nine minutes to play in the third quarter when Don Horn crashed through from the one, and the other on Treadway's 21-yard pass to Norton. Iowa made 468 yards to Wisconsin's 305 but the Badgers were in command all the way. It was, however, the sixtieth consecutive game in which Iowa scored, establishing a new all-time mark for Big Ten teams. Michigan had scored in 59 straight games between 1944 and 1950 to hold the previous record.

Losers in two out of three conference games, the Hawkeyes ran into another ambush at Purdue on their next start. Rain and mud minimized Hawkeye running and passing to an extent that only 167 yards were credited to them. Purdue made two muddy marches in the second quarter, both resulting in touchdowns from short range. Iowa's only score was set up when Treadway hit Bill Whisler with a pass on the two-yard line and Don Horn rammed it home. The Hawkeyes had been blanked through the first 56 minutes, but the late score saved the long Iowa record of scoring in 61 straight games.

With their conference title chances and national rating dissipated, a stand against Kansas State followed. It was a 53 − 0 romp for the Hawkeyes after a 45 − 0 halftime lead. They ran and passed for more than 600 yards while allowing Kansas State a total of 81. A little known sophomore named Virgil Williams was credited with two Iowa touchdowns, one on a 68-yard punt return and another on a 41-yard run. The Wildcats were victims of one of Iowa's most furious first half assaults, with the Hawks scoring 31 points in the second quarter.

The up and down season continued on the up-beat against Minnesota the following week when Iowa, playing at home, roared through the four quarters to win, 33 − 0. It was Dad's Day and the Evashevski admonition that the Hawkeyes give their fathers cause to be proud of them paid a big dividend. For three quarters the Gophers yielded ungrudgingly. Then, trailing 13 − 0, they were rapped for three Iowa touchdowns in a nine minute stretch of the fourth period. Bob Jeter's running and Treadway's passing led the winners while Jeff Langston, John Brown and Gene Mosley figured in the scoring.

Iowa, with a two-three conference record, traveled to Ohio State next and the fact that no Hawkeye team had won in Columbus for 11 years brought no comfort. There appeared to be a very good chance that the champions of 1958 would wind up in the second division in the 1959 standings. A first quarter Ohio State touchdown added to the problem. Iowa's running, it soon became obvious, however, was more than the Buckeyes could handle. Wilburn Hollis and Jerry Mauren in particular sliced up Ohio's defense. Sophomore Hollis powered his way for 82 yards in 15 tries and fired a touchdown pass of 13 yards to Bill Whisler. Mauren hauled the ball a total of 96 yards and on the second Iowa touchdown personally gained 54 of the required 67 yards, his last carry taking him into the end zone from four yards away. Tom Moore's field goal from the 17 rounded out the scoring and Iowa broke the 11-year jinx to win, 16 − 7.

That brought the conference record to 3 − 3 for the season and the over-all mark to 5 − 3, with Notre Dame still to be met. They played November 21, 1959, at Iowa City and the Hawkeyes left the field with sad memories of George Izo and Monte Stickels. This was the troublesome pair that gave Iowa concern in the 1958 game. This time they led the attack that toppled the Hawks, 20 − 19. As a starter Iowa closed a march by sending Don Horn over the goal from 1-yard away. Within two minutes the Irish offset that score when Izo threw a 29-yard pass to Stickles for a touchdown. Striking back, the Hawkeyes scored in the second quarter on Bob Jeter's 14-yard run and again in the same period when Jerry Mauren went all the way on an 80-yard punt return. Notre Dame cut the margin when Izo passed to Pat Heenan for 45 yards and a touchdown. Iowa's 19 − 13 lead held through the scoreless third quarter before Izo hurled another "mile-long" scoring pass, sending George Sefcik over the goal on a 56-yard play.

Less than four minutes remained when Notre Dame attempted the conversion that could break the 19 − 19 tie. Stickles drilled it between the posts and the Fighting Irish won, 20 − 19. George Izo's passes ruined the Hawkeyes. He completed 14, three of them for touchdowns, and piled up 295 yards on pass completions alone. The Irish gained the impressive total of 426 yards over-all and Iowa closed out its season with a 5 — 4 record.

The Hawkeyes fell short of expectations, but three touchdowns, properly placed, would have given them an undefeated season. The team finished second nationally in total offense and blanketed the Big Ten statistically by finishing first in total offense, second in team defense and first in scoring.

Don Norton and Bob Jeter shared individual post-season honors, both being selected to the

the Football Writers Association for Look Magazine.

Olen Treadway, with three Iowa passing records established against Wisconsin, gained

Don Norton

Robert Jeter

all Conference first teams of Associated Press and United Press. In addition, Norton was given a berth on the all-America team chosen by

more than 1,000 yards through the air during the season. Further, he set a new NCAA record for consecutive passes thrown without interception by tossing 127 times before his final pass of the year fell into the hands of George Sefcik of Notre Dame.

Another decade of Iowa football was over, and it showed 49 victories, 36 defeats and 7 ties. It was the first ten year period since the twenties that the Hawkeyes earned more wins than losses. It also brought Iowa to within eight victories of 300 since the first game was won in 1890.

A Coach – An Athletic Director– The Inside Story of a Feud

With the 1959 season in the record, Iowa followers made some comparisons. Howard Jones, one of the most successful coaches in Iowa history, had won 42 football games from 1916 through 1923. Evashevski had 44 victories sacked up from 1952 through 1959. This, with the championships and the Rose Bowl victories, the drawing power of his teams and the resulting gate receipts, moved the Evashevski regime toward the all-time top at Iowa.

But where the coach had kept Iowans proud and happy with the success of his football teams, he also kept them uneasy because of recurring reports that he was unhappy at Iowa, that his relations with Paul Brechler, the director of athletics, were far from smooth, and that he might become interested in one of the numerous offers he had received.

There were few dull days at Iowa after Evashevski's first championship team. Perhaps the fact that he had built a Rose Bowl winner influenced the magazine, Sports Illustrated, to send a representative, Jack Olsen, to confer with Evy. The magazine published an article entitled "A Heretic Speaks His Mind." Evashevski was quoted in the magazine as saying: "I tell you, that situation at Indiana just turned my stomach, the way that president turned on his coach. . . ." Evashevski's denial of the statement was prompt and complete.

"Had I been asked about the situation at Indiana I would have said I thought President Wells defended his coach to the fullest. . .I know of no college president who will knowingly tolerate a disregard for ethics and rules."

Whether the magazine experience caused him to take a new and hard look at coaching is not on record but it is known that he visited Detroit during 1957 to confer with business interests about a non-coaching connection there. It is also known that Evashevski reviewed his personal affairs and reached a realization, among other things, that his family was growing up.

"My boys were starting to participate in sports and I realized that I had never seen them compete. I questioned the wisdom of remaining in college coaching. I said a long time ago that coaching is a young man's job. That Detroit offer was my second off-campus interview about a job. I thought about it a long time and I think one of the reasons that I did not accept was the fact that my family and I liked Iowa City so much as a community in which to live."

The Detroit offer was not the first attempt to lure Evashevski away from Iowa. During his visit to Los Angeles for the January 1, 1957, Rose Bowl game, he conferred at some length with Greg Engelhard and Bud Hastings of the University of California. The meeting was held at the Los Angeles Airport. Evashevski duly reported the incident to Iowa's Board in Control of Athletics at a special meeting held in Pasadena.

Uneasiness over Evashevski's future had become very real as far as his Iowa supporters were concerned, and it grew alarmingly when, in mid-November, 1957, during the progress of his own Sunday afternoon television show, he said:

"The sands of time are running low in my coaching hour glass." He followed that with a newspaper statement that he "never intended to grow old in coaching."

Speculation that Evy was about to leave Iowa was immediate. Leo Fischer, writing in the Chicago American, said: "It is no secret that Evashevski and Athletic Director Paul Brechler have not seen eye to eye for a long time. . ." Evashevski, two days later, was quoted as saying that his health would be a factor in his coaching future. "What I do, or if I turn my whistle and my colitis over to somebody else, is something the future must decide."

In November, 1957, Evashevski and Brechler met in an unannounced meeting. Brechler said they talked of problems affecting football, past and future. Evashevski was not quoted, although it later was revealed that much of the discussion centered around a letter which university President Hancher had received from Big Ten Commissioner Kenneth L. (Tug) Wilson, dated October 26, 1957. The letter dealt with recruiting violations on the part of E. K. Jones, secretary of the "I" Club, specifically the transporting of athletes to the campus.

The letter suggested, and the Iowa Board in Control of Athletics concurred, that Mr. Jones "shall be prohibited from making any further contacts with prospective athletes or in engaging in furnishing transportation to and from Iowa City as long as he is an employee of the 'I' Club."

Early in December a further note of athletic family disharmony was indicated with the report that Dr. George Easton, Director Brechler and Evashevski held a meeting about "the early release of information which usually should he handled by the Iowa Board."

In the middle of that month Evashevski spoke to the Quad Cities Home-builders Association at Milan, Illinois, and told them: "Don't Count Texas A & M out." His future at Iowa seemed particularly unsettled.

One day later, however, Evashevski conferred with President Virgil M. Hancher of the State University of Iowa, after which the coach announced that he would remain at Iowa. Discord within the athletic department simmered somewhat for nearly two years, then it erupted anew.

The top football topic in the state in October, 1959, was not the football team but the inability of the leading men in the athletic department to pursue their duties in harmony. The smouldering differences began to increase at the start of the month of October. Athletic Director Brechler, who had been invited by the University of Pittsburgh to discuss the vacant athletic directorship at that school, declared that he had turned down the $20,000 opportunity. The Iowa Board announced that it had voted him an annual salary increase of $2,000, bringing his total compensation from the University to $18,500.

One day later Coach Evashevski "threw a blockbuster into the Iowa football picture" as one newspaper described it, by announcing his resignation, to become effective at the culmination of his contract. The contract was effective until 1964.

Virgil M. Hancher, president of the University, was on a mission for the United Nations in New York City. During his absence Provost Harvey H. Davis was serving as acting president and to him Evashevski addressed the following letter:

"I would like to announce my resignation as head football coach at the State University of Iowa, effective at the expiration of my present contract. In the meantime I would like to request permission of the Athletic Board to review any opportunities which are presented."

Word of the resignation of the highly successful coach reverberated across Iowa and the nation. The week-end crowd was assembling in Iowa City for a home game with Northwestern University. The "I" Club, an organization of some 6,000 friends and alumni of the University, held a meeting in the Iowa Fieldhouse. With less than 80 persons voting, the "I" Club, by a 60 — 17 vote, adopted a resolution calling for the resignation of Athletic Director Brechler. The vote was by a show of hands, with perhaps half of the estimated 150 persons in attendance abstaining from voting. A complaint voiced against Brechler at the meeting was that he "won't go to bat for the coaches" when complaints are heard on recruiting methods. John Sunstrum, Oskaloosa clothier and former president of the "I" Club, was among those opposing the action against Brechler. He said 150 club members in the Oskaloosa area had met and expressed opposition to the resolution asking Brechler's resignation.

The open rupture within the department all but stunned interested citizens. In the wake of the demand for Brechler's resignation the football team lost to Northwestern, 14 — 10. Across the state a "where do we go from here" attitude prevailed. The University's highly successful athletic department was a house divided. Observers said the blow-up was inevitable. The strained relations had existed for too long a time. Plans were made to call the Board in Control of Athletics into session. The State Board of Regents, with a meeting scheduled in Iowa City Thursday of the following week, indicated that "as a matter of good business" it would look into the problems of the athletic department.

Under date of October 6, 1959, Coach Evashevski issued a letter to "I" Club members. In it he mentioned the recent friction within the athletic department "which newspaper reporters and radio commentators are talking about.

"It is unfortunate that current differences of opinion have been placed on the public square for judgment," he wrote. "I must take my share of blame for any actions which have brought these issues to the public.

"It seems to me that working conditions within the Athletic Department which I find

intolerable can be resolved only by the administration of the University. Here in Iowa City I will do everything I can to co-operate with the President of the University in solving our problems. In the meantime, I would like to ask you to do a great favor — will you please put forth in your community every effort to get local businessmen to refrain from taking sides in an issue which appears to be between the football staff and the athletic director. This is a family affair. These differences of opinion or working conditions are not the kind of things you or I would care to have aired on the crossroads of this state.

"I probably have unconsciously aggravated discussions from time to time. For these slips of judgment, I am sorry. Now we all need your help to get this problem back in our house, where it belongs. I hope you will throw your weight into this request — not just for me, but for the best interests of the State University of Iowa." The letter carried Evashevski's signature.

Coach Evashevski was quoted in newspapers the following day as saying the "I" Club made a "tactical" error in demanding Brechler's resignation.

"I am opposed to any group exerting pressure on any organization or business to remove an employee from his job. . .This is a family problem and I hope it will be resolved within the family circle. I will not be a party to a washing of dirty linen in public places. . .the action taken by the 'I' Club was a complete surprise to me. . .I feel it was a tactical mistake. . ."

Almost simultaneously, the University's athletic board convened. After four hours of deliberation it issued a statement, which included among its highlights these excerpts:

"The Board is highly pleased with Mr. Evashevski's announced intention of serving out his present contract which expires in 1964. The Board is grateful to Mr. Evashevski for his great contributions. . .and for his courtesy in requesting the Board's permission to review other opportunities which may come to him. . .The Board reaffirms Mr. Evashevski's right, which he holds in common with all university employees, to investigate such opportunities."

The Board announced its next meeting would be October 15, "at which time Mr. Evashevski will meet with the Board to discuss whatever matters he may wish to bring before it."

Earlier in the day a five-foot effigy of Brechler was hanged outside Memorial Union. An effigy of Evashevski was found in an elm tree in front of Schaeffer Hall.

The State Board of Regents held its scheduled meeting, discussed the problems of the athletic department, and announced a hands off policy. By an 8 — 1 vote, with Regent Lester Gillette of Fostoria, Iowa, dissenting, the Regents referred the dispute to the Board in Control of Athletics. The motion of the Regents read:

'Since the State Board of Regents has thoroughly discussed the situation within the University athletic department with President Hancher, and since the Board in Control of Athletics has charge of such matters and has already discussed the problem and arranged to hear the complaints of Coach Evashevski, therefore, be it resolved that the Board of Regents leave the matter where it belong as an administrative problem with the Board in Control of Athletics for recommendation to the president and the Board of Regents. . ."
The motion also included a provision that Provost Harvey Davis attend the meeting of the Board in Control and submit a report of actions taken to the Board of Regents.

In the short interval which preceded the meeting of the Athletic Board, discussions of the departmental feud expanded. A suggestion was made that Coach Evashevski be "freed" from the supervision of Director Brechler. Another proposel involved combining of the football coaching and the athletic directorship. The problems centering around eligibility of players came up in various discussions.

The meeting of the Board in Control of Athletics, held October 15, 1959, in the office of Dean Mason Ladd, had Evashevski and Brechler in attendance. Called to order at 7:30 P.M., the lengthy meeting was adjourned at 1:15 A.M.

At its conclusion Brechler and Evashevski, press accounts stated, "came out together, laughed, and posed for pictures." The Board in Control issued a carefully prepared statement which said:

"Any problems which exist in the football situation are not personal.

"The Board inquired concerning the widespread press reference to 'intolerable working conditions.'

"Mr. Evashevski declared the words are not intended to cast any reflection on Mr. Brechler, or the University, generally.

"In the discussion that followed, it was agreed that one or two conditions which Mr. Evashevski regarded as very important might well have prompted the use of the term. All agreed that these will be corrected in detail, and within the family.

"On its part, the Board expressed confidence in both Mr. Brechler and Mr. Evashevski and its pleasure in Mr. Evashevski's announced intention of serving out his contract."

There were no supplementary remarks. One member disclosed after the meeting that everyone in attendance had taken a pledge of secrecy. Board members at the session, other than Coach Evashevski and Director Brechler, were Dean Ladd, School of Law; alumni members Walter Stewart and Dr. Wayne Foster; Elwin Joliffe, university vice-president; Dr. Willis Fowler, University Hospitals; Dean Sidney Winter, School of Business Administration; Dean Bruce Mahan, extension division; Professor William Porter, School of Journalism; Professor James Jones, College of Pharmacy; Professor Robert Ray, Institute of Public Affairs; Professor Allen Craig of the Department of Mathematics, and Dr. George Easton of the Dental·College, board chairman. Illness prevented the attendance of Dean Frank Dawson of the College of Engineering.

An uneasy peace, frequently interrupted, returned to the campus and to the alumni, but not for long. On October 26, 1959, a possible new departure from the University by Evashevski was suggested by U.S. News and World Report. The magazine said:

"In Iowa, Gov. Herschel Loveless, Democrat, is reported to be considering the following strategy: Seek for himself the Senate seat now held by Republican Thomas Martin and run Iowa's football coach, Forest Evashevski, for governor. The coach is pictured as interested in a political career."

Evashevski's name frequently was heard in political conversations but the coach has said that he never seriously considered entering politics. Still another avenue of possible departure opened promptly, however. Evashevski was named as one of four coaches under consideration as head coach of the Houston team, of the new American Professional Football League. Earlier in the year the Iowa coach had been in conference with Green Bay, of the National Football League. The Green Bay offer was tempting. It involved the job of head coach and the general managership as well. A report that the connections would carry a salary of $40,000 was given credence, but no confirmation. Quietly, Evashevski rejected the offer.

It was December 15, 1959, when the Board in Control of Athletics again took up the differences between the Director and football coach. Minutes of the meeting disclosed that Coach Evashevski again was present "to visit about some problems relating to the football program at Iowa.

"Mr. Evashevski brought up the following points," the minutes said:

"A. Football players who are academic risks, attaining and maintaining eligibility;
"B. The advisory and guidance program for football players;
"C. The need plan, and its relationship to recruiting;
"D. The physical education professional curriculum.

"Adjournment came before a thorough discussion of all problems could be made. Another meeting is planned in January."

That meeting was held on January 14, 1960, at which time the points of discussion included among other things the Stadium turf. The minutes said:

"Although the Stadium was re-seeded after the Notre Dame game last fall, it was decided the field would be re-sodded at the conclusion of spring practice.

"A new type of bluegrass was recommended by Mr. Sinek, the University landscaping supervisor. This was decided after consultation with the grounds crew, Mr. Sinek, Iowa State University and several experts on soil who are working for the United States Golf Association."

Coach Evashevski met with the Board in Control of Athletics again on February 1, 1960, when he "brought up for discussion the general problems of recruiting prospective football players." Minutes of another Board meeting, two weeks later, revealed this statement:

"It was evident the Board is concerned about the constantly increasing costs of operating the athletic department. Also, it was felt that serious consideration should be given by the director to the idea that some of the assistant football coaches be assigned additional responsibilities in the department of physical education and intercollegiate athletics."

Athletic department problems entered a new phase at that time when Director Brechler disclosed, on February 24, that he would leave the University on August 15, 1960, to become commissioner of the Skyline Conference. The clash between the coach and the director, which Evashevski later summed up as "a complete destruction of confidence in each other," became secondary to the new problem of determining Brechler's successor.

Sometime after Brechler left the University he was asked his version of some of the differences between himself and Evashevski. He recalled that he and Evashevski had planned to get together for a discussion perhaps a year before Brechler submitted his resignation.

"I was there, but he wasn't" Brechler said. "He went hunting. Then on Monday I stopped in and said, 'Well, we ought to get together, if you have any problems we can iron out. Have you time now?'"

He said Evashevski told him he was unable to meet at that time, or at two or three other times suggested by Brechler, whereupon the director said he stated:

"'Well, hell, if you don't want to meet or talk about it, there's nothing I can do.' And I left. Later Evy talked with Howard Hall (Cedar Rapids businessman) and said that I had been abrupt and discourteous and so on. Howard Hall asked me if that was true. That's as serious a disagreement as Evy and I ever had, face to face."

Brechler added: "There might be something about me that he particularly didn't like. I assume there was. I don't know what it would be. I think that Evy felt that I was not really trying to support him."

On his side of the situation Brechler said: "There were two things that really ticked me off at Iowa. First was the 'I' Club making that announcement (morning of the 1959 Northwestern game) which was all cut and dried by a few people.

"The other thing that bothered me was when Evy sent that letter to the 'I' Club saying that the working conditions at Iowa were 'intolerable'. . .I said to the Board: 'If working conditions at Iowa are intolerable, I'm the first guy that would be utterly amazed. . .because I can't think of a single thing that a football coach wants that he doesn't have, or couldn't have easily. So let's have a meeting. Let's talk right here together, and let's have Evy say what the intolerable conditions are.'

"Now the thing that really ticked me off was that during that meeting, which went until after one o'clock in the morning, at no time was there ever a single thing mentioned as being intolerable. And yet the Board wanted to release a statement that said absolutely nothing. I wanted it to say that if there were intolerable working conditions, let's say it. If there were not. . .let's say that there are none. The Board wouldn't do anything in that line. That was something that I thought was not right."

Shortly before these incidents, Brechler said, he reported at Lowry Field, Denver, for two weeks duty with the National Guard. While there he was contacted by Tad Wieman, a member of a committee appointed to search for a commissioner of the Skyline Conference. Wieman asked Brechler if he thought he might be interested. The Iowa Director indicated that his interest mounted immediately following the "I" Club demand for his resignation and the Athletic Board statement over the "intolerable working conditions" incident. He was invited by the Skyline Conference to visit Denver for an interview. Three such conferences with the Skyline group were held before Brechler made his final decision.

Any presentation of the Iowa football history must dwell at some length on Paul Brechler and his 13-year tenure as director of Hawkeye athletics. His was a reign of change and accomplishment, of unrest and of problems.

Periods of the University's greatest athletic success occurred during the tenure of Brechler, longest of any Iowa athletic director. He was instrumental in the selection of new head coaches in football, basketball, track, tennis, gymnastics, golf, fencing and wrestling. These new coaches strengthened their sports to the point where most teams finished well up in the Big Ten's first division, with football, track, tennis and wrestling copping conference titles.

Many physical improvements were made in the over-all athletic plant area. These included the extension of and modernization of an administration office building, an increase in the stadium capacity and construction of an all-purpose press box. A new track layout was built, along with permanent baseball bleachers. A championship golf course was constructed, and new fields provided for physical education, intramurals and team practices.

Within the Big Ten Brechler never missed a director's meeting and was given many duties in recognition of his abilities. Among these, he was the delegate from District 4 to the NCAA television committee; he was a member of the Conference Finance Committee; he served on the Subsidizing and Recruiting Rule Change Committee; he was a member of the Football Scheduling Committee and the Rose Bowl Committee. He was a consistent supporter of the Rose Bowl pact; was opposed to the Need Plan but steadfastly sponsored a change in the aid program of the Conference which found final approval in 1961. He was also a strong adherent for a seven game Conference football schedule, and was a leader in the adoption of the rule for equal distribution of Conference television income. Brechler was one of the early advocates of the present Big Ten rule of using over-all grade average rather than the requirement that a student athlete pass every course he attempts.

Within the NCAA he was named chairman of the important Extra Events Committee, and he was also a member of the Committee on Committees, which selected the personnel of all of the various sports committees. He was a member of the National Physical Fitness Committee and a member of the Nominating Committee of the NCAA to select officers.

All of these activities did much to gain respect and distinction for Brechler and the State University of Iowa. At the same time it eventually handicapped him somewhat in the performance of many duties as Iowa's athletic director. In addition, serious domestic problems and his subsequent remarriage in 1957 added to the difficult situation at Iowa.

An Iowa Board member, in strong support of football coach Evashevski, reviewed the years of Paul Brechler at Iowa by saying: "He is the only athletic administrator I know who could have brought the status, the standing and the respectability that Iowa had lost and so desperately needed within the Big Ten. These things Paul Brechler regained for the University."

Another prominent member of the Athletic Board, openly sympathetic with the Brechler cause, commented that "his record as Director was outstanding. It was true, however, that during the later years he spent too much time away from Iowa City, working on Conference affairs, for the NCAA, etc. As a result, many of his duties as athletic director at Iowa lacked attention or had to be handled by someone else."

Such were the viewpoints of two men who observed and worked with Paul Brechler throughout his thirteen years as director of Iowa athletics. Additional insight is provided by two others who during the period were generally recognized as the most influential within the Big Ten conference. One of them, H. O. (Fritz) Crisler of Michigan said, "I have a very high regard for Paul Brechler and his contributions. He always had his thinking well organized and was very articulate, statesmanlike and forceful in his presentation."

Big Ten Conference Commissioner Kenneth L. (Tug) Wilson commented: "I have a very high regard for what Paul Brechler did as a director. He represented the Big Ten with distinction, unselfishly gave of his time, and earned the respect of his fellow workers when serving on NCAA committees."

Within a day after the announcement of Brechler's resignation, conjecture was rampant as to his possible successor. First names into the street corner discussions were those of Dave Nelson, director of athletics at the University of Delaware; Wally Schwank, athletic director at Coe College, and Rollie Williams, assistant director of athletics at Iowa. Dr. George Easton, chairman of the Board in Control of Athletics, said no names had been filed.

Brechler's duties at the University had been twofold. He served as director of intercollegiate athletics and director of physical education. There was speculation on whether the two responsibilities might be divided. The formal procedure of preparing to fill the Brechler shoes began with the appointment of a committee by the Board. Since his resignation was not to become effective until the following August 15, the committee had no great need for urgency in its actions.

On April 30, 1960, it was agreed to invite Theodore M. Harder of the University of California at Santa Barbara, and James W. Long of the University of Toledo, to Iowa City for interviews involving the position of director of physical education and intercollegiate athletics. There were official discussions of the possible advisability of splitting the two posts but it was moved, seconded and carried that the Board seek a single replacement for the combined positions. This motion was reaffirmed at a Board meeting May 11, and again on May 24.

During the visit to Iowa City of one candidate for the soon to be vacated directorship, an Iowa board member was anxious that Evashevski interview the prospect and give his opinion of him. The Iowa coach said that he would gladly meet him but that he refused to interview or be interviewed by any candidate until the Board had in fact filled the position. "At that time," Evashevski said, "I'll be very glad to spend all of the time necessary to visit with him."

At the ensuing meeting of the Iowa Board the situation was discussed until one Board member inquired: "Now what's the answer to this? What do we do?"

A second member, quietly recognizing the wisdom of Evashevski's action, immediately said, "Hell, fire him. You have an insubordinate employee. You've requested something of him and he's refused to comply. So fire him."

There was a moment of silence, whereupon another voice said, "What do you want to do, kill Santa Claus?"

The Board's staff committee conferred with several possible successors to Brechler. One was Wally Haas of the University of Chicago. Others were Long of Toledo and Harder of the Santa Barbara branch of the University of California. Another was reported to be Greg Engelhard of California. There is strong evidence indicating that James W. Long of Toledo was agreed upon as the Board's appointee, providing one man was to be hired to fill the two posts. This, in spite of earlier reaffirmations, was not to be.

On May 26, 1960, Dean Dewey B. Stuit of the College of Liberal Arts, of which the department of athletics is a branch, wrote President Virgil M. Hancher, as follows:

"During the past several weeks this office has given considerable thought to the relationship between the departments of physical education and our program in intercollegiate athletics.

"Very briefly, I should like to state that the first preference of the department of physical education for men and the department of physical education for women would be to have an independent status.

"This means, in other words, that our present division of physical education and intercollegiate athletics would be dissolved.

"The two departments feel that their education and research programs could proceed more auspiciously if the connection with intercollegiate athletics were terminated. The combined position of director of intercollegiate athletics and head of physical education demands more time than any one person can give to the responsibilities involved. Inevitably the result is that intercollegiate athletics makes first claim on the director's time.

"The net result is that the chairman of physical education for women has reported directly to this office and many of the executive responsibilities of physical education for men have been assumed by the administrative assistant.

"When we commenced our search for a new director of the division of physical education and intercollegiate athletics, we recognized that it would not be easy to find a person who would meet the requirement of all areas. . .

"We now have completed a careful search and I, personally, do not feel that we have come up with a name which would immediately command the respect and enthusiasm of all parties concerned. I see no point in continuing a search which I believe has been fairly exhaustive. In summary, I would like to recommend the following:

"1. That the department of physical education for men be established as an independent department, with the executive officer responsible to this office. If this recommendation meets with your approval I would meet with the department and proceed to make a recommendation as to the name of the person to be appointed executive officer.

"2. That we make official what has essentially been the case in the past, namely that the chairman of the department of physical education for women report directly to this office. . .

"3. That if independent status for the two physical education departments and the program in intercollegiate athletics is approved by you, we then agree upon a policy with respect to the joint use, by physical education and intercollegiate athletics, of the facilities in the fieldhouse and the associated playing fields.

"We would also need to have some understanding with respect to the division of certain budgetary items. . .I am sure I have not covered all the specifics with respect to this proposal; however, I will say that I believe the details can be worked out, hence my recommendation that we dissolve the division of physical education and intercollegiate athletics.

"To be sure it has taken several weeks or months to come to this conclusion, but I think it understandable that if one has had a successful system he does not abandon it recklessly. . ."

Dean Stuit's recommendation apparently led directly to the proposal that Dr. Louis Alley head the department of physical education for men and Forest Evashevski be appointed director of intercollegiate athletics, in the event of a separation of the divisions of the athletic department. Evashevski's possible appointment had been openly discussed at a meeting of the state board of regents in Council Bluffs in mid-May. His name was presented for consideration by Mrs. Robert K. Valentine, regent from Centerville. No official action was taken at the time, but several regents expressed agreement with the proposal, including Mrs. Joseph Rosenfield, Des Moines; Maurice B. Crabbe, Eagle Grove, and Alfred W. Noehren, Spencer.

The recommendation of Dean Stuit preceded prompt action. At a morning meeting of the Board in Control of Athletics on June 4, 1960, in the Old Capitol, a Memorandum of Agreement was discussed. It formally set forth the understanding that Mr. Evashevski would be recommended for the position of director of athletics, should that post be created in separate form. It specified the post would carry the title, Director of Intercollegiate Athletics and Professor (without tenure) the term being for one year, on an annual renewable basis.

The minutes of the meeting:

"There was general discussion of the appointment of a new Director of Athletics. An agreement between the Board in Control of Athletics and Mr. Evashevski, concerning the functions of the post of Director of Intercollegiate Athletics, drawn up by Dr. Robert S. Ray, was submitted for the Board's approval. This document was based on earlier conversations between the Staff Committee and Mr. Evashevski. It was moved by Ray, seconded by Porter, that the motion be approved. Motion carried.

"It was moved by Fowler, seconded by Craig, that in the event a separate post of Director of Intercollegiate Athletics be created, Mr. Evashevski be appointed to that post, on the condition he sign the following Memorandum of Agreement. Motion carried.

✵   ✵   ✵

"Memorandum of Agreement Concerning the Position of Director of Athletics by and between the Board in Control of Athletics and Forest Evashevski:

1. It is agreed and understood by both parties that this document does not constitute a contract, but that it will be used as a basis for a recommendation to the position of Director of Athletics of Mr. Evashevski, should the post be created, accepted by him and confirmed through regular procedures in such matters.

2. The position shall have the title, Director of Intercollegiate Athletics and Professor (without tenure), and, consistent with general University regulations, the term for this administrative position shall be for one year on an annual renewal basis.

3. In accordance with the regulations of the Intercollegiate Conference and the University, the Board in Control of Athletics retains all necessary powers for the control of Intercollegiate Athletics and all powers exercised by the Director are delegated powers, extended through policy decisions of the Board. (For example: The Board approves all salary and other budgets of the Department of Intercollegiate Athletics; determines ticket policies, and makes policy decisions concerning public relations.) No administrative authority delegated by the Board to the Director shall in turn be delegated

by him to any other person, without the specific approval of the Board.

4. The salary of the position of Director of Athletics shall be $20,000 per year (plus retirement and insurance programs) on a twelve month basis (July 1 to June 30).

5. If the post is created, the Board will recommend that Mr. Evashevski be named Director of Athletics, as of August 15, 1960, and Mr. Evashevski agrees to perform the duties of that position and also to serve as Head Football Coach, until, but not after, January 1, 1961. Mr. Evashevski agrees to recommend a Head Football Coach to the Board, prior to September 1, 1960, the appointment of whom shall be effective January 1, 1961, and an announcement of the appointment shall be made by the Board, prior to the 1961 football season.

6. The Board and Mr. Evashevski will confer at the earliest possible time, to the end that procedures may be established for setting up detailed budgets to be administered by the Head Coach of each sport in the Intercollegiate Athletics program.

7. It is agreed that the public relations program for Intercollegiate Athletics shall continue to be a part of the over-all public relations program of the University. Insofar as tickets for athletic events are involved in such public relations, the Board will determine policies after consultation with the Director of Athletics, the Business Manager of Athletics, the Director of University Relations, the Director of Alumni Records, and others (at the discretion of the Board).

8. It is agreed that the Director of Athletics shall attend meetings of the Board at its invitation. It is further agreed that the Director shall bring to the attention of the Board all problems related to the operation of the Intercollegiate Athletic program for resolution, prior to any public discussion by either party. He shall, further, serve as chief administrative officer of the Department of Intercollegiate Athletics and perform the established duties of the position, in accordance with the rules and regulations of the Conference, the N.C.A.A.,

the policies of the Board and general regulations and policies of the University."

* * *

The Agreement bore the signatures of George S. Easton for the Board, and Mr. Evashevski.

Some of the details of the Memorandum of Agreement were not widely known, nor was the fact that the Board passed a second resolution declaring that James W. Long of the University of Toledo would be the Athletic Department head, should the positions of Director of Physical Education and Intercollegiate Athletics continue to be vested in one man. Minutes of the June 4, 1960, meeting included this statement:

"It was moved by Porter, seconded by Jones, that in the event the combined post of Director of Physical Education and Intercollegiate Athletics is continued, the Board recommended the appointment of Mr. James W. Long of the University of Toledo, at a salary of $17,500. Motion carried."

Under date of June 6, 1960, Dr. George S. Easton, chairman of the Board in Control of Athletics, dispatched this letter to President Hancher:

"If, for academic or administrative reasons, intercollegiate athletics is separated from the department of physical education, the Board in Control of Athletics by unanimous vote recommends the appointment of Forest Evashevski to the position of director of athletics and professor (without tenure), the appointment to the administrative position to be for one year on an annual renewable basis at a salary of $20,000.00 (plus retirement and insurance benefits) and to be contingent upon Mr. Evashevski's agreement to the articles of agreement unanimously approved by the Board as indicated by his signature thereto."

Of particular note is the fact that the recommendation of Evashevski for appointment hinged upon his agreement to and signing of the prepared Memorandum of Agreement. Also, among the points enumerated in the Agreement was the requirement that he relinquish his position as head football coach following the 1960 season.

The Agreement was signed; the separation of the departments followed and on June 9, 1960, the appointment of Coach Evashevski as director was announced, effective August 15, 1960. It carried the unanimous approval of the Board of Regents.

Forest Evashevski thus became the twelfth Director of Athletics at Iowa since the position was first created for Dr. Alden A. Knipe in 1900. Evashevski, however, became the first athletic director not to be given a place on the university's Board in Control of Athletics.

The departments of physical education for men and physical education for women were designated as independent departments in 1960, under the direct supervision of the Dean of Liberal Arts. Professor Louis E. Alley, who had been administrative assistant in the department of physical education for men, was appointed head of the department. Professor Gladys Scott remained as head of the department of physical education for women. No change in Evashevski's $20,000 salary was involved in his appointment as Director of Athletics.

1960

ANOTHER CHAMPIONSHIP

Coach Evashevski busied himself with preparations for another season — his ninth at Iowa and his last as head football coach of the Hawks. The Iowa coach had termed 1959 a "survival" year. The 1960 season was to be a "rebuilding" year. It was a squad that featured many sophomores, with heavy responsibilities resting upon men who were lacking in varsity experience. In his later appraisals Evashevski hinted that the 1960 Hawkeyes had greater aggressiveness and enthusiasm, although perhaps less ability and perfection of execution, than the championship teams of 1956 and 1958.

Prior to the season football's problem child, the substitution rule, was further amended to permit one player to enter the game at any time between successive downs. Within the Big Ten it was reaffirmed that since the Rose

Bowl contract had been dropped and not revived, member institutions, on an individual option basis, could accept an invitation to play in the post-season classic.

Further, it was announced that Indiana's Conference membership was being placed on probation because certain prospective athletes had "been offered or had received illegal financial assistance." In the most serious Conference disciplinary action since Iowa's 1929-30 suspension, Indiana was denied participation in football television receipts, and football games played by the Hoosiers in 1960 were not to be counted in the Conference standings.

The campaign itself began with Oregon State's visiting Iowa City for an earlier than usual opener. The Hawks were ready. They marched 85 yards for a first quarter touchdown, with Wilburn Hollis passing to Bill Perkins for the score. Early in the second period Tom Moore's 24-yard field goal raised the total to 9 points, where it stood at halftime. Oregon State wheeled through a third quarter drive, with Kasso dashing the last nine yards, but Iowa struck back, covering 48 yards in four plays after Sherwyn Thorson's recovery of an Oregon State fumble. Larry Ferguson made a 22-yard contribution along the way to that touchdown, then raced 85 yards through tackle for the final Iowa score. Oregon State, meanwhile, had covered 69 yards in nine plays for its second touchdown. Iowa won, 22 to 12, Ferguson personally gaining 141 yards on only eight attempts.

Next start for Iowa was at Northwestern, and the demonstration was impressive. Captain Jerry Mauren ran 45 yards for the first touchdown, then speared a Northwestern pass and carried it 38 yards to score, all in a matter of less than six minutes. The Hawks had a top-heavy 28 — 0 lead at the half, one touchdown by Hollis following the recovery of a fumbled Northwestern punt and another by Larry Ferguson on a 70 yard gallop with an intercepted pass. Once the Wildcats reached the Iowa 15, but they got no closer. The Hawkeyes had a 58-yard touchdown run called back but counted on two other drives in the third quarter, including a short Hollis to Perkins pass and a 53-yard scoring run by sophomore Sammie Harris. Iowa, winning 42 — 0, served notice on the Big Ten that internal trouble was over and that the Hawks were to be reckoned with.

The next test, at Michigan State, was regarded as a telltale effort for Iowa. It drew 74,493 spectators. Breaks, one of them a memorable turning point, marked the game. Iowa pounced on a Michigan State fumble midway in the first quarter and moved 59 yards in 13 rugged plays. Hollis went the last four yards for the score, but Joe Williams accounted for 37 on the drive. The Hawkeyes got the ball again when a Spartan punt struck a Michigan State player on the back, Iowa recovering on the State 48. Seven plays were enough to score, Larry Ferguson covering the last 12 yards shortly before the first quarter ended.

Iowa was on another march late in the second period when Hollis fumbled on the Michigan State 3-yard line after a 66-yard drive. With the Hawks ahead, 14 — 0, the Spartans powered their way through a drive of 83 yards in 12 plays. In the fourth quarter they marched again, this time 88 yards in 23 plays which, with a two-point conversion, put Michigan State ahead 15 — 14. Less than five minutes remained to play. Just when it appeared that the Hawks had doomed themselves completely by fumbling and losing the ball on their own 38, they countered by crashing into a Michigan State back. The ball squirted into the air and Joe Williams of Iowa caught it and sprinted 67 yards through a clear field to score. Iowa had regained the lead with 2:38 to play, then salted it up an instant later when Bernie Wyatt intercepted a Spartan pass on the Michigan State 36. Hollis hit for 11 on a quarterback sneak, then two plays later rammed for 23 more and the final score. The Hawkeyes won, 27 — 15.

Back home the following week, Iowa met Wisconsin, the defending Big Ten champion, in a furious go. The Badgers demonstrated their intentions by driving 73 yards in 16 plays for a first quarter touchdown and the lead. An intercepted pass by Iowa, followed by a 48-yard drive, sent Ferguson in for a matching touchdown on an 18-yard run. They were all even, 7 — 7, at the half. Iowa scored twice in less than five minutes to establish a seemingly comfortable 21 — 7 lead with 13 minutes remaining in the game. However, the Badgers rebounded to score on a 75 yard drive, then turned a Hawkeye fumble into another touchdown and the game was tied, 21 — 21, with five minutes remaining. Four minutes later Ferguson returned a punt 51 yards to the Wisconsin 29. On the next play he took an apparent 29 yard touchdown pass from Wilburn Hollis but the play was lost. Iowa was off side. Less than a minute remained. Again Hollis faded to pass. The ball, slightly underthrown, was deflected into the air by a Badger defender and fell neatly into the hands of Iowa's Sammie Harris for a touchdown. That play won for the Hawkeyes, 28 — 21, and the opportunist Iowans awaited the invasion of always tough Purdue.

It was Homecoming and the stadium was packed. Iowa, for the first time in the school's history, was rated Number 1 in the nation by both wire service polls. A large challenge was in order, however, from the same Purdue team that had spilled Ohio State in a surprise the week before. The inspired Hawkeyes fought to a standstill through the first quarter, took the lead in the second. Getting the ball on the Boilermaker 39, they covered the distance in six plays. One was a 20 yard run by Hollis, followed by a sneak for the touchdown. Just before the half ended another sensational break — almost a duplicate of the one on which Joe Williams had scored against Michigan State — came to Iowa. Bernie Allen, the Purdue quarterback, was swarmed over by charging Iowa linemen and the ball arched into the air. Dayton Perry, Iowa's sophomore center, caught it almost at his shoe tops before it hit the ground and rambled 80 yards for a touchdown. It was the first score by a Hawkeye pivotman in sixty years. Iowa went into the intermission leading 14 — 0.

Joe Williams, Jerry Mauren and Wilburn Hollis were the ball carriers on another Hawkeye drive midway in the third quarter. Hollis

1960 Team

(All Left to Right) TOP ROW: Arnie Buntrock, Assistant Trainer; Jerry Burns, Assistant Coach; Bob Flora, Assistant Coach; Jerry Hilgenberg, Assistant Coach; Archie Kodros, Assistant Coach; Olen Treadway, Freshman Assistant; Bill Happel, Freshman Coach; "Whitey" Piro, Assistant Coach; Dr. W. D. Paul, Team Physician; Doyle Allsup, Trainer.

FIFTH ROW: Loren Hilliard, Paul Roman, Ken Filar, Hugh Fisher, Bob Kreamer, Jerry Swartz, Felton Rogers, Sammie Harris, Jim Robenson, Donald Ferrell, Larry Stednitz, Earl McQuiston.

FOURTH ROW: Lynn Lyon, Jack Rohrs, Allan Fischer, Thomas Buroker, Kenneth Neubert, Bill Cervenak, John Calhoun, Dave Watkins, Jan Lindeman, Mike McDonald, Matthew Syzkowny, Dick Turici, Keith Kinderman.

THIRD ROW: John Kopel, manager; Wilburn Hollis, Joe Williams, Jim Winston, Kevin Barbera, Bob Yauck, Brian Mays, Jerry Soulek, Dayton Perry, Gerald Lafferty, Alex Korzeniewski, Sherwyn Thorson.

SECOND ROW: Bill Perkins, Bill Van Buren, Bruce Mitchell, Larry Ferguson, Alfred Hinton, Chester Williams, Jerry Williams, Bill DiCindio, Bill Whisler, Emery Pudder.

FIRST ROW: Dick Clauson, Tom Moore, Bernard Wyatt, Eugene Mosley, Mark Manders, Charles Lee, Jr., Capt. Jerry Mauren, Bill Ringer, Donald Zinn, Lloyd Humphreys, Bob Russo, Donald Tucker; Forest Evashevski, Head Coach.

capped it with a six yard touchdown smash and highly regarded Purdue trailed, 21 — 0. From that point on Iowa literally had to fight for its football life. Purdue stormed through a 76-yard charge in the third quarter, Allen passing to Jim Tiller for the score. It was 21 — 7. The Boilermakers came on again in the fourth quarter, maintaining possession and advancing through a gruelling 91-yard march to make it 21 — 14, with nearly eight minutes unplayed. The Hawks fought off a final Boilermaker threat and the score was unchanged at the finish. Allen's passes, 18 of them, gained 164 yards that day.

The still top ranked Hawkeyes, with a 4 — 0 record and sharing the Big Ten lead, went out of their own league to play Kansas of the Big Eight in an October 29 game at Iowa City. The Jayhawks had lost only once in six outings. As a starter the Iowans ground out an 82-yard touchdown drive, making no forays through the air. In the second quarter an attempted punt went wrong for Kansas, Iowa recovering just four yards from the Jawhawk goal. Ferguson scored a moment later. The Hawkeyes made it 21 − 0 in the third quarter, going 67 yards in 15 plays with Hollis getting the final yard. The fourth period was largely Kansas. It threatened once on a pass to the Iowa 9-yard line, which the receiver dropped. Undaunted, the Jayhawks came on again in a 43-yard march, with Hadl going the last eight into the end zone. A good Kansas team rushed for nearly 200 yards against Iowa but couldn't stop the ground assault of the Hawkeyes, who gained 257. Passing seemed incidental. Hollis tried four for Iowa, completing none, but Matt Szykowny, a sophomore, connected on two of three. It was the seventy-first straight game in which Iowa scored, the longest active streak in the nation. Michigan State ranked next to the Hawks among Big Ten teams, having gone 17 games without being shut out.

Iowa had been rated the Number 1 team in the nation in both wire service polls for three weeks in a row when the Hawks went to Minneapolis in early November for a showdown with Minnesota. The Gophers, like Iowa, were undefeated and they held the Number 2 spot in the United Press poll. Coincidentally, the Iowa point total was the highest given any team in the United Press ratings since mid-November, 1953, when Notre Dame topped the list. It was the following Saturday that Iowa and the Irish tied 14 − 14 in the memorable "fainting" game. On November 5, 1960, it was cold and windy, and Memorial Stadium was jammed with an all-time record crowd of 65,610. Minnesota's furious line play probably figured in the errors that were fatal to Iowa, as well as in minimizing the danger of the Hawkeye attack. Early in the first quarter, with Iowa on its own 46-yard line, John Calhoun went back to punt. The pass from center sailed high over his head,

forcing Calhoun to race 32 yards toward his own goal. He recovered on the Iowa 14, but to no avail. It had been fourth down, and the ball went over to Minnesota. The Gophers slammed it home in three plays to take the lead.

In the second quarter an Iowa march moved the ball 69 yards, from the Iowa 26 to the Minnesota 5-yard line, with Larry Ferguson's breakneck runs bringing 21, 11 and 16 yards in the drive. With third down and three to go, Tom Brown, widely heralded Minnesota guard, charged like lightning, knocked Iowa's Bill DiCindio into quarterback Hollis and forced a loss of six yards. Now it was fourth and nine, and the touchdown threat dimmed. Tom Moore settled for an Iowa field goal. Trailing at the half the Hawks gained a 10 − 7 lead in the third quarter on a 55-yard advance. Eugene Mosley with 12, Ferguson with 19 and Joe Williams with a 26-yard dash to the goal covered most of the yardage.

Minnesota came right back, advancing 81 yards in 11 plays to send Sandy Stephens in with the score that made it 13 − 10 for the Gophers. Iowa went into the last six minutes with a chance to win when these things happened: Sammie Harris gained eight yards, fumbled and the ball was picked out of the air by Roger Hagberg of Minnesota, who sprinted 42 yards for a touchdown. Shortly, with Iowa deep in its own end of the field resorting to passes, Matt Szykowny was rushed, flattened, and his resulting fumble was recovered by Minnesota on the Iowa 19. Four plays later Joe Salem rammed across the Iowa goal and Minnesota had won, 27 − 10. The Gophers took over Iowa's position at the head of the national parade, and they also won the coveted Floyd of Rosedale trophy for the first time in six years.

It was a vengeful rather than a dispirited band of Hawkeyes that moved into the ensuing game with Ohio State's tough outfit. The battle was to be seen by a nationwide television audience, but more than that it was to be the last home game to be coached by Forest Evashevski. The Buckeyes had lost only once and were rated third in the nation, but astonishing things happened in a hurry in a game that rates with the best of all Iowa showings in Big Ten football. It began with Ohio State the same old menacing foe. The Bucks advanced to the Iowa 17-yard line when a fourth down pass failed. Taking over the ball, the Hawks stormed up the field, going 83 yards in six plays, the last one a 48-yard burst by Joe Williams. The Buckeyes blasted back to score a touchdown before the second quarter was two minutes old. It was a 77-yard, six-play Ohio State march. The Bucks missed the extra point and Iowa exploded into action.

In a tremendous offensive show the Hawks roared across 65 yards of ground in six plays to score their second touchdown, Hollis sweeping for the last 12. With little delay Larry Ferguson of Iowa brought a Buckeye punt back 24 yards to the Ohio State 42, and the Hawkeyes went the rest of the way in seven plays, Ferguson gaining 25 yards on one dash. Ahead 21 — 6, the Hawks continued their cannonading and swept 64 yards in six plays for a fourth touchdown. Iowa left the field with an astonishing 28 — 6 halftime lead, 21 of the points coming in the second period.

The furious battle was resumed in the third quarter. Ohio State came on like a tornado, sweeping 79 yards in four plays which consumed only two minutes. Tom Matte got the touchdown on a 22-yard run. Iowa stood off another assault and took the ball when a fourth down Buckeye pass failed from the Hawk 6-yard line. In the first minute of the fourth quarter, with Iowa back on its own 9-yard line, Larry Ferguson broke around end and steamed 91 yards down the sideline for the final score. It was the second mightiest run from scrimmage credited to any of Evashevski's backs, surpassed only by Eddie Vincent's 96-yard touchdown run against Purdue six years before. Ferguson averaged more than 20 yards each time he carried the ball against the Buckeyes.

Iowa's smashing 35 — 12 victory caused Woody Hayes, Ohio State's head coach, to remark in his dressing room, after watching the

Hawkeyes slam through his team for five touchdowns, that "Evashevski is the greatest offensive coach in the country." Iowa ran for 361 yards against Ohio State, second highest ever over a conference opponent, and passed for 126 more on eight of 13 strikes through the air. With the victory, the Hawkeyes softened the loss to Minnesota the previous week and gained a share of the Big Ten championship. Minnesota, however, the co-champion, drew the Rose Bowl assignment.

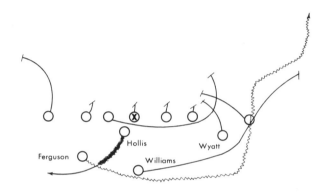

This play, originating from the Slot-T formation, featured Larry Ferguson on a sweep to the right. Ferguson took a handoff from quarterback Hollis near his own goal line, ran over the spot vacated by Iowa's split right end, and went for a touchdown. The play covered 91 yards from scrimmage and was the most spectacular of five Hawkeye touchdowns in the 35 — 12 win over Ohio State in 1960.

Once more the Big Ten campaign was over. The windup game was against Notre Dame, at South Bend. In a frosty November setting Iowa put the Irish in an early hole when Bill Whisler grabbed an errant fumble just 28 yards from the goal. Big plays were an 11-yard pass and a six yard run by Joe Williams for the touchdown. In the second quarter Sammie Harris broke away for 34 yards to the Notre Dame 28 and Matt Szykowny hit Whisler, who was unguarded in the end zone, with a 28-yard touchdown pass. The Hawks led 14 — 0 at the half and were headed toward a third quarter score when the ball was lost on a fumble at the Notre Dame two yard line. Back again they came in the fourth period, Hollis scoring from in close after a 38-yard run by Ferguson had provided the opportunity. Still another fourth quarter score was registered on a 57-yard march, highlights of which were Eugene Mosley's 36-yard run and his ensuing two-yard smash into the end zone. Iowa defeated the Fighting Irish for the fourth time in five seasons, 28 — 0, and Evashevski's last stand as Hawkeye coach was over. A team that had started the season in the "rebuilding" stage, finished by sharing the Big Ten title.

Individually three Hawkeyes were deservedly honored with post-season recognition. Larry Ferguson, Wilburn Hollis and Mark Manders all were awarded positions on the Associated Press all Big Ten first team. Ferguson and Manders were further cited by the Football Writers Association with positions on the all-America team of Look Magazine. Hollis was given a third team berth by United Press-International and Central Press.

Quarterback Hollis, with 68 total points in 1960, became the highest scoring Hawkeye since Gordon Locke in 1922. Ferguson, rushing for 665 yards, took his place as the leading single season ground gainer under Forest Evashevski. The exciting junior gained almost 7 1/2 yards each time he carried the ball during the year, the finest season-long average ever attained by an Iowa player.

Tom Moore closed his career with 26 of 28 successful extra points, matching the number Joe Warner kicked sixty years before. The Rochester, Minnesota, marksman finished the season with 19 straight conversions, another record. In addition, his five career field goals were the most since Aubrey Devine notched six between 1919 and 1921.

Forest Evashevski, the retiring Iowa coach, could look back to some memorable achievements. He had come into a "coaching graveyard" in January, 1952, to compile a 52 — 27 — 4 record in the next nine seasons. He had brought two outright conference titles and a share of an-

other to a school that had known no championship days in football since 1922. He had produced two Rose Bowl champions.

When the Hawks first picked up their top momentum in 1956, they held it through a stretch of five seasons. In that period they won 37 games, lost 8 and tied 2. In 50 years of Big Ten history only two schools won more games than the Hawks in a similar stretch. Michigan won 40 games in a five year span from 1944 through 1948, and Ohio State won 38 from 1954 through 1958.

From the Howard Jones heyday in 1922 until the Evashevski regime attained offensive might in 1956, no Iowa team had scored as many as 200 points in a season. From 1956 through 1960 the Evashevski-led Hawkeyes surpassed the 200 point mark five years in succession. No Big Ten team can match the feat over a corresponding length of time. More remarkable is the fact that Forest Evashevski retired after 12 years of coaching as one of the few collegiate coaches whose teams averaged more than 200 points a season through his entire career.

At the end of the coaching trail Evashevski could also look back to the string of all-America players who had been recognized at a school which claimed none at all since a much earlier day. He could look back to Jerry Hilgenberg and Calvin Jones in 1953, to the same Cal Jones in 1954 and 1955, to Alex Karras and Kenny Ploen in 1956 and Karras and Jim Gibbons in 1957. He could point to Karras and Curt Merz in 1958 and to Don Norton in 1959. Additionally on the "rebuilding" team of his final season, Mark Manders and Larry Ferguson earned the all-America designation.

Prominent also in the march of the Hawkeyes under Evashevski were Bill Fenton and Frank Gilliam, Don Suchy and Dick Klein, Bob Jeter and Wilburn Hollis, Don Chelf and Willie Fleming, Eddie Vincent, Bill Lapham, John Hall and Ray Jauch. Each one of them won recognition on all Big Ten teams or on second and third all-America elevens.

Just as Coach Evashevski pointed to certain games as marking his personal highlights (the Ohio State games of 1952, 1956 and 1960; the two Rose Bowl games and the Minnesota game of 1956) he had his own evaluations of the disappointments. He cited the 1955 season as the most disappointing of all (Iowa had a 3 — 5 — 1 record, scoring 166 points to its opponents'

Larry Ferguson

173). In individual games the heartbreakers against Michigan were singled out — two one point defeats, another by three points and a tie jammed into a five year stretch. The never-to-be-forgotten tie with Notre Dame in 1953 — the "fainting game" — was another great disappointment with Iowa's men leading the nation's Number 1 team into the very last seconds, only to be deprived of victory. Long afterward, in recalling the game in which Iowa led in the final seconds of each half, with frantic clock-stopping measures helping Notre

Dame ultimately to tie at 14 — 14, Coach Evashevski said:

"My real complaint was against the officiating rather than Notre Dame. I think the officials let the ball game go. They signalled for the clock to start; it didn't start and they allowed it to remain motionless until the ball was put in play. This of course was wrong and kept us from the victory. It probably would have been one of the great plums because at the time Notre Dame was rated as the No. 1 team in the nation."

Asked to evaluate some of the foremost players he coached at Iowa, Coach Evashevski cited the late Calvin Jones and Alex Karras as Iowa's top linemen during his time. He said:

"I would have to say that Karras was ahead of Jones defensively and Jones was a little ahead of Karras offensively, mainly because Karras didn't want to play offense. He was interested in playing defense." Evashevski hesitated to make a choice between Sherwyn Thorson, Frank Bloomquist and Gary Grouwinkel, among his ranking guards, saying: "I'd have to throw them in the hopper. They had strengths and weaknesses that offset each other. And Bob Commings, the smallest man we ever had in our line (174 pounds) did a terrific job for us for three years.

"Willie Fleming, without a doubt, was the greatest running back I've ever coached. I think had Willie remained at Iowa (he played only as a sophomore) he would have gone down as one of the greatest halfbacks who ever played.   He could do everything. For a man who was 5 feet 9 he could stand under a basket and dunk a basketball, he had so much spring. He had tremendous explosion. He was a fine defensive player, with tremendous quickness. He was one of the few halfbacks on defense who could make a mistake and recover fast enough to turn it into an interception on a pass play. He had all the assets a halfback needs and a real fine attitude. Willie's handicap was only playing one season. You can't choose a man for the Hall of Fame on the basis of only one year.

"Among the quarterbacks, I think you'd have to recognize Kenny Ploen on all around ability. His fine defensive qualities sometimes were overlooked. He was one of the greatest defensive backs I've ever coached. He was the quarterback on our first wing-T team.

"For throwing ability, Randy Duncan has got to have a place in Iowa football history because I think he holds most of the records. Randy had the ability to throw the long soft ball, or drill the hard, fast one. He had enough strength in his arm to split an end 8 or 10 yards out, drive him into the sideline and hit the receiver without the high trajectory that would mean the danger of an interception.

"Duncan and Ploen were different. I think Kenny had the advantage because he used himself on the big play. Kenny, if it were third and eight, and we had to have it, would drop back and take the avenue that was best open to him. If it meant running, he always got 8 1/2 yards, if you needed 8. Randy didn't have the speed to run. He was always using somebody else as the clutch player — throwing the ball to Jim Gibbons or Curt Merz or Don Norton, or feeding it to Willie Fleming or Bob Jeter or shooting the ball to John Nocera. I would have to say that Ploen had the edge because he had so much more latitude in using himself. They were both fine competitors. Kenny Ploen was by far the better runner but just on passing, you'd have to take Duncan."

Evashevski had two other notable quarterbacks at Iowa — Jerry Reichow and Wilburn Hollis.

"They were different types of ball carriers," he said. "When Reichow finished his competition and the Detroit Lions talked to me about him I said that if he were to play for us and we had a real fine quarterback we would play him at end. He had great hands. He was a kid who was playing out of position. Jerry was a big, powerful fellow who could get by with the type of offense we were running. It was probably unfair that Jerry was playing at a time when he was so badly needed in a different position because I think he would have been an All-American end if he had been

placed there. Actually, we voted to use him at end at one meeting but decided he was too valuable at quarterback. If we placed him at end, we had nobody to throw the ball because the particular offense Reichow had been running had been built around him. It didn't fit Kenny Ploen. It was not best suited for him."

George (Dusty) Rice was a halfback on the first two Evashevski teams at Iowa. Asked to evaluate him, the coach said:

"I did not have an adequate opportunity because Dusty had a knee operation and couldn't do as many things as he otherwise would have done. In 1952 and 1953 we had to play an offense that was not best for Dusty because he was like Kenny Ploen in getting back and running. However, I thought Dusty Rice was one of the real fine halfbacks Iowa has had. If he were to have played on one of our ball clubs of recent years, he would have been a standout all the way — even more than he was when he played at Iowa. He had great hands. He was one of the great receivers of the game in his time even though we were not a passing ball club then. We couldn't utilize this ability. He also was a great fellow on a sweeping game. We had to punch him in and use him occasionally at the flanks. With our personnel Dusty had to be used at a spot that really wasn't his best position. I would say, however, that I had opportunity enough to say that Dusty Rice was very high among the halfbacks we've had at Iowa since I've been here."

" 'What about Eddie Vincent and Larry Ferguson?' Evashevski was asked. 'Would they be the next to stand out among the halfbacks?'

"Bob Jeter was very good, as was Vincent," the coach answered. "Of course, you've got to realize that both were handicapped somewhat. Vincent was a great defensive player. Offensively he had two weaknesses. He had poor hands for a halfback as a pass receiver and he had poor vision. These kept Vincent from being more valuable than he was. Jeter, like Vincent, was a great defensive halfback and I think he was one of the most deceptive runners we've had. He had a shuffle and didn't look like he was running real fast. I could not rate Vincent ahead of Jeter.

"We had Larry Ferguson only one year but on the basis of one season I would say he'd have to rank just a shade below Willie Fleming because he was a game breaker all the way."

The coach designated John Nocera as the best blocking back of his Iowa regime and Binkey Broeder as the best punter.

Evashevski paid tribute to Jim Gibbons as "the best end — the clutch ball player" of his regime. "He hauled them down in the clutch," declared the coach. "Jim was one of the weakest defensive players we have had, but he wasn't interested in playing defense. Offensively he was a good blocker and he had wonderful hands.

"Don Norton was one of our better all-around ends. He could do everything. He could play defense, he was alert, had speed and good hands.

"Frank Gilliam, for what he had, was great but his defensive work was the finest. I would say that Curt Merz would have been the greatest end we had if he had not been hurt. No junior end I've coached ever approached Curt Merz. I thought he was sensational. His leg prevented him from playing his senior year. He was in and out physically and that's why he can't go down with the rest of them."

What about the tackles? The coach was asked if Alex Karras, Dick Klein and Frank Rigney led the list and he answered:

"They stand out in my mind. Karras was by far the best defensive tackle I ever had and Frank Rigney probably will go down as the No. 2 tackle because he was used as the swing man. We had to relieve both Karras and Klein and Rigney had the adaptability to fit in at either tackle. These definitely are three of the fine ones we've had but Al Hinton would be up there too. Under the first three, as I see it, but definitely up there.

"The best centers during my time as coach were Jerry Hilgenberg, Bud Lawson and Don Suchy."

In nine seasons Evashevski's teams had played 83 games, winning 52, losing 27 and playing four ties. In the Big Ten the record was 33 won, 21 lost, two tied. Before November of his final year was over the Pigskin Club of Washington, D.C., designated Evashevski as its "Coach of the Year," the fourth different season that he had received "Coach of the Year" honors.

Evashevski withdrew from the coaching field after having put Iowa in the championship picture more than any predecessor. His Hawkeye teams gained the singular distinction of being among the top three teams in the nation in three of five consecutive years. No other Big Ten team has been so honored, nor has another Conference team ever been ranked in the top five in four of five consecutive seasons. From 1956 through 1960 Evy's teams won 22 Big Ten games, lost 7 and tied 1. In addition, three Conference coaches, Woody Hayes of Ohio State, Duffy Daugherty of Michigan State and Ara Parseghian, then of Northwestern, suffered their worst coaching defeats at the hands of Evashevski-tutored Iowa teams. Terry Brennan of Notre Dame was a similar victim.

Evashevski majored in psychology during his student days at Michigan. He placed great value in it. "I'm a great believer in motivation," he once said. "I think this is where the psychological approach to football comes in. Former Michigan coach Fielding Yost was one of the great psychologists the game has known. He made two statements that have always stuck with me and that I have used many times. One was 'a little extra effort is the difference between mediocrity and greatness.' And the one that impressed me most was 'the will to prepare to win is much more important than the will to win.'

"The day of a game is no time to put the needle into a team in a psychological build-up," Evashevski said. "You've got to feel your way into it. Sometimes you start the build-up by showing disgust and attacking the pride of the players. Oftentimes I started a practice and after 10 minutes or so I said: 'All right, boys, that's all. Just go on in. If this is all the pride you have in yourselves and in your football team — it's all right with me. But I think you're wasting your time and my time.' By just sending them in and letting them reflect you sometimes accomplish more than you do with an outright scolding. On other occasions you have to hold the boys down and play the game down a little. Too much emotional build-up dissipates energy. Much of this responsibility quite naturally rests with the coach. I don't have a great deal of sympathy for the coach when he's blamed for a poor season; he's getting paid to produce.

"And just as the coach must work to win, the players must play to win. There's a very tricky shading of meaning there. When the game is over, it's not important whether you won; but during the game, it's vitally important — not just to look good, but to win.

"And when it's over if you can say 'I left everything I had out on the field and if I had it to do tomorrow I couldn't do it any better,' then there's no disgrace in losing."

So Forest Evashevski marched proudly away from his football proving ground. Nine years from his starting point at Iowa, he had put aside the coaching mantle he had worn so impressively to head the department as director of athletics, justifying, with his withdrawal, his often-made assertion that he never would grow old in coaching. He stepped out at the age of 42 after having led the Hawkeyes from the floor of the Conference to an all-time level of success.

Jerry Burns Assumes Command

With two games unplayed in his final season of 1960, Evashevski complied with the request of the Board in Control of Athletics and recommended his successor. His choice was Jerome M. (Jerry) Burns, a slight, leathery young Michigan alumnus who had joined Evashevski's staff in 1954, devoting most of his attention to the coaching of the backfield. It was November 10, 1960, with the Ohio State and Notre Dame games yet to be played, that Coach Evashevski directed the following to Dr. George S. Easton, chairman of the Board:

"In my opinion Jerry Burns, who is at present backfield coach for the State University of Iowa, is the most capable man for my replacement as Head Football Coach. I recommend that this very competent young man be named for the position as Head Football Coach at the close of the 1960 football season.

"To my way of thinking he is more capable than any of the young coaches in the nation. His technical knowledge of football is complete and his thinking on defense is very sound, which is unusual for most young coaches because most of their thinking is in terms of offensive football.

"Mr. Burns has been in complete charge of our defensive unit for the past three years and has headed up recruiting activities for the past two years. I feel that he has the experience and enthusiasm and the leadership ability to provide us with the type of football program we all desire.

"The following is a jacket on Mr. Burns' experience and education.

PERSONAL: Age 33, married, with four children.

EDUCATION: Bachelor of Science in Physical Education, University of Michigan, February, 1951.

EXPERIENCE: 1951-52, Backfield Coach and Head Baseball Coach, University of Hawaii, Honolulu, Hawaii; 1952, Backfield Coach and Basketball Coach, Whittier College, Whittier, Cal.; 1952-53, Head Football and Basketball Coach, St. Mary Redford High School, Detroit, Michigan; 1953 to present, State University of Iowa. Started in 1954 as Freshman Coach. At the end of year was moved to Varsity Staff and helped with the Backs. For the next two seasons was in complete charge of Backs when Bump Elliott moved to Michigan."

The Board, in a late afternoon session at Hotel Jefferson in Iowa City on November 10, unanimously approved Evashevski's recommendation, specifying that Burns take over the position of head coach December 1, 1960 with a rating of full professor without tenure for a three-year term, at a starting salary of $15,000 per year. At a Board meeting on December 14, the three-year stipulation was extended one month, since December 31 was considered a more desirable date for the termination of coaching contracts.

Evashevski had made his farewell to active coaching a memorable occasion on November 19, 1960. He had taken his squad to South Bend, Indiana, and tagged Notre Dame with a

Head Football Coach — 1961—
Jerry Burns

28 — 0 defeat. Almost with word of the score came the formal announcement by Virgil M. Hancher, president of the University, that Jerry Burns would succeed Evashevski as head coach.

A young man, assuming the coaching responsibilities at a major university for the first time, could hardly have chosen a more difficult role than Burns took up when he succeeded Eva-

shevski. The new coach hardly had taken charge of his squad until the press services of the nation installed Iowa as the country's top team. Jerry Burns, paradoxically, had not as yet coached his first college game. And Iowa, too, had become accustomed to great things. It might not be patient if they were not quickly forthcoming. In such an atmosphere the career of Coach Burns began.

1961

The top-rated Hawkeyes met unexpected resistance from the University of California in the 1961 opener, leading by an insecure 14 — 7 margin going into the fourth quarter. Paul Krause and Lonnie Rogers scored for the Hawks in the last period and the final score was a conclusive 28 — 7. All-American Larry Ferguson, expected to head the Iowa attack, injured his knee in the first three minutes and was lost for the season. Southern California was next and a more dramatic and often frustrating battle than this nationally televised meeting in the Los Angeles Coliseum could hardly be visualized.

Iowa scored 21 points in the first 22 minutes and the Trojans scored 34 points in the final 35 minutes. The game followed this pattern:

The Hawks stormed out to a 21 — 0 lead with the second quarter barely half gone, but at the end they were hanging for their very lives to the slimmest of all leads, 35 — 34, and won only when Southern California's desperation pass for a two-point conversion was unsuccessful. Just 48 seconds remained at the time. Joe Williams scored three touchdowns for Iowa, but quarterback Wilburn Hollis joined Larry Ferguson on the sideline for the remainder of the season with a broken wrist.

Still unbeaten, Iowa opened its Big Ten season against Indiana at Iowa City minus its two finest backs. In addition, Jim Winston was missing from his end position with a leg fracture suffered in the Southern California game. Even so, the undermanned Hoosiers were unequal to the occasion and Iowa won, 27 — 8.

Matt Szykowny, starting for the first time at quarterback, bowed in with 14 pass completions in 24 tries for 195 yards and a touchdown.

Wisconsin and Homecoming were the attractions in Game Number 4 of the Burns' regime and a Stadium record crowd of 60,150 watched an unbelievable Iowa romp in the early stages. Before the game was three minutes old Joe Williams had raced 59 yards to the Badger 2, from where Bernie Wyatt took it over. Another touchdown in the first quarter and three more in the second gave Iowa an astonishing lead of 33 — 0 at the half. Szykowny completed his first nine passes during the rout. When it ended the count was 47 — 15 for the Hawkeyes and sophomore end Cloyd Webb was selected Associated Press national "lineman of the week." The fact that Iowa had netted 441 yards on runs and passes, completed 19 of 25 passes, and intercepted three Badger throws suggested to some that the Number 1 rating given the Hawks might not have been far out of line.

A quick change was in the offing, however. Iowa made a late October trip to Purdue and met a strong Boilermaker team in hard rain on a muddy field. The Boilermakers won, 9 — 0. Not since nearly nine years before (in the closing game of Evashevski's 1952 season) had an Iowa team failed to score. This, after 78 games without being shut out, was the fifth best such performance in the history of major college football. Furthermore, it exceeded Michigan's previous Big Ten record by 19 games. Purdue, with the help of a pass interception on the Iowa 37, scored a first quarter touchdown when Don DiGravio knifed through from the 1-yard line. A third period 27 yard field goal iced the 9 — 0 Purdue victory. No Hawk back gained as many as 25 yards and the Iowa team never advanced beyond the Boilermaker 30 yard line. It was the first of Iowa's defeats under Coach Burns, but three more followed in short order.

Ohio State rapped the Hawks 29 — 13 before an all-time record crowd of 83,795 in the Buckeye Homecoming game. Minnesota followed and earned a 16 — 9 decision, its first at Iowa City in

13 years. In the process the Gophers held Iowa's ground game to a meager 39 yards. And Michigan, after trailing 14 — 3 at the half, scored 20 points in the third and fourth quarters to win, 23 — 14. Iowa, which had started the campaign rated Number 1, lost four in a row after winning the first four. Injuries had taken their toll, but mistakes too, in the form of 8 pass interceptions and 8 fumbles lost, contributed to the four game disaster. Rumors so often associated with losing were heard. None were confirmed, and the Hawks in spite of their slump drew 58,000 spectators to their concluding game against Notre Dame. They routed the Fighting Irish, 42 — 21. The aroused Hawkeyes recovered six Notre Dame fumbles, intercepted five passes and held a 42 — 7 lead going into the fourth quarter. They won by a wide margin, although the game statistics were surprisingly close. Joe Williams equalled the longest touchdown run ever scored by a Hawkeye when he returned a second period kickoff 105 yards into the Irish end zone. Charles (Peck) Hazard, playing against Coe College in 1908, had scored from a similar distance. Jerry Burns had ended his first season with a 5 — 4 mark.

With the close of the 1961 campaign the books for the season were examined. It was found that Iowa had surpassed the 200 point mark in scoring for the sixth straight year, a record unmatched by any other Big Ten school. Their consecutive scoring mark was ended but in reaching 78 games it stood as the fifth longest in major college football history. Matt Szykowny had passed for 1,078 yards, a mark surpassed only by Randy Duncan, and Cloyd Webb had caught 25 passes for 426 yards, a dition, while Wilburn Hollis had missed most of the season because of a hand injury, he had played enough to raise his career scoring total past the 100-point mark. Hollis thus became one of only a dozen Hawkeyes over the long history of Iowa football to reach the century figure.

Center Bill VanBuren and tackle Al Hinton were given all-America recognition following the season. VanBuren was placed on the first team of The Sporting News, while Hinton was awarded a third team berth on the American Football Coaches Association team.

Iowa athletics in 1961-62 grossed a record $1,226,155.87. Football accounted for $959,503.02 of that amount. An increase in Hawkeye ticket prices from $4.00 to $5.00 prior to the season was largely responsible for Iowa's netting more than $100,000 from both the Minnesota and Notre Dame games. These were the first home contests to exceed $100,000 in net income for the university.

The athletic department continued a practice of many years when, in December, 1961, it was noted that a $12,500 grant was made to the Research Council of Iowa for nonathletic purposes.

Before another season a new contract was signed between the Big Ten and the Pacific Coast Athletic Association of Western Universities to provide opponents in the Rose Bowl game. It was to extend for an indefinite period. Kenneth L. (Tug) Wilson had retired as Commissioner of the Conference after 16 years of service. William R. Reed, who had first joined the Conference staff in 1939, was elected the third Conference Commissioner.

The Faculty Representatives enacted new financial aid rules late in 1961, eliminating the controversial "need principle" and installing a requirement of predicted college success on the basis of high school rank and aptitude tests. The "normal progress" requirements of the eligibility rules also were strengthened.

1962

With a prospect of fine passing and receiving, Coach Burns altered his offense in preparing for the 1962 season. He went to an unbalanced line, using only one tackle and five backs, one a "floater" designed to help spread the defenses for the passing attack. It was intended to provide new problems for the defenses and increase the Iowa threat through the air. The Hawks had problems elsewhere, however, and personnel switches were necessary during much of the season. There was hope that a sophomore halfback, Willie Ray Smith, would give the Hawks the speed and elusiveness to complement Larry Ferguson. Paul Krause was the new "floater" back, while Lonnie Rogers, Bobby Grier and Bob LeZotte gave promise of depth at the halfbacks. Jim Winston was back in uniform after fracturing a leg in 1961.

So began the second season of the Burns era. Oregon State was the first opponent and the Hawks met their rival with a passing-running onslaught which produced a 28 — 0 lead after three quarters and a 28 — 8 victory. The revised offense saw Szykowny completing 12 of 17 passes for 144 yards, three of the throws bringing touchdowns. A week later, with Southern California in Iowa City, the new offense was blanked. Playing erratically, the Hawkeyes lost the ball on fumbles and pass interceptions seven times, and saw a substitute halfback named Heller run 19 yards for the only touchdown after the Trojans had grabbed a fumble on the Iowa 19. The Hawks held Southern California to five first downs and a total of 123 yards, produced almost twice that total themselves, but lost, 7 — 0. The Trojans were National Champions two months later.

At Indiana the following week, with the dangerous Marv Woodson against them, the Hawkeyes won their Conference opener, 14 — 10, Woodson racing 54 yards for the lone Hoosier score. Bill Perkins ran 50 yards for an Iowa touchdown and quarterback Bob Wallace, playing all the way for injured Matt Szykowny, punched through from the 1-yard line for another in the victory. Next in the seesaw season came Wisconsin, victim of a humiliating defeat at Iowa City the year before. The Badgers returned the favor. They smashed the Hawkeyes, 42 — 14, to gain satisfaction and revenge for their 47 — 15 rout in 1961. To add to the sting of the beating, Iowa started with a 7 — 0 lead in the first quarter but gave up four touchdowns in the second period and two more in the third. It was mile-a-minute scoring at one stage, with four touchdowns jammed into a stretch of 4 minutes, 9 seconds. Iowa's touchdowns resulted from a 56-yard pass, Szykowny to Webb, and a record equalling 80-yard pass play, Szykowny to Ferguson.

Morale, spectator type, was sinking when Purdue arrived to meet the 1962 Hawks, but 60,100 turned out for the game. Iowa scored in the first quarter as Jay Roberts drove a 27-yard place kick over the bar, but that was all for the Hawkeyes. Purdue, with a strong edge in running, slammed home four touchdowns in the last three quarters and won, 26 — 3. Then, with fan indifference nearing a low point, Ohio State arrived in Iowa City. The Hawks, looming as losers, outran and outpassed the Buckeyes, captured three Ohio State fumbles and won, 28 — 14. Iowa, which had lost the ball 12 times on fumbles and interceptions in the Wisconsin and Purdue games, forced Ohio State into errors. Three first half touchdowns, two by Matt Szykowny and one by Bobby Grier, virtually sewed up the decision. Bob Sherman scored the fourth Iowa touchdown, with Vic Davis, Larry Ferguson, Cloyd Webb and Bill Perkins filling big roles all the way.

Next, Minnesota, the nation's Number 1 team in defense against rushing, turned back two Iowa threats and won, 10 — 0, after the Hawks had been stopped by their own fumbles on the Gopher 3 and 18 yard lines. Statistically, it was something of a standoff but once again Iowa errors (three lost fumbles, two passes intercepted) decided the issue.

It was 3 — 4 in games won and lost as Michigan moved into Iowa City in mid-November.

In the 37 degree temperature the Hawkeyes struck the Wolverines with a ruthless running attack, supplemented by effective passing. Michigan, in four previous trips, had flattened the Hawks on their home field four times. This was different, although there was no such suggestion when Raimey of the visitors put his team in front, 6 — 0, in the first quarter. Iowa countered with Larry Ferguson, on the most productive day of his career, running 16 yards for one second quarter touchdown and Paul Krause rambling 82 yards on a punt return for another. It was 14 — 14 into the fourth quarter when Szykowny fired a tie-breaking pass to

Sammie Harris for a 47-yard touchdown. A team of Iowa reserves quarterbacked by Bob Wallace scored again in the final minutes. Ferguson, with 153 yards rushing, matched the ground yardage of the entire Michigan team. Iowa won, 28 — 14, and season Number 2 for Coach Burns stood at 4 — 4 with Notre Dame coming up.

The Fighting Irish, facing problems of their own, came up with a measure of satisfaction when they spilled the Hawkeyes, 35 — 12, before 42,653 spectators. It was one of the smaller crowds to witness a game in this series and the defeat cost Iowa a chance to square the all-time series. Although the Hawks were erratic in spots and never dynamic, they were in the game until the fourth quarter when Notre Dame slapped them down with 22 points. The shortest of Notre Dame's first four touchdowns was scored from 19 yards out. Iowa, held to 110 yards by rushing, saw Larry Ferguson collect 95 of the total on 15 carries. Neither the offense nor the defense was adequate for Iowa, with the Irish strangling Hawkeye hopes with 283 yards rushing and another 144 passing.

Jerry Burns' second season was over and once more the books were totaled. For the two seasons the Hawkeyes showed nine games won and nine lost. In the Conference the record revealed five victories, seven defeats. Signs of unrest could be seen here and there on the Iowa front but the Board in Control of Athletics took quick action to make its attitude known.

Coach Burns had a year to go on his original contract. Upon the recommendation of Athletic Director Evashevski the Board indicated its confidence in the coach by voting him a new three-year contract and a salary increase from $15,000 to $17,500. The new agreement and the increase were announced before the close of the 1962 season.

Larry Ferguson was again selected on the all-Big Ten first unit. The Iowa captain closed his oftentimes spectacular three-year career with the remarkable average of six yards gained each time he carried the ball. No other Hawkeye has matched that performance record.

Matt Szykowny also ended his highly creditable although inconsistent career. The versatile Pennsylvanian became only the second Hawk player to pass for more than 2,000 yards and his total offense mark ranks among the all-time leaders. Szykowny, however, with ten pass interceptions thrown in 1962 brought his career total to 26, second high at Iowa.

Football accounted for more than one million of the $1,218,153.45 which all athletics brought to Iowa in 1962-63. Further indication of the importance of the game to the success of the entire athletic department is the fact that the net gain from football amounted to $479,656.50 while all other sports at the University lost a total of $225,782.32.

1963

With the arrival of the 1963 season Iowa's strength loomed as largely defensive, with prospects indicating a strong interior line, an excellent secondary, good strength at the ends and excellent physical conditioning resulting from the rugged "winning edge" program of physical fitness inaugurated during the spring training period. Against these assets the Hawks had problems at quarterback, no fullbacks with Big Ten experience and a lack of breakaway speed among the halfback candidates. Development of players, particularly on offense, was an immediate necessity.

Washington State came to Iowa City to open the season. The Hawks scored twice in the first half and the Cougars twice in the last half but it was a play that did not materialize that featured the 14 — 14 tie. On third down with 11 seconds remaining and the surging Cougars on the Iowa 28, Dave Mathieson of Washington State drifted back to pass. An Iowa end threw him to the ground, then was charged with unnecessary roughness on the play. Three seconds remained as the erring Hawkeye was banished. The play lost 12 yards but the resulting 15-yard penalty put the ball on the Iowa 25. Then confusion resulted. A Cougar player came in to attempt a field goal but

Iowa lined up on offense, with the referee apparently indicating that the Hawkeyes should run a play. They did, and clicked on a Gary Snook to Paul Krause pass for 49 yards which carried to the Washington State 25. Time ran out as the ball was in the air. There was general agreement after the game that Washington State rather than Iowa should have been permitted the last offensive attempt but that play on which the Cougars might have won was not forthcoming. Officially, they had been given only three downs instead of four in their final series of plays.

Iowa took its 14 — 14 tie as a starter and visited Seattle to meet the University of Washington. Playing in rain and lightning the Hawks drew a dividend on their conditioning program with a 10 point fourth quarter that provided the winning 17 — 7 margin. Paul Krause and Fred Riddle teamed up on a 44-yard scoring pass, Riddle slammed over for another and Jay Roberts kicked a 39-yard field goal for the Iowa points.

From Seattle the Hawkeyes came home to meet Indiana — and help their quarterback, Fred Riddle, smash a Big Ten record by passing for five touchdowns in the 37 — 26 Iowa victory. In achieving his unprecedented performance, Riddle aimed scoring tosses of three and five yards to Tony Giacobazzi, passed for 76 and four yards to Paul Krause for scores and notched another touchdown on a five yard pass to Cloyd Webb. Iowa's Riddle threw 16 times, completing 10 for 155 yards on the finest day of his career. The sensational aerial performance of the two teams saw a combined total of 57 passes attempted, with 34 completed for 519 yards. The Iowa point total included a 25 yard field goal by Jay Roberts in the first quarter. Indiana, handicapped by the injury of its dynamic halfback, Marv Woodson, countered with the brilliant passing of Richie Badar (20 completions in 28 tries for 256 yards) and maintained its challenge until the finish.

Although unnoticed at the time, but of more than supplementary significance, was the fact that the Hawkeyes reached a scoring milestone as the final touchdown was notched against the

Hoosiers. At that moment, in the third game of its seventy-fifth season of intercollegiate competition, the ten-thousandth point was recorded in the Old Gold record book of football.

A tremendous Hawkeye effort failed against Wisconsin with the Badger edge of 10 — 7 in jeopardy until the gun. Iowa's last thrust, with 99 seconds remaining, saw Krause forced out of bounds on the Wisconsin 17, just a foot shy of first down. Linebacking guard Mike Reilly put on a show of defensive might that, for its unyielding fury, has rarely if ever been matched by a Hawkeye. The Iowa touchdown came on a 21-yard run by Lonnie Rodgers, playing left halfback for the first time although he had been a standout elsewhere in the backfield. Among the frustrations was a 44 yard first quarter pass, Riddle to Webb, with the spectacular end making a leaping, one-hand catch on the Wisconsin two-yard line. The gain was lost when Iowa was charged with holding on the play.

The following week the Hawks travelled to Lafayette for a battle with Purdue. An Indiana newspaper headlined the impending battle: "Bowl-Talking Iowa to Warm Frisky Purdue's Homecoming."

The disappointing 14 — 0 loss sealed any such false hopes. Quarterback Ron DiGravio sparked the Boilermakers, running 11 yards for one Purdue touchdown and passing 18 yards for another. A powerful Boilermaker line minimized the efforts of the Iowa backs. Sophomore Gary Snook shared the quarterbacking and the passing responsibilities for Iowa and completed four of his nine pass attempts for 107 yards. Fred Riddle threw seven, completing three for 33 yards. It was the beginning of the advance of Snook, an Iowa City native, to a starting position.

Another defeat was forthcoming at Columbus the following week, with the 7 — 3 victory of the Buckeyes marking the third straight Iowa loss. This time the Hawks took a third quarter lead, 3 — 0, on a 34-yard place kick by Jay Roberts. Ohio State, blanked up to that point, and held to only a single first down in the

first half, made an unusual backfield switch by moving its Tom Barrington from quarterback to left halfback. Barrington responded by carrying the ball four times for 44 yards as the Buckeyes moved through a 74 yard march. Matt Snell went the last three yards for the only touchdown and Iowa had lost a heartbreaker.

The Hawkeyes had struggled through ten consecutive quarters without a touchdown when Minnesota came to Iowa City for its annual meeting with the Hawks. Gary Snook took command, and definitely assumed the quarterbacking role for the Old Gold. The Gophers had scored a first quarter touchdown on a pass, Bob Sedek to Kraig Lofquist, before Snook began drawing beads on his receivers. Twice in the second quarter he fired for points, first on a 21-yard toss to Cloyd Webb and again on a 26-yard throw to Paul Krause. He brought a third touchdown early in the second half on a 46-yard pass to Webb. Snook threw 21 times against the Gophers, completing nine for 164 yards. Bob Sherman gave Iowa its fourth touchdown on a 30-yard run with an intercepted pass. Mike Reilly's great defensive play and his 41.5 yard punting average were big factors. End Cloyd Webb gave his finest performance in two years as the Hawkeyes won, 27 — 13.

Two more games remained on the 1963 schedule, but only one was played. The Wolverines were met at Ann Arbor, as scheduled, and the 21 — 21 tie was a thriller. Trailing 7 — 0 at the quarter, Snook ran 13 yards for an Iowa touchdown, then passed 12 yards to Webb for another, both in the second period. Michigan struck back with two third quarter touchdowns by Mel Anthony and the Hawks were a touchdown behind going into the fourth quarter. Again Snook arose to the challenge, speeding a 25-yard touchdown pass to Paul Krause. Jay Roberts' third successful extra point tied it and although each team threatened there was no further scoring.

Only the Notre Dame game remained. The Fighting Irish squad arrived in Iowa City on Friday, as planned, but earlier on that day John F. Kennedy, President of the United

States, was assassinated in Dallas, Texas. Immediate indications were that the game would be played, but discussions staged in the early morning hours resulted in a cancellation agreement. A postponement was impossible, since Notre Dame had a scheduled meeting with Syracuse on Thanksgiving Day. Iowa authorities felt that an attempt to play the game on the Saturday immediately after Thanksgiving would be unfair to Notre Dame, while the postponing of the game until December 7 would have extended the football season two weeks, creating a possible classroom hazard on players from both schools.

The resulting cancellation came with both teams at the site, Iowa Field lined and ready for the game, more than 50,000 tickets distributed and thousands of printed programs on hand. In a decision made after midnight Iowa authorities agreed that persons who had purchased tickets were entitled to a return of their money. Thus, new expense was added to the unplayed game by the refunding program, which extended until December 20. Before its early departure for home, the Notre Dame squad proceeded to St. Thomas More Chapel, the Catholic student worship center on the Iowa campus. There the Rev. Edmund P. Joyce, C.S.C., Notre Dame vice-president who had accompanied the squad to Iowa City, said a memorial Mass for the martyred president.

Even the shortened eight game season had failed to keep Iowa pass catchers Paul Krause and Cloyd Webb from entering the Hawkeye Football Record Book. Krause, with six touchdown passes caught tied an existing single season school mark held jointly by Jack Dittmer (1949) and George (Dusty) Rice (1951). The controversial but many talented Webb became only the second Iowan to exceed 1,000 yards pass receiving. His career total of 61 passes caught and ten touchdowns scored ranks him among the top three in both areas.

Mike Reilly and Wally Hilgenberg, perhaps the finest guards to pair together at Iowa, were given deserved post-season honors. Both were selected on the all-Big Ten first team of United Press-International. Hilgenberg was a third team all-American selection of the American Football Coaches Association, while Reilly was a second team pick of the Associated Press and a member of the Football Writers Association first team.

The seventy-fifth consecutive year of Iowa football was written into the record books showing 3 wins, 3 losses and 2 ties. Jerry Burns' first three years as head coach showed the identical pattern: 12 victories, 12 defeats and 2 ties.

Before another season two veteran members of the coaching staff would resign their positions for other duties at the University. Bob Flora, after a dozen years as Iowa line coach, became an administrative assistant to athletic

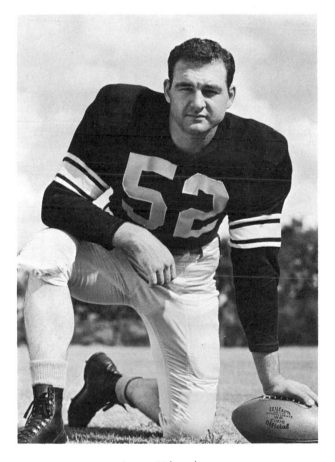

Jerry Hilgenberg
All-American 1953
Assistant Coach 1956-1963

director Evashevski. Jerry Hilgenberg, a Hawk-eye all-American in 1953 and a member of the coaching staff for eight seasons, resigned to accept a position with the University Development Fund. Hilgenberg's tenure as a football coach at Iowa was the longest ever by an alumnus of the school.

Iowa, after 75 seasons, had won 312 games, lost 255 and tied 30. Hawkeye teams had scored 10,059 points, the opposition 8,005. On October 10, 1964, Iowa marks another milestone — the six-hundredth game of intercollegiate football, with traditional Big Ten rival Indiana the opponent.

BEST OF THE DECADE — 1950 — 1956

Ends	Bill Fenton	1951-1952-1953
	Jim Gibbons	1955-1956-1957
	Frank Gilliam	1953-1954-1956
Tackles	Dick Klein	1956-1957
	Frank Rigney	1955-1956-1957
Guards	Gary Grouwinkel	1956-1957-1958
	Calvin Jones	1953-1954-1955
Centers	Jerry Hilgenberg	1951-1952-1953
	Don Suchy	1954-1955-1956
Quarterback	Ken Ploen	1954-1955-1956
Halfbacks	George (Dusty) Rice	1951-1952-1953
	Edward Vincent	1953-1954-1955
Fullback	Bill Reichardt	1949-1950-1951

BEST OF THE DECADE — 1957 — 1963

Ends	Curt Merz	1957-1958-1959
	Don Norton	1957-1958-1959
Tackles	Al Hinton	1959-1960-1961
	Alex Karras	1956-1957
Guards	Wally Hilgenberg	1961-1962-1963
	Mike Reilly	1961-1962-1963
	Sherwyn Thorson	1959-1960-1961
Centers	Bill Lapham	1957-1958-1959
	Bill Van Buren	1955-1960-1961
Quarterback	Randy Duncan	1956-1957-1958
Halfbacks	Larry Ferguson	1959-1960-1962
	Bob Jeter	1957-1958-1959
Fullback	John Nocera	1956-1957-1958

Appendix

UNIVERSITY OF IOWA FOOTBALL HONOR WINNERS FROM 1900

1900

Clyde Williams — Quarterback — All-America 3rd Team of Walter Camp; All-Western 1st Team of Chicago Post.

Joe Warner — Tackle — All-Western 1st Team of Chicago Post. ....

Ray Morton — Halfback — All-Western 1st Team of Chicago Post.

Willis Edson — Halfback — All-Western 1st Team of Chicago Post.

1907

Carrol Kirk—Halfback—All-America Honorable Mention by Caspar Whitney in Outing Magazine; All-Western 1st Team by Chicago Record Herald — Chicago Examiner — Chicago American; All-Western 2nd Team picked by E. C. Patterson for Collier's Weekly.

Aaron E. Seidel—Guard—All-Western 2nd Team picked by E. C. Patterson for Collier's Weekly.

1908

Carrol Kirk—Halfback—All-Western 1st Team by E. C. Patterson in Collier's Weekly; F. H. Yost Team; Big Ten Conference 1st Team by W. Eckersall for Chicago Tribune.

Aaron E. Seidel—Guard—All-Western 2nd Team picked by E. C. Patterson for Collier's Weekly.

Henry R. Gross—Tackle—All-Western 1st Team by Urbana (Illinois) Herald.

1911

Willis O'Brien—Center—All-Western 1st Team by Chicago Evening Post — San Francisco Examiner — Chicago Daily News — Chicago Record Herald; All-Western 2nd Team of Walter Eckersall; All Big Ten Conference 1st Team by Chicago Evening Post — San Francisco Examiner — Chicago Daily News — Chicago Record Herald.

1912

Jim Trickey—Tackle—All-America 2nd Team of Walter Camp; All-Western 1st Team picked by E. C. Patterson in Collier's Weekly; All-Western 2nd Team of Walter Eckersall.

Henry Hanson—Guard—All-Western 1st Team by Chicago Evening Post — Chicago Daily News; All-Western 2nd Team of Walter Eckersall; Big Ten Conference 1st Team in Chicago Evening Post — Chicago Daily News —Chicago Record Herald.

1913

Archie R. Kirk—Tackle—All Big Ten 1st Team of Walter Eckersall; All-Western 1st Team by Frank Menke for I.N.S., and Chicago Record Herald (at guard); All-Western 2nd Team by E. C. Patterson in Collier's Weekly.

Arthur Gunderson—End—All-Western 1st Team of Chicago Record Herald.

Leo Dick—Halfback—All-Western 2nd Team of Chicago Record Herald.

1914

Irving J. (Stub) Barron—Tackle—Big Ten Conference 1st Team by Minneapolis Daily News — Daily Illini, Chicago Herald.

Archie R. Kirk—Tackle—All-Western 2nd Team by E. C. Patterson in Collier's Weekly; Big Ten Conference 1st Team of Chicago American.

Arthur Gunderson—End — Big Ten Conference 1st Team of Chicago Examiner and Chicago American.

1915

Irving J. (Stub) Barron—Guard—All-Western 2nd Team of Walter Eckersall.

1916

Fred Becker—Tackle—All-America 1st Team of Walter Eckersall; All-Western 1st Team in Collier's Weekly — Columbus Dispatch — Chicago Herald — Ohio State Journal — Chicago Daily News (center) — Walter Eckersall (center); Big Ten Conference — 1st Team in Chicago Herald — Ohio State Journal; and Big Ten Conference 1st Team at Center by W. Eckersall in Chicago Tribune — The Daily Illini — Chicago Daily News — Daily Cardinal (U. of Wisconsin) — Daily Maroon (U. of Chicago).

J. (Waddy) Davis—Halfback—All-Western 2d Team of Walter Eckersall.

1917

Chuck Laun—End—All-Western 1st Team in Chicago Herald; Big Ten Conference 1st Team in Chicago Herald.

1918

Ronald Reed—End—All Big Ten 1st Team by W. Eckersall in Chicago Tribune— and Detroit Journal.

Harry Hunzelman—Guard All Big Ten 1st Team by W. Eckersall in Chicago Tribune.

1919

Lester Belding—End—All-America 1st Team by Frank Menke for Newspaper Features Syndicate; All-America 3rd Team of W. Eckersall for Chicago Tribune; All-Western 1st Team by Frank Menke for Newspaper Features Syndicate — Walter Eckersall in Chicago Tribune; Big Ten Conference — 1st Team by E. C. Patterson for Collier's Weekly; Chicago Evening Post — St. Paul Press — Chicago American — International News Service — W. Eckersall in Chicago Tribune — Purdue Exponent — Chicago Evening Post.

Fred (Duke) Slater—Tackle—All-America 1st Team by Ohio State Journal; All-America 2nd Team of W. Eckersall (Chicago Tribune);

All-American 3rd Team of Walter Camp; All-Western 1st Team by Frank Menke for Newspaper Feature Service — Minneapolis Daily News — Detroit Times — W. Eckersall for Chicago Tribune — Chicago Evening Journal; Big Ten Conference 1st Team by E. C. Patterson in Collier's Weekly — Chicago Evening Post — St. Paul Press — International News Service — Ohio State Journal — Chicago American — Chicago Daily News — W. Eckersall for Chicago Tribune — Ohio State Lantern of O.S.U.; Chicago Journal; Chicago Sunday Herald.

Aubrey Devine—Quarterback—All-Western 1st Team — by Minneapolis Daily News; Big Ten Conference 1st Team in St. Paul Press — International News Service — Chicago American — Chicago Daily News — Chicago Sunday Herald.

Fred Lohman—Fullback—All-Western 1st Team by W. Eckersall in Chicago Tribune; Big Ten Conference — 1st Team by W. Eckersall for Chicago Tribune.

Harry Hunzelman—Guard—All Big Ten 1st Team of Ohio State Lantern of O.S.U.

1920

Aubrey Devine—Quarterback—All-Western 1st Team by Knute Rockne — Indiana Daily — W. Eckersall for Chicago Tribune — Chicago Herald Examiner — Chicago Evening Post — Detroit Free Press — E. C. Patterson in Collier's Weekly; Big Ten — 1st Team by Chicago Daily News — Chicago Evening Post — Detroit Free Press — Minneapolis Daily News — University of Michigan Daily — Minneapolis Tribune — W. Eckersall for Chicago Tribune — Christian Science Monitor (halfback) — The Daily Illini (halfback).

Lester Belding—End—All-America 2nd Team of Walter Eckersall; All-Western 1st Team by Frank Menke for King Features & Newspaper Alliance — Chicago Evening Post; All-Western 2nd Team by W. Eckersall for Chicago Tribune— E. C. Patterson for Collier's Weekly; Big Ten Conference 1st Team by Christian Science Monitor — Chicago Evening Post.

Fred (Duke) Slater—Tackle—All-Western 1st Team by Detroit Free Press; All-Western 2nd Team by W. Eckersall for Chicago Tribune — E. C. Patterson for Collier's Weekly; Big Ten Conference 1st Team — Daily Illini — Detroit Free Press — Minneapolis Daily News — W. Eckersall for Chicago Tribune — Minneapolis Tribune.

Glenn Devine—Halfback—All-Western 2nd Team — E. C. Patterson for Collier's Weekly.

1921

Lester Belding—End—All-America 2nd Team of H. L. Farrell (United Press) and Jack Veiock of I.N.S.; All-America 3rd Team of Football World (267 Coaches); All-Western 1st Team of Billy Evans (umpire-critic); All Big Ten 1st Team of W. Trumbull (Eastern critic of New York Herald) — Lafayette Courier Journal — United Press.

Aubrey Devine—Quarterback—All-America 1st Team of Walter Camp — Walter Eckersall — Chas. Brickley — Football World (Coaches) (at Halfback) — Billy Evans (umpire-critic) — H. L. Farrell of United Press — W. Trumbell (New York Herald) — Jack Veiock of I.N.S.—N.E.A.—Lawrence Perry; All-America 2nd Team of N. E. Brown (Top Eastern Critic); All-Western 1st Team of Chicago Herald & Examiner — Walter Eckersall (Chicago Tribune) — Billy Evans; All Big Ten 1st Team of W. Trumbull (Eastern Critic of New York Herald) — W. Eckersall — Los Angeles Examiner (M. McLean) — Chicago American — Lafayette Courier Journal — United Press — Chicago Herald-Examiner.

Gordon Locke—Fullback—All-America 1st Team of N. E. Brown (Top Eastern Critic); All-America 2nd Team of Walter Eckersall (Chicago Tribune); All-America 3rd Team of W. Trumbull of New York Herald (halfback); All-Western 1st Team of Chicago Herald & Examiner — W. Eckersall — Billy Evans (umpire-critic); All Big Ten 1st Team of W. Eckersall — Los Angeles Examiner (M. McLean) — Chicago American — Lafayette Courier Journal — United Press — Chicago Herald-Examiner.

Fred (Duke) Slater—Tackle—All-America 1st Team of Walter Eckersall — Billy Evans — W. Trumbell (N. Y. Herald) (umpire critic) — Jack Veiock of I.N.S. — and N.E.A.; All-America 2nd Team of Walter Camp —H. L. Farrell of United Press — Football World (Coaches); All-Western 1st Team of Chicago Herald Examiner — Walter Eckersall —Billy Evans; All Big Ten 1st Team of W. Trumbull (Eastern critic of New York Herald) — W. Eckersall — Billy Evans — Los Angeles Examiner (M. McLean) — Chicago American — Lafayette Courier Journal — United Press — Chicago Herald-Examiner.

1922

Gordon Locke—Halfback—All-America 1st Team of Norman E. Brown (Top Eastern Critic) — Chicago Daily News (F. Hayner) — W. Eckersall (Locke Capt.) — Frank Menke—

Walter Camp — Athletic World; All-Western 1st team of Walter Eckersall — Frank Menke (fullback); All Big Ten 1st Team of Walter Eckersall (Chicago Tribune) — Chicago Journal — Chicago Post — Chicago Evening American — (Quarterback of Evening American and Fullback of the Post) Daily Illini of University of Illinois.

John Heldt—Center—All-America 1st Team of Chicago Daily News — (by F. Hayner) — also of Charlie Brickley (eastern critic) — All-America 3rd Team of Walter Eckersall — Frank Menke — All-Western 2nd. Team of Walter Eckersall; All Big Ten 1st Team of Chicago Journal.

Paul Minick—Guard—All-America 1st Team of Norman E. Brown (Eastern Critic); All-America 2nd Team of F. Hayner (Chicago Daily News) — C. Brickley; All Big Ten 1st Team of Chicago Post, Journal and Evening American; also All-Western 2nd Team of W. Eckersall in Chicago Tribune.

Max Kadesky—End—All-America 2nd Team of Chicago Daily News (F. Hayner) — Norman E. Brown (top eastern critic) — All-America 1st Team of Heywood Broun (eastern critic); All-America 3rd Team of Daily Maroon (University of Chicago) and of Walter Camp; All-Western 2nd Team of Walter Eckersall; All Big Ten 1st Team of Walter Eckersall — Chicago Evening American.

George Thompson—Tackle—All-Western 2nd Team of W. Eckersall for Chicago Tribune; All Big Ten 1st Team of Chicago Post — W. Eckersall in Chicago Tribune.

1923

William Fleckenstein—Guard—Big Ten Conference 1st Team of Daily Maroon (University of Chicago); and Warren Brown of Chicago Herald Examiner.

Lowell Otte—End—All Big Ten 1st Team of Walter Eckersall; All-Western 2d Team of W. Eckersall for Chicago Tribune.

Leo Kriz—Tackle—All Western 2nd Team of W. Eckersall for Chicago Tribune; Norman E. Brown (top eastern critic); All Big Ten 1st Team of W. Brown of Chicago Herald-Examiner.

1924

Lowell Otte—End—All-America 3rd Team of Walter Eckersall; All-Midwest 1st Team of Knute Rockne — also Walter Eckersall; All-Midwest 2nd Team of N. E. Brown; Big Ten Conference 1st Team of W. Eckersall for Chicago Tribune, also of Billy Evans (umpire-critic).

Richard Romey—End—All-Western 2nd Team of N. Brown (top eastern critic).

John Hancock—Tackle—All-America 2nd Team of N. E. Brown; All-America 3rd Team of All-

Sports Magazine; All-Western 1st Team of N. Brown; All Big Ten 1st Team of Billy Evans.

Leland Parkin—Quarterback—All-America 3rd Team of N. E. Brown; also A. A. Beard (C. Walsh) & W. Eckersall; All-Midwest 1st Team of Knute Rockne; All-Midwest 2nd Team of N. E. Brown; also of Walter Eckersall; Big Ten Conference 1st Team of W. Eckersall for Chicago Tribune; also of Billy Evans.

1925

Wes Frey—Fullback—All-Western 1st Team by F. Turbeyville of Chicago; All-Western 3rd Team by Knute Rockne.

Richard Romey—End—All-America 2nd Team of Collier's (Grantland Rice); All Big Ten 1st Team by Norman E. Brown (top eastern critic).

Nick Kutsch—Halfback—All-America 3rd Team — Herbert Reed of Universal Service; All-Western 2nd Team — Knute Rockne; All Big Ten 1st Team — Norman E. Brown; also the Minnesota Daily.

1926

Emerson "Spike" Nelson—Tackle — All-America 1st Team of The New York Sun; All-America 2nd Team of Central Press Assn. by Norman E. Brown — Billy Evans (umpire & critic); and U. S. Coaches (for the A.P.); All Big Ten 1st Team of Cleveland Press — Chicago Examiner — & Big Ten Coaches (for A.P.) — Billy Evans.

Nick Kutsch—Halfback—All-Western 2nd Team of W. Eckersall (Chicago Tribune); All Big Ten 1st Team of Big Ten Coaches (for A.P.).

1928

Willis Glassgow—Halfback—All-America 2nd Team of Central Press Assn.; All-Western 2nd Team of Walter Eckersall; All-America 3rd Team of Associated Press — and of W. Trumbull (NANA & New York Herald) — New York Post; All-Western 1st Team of Central Press — Knute Rockne, 1st Team all Big Ten Associated Press.

Mayes McLain—Halfback—2nd Team All-Western of Knute Rockne — W. Eckersall (fullback).

Pete Westra—Guard—All-America 1st Team of N.E.A.; All-America 2nd Team of New York Sun (George Trevor); All-Midwest 1st Team of Knute Rockne.

V. L. Schleusner—Tackle—All-America 1st Team of W. Trumbull (NANA & N.Y. Herald).

Richard Brown—Center—All-Western 2nd Team of Walter Eckersall; All Big Ten 1st Team of Walter Eckersall.

1929

Pete Westra—Tackle—All-Western 2nd Team of Walter Eckersall; All Big Ten 1st Team of N.E.A.

Fred Roberts—Guard—All-America 2nd Team of John Heisman (Universal Service) — All-America 3rd Team of United Press — All-Western 2nd Team of Walter Eckersall; All Big Ten — 1st Team of Associated Press, United Press.

Willis Glassgow—Halfback — All-America 1st Team of New York Sun ("Finest back in the country") — Collier's Magazine (G. Rice) — John Heisman (Universal Service) — Lawrence Perry — and N.E.A.; All-America 2nd Team of United Press; All-America 3rd Team of Walter Eckersall — Davis Walsh (Sp. Ed. of I.N.S.); All-Midwest 1st Team of Knute Rockne — W. Eckersall; All Big Ten 1st Team of Associated Press — N.E.A. — United Press.

Fred Roberts—Guard—All-America 2nd Team of John Heisman (Universal Service); All-America 3rd Team of United Press; All Big Ten 1st Team of Associated Press — United Press.

1930

Harold Ely—Tackle—All-Western 2nd Team of United Press.

1933

Joe Laws—Quarterback—All-America 2nd Team of Collier's Mag. (G. Rice) — also N.A.N.A.; All Big Ten 1st Team of Associated Press — United Press.

Francis Schammel—Guard—All-America 1st Team of Assoc. Press — United Press — Liberty Magazine — and N.A.N.A.; All-America 2nd Team of Collier's Magazine (G. Rice); All Big Ten 1st Team of Associated Press — and Coaches Team for U.P. (tackle)

1934

Dick Crayne—Fullback—All-Western 1st Team of Illustrated Football Annual; All Big Ten 1st Team of I.N.S.

1935

Oze Simmons—Halfback—All-America 1st Team of The Sporting News (fullback) — Ted Husing Eleven; All-America 2nd Team of Associated Press — Central Press — N.E.A. — N.A.N.A.; All-America 3rd Team of Hearst Newspapers; All-Midwest 1st Team of N.E.A. (Harry Grayson); All-Midwest 2nd Team of I.N.S.; All Big Ten 1st Team of Associated Press — United Press — Big Ten Coaches.

Floyd DeHeer—Tackle—All-America 2nd Team of Ted Husing.

Dick Crayne—Fullback—All-America 3rd Team of United Press — and Associated Press; All-Mid-Western 1st Team of Illustrated Football Annual; All-Midwest 2nd Team of N.E.A. (Harry Grayson) (halfback).

Ted Osmaloski—Center—All-Midwest 1st Team of N.E.A. (Harry Grayson).

Bob Lannon—End—All-Midwest 2nd Team of N.E.A. (Harry Grayson).

1936

Don Nelson—Center—All-Midwest 2nd Team of N.E.A. (Harry Grayson).

1937

Nick Kinnick—Quarterback—All-America 3rd Team of N.E.A. (Harry Grayson); All-Midwest 1st Team of N.E.A. (Harry Grayson); 1st Team All-Big Ten of International News Service — United Press (halfback).

Bob Lannon—End—All-Big Ten 1st Team of Associated Press.

1938

Erwin Prasse—End—All-Midwest 1st Team of Liberty (Norman Sper); All-Big Ten 1st Team of Associated Press, and I.N.S.

Nile Kinnick—Back—All-Midwest 2nd Team of N.E.A.

1939

Nile Kinnick—Halfback—All-America 1st Team of Associated Press — United Press — Intl. News Service — Central Press — Newsweek — Hearst — N. Y. Sun — All-Amer. Board — Paramount News — N. Y. News — Fox Movietone News — Collier's (Rice); All-America 2nd Team of Liberty Magazine — Life Magazine (Stern); All-Midwest 1st Team of Collier's (Rice), etc., etc.; All-Big Ten 1st Team of Associated Press — United Press — Central Press.

Erwin Prasse—End—All-America 2nd Team of United Press; All-America 3rd Team of Central Press; All Big Ten 1st Team of Associated Press — United Press — Central Press.

Mike Enich—Tackle—All-America 3rd Team of N.E.A. — Liberty Magazine; All-Midwest 1st Team of Collier's (Rice); All-Big Ten 1st Team of United Press — Central Press.

1940

Mike Enich—Tackle—All-America 1st Team of New York News — The Sporting News; All-America 2nd Team of United Press — Life (Stern) — K. Smith (Crowley) — Paramount News; All-Midwest 1st Team of Collier's Magazine (Rice) — New York News; All-Midwest 2nd Team of Chicago Daily News; All-Big Ten 1st Team of United Press.

Bill Green—Fullback—All-Western 1st Team of Chicago Daily News.

1942

Tom Farmer—Halfback—All-Big Ten 1st Team of Central Press; All-America 3rd Team of Bill Stern.

1946

Earl Banks—Guard—All-Big Ten 1st Team of United Press.

Bill Kay—Tackle—All-America 3rd. Team of Central Press.

Dick Hoerner—Back—All-Midwest 1st Team of New York News; All Big Ten 1st Team of Associated Press (fullback).

1948

Bill Kay—Tackle—All-America 2nd Team of Associated Press; All-America 3rd Team of All Players (Sponsored by Chicago Tribune); All-Big Ten 1st Team of Associated Press.

1950

Bill Reichardt—Fullback—All-Midwest 2nd Team of United Press; All-Big Ten 1st Team of United Press.

1951

Bill Reichardt—Fullback—All-America 2nd Team of All-Players (Chicago Tribune); All-Midwest 1st Team of All-Players (Chicago Tribune) and United Press; All-Big Ten 1st Team of United Press & Associated Press.

1952

Bill Fenton—End—All-Western 2nd Team (defensive) of Associated Press; All-Big Ten 1st Team (defensive) of Associated Press.

1953

Jerry Hilgenberg—Center—All-America 1st Team of Look Magazine (G. Rice & FWA); All-America 2nd Team of Associated Press; All-America 3rd Team of Sporting News & N.E.A.; All-Midwest 1st Team of Associated Press & Chicago Daily News; All-Big Ten 1st Team of Associated Press & United Press.

Bill Fenton—End—All-America 3rd Team of Sporting News.

Frank Gilliam—End—All-America 3rd Team of Central Press; All-Midwest 2nd Team of Intl. News Service.

Don Chelf—Guard—All-Midwest 1st Team of Collier's Magazine, & All-Players of Chicago Tribune; All-Midwest 2nd Team of Intl. News Service; All-Big Ten 1st Team (defensive) of Chicago Daily News.

Calvin Jones—Guard—All-America 1st Team of N.B.C.; All-America 3rd Team of All-Players All-Amer. (Chicago Tribune); All-Midwest 1st Team of All-Players (Chicago Tribune) — Chicago Daily News and Associated Press; All-Big Ten 1st Team of Associated Press.

1954

Calvin Jones—Guard—All-America 1st Team of Look Magazine (FWA) — Sporting News — All-America Board — United Press — ABC-TV — Central Press — N.E.A. — All-Players (Chicago Tribune) — New York Daily News — CBS — Gridiron Record; All-America 2nd Team of Associated Press — Intl. News Service; All-Midwest 1st Team of Associated Press — All-Players — Collier's — Intl. News Service; All-Big Ten 1st Team of Associated Press — United Press — Intl. News Service.

Eddie Vincent—Halfback—All-Midwest 1st Team of New York Daily News; All-Midwest 2nd Team of Associated Press.

John Hall—Tackle—All-Midwest 1st Team of New York Daily News.

1955

Calvin Jones—Guard—All-America 1st Team of Sporting News — United Press — Look Mag. (FWA) — New York News — All-America Board; All-America 2nd Team of Associated Press — N.E.A.; All-Big Ten 1st Team of Associated Press — I.N.S. — United Press.

Eddie Vincent—Halfback—All-Midwest 1st Team of New York Daily News; All-Big Ten 1st Team of I.N.S.

1956

Alex Karras—Tackle—All-America 1st Team of Associated Press — Look (FWA) — NBC — Central Press — Hearst; All-America 2nd Team of United Press — N.E.A.; All-Big Ten 1st Team of Associated Press — United Press — I.N.S.

Ken Ploen—Quarterback—All-America 1st Team of N.B.C. — A.B.C. (Frank Leahy); All-America 2nd Team of Associated Press; All-Big Ten 1st Team of Associated Press — United Press — I.N.S.

Don Suchy—Center—All-America 2nd Team of Central Press; All-Big Ten 1st Team of United Press — I.N.S.

Frank Gilliam—End—All-America 2nd Team of N.E.A.; All-America 3rd Team of United Press; All-Big Ten 1st Team of Associated Press — United Press.

1957

Alex Karras—Tackle—All-America 1st Team of Associated Press — United Press Look (F.W.A.) — Central Press — N.B.C. — Football Digest — Intl. News Service — N.E.A. — Sporting News — Hearst; All-Big Ten 1st Team of Associated Press — United Press — I.N.S.

Jim Gibbons—End—All-America 1st Team of Look (FWA) — United Press — Sporting News — Hearst, New York Daily News; All-America 2nd Team of Central Press — Football Digest; All-America 3rd Team of Associated Press; All-Big Ten 1st Team of Associated Press — United Press.

Dick Klein—Tackle—All-America 3rd Team of United Press.

Frank Bloomquist—Guard — All Big Ten 1st Team of Associated Press.

1958

Randy Duncan—Quarterback—All-America 1st Team of Associated Press — United Press-Intl. — America F.B. Coaches — Look (FWA) — Football Digest — Sporting News — Central Press — New York News — N.E.A.; All-Big Ten 1st Team Associated Press — United Press-Intl.

Curt Merz—End—All-America 1st Team of Look (FWA) — N.B.C.; All-America 2nd Team of N.E.A. — (Grayson).

Ray Jauch—Halfback—All-Western 1st Team of New York Daily News.

Willie Fleming—Halfback—All-Big Ten 1st Team of Associated Press.

1959

Don Norton—End—All-America 1st Team of Look (FWA) — N.B.C.; All-America 2nd Team of N.E.A., Sporting News; All-America 3rd Team of United Press-Intl. and Central Press; All-Big Ten 1st Team of Associated Press and United Press-Intl.

Bob Jeter—Back All-America 3rd Team of Central Press, Sporting News; All-Midwest 1st Team of New York News; All-Big Ten 1st Team of United Press-Intl. and Associated Press.

1960

Mark Manders—Guard—All-America 1st Team of Sporting News — Look (FWA) — Football Digest; All-America 2nd Team of Associated Press — Central Press — American Football Coaches Assn.; All-America 3rd Team of United Press-Intl.; All-Big Ten 1st Team of Associated Press & United Press-Intl.

Wilburn Hollis—Back—All-America 3rd Team of United Press-Intl. — Central Press; All-Big Ten 1st Team of Associated Press.

Larry Ferguson—Halfback—All-America 1st Team of Look (FWA); All-America 3rd Team of Central Press; All-Big Ten 1st Team of Associated Press & United Press-Intl.

1961

Bill Van Buren—Center—1st Team All-America of The Sporting News.

Al Hinton—Tackle—All-America 3rd Team of Amer. Football Coaches Assn.

1962

Larry Ferguson—Halfback—1st Team All-Big Ten of United Press-Intl.

1963

Wally Hilgenberg—Tackle—3rd Team All-America of American Football Coaches Association —

1st Team All-Big Ten of United Press-Intl.

Mike Reilly—Tackle—1st Team All-America of Football Writers Association (Look Magazine) — 2nd Team All-America of Associated Press — 1st Team All-Big Ten of United Press-Intl.

AWARDS

HEISMAN MEMORIAL TROPHY
(Player of the Year)

1939—Nile Kinnick, halfback

MAXWELL MEMORIAL AWARD
(Player of the Year)

1939—Nile Kinnick, halfback

WALTER CAMP TROPHY
(Player of the Year)

1939—Nile Kinnick, halfback
1958—Randy Duncan, quarterback

HELMS ATHLETIC FOUNDATION PLAYER OF THE YEAR AWARD

1958—Randy Duncan, quarterback

OUTLAND AWARD
(Interior lineman of the Year)

1955—Calvin Jones, guard
1957—Alex Karras, tackle

HELMS ATHLETIC FOUNDATION ROSE BOWL AWARD
(Player of the Game)

1957—Ken Ploen, quarterback
1959—Bob Jeter, halfback

NATIONAL FOOTBALL FOUNDATION AND HALL OF FAME

Howard H. Jones, coach
Nile Kinnick, player
Gordon Locke, player
Fred (Duke) Slater, player

FOREST EVASHEVSKI SCHOLASTIC ACHIEVEMENT AWARD
(Senior Player with Highest Grade Average)

1960—Lloyd Humphreys
1961—Jerry Williams
1962—Lynn Lyon
1963—Richard Dougherty

HELMS ATHLETIC FOUNDATION FOOTBALL HALL OF FAME

Edward N. Anderson, coach
Calvin Jones, player
Howard H. Jones, coach
Nile Kinnick, player
Gordon Locke, player
Edward (Slip) Madigan, coach
Fred (Duke) Slater, player
Ossie Solem, coach
Emlen Tunnell, pro player

COACH OF THE YEAR AWARD

1939—Edward N. Anderson (Coaches' poll)
1953—Forest Evashevski (Detroit Times)
1956—Forest Evashevski (Washington Touchdown Club; Los Angeles Times; Kansas City Rockne Club;
    Columbus Touchdown Club)
1958—Forest Evashevski (Columbus Touchdown Club; Los Angeles Times; Detroit News)
1960—Forest Evashevski (Pigskin Club of Washington, D.C.)

IOWA'S MOST VALUABLE PLAYERS (1924 — 1963)

From 1924 through 1929 a Chicago Tribune committee selected the "most valuable" player from each Big Ten team. Beginning in 1930, each school squad picked its own "most valuable" player, thus qualifying him to compete against choices of other member teams for the Silver Football Trophy given each year by The Tribune to the "most valuable" conference player. No school has had more winners than Iowa.

1924	Leland Parkin, qb	1938	Erwin Prasse, e	1952	William Fenton, e
1925	Donald Graham, fb	1939	°Nile Kinnick, hb	1953	William Fenton, e
1926	Nick Kutsch, hb	1940	Mike Enich, t	1954	Warren Lawson, c
1927	Emerson Nelson, t	1941	William Diehl, c	1955	Jerry Reichow, qb
1928	Willis Glassgow, hb	1942	Tom Farmer, qb	1956	°Kenneth Ploen, qb
1929	°Willis Glassgow, hb	1943	Bob Liddy, g	1957	Robert Commings, g
1930	Oliver Sansen, fb	1944	Bob Snyder, c	1958	°Randy Duncan, qb
1931	Oliver Sansen, fb	1945	Arthur Johnson, fb	1959	Don Norton, e
1932	Joe Laws, hb	1946	William Kay, t	1960	Bernie Wyatt, hb
1933	°Joe Laws, hb	1947	Harold Shoener, e	1961	Al Hinton, t
1934	Dick Crayne, fb	1948	Al DiMarco, qb	1962	Larry Ferguson, hb
1935	Dick Crayne, fb	1949	Jack Dittmer, e	1963	Michael Reilly, g
1936	Homer Harris, e	1950	Harold Bradley, t		
1937	Bob Lannon, e	1951	°William Reichardt, fb		

°Won Chicago Tribune trophy awarded annually to "most valuable" player in Big Ten.

ATHLETIC BOARD CUP

This annual award is presented by the Iowa Board in Control of Athletics to the graduating varsity letter winner who is outstanding in athletics and scholarship. Eighteen of the 43 recipients since 1920 have been major letter winners in football.

1920	Leon H. Brigham	1935	Ralph L. Houser	1951	Joseph Paulsen°
1921	Leland B. Irish	1936	Raymond W. Latham	1952	John W. Dinzole, Jr.
1922	Lester C. Belding°	1937	George P. Nissen	1953	Duane M. Brandt°
1923	Edmund G. Rich°	1938	Eliot Waples	1954	Jerry J. Hilgenberg°
	and Eric C. Wilson	1939	Albert G. Schenk°	1955	Warren G. Lawson°
1924	Elmer B. Goodrich	1940	Nile C. Kinnick°	1956	Milton C. Scheuerman
1925	James A. Laude	1941	Mike Enich°	1957	James A. McCullough
1926	James J. Lutz	1942	T. Cyril Noon	1958	Richard E. Deasy°
1927	Harry H. Rice°	1943	Kenneth L. Steinbeck	1959	Arthur W. Andrews
1928	Emerson W. Nelson°	1944	No Award	1960	Allan C. Bachman
1929	Clayton B. Thompson	1945	No Award	1961	John W. Nadig
1930	Francis Wilcox	1946	Harry Rinkema	1962	James B. Tucker
1931	No Award	1947	Walter R. Thorpe	1963	Steven L. Combs
1932	Francis A. Merten°	1948	Peter W. Everett	1964	Robert Sherman°
1933	Robert C. Loufek°	1949	Anthony J. Guzowski°		
1934	Christian G. Schmidt°	1950	John D. Dittmer°		° Major letter winner in football.

CONFERENCE MEDAL WINNERS

In 1914 the Conference endowed a Medal of Honor, to be awarded annually to the one senior student from each school who has "attained greatest proficiency in athletics and scholastic work." The medal, designed by R. Tait McKenzie in 1915, is the only Conference recognition of scholastic ability. Of the forty-seven Iowa winners, twenty-two have been major letter winners in football:

1915	Herman L. Von Lackum°	1932	Stuart W. Skowbo	1949	Evan L. Hultman
1916	Forrest W. Deardorff	1933	William A. McCloy	1950	Donald C. Hays
1917	Wayne J. Foster	1934	Tom W. Moore°	1951	Ralph W. Thomas
1918	John K. Von Lackum°	1935	James P. McClintock	1952	Charles F. Darling
1919	Homer W. Scott°	1936	Francis X. Cretzmeyer	1953	J. Burton Britzman°
1920	Charles Mockmore°	1937	Cornelius J. Walker°	1954	William Fenton°
1921	Robert J. Kaufman°	1938	Robert G. Lannon°	1955	LeRoy A. Ebert
1922	Aubrey Devine°	1939	Wilbur V. Nead°	1956	Andrew M. Houg°
1923	Gordon C. Locke°	1940	Andrew J. Kantor	1957	Frank O. Sebolt
1924	Wayland Hicks	1941	James R. Murphy, Jr.°	1958	Gary E. Meyer
1925	John Hancock°	1942	Richard E. Hein	1959	James Van Young
1926	Donald M. Graham°	1943	Thomas Farmer°	1960	William L. Voxman
1927	Carl D. Voltmer°	1944	No Award	1961	William D. Buck
1928	Lawrence Harrison	1945	No Award	1962	Joel D. Novak
1929	Forest Twogood	1946	Arthur H. Johnson°	1963	Ralph W. Trimble
1930	Willis A. Glassgow°	1947	John K. Hunter°	1964	Andrew Hankins
1931	No Award	1948	Herbert W. Wilkinson		°Major letter winner in football.

ALL-TIME PLAYER SQUAD

In the preparation of this book, which has taken nearly six years, we have earnestly endeavored to chronicle all of the achievements and highlights, as well as the failures and disappointments, which have been so prominent a part of the Iowa football story. Newspapers have been read in detail back more than ninety years. We have corresponded with the only four living players of the pre-1900 period. In addition, hundreds of subsequent players, coaches, athletic administrators, writers and fans have been consulted.

We have been importuned from many sources to pick an all-time Iowa team based upon this exhaustive research. Specific recognition has been given many players throughout these pages and others have been singled out as among the "best of the decade" in which they played.

Many times recent achievements have tended to cloud past accomplishments. So, too, the passage of time has often afforded opportunity to embellish upon those deeds of other years. Tradition, legend, public opinion and the press have created many images and destroyed others.

In addition time, vital changes in rules, as well as the multiplication of formations within these rules, have so fundamentally altered the tactics of football in these 75 years that it is neither fair nor reasonable to proclaim that a player of one period of the game would, or could, shine in another or in all. The only certain thing that can be said is that the following group of all-time players consists of those who, offensively and defensively, contributed a consistently prominent share towards the history of Hawkeye football.

ENDS

Charles Laun	1915-1916-1917
Lester Belding	1918-1919-1920-1921
Max Kadesky	1920-1921-1922
Lowell Otte	1922-1923-1924
Richard Romey	1923-1924-1925
Erwin Prasse	1937-1938-1939
Jack Dittmer	1946-1947-1948-1949
Jim Gibbons	1955-1956-1957
Don Norton	1957-1958-1959

TACKLES

Joe Warner	1897-1898-1899-1900
Archie Alexander	1909-1910-1911
Fred (Duke) Slater	1918-1919-1920-1921
George Thompson	1920-1921-1922
Emerson Nelson	1925-1926-1927
Mike Enich	1938-1939-1940
Jim Walker	1939-1940-1941
Bill Kay	1945-1946-1947-1948
Alex Karras	1956-1957

GUARDS

Jim Brockway	1898-1899-1900
Aaron Seidel	1907-1908
Jim Trickey	1910-1911-1912
Paul Minick	1920-1921-1922
Francis (Zud) Schammell	1932-1933-1934
Calvin Jones	1953-1954-1955

CENTERS

Iver Iverson	1894-1895-1896
Willis O'Brien	1909-1910-1911
John Heldt	1918-1919-1921-1922
Bill Diehl	1939-1940-1941

QUARTERBACKS

S. Clyde Williams	1898-1899-1900-1901
Aubrey Devine	1919-1920-1921
Leland Parkin	1922-1923-1924
Kenneth Ploen	1954-1955-1956
Randy Duncan	1956-1957-1958

HALFBACKS

Carrol (Chick) Kirk	1906-1907-1908
Nick Kutsch	1925-1926
Willis Glassgow	1927-1928-1929
Joe Laws	1931-1932-1933
Dick Crayne	1933-1934-1935
Ozzie Simmons	1934-1935-1936
Nile Kinnick	1937-1938-1939
Larry Ferguson	1959-1960-1962

FULLBACKS

J. Ray Murphy	1909-1910-1911
Gordon Locke	1920-1921-1922
Wes Fry	1923-1924-1925
Bill Reichardt	1949-1950-1951

THE THIRTEEN FINEST SINGLE SEASON PERFORMERS

Another group of players deserving special mention are those who participated only one year. These gridders, while not considered for all-time positions, nevertheless proved their outstanding value and undoubtedly would have earned recognition among Iowa's greatest had opportunity allowed them to play more than a single season.

Burt German	halfback	1891	Wallace Bergstrom	tackle	1939
Asher Ely	center	1900	Burdell Gilleard	halfback	1940
J. O. Perrine	end	1908	Charles Uknes	fullback	1942
Fred Becker	tackle	1916	John Estes	quarterback	1947
J. Ben Synhorst	tackle	1918	Willie Fleming	halfback	1958
LeDrue Galloway	tackle	1924	James Helgens	end	1961
Mayes McLain	fullback	1928			

HAWKEYE POST-SEASON AND ALL-STAR GAME PLAYERS

EAST — WEST SHRINE GAME at San Francisco

1926—Wesley L. Fry, fb
1930—Willis Glassgow, hb
1931—Harold Ely, t
1934—Joe Laws, hb; Francis (Zud) Schammel, g
1936—Dick Crayne, hb
1941—Mike Enich, t
1942—Al Couppee, qb
1943—Bill Burkett, e
1944—William Baughman, c
1948—Hal Schoener, e; Bob Smith, hb
1949—Dick Woodard, c
1953—Don Chelf, t; Jerry Hilgenberg, c
1954—George (Binkey) Broeder, fb; John Hall, t
1955—Jerry Reichow,* qb; Calvin Jones, g
1957—Jim Gibbons, e; Alex Karras, t
1959—Bob Jeter, hb; Ray Jauch, hb; Don Norton, e
1960—Mark Manders, g
1961—Bill Van Buren, c
1962—Larry Ferguson, hb; Earl McQuiston, g
1963—Mike Reilly, g; Paul Krause, hb
   * Voted "Most Valuable Player" in the game.

ALL-AMERICAN BOWL — MAJOR SCHOOLS VS. SMALL SCHOOLS at Tucson, Arizona

1959—Bill Lapham, c
1960—Charles Lee, t

CHICAGO TRIBUNE ALL-STAR GAME at Chicago

1934—Joe Laws, hb
1936—Dick Crayne, fb
1939—Frank Balazs, fb
1940—Nile Kinnick, hb; Floyd (Buzz) Dean, hb; Dick
    Evans, e; Dr. Edward N. Anderson, head coach
1941—Ken Pettit, e
1942—Bill Diehl, c; Jim Walker, t
1943—Tom Hand, c; Jim Youell, qb; Bob Penaluna, g
1945—Stanley Mohrbacher, t
1947—Bruno Niedziela, t
1949—Bill Kay, t; Al Di Marco, qb
1950—Don Winslow, g
1952—Bill Reichardt, fb
1954—Jerry Hilgenberg, c; Bill Fenton, e
    Forest Evashevski, assistant coach
1956—Jerry Reichow, qb; Edward Vincent, hb
1958—Jim Gibbons, e; Alex Karras, t
1959—Charles (Mac) Lewis, t
1960—Bill Lapham, c
1963—Larry Ferguson, hb
1964—Wally Hilgenberg, g; Mike Reilly, g;
    Paul Krause, hb

AMERICAN FOOTBALL COACHES ASSN. ALL-AMERICA GAME at Buffalo, New York

1961—Mark Manders, g
1962—Al Hinton, t; Sherwyn Thorson, g
1963—Larry Ferguson, hb
1964—Wally Hilgenberg, g; Gary Fletcher, c

BLUE — GRAY ALL-STAR GAME at Montgomery, Alabama

1947—Lou King, qb
1949—Bob McKenzie, e; Don Winslow, t
1951—Bill Reichardt, fb
1955—Rodger Swedberg, t; Roger Wiegmann, fb
1959—John Sawin, t
1960—Jerry Mauren, hb
1961—Sherwyn Thorson, g; Bernie Wyatt, hb
1963—Lonnie Rogers, hb; Gus Kasapis, t

OPTIMIST BOWL ALL-STAR GAME at Tucson

1957—Collins (Mike) Hagler, hb

CHALLENGE BOWL ALL-STAR GAME at Corpus Christie, Texas

1963—Gus Kasapis, t

SENIOR BOWL GAME at Mobile, Alabama (played in January)

1952—Bill Reichardt, fb
1954—Jerry Hilgenberg, c; Don Chelf, t
1956—Jerry Reichow, qb; Jim Freeman, e
1958—Jim Gibbons, e; Alex Karras, t; Frank Rigney, t
1960—Bill Lapham, c; Don Norton, e;
    Olen Treadway, qb; Curt Merz, e
1964—Paul Krause, e*
   * Voted "most valuable" North lineman.

NORTH — SOUTH ALL-STAR SHRINE GAME at Miami, Florida

1948—Bill Kay, t
1953—Bill Fenton, e; George (Dusty) Rice, hb
1954—Warren (Bud) Lawson, c; Lou Matykiewicz, e
1955—Jim Freeman, e
1957—Frank Bloomquist, g; Bob Commings, g
    Frank Rigney, t
1959—Don Horn, fb; Curt Merz, e; Bill Lapham, c
1960—Lloyd Humphreys, c
1961—Bill Whisler, e
1962—Bill Perkins, fb
1963—Cloyd Webb, e; Gary Fletcher, c;
    Wally Hilgenberg, g

HULA BOWL GAME at Honolulu, Hawaii (played in January) since 1954

1955—George (Binkey) Broeder, fb
1956—Calvin Jones, g
1957—Frank Gilliam, e
1958—Alex Karras, t; Jim Gibbons, e
1960—Ray Jauch, hb
1961—Mark Manders, g; Charles Lee, t
1962—Bill Van Buren, c
1963—Larry Ferguson, hb; Earl McQuiston, g
1964—Mike Reilly, g; Wally Hilgenberg, g

IOWA COACHING RECORDS 1889 — 1963

Year	Coach	Seasons	Won	Lost	Tied	Ave. Pts. Per Game Iowa	Opp.
1889-1891	None	3	4	4	0	26.1	13.3
1892	E. A. Dalton	1	3	2	1	20.7	11.3
1893	Benjamin Donnelly	1	3	4	0	25.4	23.0
1894	Roger Sherman	1	4	4	1	16,2	17.6
1895	None	1	2	5	0	6.0	19.7
1896	A. E. Bull	1	7	1	1	14.7	1.3
1897	Otto F. Wagonhurst	1	4	4	0	8.3	13.0
1898-1902	Alden A. Knipe	5	28	11	4	19.3	10.9
1903-1906	John G. Chalmers	4	26	11	0	21.1	10.0
1907-1908	Mark Catlin	2	5	7	0	18.5	9.4
1909	John G. Griffith	1	2	4	1	8.3	14.0
1910-1915	Jess Hawley	6	24	18	0	20.6	10.5
1916-1923	Howard H. Jones	8	42	17	1	18.1	9.3
1924-1931	Burton A. Ingwersen	8	33	27	4	12.8	9.4
1932-1936	Oscar M. Solem	5	15	21	4	12.5	13.0
1937-1938	Irl Tubbs	2	2	13	1	5.1	16.0
1939-1942 1946-1949	Edward N. Anderson	8	35	33	2	15.4	15.5
1943-1944	Edward P. Madigan	2	2	13	1	8.5	24.5
1945	Clem F. Crowe	1	2	7	0	8.2	34.4
1950-1951	Leonard Raffensperger	2	5	10	3	15.6	24.1
1952-1960	Forest Evashevski	9	52	27	4	22.7	14.2
1961-1963	Jerome Burns	3	12	12	2	18.0	17.0
		75	312	255	30	16.85	13.40

THIRTY HAWKEYES WERE AWARDED LETTERS IN FOUR DIFFERENT YEARS

The four letter winners:

Lloyd L. Elliott	1890-1891-1892-1893	Lester C. Belding	1918-1919-1920-1921
Samuel W. Hobbs	1895-1896-1897-1898	John C. Heldt	1918-1919 1921-1922
Moray L. Eby	1897-1898-1899-1900	Joseph Grothus	1943-1946-1947-1948
John G. Griffith	1897-1898-1899-1900	James Cozad	1943-1946-1947-1948
Joseph S. Warner	1897-1898-1899-1900	Richard Woodard	1944-1946-1947-1948
S. Clyde Williams	1898-1899-1900-1901	Ralph Woodard	1945-1947-1948-1949
Emmett F. Burrier	1898-1899-1900-1901	Donald Winslow	1944-1947-1948-1949
L. Bert Watters	1899-1900-1901-1903	William Kay	1945-1946-1947-1948
George H. Coulthard	1900-1901-1902-1903	Louis Ginsberg	1945-1948-1949-1950
Nyle W. Jones	1901-1902-1903-1904	Robert Geigel	1946-1947-1948-1949
Dwight M. Griffith	1901-1902-1903-1904	Earl Banks	1946-1947-1948-1949
George H. Allen	1903-1904-1905-1906	Jack Dittmer	1946-1947-1948-1949
Harry Hunzelman	1916-1917-1918-1919	Richard Laster	1946-1947-1948-1949
Lawrence A. Block	1917-1918-1919-1920	George (Binkey) Broeder	1951-1952-1953-1954
Fred (Duke) Slater	1918-1919-1920-1921	Robert Stearnes	1951-1952-1953-1954

1908

Coach — Mark Catlin (Chicago)
Captain C. N. Kirk, fb.

92	Coe	0
5	Missouri	10
16	Morningside	0
8	Nebraska	11
0	Illinois	22
6	Drake	12
5	Kansas	10
132		65

Won 2   Lost 5   Tied 0

1909

Coach — J. G. Griffith (Iowa)
Captain — H. R. Gross, t.

0	Minnesota	41
3	Cornell	0
6	Nebraska	6
12	Missouri	13
14	Drake	17
16	Iowa State	0
7	Kansas	20
58		97

Won 2   Lost 4   Tied 1

1910

Coach — Jess Hawley (Dartmouth)
Captain — M. W. Hyland, e.

12	Morningside	0
5	Northwestern	10
0	Missouri	5
16	Purdue	0
2	Iowa State	0
21	Drake	0
38	Washington (St. L.)	0
94		15

Won 5   Lost 2   Tied 0

1911

Coach — Jess Hawley (Dartmouth)
Captain — J. R. Murphy, hb.

11	Morningside	5
0	Cornell	3
6	Minnesota	24
0	Wisconsin	12
11	Purdue	9
0	Iowa State	9
6	Northwestern	0
34		53

Won 3   Lost 4   Tied 0

1912

Coach — Jess Hawley (Dartmouth)
Captain — H. D. Hanson, g.

35	Iowa Teachers	7
31	Cornell	0
14	Chicago	34
7	Minnesota	56
13	Indiana	6
20	Iowa State	7
10	Wisconsin	28
130		138

Won 4   Lost 3   Tied 0

1913

Coach — Jess Hawley (Dartmouth)
Captain — R. A. McGinnis, fb.

45	Iowa Teachers	3
76	Cornell	0
6	Chicago	23
78	Northwestern	6
60	Indiana	0
45	Iowa State	7
0	Nebraska	12
310		51

Won 5   Lost 2   Tied 0

1914

Coach — Jess Hawley (Dartmouth)
Captain — A. H. Gunderson, e.

95	Iowa Teachers	0
49	Cornell	0
0	Chicago	7
0	Minnesota	7
27	Northwestern	0
26	Iowa State	6
7	Nebraska	16
204		36

Won 4   Lost 3   Tied 0

1915

Coach — Jess Hawley (Dartmouth)
Captain — I. J. Barron, t.

33	Cornell	0
17	Morningside	6
9	Northwestern	6
13	Minnesota	51
13	Purdue	19
0	Iowa State	16
7	Nebraska	52
92		150

Won 3   Lost 4   Tied 0

1916

Coach — Howard H. Jones (Yale)
Captain — C. E. Laun, fb.

31	Cornell	6
17	Grinnell	7
24	Purdue	6
0	Minnesota	67
13	Northwestern	20
19	Iowa State	16
17	Nebraska	34
121		156

Won 4   Lost 3   Tied 0

1917

Coach — Howard H. Jones (Yale)
Captain — J. E. Davis, hb.

22	Cornell	13
0	Nebraska	47
0	Grinnell	10
0	Wisconsin	20
14	Great Lakes	23
35	South Dakota	0
14	Northwestern	25
6	Iowa State	3
91		141

Won 3   Lost 5   Tied 0

1918

Coach — Howard H. Jones (Yale)
Captain — R. G. Reed, e.

0	Great Lakes	10
12	Nebraska	0
27	Coe	0
34	Cornell	0
0	Illinois	19
6	Minnesota	0
21	Iowa State	0
23	Northwestern	7
0	Camp Dodge	0
123		36

Won 6   Lost 2   Tied 1

1919

Coach — Howard H. Jones (Yale)
Captain — F. H. Lohman, fb.

18	Nebraska	0
7	Illinois	9
9	Minnesota	6
26	South Dakota	13
14	Northwestern	7
6	Chicago	9
10	Iowa State	0
90		44

Won 5   Lost 2   Tied 0

HISTORICAL OUTLINE: 1889 — 1963

Year	Coach	Captain	All Games W	L	T	Conf. Games W	L	T
1889	None	Martin Sampson, hb	0	1	0			
1890	None	Arthur Smith, qb	1	1	0			
1891	None	Frank Pierce, qb	3	2	0			
1892	E. A. Dalton	Allen Sanford, hb	3	2	1			
1893	Benjamin Donnelly	Lloyd Elliott, fb	3	4	0			
1894	Roger Sherman	Prince Sawyer, qb	4	4	1			
1895	None	Kalita Leighton, g	2	5	0			
1896	A. E. Bull	Iver Iverson, c	7	1	1			
1897	Otto F. Wagonhurst	James C. Walker, g	4	4	0			
1898	Alden A. Knipe	Samuel Hobbs, fb	3	4	2			
1899	Alden A. Knipe	Moray Eby, t, e	8	0	1			
1900	Alden A. Knipe	John Griffith, fb	7	0	1	2	0	1
1901	Alden A. Knipe	S. Clyde Williams, qb; Emmett Burrier, t	5	3	0	0	3	0
1902	Alden A. Knipe	Henry S. Hollenbeck, g	5	4	0	0	3	0
1903	John G. Chalmers	George H. Coulthard, e	9	2	0	1	1	0
1904	John G. Chalmers	Nyle Jones, hb	7	4	0	0	3	0
1905	John G. Chalmers	Earle A. McGowan, fb	8	2	0	0	2	0
1906	Mark Catlin	George Allen, hb	2	3	0	0	1	0
1907	Mark Catlin	Roy A. White, e	3	2	0	1	1	0
1908	Mark Catlin	Carrol Kirk, fb	2	5	0	0	1	0
1909	John G. Griffith	Henry R. Gross, t	2	4	1	0	1	0
1910	Jess Hawley	Mark W. Hyland, e	5	2	0	1	1	0
1911	Jess Hawley	J. Ray Murphy, fb, hb	3	4	0	2	2	0
1912	Jess Hawley	Henry Hanson, g	4	3	0	1	3	0
1913	Jess Hawley	Ralph McGinnis, fb	5	2	0	2	1	0
1914	Jess Hawley	Arthur H. Gunderson, e	4	3	0	1	2	0
1915	Jess Hawley	Irving Barron, t	3	4	0	1	2	0
1916	Howard H. Jones	Charles Laun, fb	4	3	0	1	2	0
1917	Howard H. Jones	John E. Davis, hb	3	5	0	0	2	0
1918	Howard H. Jones	Ronald Reed, e	6	2	1	2	1	0
1919	Howard H. Jones	Fred Lohman, fb	5	2	0	2	2	0
1920	Howard H. Jones	William Kelly, qb	5	2	0	3	2	0
1921	Howard H. Jones	Aubrey Devine, qb	7	0	0	5	0	0
1922	Howard H. Jones	Gordon Locke, fb	7	0	0	5	0	0
1923	Howard H. Jones	Glenn Miller, hb	5	3	0	3	3	0
1924	Burton A. Ingwersen	Leland Parkin, qb	6	1	1	3	1	1
1925	Burton A. Ingwersen	Harold Griffen, c	5	3	0	2	2	0
1926	Burton A. Ingwersen	Paul Smith, e	3	5	0	0	5	0
1927	Burton A. Ingwersen	Emerson Nelson, t	4	4	0	1	4	0
1928	Burton A. Ingwersen	Richard Brown, c	6	2	0	3	2	0
1929	Burton A. Ingwersen	Willis Glasgow, hb	4	2	2	2	2	2
1930	Burton A. Ingwersen	Grover Higdon, g	4	4	0	0	1	0
1931	Burton A. Ingwersen	Oliver Sansen, fb	1	6	1	0	3	1
1932	Oscar M. Solem	Marcus Magnussen, c	1	7	0	0	5	0
1933	Oscar M. Solem	Tom Moore, c	5	3	0	3	2	0
1934	Oscar M. Solem	Russell Fisher, hb	2	5	1	1	3	1
1935	Oscar M. Solem	Richard Crayne, fb	4	2	2	1	2	2
1936	Oscar M. Solem	John Hild, hb; Ted Osmaloski, c	3	4	1	0	4	1
1937	Irl Tubbs	Homer Harris, e	1	7	0	0	5	0
1938	Irl Tubbs	Jack Eicherly, hb	1	6	1	1	3	1
1939	Edward N. Anderson	Erwin Prasse, e	6	1	1	4	1	1
1940	Edward N. Anderson	Mike Enich, t	4	4	0	2	3	0
1941	Edward N. Anderson	William Diehl, c	3	5	0	2	4	0
1942	Edward N. Anderson	None	6	4	0	3	3	0
1943	E. P. (Slip) Madigan	Robert Liddy, g; William Barbour, e	1	6	1	0	4	1
1944	E. P. (Slip) Madigan	None	1	7	0	0	6	0

Year	Coach	Captain	All Games W	L	T	Conf. Games W	L	T
1945	Clem F. Crowe	None	2	7	0	1	5	0
1946	Edward N. Anderson	None	5	4	0	3	3	0
1947	Edward N. Anderson	None	3	5	1	2	3	1
1948	Edward N. Anderson	None	4	5	0	2	4	0
1949	Edward N. Anderson	None	4	5	0	3	3	0
1950	Leonard Raffensperger	None	3	5	1	2	4	0
1951	Leonard Raffensperger	None	2	5	2	0	5	1
1952	Forest Evashevski	William Fenton, e	2	7	0	2	5	0
1953	Forest Evashevski	Andrew Houg, t	5	3	1	3	3	0
1954	Forest Evashevski	George Broeder, fb	5	4	0	4	3	0
1955	Forest Evashevski	Calvin Jones, g	3	5	1	2	3	1
1956	Forest Evashevski	Richard Deasy, t; Don Suchy, c	9	1	0	5	1	0
1957	Forest Evashevski	Jim Gibbons, e	7	1	1	4	1	1
1958	Forest Evashevski	John Nocera, fb	8	1	1	5	1	0
1959	Forest Evashevski	Don Norton,e; Ray Jauch, hb	5	4	0	3	3	0
1960	Forest Evashevski	Jerry Mauren, hb	8	1	0	5	1	0
1961	Jerry Burns	Bill Van Buren, c; Wilburn Hollis, qb.	5	4	0	2	4	0
1962	Jerry Burns	Larry Ferguson, hb	4	5	0	3	3	0
1963	Jerry Burns	Paul Krause, hb; Wally Hilgenberg, g	3	3	2	2	3	1

Totals.............. 312 255 30   114 162 17

YEAR-BY-YEAR RECORD

1889

Coach — No paid coach.
Captain — M. V. Sampson, hb.

0	Grinnell	24

Won 0   Lost 1   Tied 0

1890

Coach — No paid coach.
Captain — A. G. Smith, qb.

6	Grinnell	14
91	Iowa Wesleyan	0
—		—
97		14

Won 1   Lost 1   Tied 0

1891

Coach — No paid coach.
Captain — F. G. Pierce, qb.

64	Cornell	6
4	Minnesota	42
4	Grinnell	6
22	Nebraska	0
18	Kansas	14
—		—
112		68

Won 3   Lost 2   Tied 0

1892

Coach — E. A. Dalton (Princeton)
Captain — A. T. Sanford, hb.

48	Coe	0
44	Knox	0
4	Kansas	24
0	Missouri	22
18	Grinnell	12
10	Nebraska	10
—		—
124		68

Won 3   Lost 2   Tied 1

1893

Coach — Benjamin Donnelly,
(Princeton)
Captain — L. L. Elliott, fb.

56	Coe	0
0	Denver A. C.	58
32	Luther	0
24	Kansas	35
14	Grinnell	36
34	Missouri	12
18	Nebraska	20
—		—
178		161

Won 3   Lost 4   Tied 0

1894

Coach — Roger Sherman
(Michigan)
Captain — P. E. Sawyer, qb.

8	Iowa State	16
60	Cornell	0
34	Augustana	0
18	Chicago	18
0	Wisconsin	44
14	Kansas	12
6	Grinnell (forfeit)	0
6	Missouri	32
0	Nebraska	36
—		—
146		158

Won 4   Lost 4   Tied 1

1895

Coach — No paid coach.
Captain — K. E. Leighton, g.

0	Doane	10
28	Parsons	0
0	Iowa State	24
0	Kansas	52
0	Missouri	34
14	Penn	12
0	Nebraska	6
—		—
42		138

Won 2   Lost 5   Tied 0

1896

Coach — A. E. Bull, (Pennsylvania)
Captain — I. Iverson, c.

32	Drake	0
0	Chicago	6
6	Kansas	0
27	Wilton	0
12	Missouri	0
15	Grinnell	6
34	Des Moines YMCA	0
0	Nebraska	0
6	Nebraska	0
—		—
132		12

Won 7   Lost 1   Tied 1

1897

Coach — Otto F. Wagonhurst,
(Pennsylvania)
Captain — J. C. Walker, g.

22	Wilton	4
12	Northwestern	6
0	Phys. & Surgeons	14
0	Kansas	56
0	Iowa State (forfeit)	6
16	Drake	0
16	Grinnell	12
0	Nebraska	6
—		—
66		104

Won 4   Lost 4   Tied 0

1898

Coach — A. A. Knipe
(Pennsylvania)
Captain — S. W. Hobbs, fb.

0	Knox	0
0	Chicago	38
5	Drake	18
23	Upper Iowa	5
11	Rush Medical	15
5	Iowa Teachers	11
5	Grinnell	5
12	Simpson	0
6	Nebraska	5
—		—
67		97

Won 3   Lost 4   Tied 2

1899

Coach — A. A. Knipe
(Pennsylvania)
Captain — Moray L. Eby, t.

22	Iowa Teachers	0
5	Chicago	5
35	Penn	0
17	Rush Medical	0
5	Iowa State	0
30	Nebraska	0
16	Grinnell	0
33	Knox	0
58	Illinois	0
—		—
221		5

Won 8   Lost 0   Tied 1

1900

Coach — A. A. Knipe
(Pennsylvania)
Captain — J. G. Griffith, fb.

57	Upper Iowa	0
68	Iowa Teachers	0
47	Simpson	0
26	Drake	0
17	Chicago	0
28	Michigan	5
63	Grinnell	2
5	Northwestern	5
—		—
311		12

Won 7   Lost 0   Tied 1

1901

Coach—A. A. Knipe (Pennsylvania)
Captain — S. Clyde Williams, qb.,
and Emmet Burrier, t.

16	Iowa Teachers	0
6	Drake	5
12	Iowa State	0
0	Minnesota	16
23	Knox	6
0	Illinois	27
17	Grinnell	11
0	Michigan	50
—		—
74		115

Won 5   Lost 3   Tied 0

1902

Coach—A. A. Knipe (Pennsylvania)
Captain — H. S. Hollenbeck, g.

63	Iowa Teachers	5
12	Drake	0
10	Simpson	0
0	Minnesota	34
12	Iowa State	6
0	Michigan	107
61	Washington (St. L.)	0
0	Missouri	6
0	Illinois	80
—		—
158		238

Won 5   Lost 4   Tied 0

1903

Coach — J. G. Chalmers
(Lafayette)
Captain — G. H. Coulthard, e.

6	Cornell	0
16	Coe	0
29	Iowa Teachers	0
22	Drake	6
0	Minnesota	75
17	Grinnell	0
6	Nebraska	17
35	Simpson	2
16	Missouri	0
12	Illinois	0
12	Washington (St.L.)	2
—		—
171		102

Won 9   Lost 2   Tied 0

1904

Coach J. G. Ch
(Lafayette)
Captain — N. W. J

16	Coe	
33	Augustana	
88	Cornell	
17	Drake	
0	Chicago	
11	Iowa Teachers	
10	Iowa State	
12	Nebraska	
69	Grinnell	
0	Illinois	
0	Minnesota	
—		
256		

Won 7   Lost 4

1905

Coach — J. G. Chalme
(Lafayette)
Captain — E. A. McGowan

27	Coe	
40	Monmouth	
0	Chicago	
0	Minnesota	
41	Iowa Teachers	
45	Grinnell	
72	Des Moines	
44	Drake	
8	Iowa State	
31	St. Louis	
—		
308		

Won 8   Lost 2   Tied

1906

Coach — Mark Catlin (Chicago)
Captain — G. H. Allen, hb.

26	Missouri	4
4	Wisconsin	18
15	Coe	12
0	Iowa State	2
0	St. Louis	39
—		—
45		75

Won 2   Lost 3   Tied 0

1907

Coach — Mark Catlin (Chicago)
Captain — R. A. White, e.

21	Missouri	6
25	Drake	4
5	Wisconsin	6
25	Illinois	12
14	Iowa State	20
—		—
90		48

Won 3   Lost 2   Tied 0

1920

Coach — Howard H. Jones (Yale)
Captain — W. S. Kelly, qb.

14	Indiana	7
63	Cornell	0
3	Illinois	20
0	Chicago	10
20	Northwestern	0
28	Minnesota	7
14	Iowa State	10
——		—
142		54

Won 5   Lost 2   Tied 0

1921

Coach — Howard H. Jones (Yale)
Captain — Aubrey A. Devine, qb.

52	Knox	14
10	Notre Dame	7
14	Illinois	2
13	Purdue	6
41	Minnesota	7
41	Indiana	0
14	Northwestern	0
——		—
185		36

Won 7   Lost 0   Tied 0

(Western Conference Champions)

1922

Coach — Howard H. Jones (Yale)
Captain — Gordon C. Locke, fb.

61	Knox	0
6	Yale	0
8	Illinois	7
56	Purdue	0
28	Minnesota	14
12	Ohio State	9
37	Northwestern	3
——		—
208		33

Won 7   Lost 0   Tied 0
(Shared championship with
Michigan)

1923

Coach — Howard H. Jones (Yale)
Captain — G. W. Miller, hb.

44	Knox	3
20	Oklahoma A. & M.	0
7	Purdue	0
6	Illinois	9
20	Ohio State	0
3	Michigan	9
7	Minnesota	20
17	Northwestern	14
——		—
124		55

Won 5   Lost 3   Tied 0

1924

Coach — Burt Ingwersen (Illinois)
Captain — Leland C. Parkin, qb.

43	SE Oklahoma Teachers	0
0	Ohio State	0
13	Lawrence	5
13	Minnesota	0
0	Illinois	36
7	Butler	0
21	Wisconsin	7
9	Michigan	2
——		—
106		50

Won 6   Lost 1   Tied 1

1925

Coach — Burt Ingwersen (Illinois)
Captain — H. W. Griffin, c.

26	Arkansas	0
41	St. Louis	0
12	Illinois	10
15	Ohio State	0
28	Wabash	7
0	Wisconsin	6
0	Minnesota	33
0	Southern California	18
——		—
122		74

Won 5   Lost 3   Tied 0

1926

Coach — Burt Ingwersen (Illinois)
Captain — P. E. Smith, e.

24	Colorado Teachers	0
40	North Dakota	7
6	Illinois	13
6	Ohio State	23
21	Carroll	0
0	Minnesota	41
10	Wisconsin	20
6	Northwestern	13
——		—
113		117

Won 3   Lost 5   Tied 0

1927

Coach — Burt Ingwerson (Illinois)
Captain — E. W. Nelson, t.

32	Monmouth	6
6	Ohio State	13
38	Wabash	0
0	Minnesota	38
15	Denver	0
0	Illinois	14
16	Wisconsin	0
0	Northwestern	12
——		—
107		83

Won 4   Lost 4   Tied 0

1928

Coach — Burt Ingwersen (Illinois)
Captain — R. M. Brown, e.

26	Monmouth	0
13	Chicago	0
61	Ripon	6
7	Minnesota	6
19	South Dakota	0
14	Ohio State	7
0	Wisconsin	13
7	Michigan	10
——		—
147		42

Won 6   Lost 2   Tied 0

1929

Coach — Burt Ingwersen (Illinois)
Captain — W. A. Glassgow, hb.

46	Carroll	0
46	Monmouth	0
6	Ohio State	7
7	Illinois	7
14	Wisconsin	0
9	Minnesota	7
0	Purdue	7
0	Michigan	0
——		—
128		28

Won 4   Lost 4   Tied 2

1930

Coach — Burt Ingwersen (Illinois)
Captain — G. E. Higdon, g.

38	Bradley Tech	12
0	Oklahoma A. & M.	6
12	Centenary	19
0	Purdue	20
7	Detroit	3
0	Marquette	7
19	Penn State	0
12	Nebraska	7
——		—
88		74

Won 4   Lost 4   Tied 0

1931

Coach — Burt Ingwersen (Illinois)
Captain — O. M. Sansen, fb.

0	Pittsburgh	20
0	Texas A. & M.	29
0	Indiana	0
0	Minnesota	34
7	Geo. Washington	0
0	Nebraska	7
0	Purdue	22
0	Northwestern	19
—		——
7		131

Won 1   Lost 6   Tied 1

1932

Coach — O. M. Solem (Minnesota)
Captain — M. J. Magnussen

31	Bradley Tech	7
0	Wisconsin	34
0	Indiana	12
6	Minnesota	21
6	Geo. Washington	21
13	Nebraska	14
0	Purdue	18
6	Northwestern	44
—		——
62		171

Won 1   Lost 7   Tied 0

1933

Coach — O. M. Solem (Minnesota)
Captain — Thomas W. Moore, c.

7	Northwestern	0
38	Bradley Tech	0
26	Wisconsin	7
7	Minnesota	19
27	Iowa State	7
6	Michigan	10
14	Purdue	6
6	Nebraska	7
——		—
131		56

Won 5   Lost 3   Tied 0

1934

Coach — O. M. Solem (Minnesota)
Captain — Russell Fisher, hb.

34	South Dakota	0
20	Northwestern	7
13	Nebraska	14
6	Iowa State	31
12	Minnesota	48
0	Indiana	0
6	Purdue	13
7	Ohio State	40
—		——
98		153

Won 2   Lost 5   Tied 1

1935

Coach — O. M. Solem (Minnesota)
Captain — Dick Crayne, fb.

26	Bradley Tech	0
47	South Dakota	2
12	Colgate	6
19	Illinois	0
6	Indiana	6
6	Minnesota	13
6	Purdue	12
0	Northwestern	0
——		—
122		39

Won 4   Lost 2   Tied 2

1936

Coach — O. M. Solem (Minnesota)
Captains — Ted Osmaloski, c;
John Hild, hb.

14	Carleton	0
7	Northwestern	18
33	South Dakota	7
0	Illinois	0
6	Indiana	13
0	Minnesota	52
0	Purdue	13
25	Temple	0
—		——
85		103

Won 3   Lost 4   Tied 1

1937

Coach — Irl Tubbs (Wm. Jewell)
Captain — Homer Harris, e.

0	Washington (Seattle)	14
14	Bradley Tech	7
6	Wisconsin	13
6	Michigan	7
0	Purdue	13
10	Minnesota	35
0	Indiana	3
0	Nebraska	28
—		——
36		120

Won 1   Lost 7   Tied 0

1938

Coach — Irl Tubbs (Wm. Jewell)
Captain — Jack Eicherly, hb.

3	U.C.L.A.	27
13	Wisconsin	31
27	Chicago	14
0	Colgate	14
0	Purdue	0
0	Minnesota	28
3	Indiana	7
0	Nebraska	14
—		——
46		135

Won 1   Lost 6   Tied 1

1939

Coach — Dr. E. N. Anderson
(Notre Dame)
Captain — Erwin Prasse, e.

41	South Dakota	0
32	Indiana	29
7	Michigan	27
19	Wisconsin	13
4	Purdue	0
7	Notre Dame	6
13	Minnesota	9
7	Northwestern	7
——		——
130		91

Won 6   Lost 1   Tied 1

1940

Coach — Dr. E. N. Anderson
(Notre Dame)
Captain — Mike Enich, t.

46	South Dakota	0
30	Wisconsin	12
6	Indiana	10
6	Minnesota	34
6	Purdue	21
6	Nebraska	14
7	Notre Dame	0
18	Illinois	7
——		—
125		98

Won 4   Lost 4   Tied 0

1941

Coach — Dr. E. N. Anderson
(Notre Dame)
Captain — Bill Diehl, c.

25	Drake	8
0	Michigan	6
0	Wisconsin	23
6	Purdue	7
13	Indiana	7
21	Illinois	0
13	Minnesota	34
13	Nebraska	14
—		—
91		99

Won 3   Lost 5   Tied 0

1942

Coach — Dr. E. N. Anderson
(Notre Dame)
Captain — Named for each game.

26	Washington U.	7
27	Nebraska	0
0	Great Lakes	25
33	Camp Grant	16
7	Illinois	12
14	Indiana	13
13	Purdue	7
6	Wisconsin	0
7	Minnesota	27
14	Michigan	28
——		——
147		135

Won 6   Lost 4   Tied 0

1943

Coach — E. P. (Slip) Madigan
(Notre Dame)
Captains — Robert Liddy, g, and
Bill Barbour, e.

7	Great Lakes	21
5	Wisconsin	7
0	Iowa Pre-Flight	25
7	Indiana	7
7	Purdue	28
10	Illinois	19
14	Minnesota	33
33	Nebraska	13
—		——
83		153

Won 1   Lost 6   Tied 1

HISTORICAL OUTLINE: 1889 — 1963

Year	Coach	Captain	All Games W	L	T	Conf. Games W	L	T
1889	None	Martin Sampson, hb	0	1	0			
1890	None	Arthur Smith, qb	1	1	0			
1891	None	Frank Pierce, qb	3	2	0			
1892	E. A. Dalton	Allen Sanford, hb	3	2	1			
1893	Benjamin Donnelly	Lloyd Elliott, fb	3	4	0			
1894	Roger Sherman	Prince Sawyer, qb	4	4	1			
1895	None	Kalita Leighton, g	2	5	0			
1896	A. E. Bull	Iver Iverson, c	7	1	1			
1897	Otto F. Wagonhurst	James C. Walker, g	4	4	0			
1898	Alden A. Knipe	Samuel Hobbs, fb	3	4	2			
1899	Alden A. Knipe	Moray Eby, t, e	8	0	1			
1900	Alden A. Knipe	John Griffith, fb.	7	0	1	2	0	1
1901	Alden A. Knipe	S. Clyde Williams, qb; Emmett Burrier, t	5	3	0	0	3	0
1902	Alden A. Knipe	Henry S. Hollenbeck, g	5	4	0	0	3	0
1903	John G. Chalmers	George H. Coulthard, e	9	2	0	1	1	0
1904	John G. Chalmers	Nyle Jones, hb	7	4	0	0	3	0
1905	John G. Chalmers	Earle A. McGowan, fb	8	2	0	0	2	0
1906	Mark Catlin	George Allen, hb	2	3	0	0	1	0
1907	Mark Catlin	Roy A. White, e	3	2	0	1	1	0
1908	Mark Catlin	Carrol Kirk, fb	2	5	0	0	1	0
1909	John G. Griffith	Henry R. Gross, t	2	4	1	0	1	0
1910	Jess Hawley	Mark W. Hyland, e	5	2	0	1	1	0
1911	Jess Hawley	J. Ray Murphy, fb, hb	3	4	0	2	2	0
1912	Jess Hawley	Henry Hanson, g	4	3	0	1	3	0
1913	Jess Hawley	Ralph McGinnis, fb	5	2	0	2	1	0
1914	Jess Hawley	Arthur H. Gunderson, c	4	3	0	1	2	0
1915	Jess Hawley	Irving Barron, t	3	4	0	1	2	0
1916	Howard H. Jones	Charles Laun, fb	4	3	0	1	2	0
1917	Howard H. Jones	John E. Davis, hb	3	5	0	0	2	0
1918	Howard H. Jones	Ronald Reed, e	6	2	1	2	1	0
1919	Howard H. Jones	Fred Lohman, fb	5	2	0	2	2	0
1920	Howard H. Jones	William Kelly, qb	5	2	0	3	2	0
1921	Howard H. Jones	Aubrey Devine, hb	7	0	0	5	0	0
1922	Howard H. Jones	Gordon Locke, fb	7	0	0	5	0	0
1923	Howard H. Jones	Glenn Miller, hb	5	3	0	3	3	0
1924	Burton A. Ingwersen	Leland Parkin, qb	6	1	1	3	1	1
1925	Burton A. Ingwersen	Harold Griffen, c	5	3	0	2	2	0
1926	Burton A. Ingwersen	Paul Smith, e	3	5	0	0	5	0
1927	Burton A. Ingwersen	Emerson Nelson, t	4	4	0	1	4	0
1928	Burton A. Ingwersen	Richard Brown, c	6	2	0	3	2	0
1929	Burton A. Ingwersen	Willis Glassgow, hb	4	2	2	2	2	2
1930	Burton A. Ingwersen	Grover Higdon, g	4	4	0	0	1	0
1931	Burton A. Ingwersen	Oliver Sansen, fb	1	6	1	0	3	1
1932	Oscar M. Solem	Marcus Magnussen, c	1	7	0	0	5	0
1933	Oscar M. Solem	Tom Moore, c	5	3	0	3	2	0
1934	Oscar M. Solem	Russell Fisher, hb	2	5	1	1	3	1
1935	Oscar M. Solem	Richard Crayne, fb	4	2	2	1	2	2
1936	Oscar M. Solem	John Hild, hb; Ted Osmaloski, c	3	4	1	0	4	1
1937	Irl Tubbs	Homer Harris, e	1	7	0	0	5	0
1938	Irl Tubbs	Jack Eicherly, hb	1	6	1	1	3	1
1939	Edward N. Anderson	Erwin Prasse, e	6	1	1	4	1	1
1940	Edward N. Anderson	Mike Enich, t	4	4	0	2	3	0
1941	Edward N. Anderson	William Diehl, c	3	5	0	2	4	0
1942	Edward N. Anderson	None	6	4	0	3	3	0
1943	E. P. (Slip) Madigan	Robert Liddy, g; William Barbour, e	1	6	1	0	4	1
1944	E. P. (Slip) Madigan	None	1	7	0	0	6	0

Year	Coach	Captain	All Games W	L	T	Conf. Games W	L	T
1945	Clem F. Crowe	None	2	7	0	1	5	0
1946	Edward N. Anderson	None	5	4	0	3	3	0
1947	Edward N. Anderson	None	3	5	1	2	3	1
1948	Edward N. Anderson	None	4	5	0	2	4	0
1949	Edward N. Anderson	None	4	5	0	3	3	0
1950	Leonard Raffensperger	None	3	5	1	2	4	0
1951	Leonard Raffensperger	None	2	5	2	0	5	1
1952	Forest Evashevski	William Fenton, e	2	7	0	2	5	0
1953	Forest Evashevski	Andrew Houg, t	5	3	1	3	3	0
1954	Forest Evashevski	George Broeder, fb	5	4	0	4	3	0
1955	Forest Evashevski	Calvin Jones, g	3	5	1	2	3	1
1956	Forest Evashevski	Richard Deasy, t; Don Suchy, c	9	1	0	5	1	0
1957	Forest Evashevski	Jim Gibbons, e	7	1	1	4	1	1
1958	Forest Evashevski	John Nocera, fb	8	1	1	5	1	0
1959	Forest Evashevski	Don Norton,e; Ray Jauch, hb	5	4	0	3	3	0
1960	Forest Evashevski	Jerry Mauren, hb	8	1	0	5	1	0
1961	Jerry Burns	Bill Van Buren, c; Wilburn Hollis, qb	5	4	0	2	4	0
1962	Jerry Burns	Larry Ferguson, hb	4	5	0	3	3	0
1963	Jerry Burns	Paul Krause, hb; Wally Hilgenberg, g	3	3	2	2	3	1
		Totals	312	255	30	114	162	17

YEAR-BY-YEAR RECORD

1889

Coach — No paid coach.
Captain — M. V. Sampson, hb.

0	Grinnell	24

Won 0   Lost 1   Tied 0

1890

Coach — No paid coach.
Captain — A. G. Smith, qb.

6	Grinnell	14
91	Iowa Wesleyan	0
97		14

Won 1   Lost 1   Tied 0

1891

Coach — No paid coach.
Captain — F. G. Pierce, qb.

64	Cornell	6
4	Minnesota	42
4	Grinnell	6
22	Nebraska	0
18	Kansas	14
112		68

Won 3   Lost 2   Tied 0

1892

Coach — E. A. Dalton (Princeton)
Captain — A. T. Sanford, hb.

48	Coe	0
44	Knox	0
4	Kansas	24
0	Missouri	22
18	Grinnell	12
10	Nebraska	10
124		68

Won 3   Lost 2   Tied 1

1893

Coach — Benjamin Donnelly,
(Princeton)
Captain — L. L. Elliott, fb.

56	Coe	0
0	Denver A. C.	58
32	Luther	0
24	Kansas	35
14	Grinnell	36
34	Missouri	12
18	Nebraska	20
178		161

Won 3   Lost 4   Tied 0

1894

Coach — Roger Sherman
(Michigan)
Captain — P. E. Sawyer, qb.

8	Iowa State	16
60	Cornell	0
34	Augustana	0
18	Chicago	18
0	Wisconsin	44
14	Kansas	12
6	Grinnell (forfeit)	0
6	Missouri	32
0	Nebraska	36
146		158

Won 4   Lost 4   Tied 1

1895

Coach — No paid coach.
Captain — K. E. Leighton, g.

0	Doane	10
28	Parsons	0
0	Iowa State	24
0	Kansas	52
0	Missouri	34
14	Penn	12
0	Nebraska	6
42		138

Won 2   Lost 5   Tied 0

1896

Coach — A. E. Bull, (Pennsylvania)
Captain — I. Iverson, c.

32	Drake	0
0	Chicago	6
6	Kansas	0
27	Wilton	0
12	Missouri	0
15	Grinnell	6
34	Des Moines YMCA	0
0	Nebraska	0
6	Nebraska	0
132		12

Won 7   Lost 1   Tied 1

1897

Coach — Otto F. Wagonhurst,
(Pennsylvania)
Captain — J. C. Walker, g.

22	Wilton	4
12	Northwestern	6
0	Phys. & Surgeons	14
0	Kansas	56
0	Iowa State (forfeit)	6
16	Drake	0
16	Grinnell	12
0	Nebraska	6
66		104

Won 4   Lost 4   Tied 0

1898

Coach — A. A. Knipe
(Pennsylvania)
Captain — S. W. Hobbs, fb.

0	Knox	0
0	Chicago	38
5	Drake	18
23	Upper Iowa	5
11	Rush Medical	15
5	Iowa Teachers	11
5	Grinnell	5
12	Simpson	0
6	Nebraska	5
67		97

Won 3   Lost 4   Tied 2

1899

Coach — A. A. Knipe
(Pennsylvania)
Captain — Moray L. Eby, t.

22	Iowa Teachers	0
5	Chicago	5
35	Penn	0
17	Rush Medical	0
5	Iowa State	0
30	Nebraska	0
16	Grinnell	0
33	Knox	0
58	Illinois	0
221		5

Won 8   Lost 0   Tied 1

1900

Coach — A. A. Knipe
(Pennsylvania)
Captain — J. G. Griffith, fb.

57	Upper Iowa	0
68	Iowa Teachers	0
47	Simpson	0
26	Drake	0
17	Chicago	0
28	Michigan	5
63	Grinnell	2
5	Northwestern	5
311		12

Won 7   Lost 0   Tied 1

1901

Coach—A. A. Knipe (Pennsylvania)
Captain — S. Clyde Williams, qb.,
and Emmet Burrier, t.

16	Iowa Teachers	0
6	Drake	5
12	Iowa State	0
0	Minnesota	16
23	Knox	6
0	Illinois	27
17	Grinnell	11
0	Michigan	50
74		115

Won 5   Lost 3   Tied 0

1902

Coach—A. A. Knipe (Pennsylvania)
Captain — H. S. Hollenbeck, g.

63	Iowa Teachers	5
12	Drake	0
10	Simpson	0
0	Minnesota	34
12	Iowa State	6
0	Michigan	107
61	Washington (St. L.)	0
0	Missouri	6
0	Illinois	80
158		238

Won 5   Lost 4   Tied 0

1903

Coach — J. G. Chalmers
(Lafayette)
Captain — G. H. Coulthard, e.

6	Cornell	0
16	Coe	0
29	Iowa Teachers	0
22	Drake	6
0	Minnesota	75
17	Grinnell	0
6	Nebraska	17
35	Simpson	2
16	Missouri	0
12	Illinois	0
12	Washington (St.L.)	2
171		102

Won 9   Lost 2   Tied 0

1904

Coach J. G. Chalmers
(Lafayette)
Captain — N. W. Jones, hb.

16	Coe	0
33	Augustana	2
88	Cornell	0
17	Drake	0
0	Chicago	39
11	Iowa Teachers	5
10	Iowa State	6
12	Nebraska	17
69	Grinnell	0
0	Illinois	29
0	Minnesota	11
256		109

Won 7   Lost 4   Tied 0

1905

Coach — J. G. Chalmers
(Lafayette)
Captain — E. A. McGowan, fb.

27	Coe	0
40	Monmouth	0
0	Chicago	42
0	Minnesota	39
41	Iowa Teachers	5
45	Grinnell	0
72	Des Moines	0
44	Drake	0
8	Iowa State	0
31	St. Louis	0
308		86

Won 8   Lost 2   Tied 0

1906

Coach — Mark Catlin (Chicago)
Captain — G. H. Allen, hb.

26	Missouri	4
4	Wisconsin	18
15	Coe	12
0	Iowa State	2
0	St. Louis	39
45		75

Won 2   Lost 3   Tied 0

1907

Coach — Mark Catlin (Chicago)
Captain — R. A. White, e.

21	Missouri	6
25	Drake	4
5	Wisconsin	6
25	Illinois	12
14	Iowa State	20
90		48

Won 3   Lost 2   Tied 0

1908

Coach — Mark Catlin (Chicago)
Captain C. N. Kirk, fb.

92	Coe	0
5	Missouri	10
16	Morningside	0
8	Nebraska	11
0	Illinois	22
6	Drake	12
5	Kansas	10
132		65

Won 2   Lost 5   Tied 0

1909

Coach — J. G. Griffith (Iowa)
Captain — H. R. Gross, t.

0	Minnesota	41
3	Cornell	0
6	Nebraska	6
12	Missouri	13
14	Drake	17
16	Iowa State	0
7	Kansas	20
58		97

Won 2   Lost 4   Tied 1

1910

Coach — Jess Hawley (Dartmouth)
Captain — M. W. Hyland, e.

12	Morningside	0
5	Northwestern	10
0	Missouri	5
16	Purdue	0
2	Iowa State	0
21	Drake	0
38	Washington (St. L.)	0
94		15

Won 5   Lost 2   Tied 0

1911

Coach — Jess Hawley (Dartmouth)
Captain — J. R. Murphy, hb.

11	Morningside	5
0	Cornell	3
6	Minnesota	24
0	Wisconsin	12
11	Purdue	0
0	Iowa State	9
6	Northwestern	0
34		53

Won 3   Lost 4   Tied 0

1912

Coach — Jess Hawley (Dartmouth)
Captain — H. D. Hanson, g.

35	Iowa Teachers	7
31	Cornell	0
14	Chicago	34
7	Minnesota	56
13	Indiana	6
20	Iowa State	7
10	Wisconsin	28
130		138

Won 4   Lost 3   Tied 0

1913

Coach — Jess Hawley (Dartmouth)
Captain — R. A. McGinnis, fb.

45	Iowa Teachers	3
76	Cornell	0
6	Chicago	23
78	Northwestern	6
60	Indiana	0
45	Iowa State	7
0	Nebraska	12
310		51

Won 5   Lost 2   Tied 0

1914

Coach — Jess Hawley (Dartmouth)
Captain — A. H. Gunderson, e.

95	Iowa Teachers	0
49	Cornell	0
0	Chicago	7
0	Minnesota	7
27	Northwestern	0
26	Iowa State	6
7	Nebraska	16
204		36

Won 4   Lost 3   Tied 0

1915

Coach — Jess Hawley (Dartmouth)
Captain — I. J. Barron, t.

33	Cornell	0
17	Morningside	6
9	Northwestern	6
13	Minnesota	51
13	Purdue	19
0	Iowa State	16
7	Nebraska	52
92		150

Won 3   Lost 4   Tied 0

1916

Coach — Howard H. Jones (Yale)
Captain — C. E. Laun, fb.

31	Cornell	6
17	Grinnell	7
24	Purdue	6
0	Minnesota	67
13	Northwestern	20
19	Iowa State	16
17	Nebraska	34
121		156

Won 4   Lost 3   Tied 0

1917

Coach — Howard H. Jones (Yale)
Captain — J. E. Davis, hb.

22	Cornell	13
0	Nebraska	47
0	Grinnell	10
0	Wisconsin	20
14	Great Lakes	23
35	South Dakota	0
14	Northwestern	25
6	Iowa State	3
91		141

Won 3   Lost 5   Tied 0

1918

Coach — Howard H. Jones (Yale)
Captain — R. G. Reed, e.

0	Great Lakes	10
12	Nebraska	0
27	Coe	0
34	Cornell	0
0	Illinois	19
6	Minnesota	0
21	Iowa State	0
23	Northwestern	7
0	Camp Dodge	0
123		36

Won 6   Lost 2   Tied 1

1919

Coach — Howard H. Jones (Yale)
Captain — F. H. Lohman, fb.

18	Nebraska	0
7	Illinois	9
9	Minnesota	6
26	South Dakota	13
14	Northwestern	7
6	Chicago	9
10	Iowa State	0
90		44

Won 5   Lost 2   Tied 0

1944
Coach — E. P. (Slip) Madigan
(Notre Dame)
Captain — Named for each game.

0	Ohio State	34
6	Illinois	40
7	Purdue	26
0	Indiana	32
27	Nebraska	6
7	Wisconsin	26
0	Minnesota	46
6	Iowa Pre-Flight	30
—		——
53		240

Won 1   Lost 7   Tied 0

1945
Coach — Clem F. Crowe
(Notre Dame)
Captain — Named for each game.

14	Bergstrom AAF	13
0	Ohio State	42
0	Purdue	40
20	Indiana	52
0	Notre Dame	56
7	Wisconsin	27
7	Illinois	48
20	Minnesota	19
6	Nebraska	13
—		——
74		310

Won 2   Lost 7   Tied 0

1946
Coach — Dr. E. N. Anderson
(Notre Dame)
Captain — Named for each game.

39	North Dakota State	0
16	Purdue	0
7	Michigan	14
21	Nebraska	7
13	Indiana	0
6	Notre Dame	41
0	Illinois	7
21	Wisconsin	7
6	Minnesota	16
——		—
129		92

Won 5   Lost 4   Tied 0

1947
Coach — Dr. E. N. Anderson
(Notre Dame)
Captain — Named for each game.

59	North Dakota State	0
7	U.C.L.A.	22
12	Illinois	35
27	Indiana	14
13	Ohio State	13
0	Notre Dame	21
0	Purdue	21
14	Wisconsin	46
13	Minnesota	7
——		——
145		179

Won 3   Lost 5   Tied 1

1948
Coach — Dr. E. N. Anderson
(Notre Dame)
Captain — Named for each game.

14	Marquette	12
0	Indiana	7
14	Ohio State	7
13	Purdue	20
12	Notre Dame	27
19	Wisconsin	13
0	Illinois	14
21	Minnesota	28
34	Boston Univ.	14
——		——
127		142

Won 4   Lost 5   Tied 0

1949
Coach — Dr. E. N. Anderson
(Notre Dame)
Captain — Named for each game.

25	U.C.L.A.	41
21	Purdue	7
14	Illinois	20
35	Indiana	9
28	Northwestern	21
34	Oregon	31
7	Minnesota	55
13	Wisconsin	35
7	Notre Dame	28
——		——
184		247

Won 4   Lost 5   Tied 0

1950
Coach — Leonard Raffensperger
(Iowa)
Captain — Named for each game.

20	Southern California	14
7	Indiana	20
0	Wisconsin	14
33	Purdue	21
21	Ohio State	83
13	Minnesota	0
7	Illinois	21
14	Notre Dame	14
6	Miami, Fla.	14
——		——
121		201

Won 3   Lost 5   Tied 1

1951
Coach — Leonard Raffensperger
(Iowa)
Captain — Named for each game.

16	Kansas State	0
30	Purdue	34
34	Pittsburgh	17
0	Michigan	21
21	Ohio State	47
20	Minnesota	20
13	Illinois	40
7	Wisconsin	34
20	Notre Dame	20
——		——
161		233

Won 2   Lost 5   Tied 2

1952
Coach — Forest Evashevski
(Michigan)
Captain — William Fenton, e.

14	Pittsburgh	26
13	Indiana	20
14	Purdue	41
13	Wisconsin	42
8	Ohio State	0
7	Minnesota	17
13	Illinois	33
39	Northwestern	14
0	Notre Dame	27
——		——
121		220

Won 2   Lost 7   Tied 0

1953
Coach — Forest Evashevski
(Michigan)
Captain — Andrew Houg, t.

7	Michigan State	21
54	Washington State	12
13	Michigan	14
21	Wyoming	7
19	Indiana	13
6	Wisconsin	10
26	Purdue	0
27	Minnesota	0
14	Notre Dame	14
——		—
187		91

Won 5   Lost 3   Tied 1

1954
Coach — Forest Evashevski
(Michigan)
Captain — George Broeder, fb.

14	Michigan State	10
48	Montana	6
13	Michigan	14
14	Ohio State	20
27	Indiana	14
13	Wisconsin	7
25	Purdue	14
20	Minnesota	22
18	Notre Dame	34
——		——
192		141

Won 5   Lost 4   Tied 0

1955
Coach — Forest Evashevski
(Michigan)
Captain — Calvin Jones, g

28	Kansas State	7
14	Wisconsin	37
20	Indiana	6
20	Purdue	20
13	U.C.L.A.	33
21	Michigan	33
26	Minnesota	0
10	Ohio State	20
14	Notre Dame	17
——		——
166		173

Won 3   Lost 5   Tied 1

1956

**Coach — Forest Evashevski
(Michigan)
Captains — Richard Deasy, t;
Don Suchy, c.**

27	Indiana	0
14	Oregon State	13
13	Wisconsin	7
34	Hawaii	0
21	Purdue	20
14	Michigan	17
7	Minnesota	0
6	Ohio State	0
48	Notre Dame	8
°35	Oregon State	19
—		—
219		84

Won 9   Lost 1   Tied 0
°Rose Bowl game.

1957

**Coach — Forest Evashevski
(Michigan)
Captain — Jim Gibbons, e.**

70	Utah State	14
20	Washington State	13
47	Indiana	7
21	Wisconsin	7
6	Northwestern	0
21	Michigan	21
44	Minnesota	20
13	Ohio State	17
21	Notre Dame	13
—		—
263		112

Won 7   Lost 1   Tied 1

1958

**Coach — Forest Evashevski
(Michigan)
Captain — John Nocera, fb.**

17	Texas Christian	0
13	Air Force Academy	13
34	Indiana	13
20	Wisconsin	9
26	Northwestern	20
37	Michigan	14
28	Minnesota	6
28	Ohio State	38
31	Notre Dame	21
°38	California	12
—		—
272		146

Won 8   Lost 1   Tied 1
°Rose Bowl game.

1959

**Coach — Forest Evashevski
(Michigan)
Captains — Don Norton, e;
Ray Jauch, hb.**

42	California	12
10	Northwestern	14
37	Michigan State	8
16	Wisconsin	25
7	Purdue	14
53	Kansas State	0
33	Minnesota	0
16	Ohio State	7
19	Notre Dame	20
—		—
233		100

Won 5   Lost 4   Tied 0

1960

**Coach — Forest Evashevski
(Michigan)
Captain — Jerry Mauren, hb.**

22	Oregon State	12
42	Northwestern	0
27	Michigan State	15
28	Wisconsin	21
21	Purdue	14
21	Kansas	7
10	Minnesota	27
35	Ohio State	12
28	Notre Dame	0
—		—
234		108

Won 8   Lost 1   Tied 0

1961

**Coach — Jerry Burns (Michigan)
Captains — Bill Van Buren, c;
Wilburn Hollis, qb.**

28	California	7
35	Southern California	34
27	Indiana	8
47	Wisconsin	15
0	Purdue	9
13	Ohio State	29
9	Minnesota	16
14	Michigan	23
42	Notre Dame	21
—		—
215		162

Won 5   Lost 4   Tied 0

1962

**Coach — Jerry Burns (Michigan)
Captain — Larry Ferguson, hb.**

28	Oregon State	8
0	Southern California	7
14	Indiana	10
14	Wisconsin	42
3	Purdue	26
28	Ohio State	14
0	Minnesota	10
28	Michigan	14
12	Notre Dame	35
—		—
127		166

Won 4   Lost 5   Tied 0

1963

**Coach — Jerry Burns (Michigan)
Captains — Paul Krause, hb;
Wally Hilgenberg, g.**

14	Washington State	14
17	Washington (Seattle)	7
37	Indiana	26
7	Wisconsin	10
0	Purdue	14
3	Ohio State	7
27	Minnesota	13
21	Michigan	21
—		—
126		112

Won 3   Lost 3   Tied 2

IOWA LETTERMEN ROSTER

During seventy-five years of intercollegiate football competition 823 different players have earned one or more major letters at Iowa. Most conspicuous names have been Smith and Williams. Ten different letter winners have been named Smith, while nine were called Williams. Following is a complete list of letter winners, including years of award.

A

Ahlgren, Donald, 1956.
Akin, Austin F., 1931.
Akin, Paul, 1935.
Aldrich, Charles S., 1892, 1893, 1894.
Alexander, Archie A., 1909, 1910, 1911.
Allen, George H., 1903, 1904, 1905, 1906.
Allen, Joseph H., 1893, 1894.
Allen, Robert, 1937, 1938.
Allison, William B., 1895.
Andruska, Bruno, 1938, 1939, 1940.
Anderson, Richard, 1935, 1936, 1937.
Anderson, Ross, 1940, 1941, 1947.
Ankeny, Gerald, 1939, 1940, 1941.
Annis, Daryl, 1943.
Armil, Paul W., 1926, 1927, 1928.
Arzberger, Robert, 1943.
Ash, William, 1932, 1934.
Atkinson, William I., 1903, 1904, 1905.

B

Bailey, Charles H., 1891.
Baird, Burton A., 1911.
Baker, Mark I., 1898, 1899, 1901.
Balazs, Frank, 1936, 1937, 1938.
Balliet, Michael R., 1890.
Banks, Earl, 1946, 1947, 1948, 1949.
Banton, Oscar H., 1910, 1911.
Barbera, Kevin, 1961.
Barbour, William, 1942, 1943.
Barron, Irving J. (Stub), 1913, 1914, 1915.
Bartells, Del, 1946.
Bateman, Howard W., 1906.
Baughman, William, 1943.
Becker, Fred H., 1916.
Belding, Lester C., 1918, 1919, 1920, 1921.
Bell, Charles L., 1909.
Benda, Russell, 1946, 1947.
Benjamin, Wendell P., 1929, 1930.
Bennett, Bernie, 1950, 1951, 1952.
Benskin, William, 1944.
Bergstrom, Wallace, 1939.
Berry, John W., 1901, 1902, 1904.

Bjork, Donald, 1950.
Blackburn, James M., 1915.
Blackmore, Auzman H., 1897.
Blackmore, Ralph D., 1896, 1897.
Blair, Fred, 1892.
Bleeker, John J., 1917.
Block, Lawrence A., 1917, 1918, 1919, 1920.
Bloomquist, Frank, 1955, 1956, 1957.
Boothe, Charles, Jr., 1952, 1953.
Bowen, Carl, 1945.
Bostwick, Robert, 1949, 1950.
Bowen, Carl T., 1913.
Bowen, Donald, 1955, 1956, 1957.
Bowlin, Richard, 1935, 1936.
Bowlsby, Clifton A., 1915.
Bradley, Harold, 1949, 1950.
Brady, Charles, 1937, 1938.
Brandt, Duane, 1949, 1950, 1951.
Bremner, William H., 1889, 1890, 1894.
Briggs, Charles O., 1901, 1902.
Briggs, William, 1963.
Bristol, Joseph, 1949, 1950, 1951.
Britzmann, Burt, 1950, 1951, 1952.
Brockway, James M., 1898, 1899, 1900.
Broeder, George (Binkey), 1951, 1952, 1953, 1954.
Brown, John, 1958, 1959.
Brown, Richard M., 1926, 1927, 1928.
Brueckner, Carl, 1913, 1914.
Brugman, Francis A., 1907.
Buckley, George M., 1910, 1911, 1912.
Buckley, C. Roy, 1903, 1905.
Buckley, Fred W., 1901, 1902, 1903.
Budzik, Bernard, 1962, 1963.
Buntz, Andrew, 1949, 1950, 1951.
Burkett, Wilford, 1940, 1941, 1942.
Burkett, Charles, 1943.
Burrier, Emmett F., 1898, 1899, 1900, 1901.
Burroughs, John, 1955, 1956, 1958.
Busk, Russell, 1937, 1938, 1939.
Byers, Clar T., 1926.
Byers, Herbert, 1944.
Byrd, Joseph, 1947.

C

Calhoun, John, 1960, 1961.
Caplan, Arnold, 1949, 1950, 1951.
Carberry, Joseph L., 1913, 1914.
Carberry, William L., 1906, 1907, 1908.
Carlsen, John W., 1930.
Carlsen, Oakley L., 1927, 1928.
Carlson, Raymond, 1946, 1947, 1948.
Carr, Spencer H., 1893.
Case, Lyman G., 1930, 1931.
Cervenak, William, 1961.
Chalmers, Andrew M., 1903, 1904, 1905.
Charlton, Clyde B., 1919.
Chase, William B., 1897.
Chatterton, Robert B., 1926, 1927.
Chelf, Donald, 1951, 1952, 1953.
Clark, Jerry, 1952, 1953.
Clark, Richard, 1959.
Clauson, Richard, 1959, 1960.
Clearman, Eugene R., 1931.
Clemons, Homer, 1910, 1912.
Coast, Preston C., 1889.
Coast, Wm. O., 1898.
Coldren, Clymer A., 1894.
Coldren, Paul, 1896.
Coldren, Stevens, 1894.
Collins, Benjamin P., 1908, 1909.
Collins, Wm. J., 1893, 1894.
Comly, Ross H., 1908.
Commack, Donald, 1949, 1950, 1951.
Commings, Robert, 1953, 1956, 1957.
Connor, Edward G., 1907.
Conrad, Carl, 1938.
Converse, Willard L., 1894.
Cooley, Clark A., 1927.
Coulthard, George H., 1900, 1901, 1902, 1903.
Couppee, Albert, 1939, 1940, 1941.
Cox, Arthur J., 1890.
Cozad, James, 1943, 1946, 1947, 1948.
Crayne, Richard, 1933, 1934, 1935.
Cross, Clarence, 1944.
Crossley, James J., 1890.
Cuhel, Frank J., 1926, 1927.
Cummins, Cameron, 1952, 1953, 1954.

Curran, Francis, 1940, 1941, 1942.
Curran, Ted, 1942, 1946, 1947.
Curry, Paul J., 1910, 1911, 1912.
Cutler, F. H., 1890.
Cutting, Elmer W., 1895.

D

Dallas, William, 1944.
Daniels, Charles, 1952.
Danner, David, 1943.
Dauber, Raymond G., 1923, 1924, 1925.
Davis, John E. (Waddy), 1915, 1916, 1917.
Davis, Victor, 1962.
Dawson, Carl E., 1892.
Day, David, 1946.
Dean, Floyd (Buzz), 1937, 1938, 1939.
De Antona, Joseph, 1963.
Deasy, Richard, 1954, 1955, 1956.
Dee, Clarence, 1934.
Dee, James E., 1930.
Deems, Oren M., 1898.
DeHeer, Floyd, 1935, 1936, 1937.
Della Vedova, T., 1931.
DeNio, Earl W., 1914.
Denning, Charles, 1949, 1950, 1951.
DeProspero, David, 1949, 1950, 1951.
Deutsch, Phillip, 1962, 1963.
Devine, Aubrey, 1919, 1920, 1921.
Devine, Glenn, 1919, 1920, 1921.
DiCindio, William, 1960, 1961.
Dick, Leo G., 1912, 1913.
Dickerhoof, Del, 1941, 1942.
Dickerson, Voris R., 1932.
Diehl, William, 1939, 1940, 1941.
DiMarco, Alfonzo, 1947, 1948.
Dittmer, John D., 1946, 1947, 1948, 1949.
Dobrino, Donald, 1954, 1955, 1956.
Dolly, Edward L., 1930, 1931, 1932.
Donnelly, William L., 1914, 1915, 1918.
Donovan, Louis P., 1902, 1903.
Doran, Ralph, 1948.
Dorsey, Don D., 1932.
Dougherty, Richard, 1962, 1963.
Drahn, Glenn, 1948, 1949, 1950.
Drake, Hugh, 1956, 1957, 1958.
Duncan, Floyd C., 1915, 1916.
Duncan, H. Randolph, 1956, 1957, 1958.
Dutcher, Charles M., 1891.
Dye, Charles W., 1900.
Dyer, Walter R., 1909.

E

Eby, Moray L., 1897, 1898, 1899, 1900.
Edmonds, Charles W., 1895, 1896. (alias Jim Brown)
Edson, Willis C., 1899, 1900.
Egan, George W., 1898.
Ehret, James, 1909.
Eicherly, Jack, 1936, 1937, 1938.
Elliott, Edward G., 1906, 1907.
Elliott, Lloyd L., 1890, 1891, 1892, 1893.
Ellis, Thomas, 1952.
Ely, Asher W., 1900.
Ely, Harold E., 1928, 1929, 1930.
Engeldinger, Karl, 1922.
Enich, Michael, 1938, 1939, 1940.
Estes, John, 1947.
Evans, Richard, 1937, 1938, 1939.
Ewen, Roger, 1959.

F

Fagerlind, Paul, 1944, 1945.
Fairchild, Ron, 1949, 1950, 1951.
Farmer, Thomas, 1940, 1941, 1942.
Farroh, Mike, 1928, 1929.
Farroh, Shipley, 1936, 1937.
Faske, Jerry, 1948, 1949, 1950.
Fechter, Russell, 1946.
Fee, Joseph M., 1908, 1909.
Fenton, William, 1951, 1952, 1953.
Ferguson, James, 1942.
Ferguson, Larry, 1959, 1960, 1962.
Ferren, Wm. A., 1891.
Fischer, Alan, 1962.
Fisher, Darrell C., 1923, 1924.
Fisher, Hugh, 1962.
Fisher, Raymond R., 1931, 1932, 1933.
Fisher, Russell, 1933, 1934.
Fleckenstein, William P., 1923, 1924.
Fleming, Willie, 1958.
Fletcher, Gary, 1962, 1963.
Flood, Robert, 1944.
Ford, John, 1943.
Fosdick, Robert E., 1915, 1916.
Foster, Jerry P., 1931, 1933, 1934.
Freeman, James, 1953, 1954, 1955.
Frey, Harry, 1943.
Fritzel, Carl C., 1906, 1907.
Fry, Wesley L., 1923, 1924, 1925.
Fryauf, Don, 1948.
Frye, George (Red), 1939, 1940, 1941.
Frymire, Richard, 1951, 1952.
Fuhrman, John J., 1927, 1928, 1929.
Furlong, Kevin, 1957, 1958.

G

Gaines, Richard J., 1895, 1896.
Gallagher, Frank, 1936, 1937.
Gallagher, Jack, 1933, 1934, 1935.
Gallagher, James Ambrose, 1917.
Gallagher, William, 1937, 1939, 1940.
Gallagher, William, 1943.
Galloway, Ledrue, 1924.
Gardner, John R., 1895, 1896, 1897.
Garretson, Herman John, 1914, 1915.
Geigel, Robert, 1946, 1947, 1948, 1949.
George, Leon, 1945.
German, Burt, 1891.
Giacobazzi, Tony, 1962, 1963.
Gibbs, Frank W., 1903.
Gibbons, James, 1955, 1956, 1957.
Gilleard, Burdell (Oops), 1940.
Gillette, Charles, 1892.
Gilliam, Frank, 1953, 1954, 1956.
Ginsberg, Louis, 1945, 1948, 1949, 1950.
Glasener, Paul, 1943.
Glassgow, Willis A. 1927, 1928, 1929.
Golden, Paul, 1945.
Gordenier, Sheldon, 1934, 1935.
Gorrell, Andrew, 1889.
Graham, Donald M., 1923, 1924, 1925.
Gravel, William, 1956, 1957, 1958.
Green, Boyd, 1954.
Green, Thomas W. 1905.
Green, William, 1939, 1940, 1941.
Greene, William, 1948, 1949, 1950.
Greenwood, Glen J., 1917, 1918.
Grier, Robert, 1962, 1963.
Griffen, Harold, 1923, 1924, 1925.
Griffin, Festus, 1896.
Griffith, Dwight M., 1901, 1902, 1903, 1904.
Griffith, John G., 1897, 1898, 1899, 1900.
Grimm, Lloyd D., 1926, 1927, 1928.
Gross, Henry R., 1907, 1908, 1909.
Gross, Samuel E., 1913, 1914, 1915.
Grothus, Joseph, 1943, 1946, 1947, 1948.
Grouwinkel, Gary, 1956, 1957, 1958.
Grubb, Frank J., 1915, 1916.
Gunderson, Arthur, 1912, 1913, 1914.
Gunsolis, Frank H., 1894.
Gustafson, Robert, 1945.
Guzowski, Anthony J., 1946, 1947, 1948.

H

Hagerty, Lorin J., 1927, 1929.
Hagler, Collins (Mike), 1955, 1956, 1957.
Hain, Robert, 1958, 1959.
Hall, John, 1952, 1953, 1954.
Hall, Shelley B., 1891.
Halliburton, James, 1948.
Haltom, Warren, 1934.
Hammond, Jack, 1945.
Hancock, John W., 1922, 1923, 1924.
Hand, Thomas, 1942, 1945.
Hanlon, Thomas A., 1909.
Hansen, James, 1944.
Hanson, Henry D., 1909, 1911, 1912.
Hantelmann, Harold E., 1930, 1931.
Happel, William, 1955, 1956, 1957.
Harrell, George, 1959.
Harris, Fred, 1955, 1956, 1957
Harris, Homer, 1935, 1936, 1937.
Harris, Sammie, 1960, 1961, 1962.
Hass, Wilmon H., 1932.
Hastings, Irving C., 1906, 1907, 1908.
Hatch, James, 1952, 1954.
Hatch, Toni, 1955, 1956.
Hauge, Gerhard S., 1930.
Haussman, Robert, 1956.
Hawkins, Max, 1939, 1940.
Hay, Jim B., 1930.
Hayes, Robert C., 1894.
Hayman, Philip, Jr., 1952.
Hazard, Charles M. (Peck), 1907, 1908, 1909.
Head, James, 1954.
Headington, Ron, 1946, 1947, 1948.
Heald, Albert P., 1890.
Heldt, John C., 1918, 1919, 1921, 1922.
Helgens, James, 1961.
Herbert, Vane E., 1900, 1901.
Herman, Robert, 1937.
Herrig, Carl M., 1894.
Hess, Jack, 1951, 1952.
Hess, John J., 1894.
Hetzel, Roy B., 1896.
Hickman, Randall F., 1930, 1931.
Higdon, Grover E., 1929, 1930.
Hild, John, 1934, 1935, 1936.
Hilgenberg, Jerry, 1951, 1952, 1953.
Hilgenberg, Walter, 1961, 1962, 1963.
Hilliard, Leon, 1962.
Hines, Don T., 1925, 1926.
Hinton, Alfred, 1959, 1960, 1961.
Hobbs, Samuel W., 1895, 1896, 1897, 1898.

Hoerlein, Hans, 1910.
Hoerner, Lester (Dick), 1942, 1946.
Hoff, Robert, 1948, 1949, 1950.
Hoffman, Lloyd E., 1933.
Holbrook, Carleton W., 1895, 1896.
Hollenback Henry S., 1901, 1902.
Hollis, Wilburn, 1959, 1960, 1961.
Holmes, George S., 1915.
Hoover, Dwight, 1933, 1934, 1935.
Horn, Donald, 1957, 1958, 1959.
Houg, Andrew, 1951, 1952, 1953.
Houghton, Max, 1912, 1913, 1914.
Howard, Joseph, 1943.
Howard, Sherman, 1946.
Howell, Lloyd, 1899.
Howell, James R., 1901, 1902.
Hudson, James, 1943.
Hughes, Thomas, 1943.
Hull, John A., 1892.
Humphreys, Lloyd, 1958, 1959, 1960.
Hunter, John, 1945, 1946.
Hunzelman, Harry, 1916, 1917, 1918, 1919.
Hutchinson, Roy, 1952.
Hyland, Mark W. (Mike), 1908, 1909, 1910.

I

Ingersoll, Clarence J., 1893, 1894.
Inman, Don, 1952, 1954.
Ireland, Robert, 1943.
Irvine, Charles, 1937, 1938.
Iverson, Iver, 1894, 1895, 1896.

J

Jacobsen, Grover C., 1914, 1915.
Jakoubek, Frank, 1934, 1936.
Janda, Jon, 1957.
Jaqua, Franklin J., 1920.
Jauch, Raymond, 1957, 1958, 1959.
Jehle, Kenneth, 1955.
Jenkins, Albert P., 1916, 1917.
Jenkinson, Jerry, 1957.
Jensvold, Leo, 1928, 1929, 1930.
Jensvold, Lloyd, 1929, 1930.
Jessen, Ernest R., 1926, 1927, 1928.
Jeter, Robert, 1957, 1958, 1959.
Jewell, John J., 1907.
Jewell, Walter, 1917.
Johnson, Arthur, 1945.
Johnson, Eliza C., 1892.
Johnston, Albert C., 1903.
Johnston, Hubert, 1949, 1950, 1951.
Jones, Calvin, 1953, 1954, 1955.
Jones, Nyle W., 1901, 1902, 1903, 1904.

K

Kadesky, Max, 1920, 1921, 1922.
Kaisershot, Quentin, 1947, 1949.

Kane, Roger, 1942, 1946.
Kanellis, Eldan, 1955.
Karras, Alex, 1956, 1957.
Karras, Paul, 1958.
Kasapis, Constantinos (Gus), 1961, 1962, 1963.
Katz, Ralph, 1944, 1945.
Kaufmann, Robert J., 1919, 1920.
Kay, William, 1945, 1946, 1947, 1948.
Keane, James, 1942.
Kelley, James, 1934, 1935, 1938.
Kelly, Leo J., 1916, 1917.
Kelly, William, 1937.
Kelly, Wm. F., 1897.
Kelly, William S., 1918, 1919, 1920.
Kelso, Jack, 1944, 1947.
Kemp, Paul, 1952, 1953.
Kent, Maurice A., 1904, 1905, 1906.
Kepler, Richard P., 1894, 1895.
Kersten, William, 1951.
Kersten, William, 1944.
Kerwick, Joseph M., 1914, 1915.
King, Louis, Jr., 1946, 1947.
Kinnick, Nile C., 1937, 1938, 1939.
Kirk, Archie (Bunt), 1912, 1913, 1914.
Kirk, Carrol N. (Chick), 1906, 1907, 1908.
Klein, Richard, 1956, 1957.
Klingenberg, Theodore W., 1897.
Kloewer, Delmar, 1956, 1957.
Klumpar, Emil, 1936, 1937.
Knapp, David M., 1890.
Knapp, Karl W., 1904.
Knotts, Melvin, 1957.
Knowlton, Will P., 1906, 1907.
Kouba, Lumir J., 1932.
Krasuski, Paul R., 1923, 1924, 1925.
Krause, Paul, 1961, 1962, 1963.
Kreamer, Robert, 1962.
Kresensky, Walter William A., 1909.
Kress, George, 1953, 1955, 1956.
Kriz, Frank C., 1917.
Kriz, Jerome R., 1930, 1931.
Kriz, Leo J., 1921, 1922, 1923.
Kuhn, Marvin, 1934.
Kutsch, Nicholas A., 1925, 1926.

L

Lage, Robert, 1949, 1950, 1951.
Lagomarcino, James, 1944.
Lamb, Bush, 1935, 1936, 1937.
Lamerton, William E., 1897.
Langston, Jeff, Jr., 1956, 1958, 1959.
Lannon, Robert, 1935, 1936, 1937.
Lapham, William, 1957, 1958, 1959.
Larson, Howard, 1943.
Larrabee, William, Jr., 1891, 1892.

Laster, Richard, 1946, 1947, 1948, 1949.
Latta, George, 1961, 1962, 1963.
Laun, Charles E., 1915, 1916, 1917.
Lauterbach, Robert, 1942.
Lawrence, James, 1946, 1947.
Lawsen, Warren (Bud), 1952, 1953, 1954.
Laws, Joseph R., 1931, 1932, 1933.
Lee, Charles, Jr., 1958, 1959, 1960.
Lees, Paul, 1959.
Leighton, Kalita E., 1894, 1895, 1896.
Leinbaugh, Lyle, 1952, 1953.
Leshyn, John, 1958.
Lewis, Charles (Mac), 1956, 1957, 1958.
Lewis, Edward R., 1889.
Leytze, Rudolph, 1934, 1935.
LeZotte, Robert, 1962.
Liddy, Robert, 1942, 1943, 1946.
Liggett, Eugene, 1935, 1936.
Lindenmeyer, Fred, 1936, 1937.
Lindsey, Edwin, 1951, 1952, 1953.
Littig, Victor L., 1893, 1894.
Little, Ernest, 1900.
Locke, Gordon C., 1920, 1921, 1922.
Loehlein, Harold, 1945.
Lohman, Fred H., 1918, 1919.
Long, Jerry, 1949, 1950.
Long, David, 1960.
Longley, Earl, 1920.
Longley, Robert, 1947, 1948, 1949.
Loufek, Robert C., 1931, 1932.
Luebcke, Henry, 1938, 1939, 1940.
Lund, Ira, 1945.
Lyon, Lynn, 1961, 1962.

M

McBride, Dan, 1952.
McClain, Mayes W., 1928.
McDonnell, Jack, 1948.
McDowell, Floyd, 1934, 1935.
McDowell, Ivory, 1963.
McEniry, Matthew L., 1890.
McFadden, William J., 1906.
McGinnis, Ralph A., 1911, 1912, 1913.
McGowan, Earle A., 1903, 1904, 1905.
McIntyre, J. Scott, 1922, 1923.
McKee, Howard M., 1915, 1916.
McKenzie, Robert, 1947, 1948, 1949.
McKinley, Michael L., 1894.
McKinstry, James, 1946.
McLain, Edwin, 1937, 1938, 1939.
McLaughlin, Russell, 1944.
McNeil, Harry H., 1896.

McQuiston, Earl, 1960, 1961, 1962.
Mack, Guy E., 1902.
Macy, Clarence S., 1900, 1901.
Magnussen, Marcus J., 1929, 1932.
Maher, John, 1940, 1941.
Maine, Ernest K., 1895.
Manders, Mark, 1958, 1959, 1960.
Mannino, Alfred, 1942.
Maresh, George, 1901.
Martin, Richard, 1943.
Masden, Howard S., 1932.
Mason, Wayne, 1935, 1936.
Masterson, Forrest, 1942, 1944.
Mastrogany, Gus N., 1929, 1930.
Matheson, Eldean, 1953, 1954, 1955.
Matson, Gordon, 1934, 1936.
Matykiewicz, Louis, 1952, 1953, 1954.
Mauren, Gerald, 1959, 1960.
Mead, Chester I., 1920, 1921, 1922.
Meek, Kenneth, 1954.
Meggers, Frank H., 1898, 1899.
Meister, Melvin G., 1897.
Meloy, Charles D., 1911, 1912.
Meltzer, Sam H., 1931.
Mendenhall, Leland, 1916.
Mendenhall, Otho H., 1915.
Merten, Francis A., 1931.
Mertes, Bernard (Bus), 1940, 1941.
Merz, Curtis, 1957, 1958, 1959.
Meyer, Richard, 1948, 1950.
Meyers, Joseph H., 1896, 1897.
Mielke, Ernest, 1958, 1959.
Milani, James, 1952.
Miller, Allan, 1958, 1959.
Miller, Glenn W., 1921, 1922, 1923.
Miller, Henry, 1941.
Miller, John E., 1932.
Miller, Leo, 1963.
Miller, Robert, 1944.
Minick, Paul, 1920, 1921, 1922.
Mockmore, Charles A., 1918, 1919.
Moffitt, Howard B., 1931, 1932.
Mohrbacher, Stanley, 1943, 1944.
Moore, Fred, 1904, 1905.
Moore, Joseph, 1940.
Moore, Robert, 1934.
Moore, Robert H., 1927, 1928.
Moore, Thomas, 1959, 1960.
Moore, Thomas W., 1931, 1932, 1933.
Moran, Terrance, 1953, 1954.
Morton, Ray (Buck), 1898, 1899, 1900.
Mosley, Eugene, 1959, 1960.
Murphy, Bernard V., 1904, 1905, 1907.
Murphy, James Ray, 1909, 1910, 1911.

Murphy, J. Ray, Jr., 1938, 1939, 1940.
Myers, Dennis E., 1927, 1928, 1929.
Myers, Harl, 1892, 1893.

N

Naber, Mearle, 1948, 1949.
Narum, Carl C., 1905.
Nead, Wilbur, 1937, 1938.
Neal, Fred W., 1889, 1890.
Neidig, Milo H., 1910.
Niedbala, William, 1962, 1963.
Niedziela, Bruno, 1942, 1946.
Nelson, Donald, 1934, 1935, 1936.
Nelson, Elmo, 1930, 1931.
Nelson, Emerson W., 1925, 1926, 1927.
Nelson, Irving L., 1928, 1929.
Ney, John J., 1910, 1911.
Niland, John, 1963.
Niles, Jerry, 1938, 1945.
Noble, Dudley, 1950, 1951.
Nocera, John, 1956, 1957, 1958.
Noonan, Karl, 1963.
Nordman, Gerald, 1949, 1951.
Norgaard, Jens, 1938, 1939.
Norton, Donald, 1957, 1958, 1959.
Novack, Gerald, 1958, 1959.
Nugent, Clement E., 1922.
Nugent, Lee, 1917.

O

O'Brien, Willis J. (Fat), 1909, 1910, 1911.
Ochiltree, H. C., 1902, 1904.
Ogeigo, Mitchell, 1958.
Olson, Forrest M. (Tiny), 1923, 1924, 1925.
Olson, Glenn, 1936, 1937, 1938.
O'Neal, Charles E., 1926, 1927.
Osmaloski, Ted, 1934, 1935, 1936.
Otte, Lowell, 1922, 1923, 1924.
Otto, J. Robert, 1941.

P

Page, Bernard, 1932, 1933, 1934.
Palmer, George, 1952.
Pape, Oran (Nanny), 1928, 1929.
Parker, Guerdon D., 1919, 1920, 1921.
Parker, William, 1940, 1941, 1942.
Parkin, Leland C., 1922, 1923, 1924.
Parsons, Charles L., 1912, 1913, 1914.
Parsons, Lawrence C., 1932.
Paulsen, Joseph, 1948, 1949, 1950.
Pellegrino, Orlando, 1956.
Penaluna, Robert, 1941, 1942.
Pence, Lawrence W., 1898.

Penningroth, Walter, 1911, 1913.
Perkins, William, 1960, 1961, 1962.
Perrin, Del, 1949, 1950.
Perrine, James O., 1908.
Perry, Dayton, Jr., 1960, 1961, 1962.
Peterson, Ron, 1949, 1950, 1951.
Peterson, Frank R., 1917.
Pettit, Kenneth, 1938, 1939, 1940.
Phillips, Robert, 1946, 1947, 1948.
Phillips, Robert, 1951, 1952, 1953.
Pierce, Charles, 1956, 1957.
Pierce, Frank G., 1889, 1890, 1891.
Pignatelli, Carl A., 1927, 1929.
Ploen, Kenneth, 1954, 1955, 1956.
Poluga, Chester, 1938.
Powell, Leska, 1910.
Power, Howard, 1895.
Powers, Milton I., 1889, 1890.
Prasse, Erwin, 1937, 1938, 1939.
Prescott, Robert, 1956, 1957, 1958.
Pritchard, Irving M., 1893.
Pudder, Emery, 1960, 1961.
Pyles, Arthur G., 1917, 1919.

R

Radloff, Fred, 1932, 1933, 1934.
Rath, Gordon, 1920.
Recher, David, 1962, 1963.
Reed, Ronald G., 1916, 1917, 1918.
Reedquist, Lawrence A., 1928, 1929.
Reichardt, William, 1949, 1950, 1951.
Reichow, Garet (Jerry), 1953, 1954, 1955.
Reichow, William, 1954, 1955.
Reilly, Michael, 1961, 1962, 1963.
Reister, Harold, 1951, 1952.
Repass, Maurice A., 1910.
Reynolds, Robert, 1947.
Rice, George (Dusty), 1951, 1952, 1953.
Rice, Harry H., 1925, 1926.
Rich, Edmund G., 1922.
Richards, Joseph, 1933, 1934.
Riddle, Fred, Jr., 1962, 1963.
Rigg, George, 1892.
Rigney, Frank, 1955, 1956, 1957.
Riley, Don, 1949, 1950, 1951.
Ringer, William, 1960.
Roberts, Fred E., 1927, 1928, 1929.
Roberts, Jay, 1962, 1963.
Robinson, Leonard B., 1893.
Robshaw, James, 1962.
Rockwood, Merle C., 1904, 1905, 1906.
Rodawig, Don F., 1925.
Rogers, Alexander, 1930, 1931.
Rogers, Alfred, 1893.

Rogers, Felton, 1960, 1961.
Rogers, Lonnie, 1961, 1962, 1963.
Rogge, George R., 1929, 1930.
Romey, Richard E., 1923, 1924, 1925.
Rook, Robert, 1933.
Rose, Kenneth, 1944.
Ruck, Fred, 1949, 1950, 1951.
Russo, Robert, 1960.
Ryan, Karlin, 1963.

S

Sabin, Edwin L., 1889.
Sampson, Martin W., 1889, 1890.
Samuelson, Leo, 1931, 1932.
Sanford, Allen T., 1890, 1891, 1892.
Sangster, James, 1951, 1952.
Sangster, William, 1943.
Sansen, Oliver M., 1929, 1930, 1931.
Sawin, John, 1958, 1959.
Sawyer, Emmett, 1952.
Sawyer, Prince E., 1892, 1893, 1894.
Scanlon, George H., 1918.
Scantlebury, Wilbur E., 1923, 1924.
Schammel, Francis (Zud), 1932, 1933, 1934.
Schenk, Albert, 1936, 1938.
Schirmer, John A., 1923, 1924, 1925.
Schleusner, Vincent L., 1927, 1928.
Schmidt, Christian G., 1932.
Schmidt, Marvin H., 1926, 1927.
Schneidman, Herman, 1932, 1934.
Schroeder, William, 1898.
Schweizer, Edsel, 1942.
Schwin, Frederick W. (Germany), 1903, 1904, 1905.
Scott, Homer W., 1916, 1918.
Scott, William, 1958.
Secl, William, 1933, 1934, 1935.
Seidel, Aaron E., 1907, 1908.
Seidel, Earl R., 1905.
Sessi, Geno, 1957.
Sgro, Dominick, 1957.
Shambaugh, George E., 1892.
Sheehan, Dan, 1943, 1945.
Sheets, Wallace, 1956.
Sherman, Robert, 1962, 1963.
Shipanik, Donald, 1958, 1959.
Shoaf, James, 1946, 1947, 1948.
Shoener, Harold, 1946, 1947.
Shoener, Herbert, 1946, 1947.
Shuck, Terry, 1954, 1955.
Shuttleworth, V. Craven, 1920, 1921, 1922.
Siberts, Frank L., 1900, 1901, 1902.
Simmons, Don, 1935, 1936.
Simmons, Oze, 1934, 1935, 1936.
Simons, Obern, 1945.

Simpson, Gary, 1963.
Six, Norman, 1954, 1955.
Skelley, Leland (Ike), 1926.
Slater, Fred (Duke), 1918, 1919, 1920, 1921.
Smeltzer, Charles B., 1890.
Smith, Arthur G., 1889, 1890.
Smith, Don R., 1926, 1927.
Smith, Earl, 1953, 1954, 1955.
Smith, Fred, 1937, 1938.
Smith, James Robert, 1946, 1947.
Smith, John James, 1946.
Smith, Nelson, Jr., 1944, 1945.
Smith, Paul E., 1925, 1926.
Smith, P. P., 1901.
Smith, Willie Ray, 1962.
Snider, Herman (Ham), 1938, 1939, 1940.
Snyder, Robert, 1944, 1947, 1948.
Snook, Gary, 1963.
Spaan, James, 1958.
Spanjers, Peter, 1950, 1951, 1952.
Spurbeck, Wayne, 1945.
Staak, John, 1941, 1942.
Stanton, James, 1895, 1896.
Stauss, William, 1940, 1941, 1942.
Stearnes, Robert, 1951, 1952, 1953, 1954.
Stephens, Roger, 1943.
Stewart, John, 1943, 1944.
Stewart, Walter L. (Stub), 1907, 1908, 1909.
Stiles, Frank N., 1891, 1892.
Stoltenberg, Walter P., 1904.
Streff, Jack N., 1904, 1905, 1906.
Stutsman, Carl A., 1889.
Stutsman, John P., 1931, 1932.
Stutsman, Isaac E., 1907, 1908.
Suchy, Donald, 1954, 1955, 1956.
Sullivan, Robert, 1946.
Swaney, Harold J., 1931, 1933.
Swartzendruber, Donald, 1950, 1951.
Swedberg, Rodger, 1953, 1954, 1955.
Sykes, Joe, 1918, 1920.
Synhorst, John B., 1918.
Szykowny, Matthew, 1960, 1961, 1962.

T

Tedore, John, 1946, 1947, 1948.
Terrell, Charles E., 1901, 1903.
Terrell, Henry, 1943.
Teyro, George, 1932, 1933, 1934.
Theer, Richard, 1956, 1957.
Thomas, Brice L., 1928, 1929.
Thomas, Charles, 1895, 1896.
Thomas, Floyd E., 1910.
Thompson, Arthur P., 1906.

Thompson, Dale, 1943.
Thompson, George D., 1920, 1921, 1922.
Thorson, Sherwyn, 1959, 1960, 1961.
Thurtle, Philip W., 1931.
Tofson, Duane, 1955.
Tollefson, Charles, 1938, 1939, 1940.
Tompkins, S. Nelson, 1930, 1931.
Towner, John, 1949, 1950, 1951.
Treadway, Olen, 1957, 1958, 1959.
Trickey, Ben, 1941, 1942.
Trickey, James J., 1910, 1911, 1912.
Trickey, Kenneth W., 1931.
Triplett, Orle F., 1916.
Tucker, Donald, 1960.
Tunnell, Emlen, 1946, 1947.
Tupper, W. William, 1905.
Turici, Richard, 1961, 1962.
Turner, Austin, 1949, 1950, 1951.
Turner, Stephen, 1958.
Tyrrell, William, 1892, 1893.

U

Uknes, Charles, 1942.
Urban, Albert, 1942.
Ure, Samuel R., 1892.

V

Vacanti, Sam, 1942.
Van Buren, William, 1955, 1960, 1961.
Van Meter, Harold L., 1912.
Van Oosterhout, Peter D., 1892, 1893.
Veit, Eugene, 1956, 1957.
Vincent, Edward, Jr., 1953, 1954, 1955.
Vollenweider, Henry, 1939, 1941.

Voltmer, Carl D., 1926.
Von Lackum, Herman Le Roy, 1911, 1912.
Von Lackum, J. Kenneth, 1917.

W

Wagler, Scott, 1935, 1936.
Walker, Cornelius, 1934, 1935, 1936.
Walker, James, 1939, 1940, 1941.
Walker, James C., 1895, 1896, 1897.
Walker, James H., 1902, 1904.
Walker, Marion, 1956.
Wallace, Robert, 1962.
Warner, Joe S. 1897, 1898, 1899, 1900.
Warrington, John H., 1930.
Washburn, Roy B., 1905, 1906.
Watkins, David, 1960, 1961.
Watters, L. Bert, 1899, 1900, 1901, 1903.
Waugh, Harry, 1943.
Webb, Cloyd, 1961, 1962, 1963.
Weber, Harold, 1934.
Weeks, Seth B., 1910.
Wehrle, Roger, 1963.
Weiland, Frank H., 1901.
Weller, Wendell, 1945.
Westra, Peter A., 1927, 1928, 1929.
Whisler, William, 1959, 1960, 1961.
White, Edward H., 1904.
White, Edward S., 1893.
White, Roy A., 1904, 1905, 1907.
Wiegmann, Roger, 1953, 1954, 1955.
Wilder, Clifford, 1963.
Wilkins, Glen H., 1901, 1903.
Willer, James F., 1930.
Willett, James, 1956.
Williams, Chester, 1960.

Williams, Fred, 1898, 1899.
Williams, Hermon P., 1894.
Williams, Jerry, 1961.
Williams, Joe, 1960, 1961.
Williams, Loranzie, 1951.
Williams, Louis, Jr., 1962, 1963.
Williams, Samuel Clyde, 1898, 1899, 1900, 1901.
Williams, Virgil, 1959.
Wills, Ernest C., 1914.
Wilson, J. Max, 1913, 1914, 1915.
Wilson, Robert, 1949, 1950, 1951.
Winslow, Donald, 1944, 1947, 1948, 1949.
Winston, James, 1960, 1962.
Woodard, Ralph, 1945, 1947, 1948, 1949.
Woodard, Richard, 1944, 1946, 1947, 1948.
Woodhouse, Donald A., 1949, 1950.
Woodhouse, Donald E., 1949.
Woolston, Frank, 1891, 1892.
Wright, Benson E., 1891.
Wright, Charles E., 1897.
Wyatt, Bernard, 1959, 1960, 1961.
Wyland, Guido B., 1916.

Y

Yauck, Robert, 1960, 1961.
Yelton, Robert, 1942.
Yegge, John P., 1926, 1927.
Youel, James, 1940, 1941, 1942.
Young, Earl, 1926, 1927.

Z

Zaehringer, Paul, 1943.
Zender, Robert, 1947.
Ziolkowski, Robert, 1963.
Zinn, Donald, Jr., 1960.
Zollman, Philip A., 1892.